# ASIA–PACIFIC STRATEGIC RELATIONS
## Seeking Convergent Security

This comprehensive book is an overview of security issues in the Asia-Pacific and an argument for a strategy that promises to achieve greater regional stability. It finds that current approaches by policy-makers increase the likelihood of conflict. Instead, it proposes that a strategy of 'convergent security' be adopted to build an enduring regional security framework. A concise survey of key policy approaches to regional security politics, *Asia-Pacific Strategic Relations* also includes extensive historical and contemporary empirical discussion. This authoritative and broad-ranging survey is designed for a wide body of analysts and students of the problems of contemporary Asian politics and strategy.

**William T. Tow** is Professor in the School of Political Science and International Studies at the University of Queensland, Australia. He has served on the Australian Foreign Affairs Council, Australia's National Fulbright Commission's Board of Directors and on the Australian Member Committee of the Council for Security Co-operation in the Asia-Pacific. He is the author of numerous books and articles on Asian security affairs, international security issues and alliance politics.

*To my father, Harry A. Tow*
*Calming my many storms …*

# CAMBRIDGE ASIA–PACIFIC STUDIES

Cambridge Asia–Pacific Studies aims to provide a focus and forum for scholarly work on the Asia–Pacific region as a whole, and its component sub-regions, namely Northeast Asia, Southeast Asia and the Pacific Islands. The series is produced in association with the Research School of Pacific and Asian Studies at the Australian National University and the Australian Institute of International Affairs.

Editor: John Ravenhill

Editorial Board: James Cotton, Donald Denoon, Mark Elvin, Hal Hill, Ron May, Anthony Milner, Tessa Morris-Suzuki, Anthony Low

# ASIA–PACIFIC STRATEGIC RELATIONS

## Seeking Convergent Security

WILLIAM T. TOW
*University of Queensland*

PUBLISHED BY THE PRESS SYNDICATE OF THE UNIVERSITY OF CAMBRIDGE
The Pitt Building, Trumpington Street, Cambridge, United Kingdom

CAMBRIDGE UNIVERSITY PRESS
The Edinburgh Building, Cambridge CB2 2RU, UK
40 West 20th Street, New York, NY 10011–4211, USA
10 Stamford Road, Oakleigh, VIC 3166, Australia
Ruiz de Alarcón 13, 28014 Madrid, Spain
Dock House, The Waterfront, Cape Town 8001, South Africa

http://www.cambridge.org

First published 2001

Printed in Singapore by Green Giant Press

*Typeface* New Baskerville  (*Adobe*) 10/12 pt.   *System* QuarkXPress®   [PK]

*A catalogue record for this book is available from the British Library*

*National Library of Australia Cataloguing in Publication data*
Tow, William T.
Asia-Pacific strategic relations: seeking convergent security.
Bibliography.
Includes index.
ISBN 0 521 80790 5.
ISBN 0 521 00368 7 (pbk.).
1. National security – Asia.
2. National security – Pacific Area.
3. Security, International.
I. Title.
355.03305


ISBN 0 521 80790 5 hardback
ISBN 0 521 00368 7 paperback

# Contents

# Acknowledgments

As is usually the case with a project of this scope, there are many people and organisations to which I owe much. So I will depart from the usual practice of thanking 'everyone else' at the end of this note to do so at the outset. I have incurred too many debts along the way to completing this book for them ever to be fully rectified.

There are some colleagues and institutions that must be acknowledged, however, as having played an integral part in this work's fruition. As Director of the Centre for Asia-Australia Studies, Professor Russell Trood supported my presence there academically and financially throughout 1994–95 to launch research for this project. The late Michel Oksenberg hosted me at Stanford University's Asia/Pacific Center during the first part of 1999, enabling me to complete a substantial portion of the writing. Financial support provided by the Australian Research Council underwrote my presence there. The University of Queensland's School of Political Science and International Studies has provided a stimulating intellectual and personally gratifying professional environment over the past decade to complete the research for this book. In particular, my colleagues in that School's International Studies component, including Roland Bleiker, C. L. Chiou, Marianne Hanson, Rod Lyon and Cindy O'Hagan have all provided much appreciated moral support, as have Paul Boreham, Linda Buckham and Ian Ward in their administrative capacities. Sue Lochran and Karen Larocca provided critical logistical support at key intervals.

Two colleagues must be cited independently. David Dellit went through the entire manuscript, providing incisive and valued input to make this analysis much better than would otherwise have been the case. Donna Weeks reviewed and copy-edited preliminary and advanced drafts with patience and fortitude. To both of you, the book would not have seen the light of day without each of your substantial efforts. The research assistance of Cameron Hill, Chieko Iida and Sophie Prévot must also be acknowledged with gratitude. Plaudits are also due to Phillipa McGuinness, Senior Commissioning Editor for Cambridge University Press in Australia, her colleague Paul Watt, editorial consultant Lee White, and to relevant CUP staff for all of their highly professional efforts in seeing this project through to its culmination.

Finally, to my family (wife Leslie and daughter Shannon), my eternal gratitude for your understanding and support in allowing me to pursue my craft at great sacrifice to your own interests and priorities. It is to the two of you that I ultimately owe the most thanks for allowing me to complete this work.

# Tables

# Abbreviations

| | |
|---|---|
| ABM | Anti-ballistic missile |
| ABRI | *Anskatan Bersenjata Republik Indonesia* (Armed Forces of the Republic of Indonesia) |
| ACSA | Acquisition and Cross-Servicing Agreement |
| ADF | Australian Defence Force |
| AFP | Armed Forces Philippines |
| AMS | Agreement on Maintaining Security (Indonesia and Australia) |
| ANZUS | Australia, New Zealand, United States Security Treaty |
| APEC | Asia-Pacific Economic Cooperation |
| ARF | ASEAN Regional Forum |
| ASEAN | Association of Southeast Asian Nations |
| ASEM | Asia-Europe Meeting |
| AUSMIN | Australia–US Ministerial Meeting |
| AWACs | Airborne Warning and Control Systems |
| BUR | Bottom-up Review |
| CCP | Chinese Communist Party |
| CFC | (Republic of Korea–US) Combined Forces Command |
| CIA | (US) Central Intelligence Agency |
| CMC | Central Military Commission (China) |
| CSCAP | Council on Security and Cooperation in Asia and the Pacific |
| CSCE | Conference for Security and Cooperation on Europe |
| CTBT | Comprehensive Test Ban Treaty |
| CTIB | Civilian and Technology Industrial Base |
| DFAT | Department of Foreign Affairs and Trade (Australia) |
| DMZ | Demilitarized Zone (Korean Peninsula) |
| DPRK | Democratic People's Republic of Korea |

| | |
|---|---|
| DTIB | Defense Technology and Industrial Base |
| EAEC | East Asian Economic Caucus |
| EASI | East Asia Strategy Initiative |
| EASR | East Asia Strategy Review |
| EEZ | Enhanced Economic Zone |
| ERINT | extended range interceptor |
| FPDA | Five Power Defence Arrangements |
| GNP | Gross National Product |
| IAEA | International Atomic Energy Agency |
| ICBM | intercontinental ballistic missile |
| IISS | International Institute for Strategic Studies |
| IMF | International Monetary Fund |
| INTERFET | International Emergency Force in East Timor |
| IRBM | intermediate-range-ballistic missile |
| JCS | (US) Joint Chiefs of Staff |
| JDA | Japan Defense Agency |
| JICPAC | Joint Intelligence Center at the United States Pacific Command |
| KEDO | Korean Peninsula Energy Development Organization |
| KPA | Korea People's Army |
| LAC | Line of Actual Control |
| LEAP | Lightweight Exoatmosphere Projectile |
| LOC | Line of Control |
| MBTs | Main Battle Tanks |
| MDT | (US–Philippines) Mutual Defense Treaty |
| MFN | Most-favoured nation (status) |
| MITI | Ministry of International Trade and Industry (Japan); In January 2001, renamed Ministry of Economy, Trade and Industry, METI |
| MOF | Ministry of Finance (Japan) |
| MOFA | Ministry of Foreign Affairs (Japan) |
| MOU | Memorandum of Understanding |
| MRVs | multiple re-entry vehicles |
| MSDF | Maritime Self-Defense Force (Japan) |
| MST | (US–Japan) Mutual Security Treaty |
| NATO | North Atlantic Treaty Organization |
| NDPO | National Defense Program Outline (*Taiko*) |
| NEACD | Northeast Asian Cooperation Dialogue |
| NEASED | Northeast Asian Security Dialogue |
| NFU | No-first-use (commitment) |
| NGOs | Non governmental organisations |
| NIEs | newly industrialised economies |
| NKP | New Korea Party |

| | |
|---|---|
| NMD | National Missile Defense |
| NNPT | nuclear non-proliferation treaty |
| NORINCO | China North Industries Corporation |
| NPC | National People's Congress (China) |
| NTW | Navy Theatre Wide |
| ODA | Overseas Development Assistance |
| OECD | Organization for Economic Cooperation and Development |
| OMF | Overseas Minesweeping Force |
| PKO | peacekeeping operations (Japan) |
| PLA | People's Liberation Army (China) |
| PMC | Post-ministerial Council (ASEAN) |
| PRC | People's Republic of China |
| PW | People's War (China) |
| PWUMC | People's War Under Modern Conditions (China) |
| QDR | Quadrennial Defense Review |
| RDF | Rapid Deployment Force (Malaysia) |
| RIMPAC | biennial Rim of the Pacific maritime exercises |
| RMA | Revolution in Military Affairs |
| ROC | Republic of China (Taiwan) |
| ROK | Republic of Korea |
| ROKA | Republic of Korea Armed forces |
| RRU | Rapid reaction units |
| SAARC | South Asian Association for Regional Cooperation |
| SACO | Special Action Committee on Okinawa |
| SAF | Singapore Armed Forces |
| SAR | Search and Rescue (naval exercise) |
| SCAP | Supreme Commander for Allied Powers in Japan (1947-52) |
| SDF | Self-Defense Force (Japan) |
| SEATO | Southeast Asian Treaty Organization |
| SLOCs | Sea lines of communication |
| SLORC | State Law and Order Restoration Council |
| SOMs | (ARF's) Senior Officials Meetings |
| SPDC | State Peace and Development Council |
| START | Strategic Arms Reduction Talks |
| THAAD | Theatre High Altitude Area Defense |
| TMD | Theatre Missile Defense |
| TNI | Tentara Nasional Indonesia (Indonesian Armed Forces) |
| TRA | Taiwan Relations Act |
| UNCLOS | United Nations Convention on the Law of the Sea |
| UNTAET | United Nations Transitional Administration in East Timor |
| USFJ | United States Forces, Japan |
| VFA | Visiting Forces Agreement |

| | |
|---|---|
| WMD | Weapons of Mass Destruction |
| WTO | World Trade Organization |
| ZOPFAN | Zone for Peace, Freedom and Neutrality (ASEAN) |

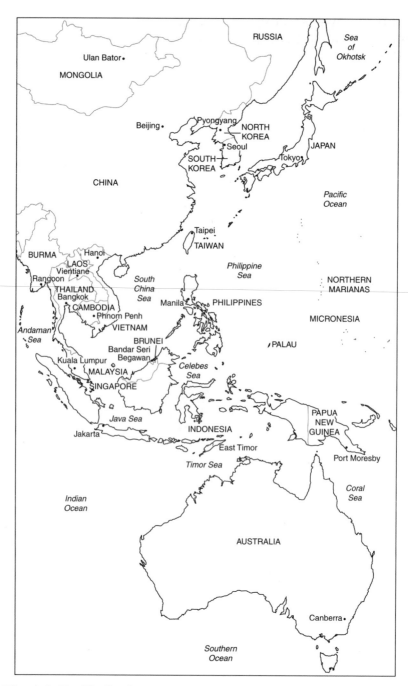

The Asia-Pacific Region

# CHAPTER 1

# *Introduction*

It is a curious fact that radically polarised viewpoints on almost any issue command undue attention and precipitate widespread circulation. This truism is underscored in international relations by the continuing prominence of the 'realist' and 'liberal' approaches in both that field's academic literature and, even more critically, in real-world security decision-making. The danger is that, unless managed judiciously, such approaches may not only be too doctrinaire but may be so divisive as to create or exacerbate, rather than to solve, international disputes and security dilemmas.

A decade beyond the end of the Cold War, these approaches are having a critical impact upon what type of security order will replace the former crisis-prone but predictable bipolar structure in the Asia-Pacific region. European history, as has been observed, is the 'laboratory from which liberals and realists alike have derived their widely divergent theories of inter-state relations'.[1] Yet Asia's culture, geography and geopolitics are not those of Europe and attempting to link historical precedents between the two regions is not very instructive in understanding the forces that shape the former. The region under review is the world's largest and most populous geographic entity, potentially its wealthiest and clearly among its most diverse and complex.[2] Asian cultures and institutions are still reconciling their origins and identities with the Western modernisation experience and are adopting regionally distinct agendas for confronting the forces of international change. The economic fate and strategic destiny of the region will depend upon how effective those agendas prove to be. Debate is intensifying both within and outside Asia over the best way to ensure their success.[3] Extreme policy outlooks and approaches to Asian security are tending to overwhelm forces of pragmatism and moderation. The intensification of 'Asian exceptionalism' and

1

sharpening great power rivalries in the region are illustrative. If left unchecked, these trends could lead to regional conflict.

This book challenges prevailing trends by arguing that only a carefully integrated application of *both* realism and liberalism will achieve conflict-avoidance in the Asia-Pacific. This 'convergent security' approach, it will be maintained, represents the only effective means for Asia-Pacific regional security actors to define and implement a stable regional security order.

Why is this the case? If realism and liberalism are not successfully combined, either approach could plunge the Asia-Pacific into war. Hard-line American postures, for example, calling for its bilateral regional allies to collaborate in missile defence, or to commit them to assist in American military intervention against a future Chinese invasion of Taiwan, are destabilising.[4] So too are Chinese efforts to isolate and eventually extricate American military forces from the region by manipulating multinational regional organisations.[5] Beijing is now embracing multilateralism (or 'institutionalism') demonstrating its willingness to collaborate with ASEAN, and thus arguing the increasing irrelevance of American-led bilateral alliances.

This book will postulate that a pragmatic combination of realist and liberal approaches can overcome such tendencies. Such a combination remains evasive, however, due to a lack of leadership by great power elites and a reticence by smaller powers to pressure their larger counterparts into adopting more moderate postures that emphasise diplomacy and reassurance over strategic advantage. Regional security behaviour in Asia is now too often shaped by factors that impede rather than encourage the needed combination of *realpolitik* and institution-building to achieve regional order. Some examples of predominant themes in this vein are: the primacy of narrow budgetary considerations, domestic bureaucratic rivalries and shortsighted 'worst case' perceptions about other states' intentions and behaviour. Convergent security argues that a consistent and systematic policy approach can be adopted to overcome such policy extremes.

The orientation of this study is predominantly state-centric and geopolitical, although it acknowledges the impact of economic and socio-cultural factors, particularly in the current era of globalisation. It asserts that policy makers in the Asia-Pacific are primarily influenced by either realist or liberal approaches. There is some evidence that modest efforts have been made to integrate the two approaches, but such initiatives have been intermittent and unsystematic.

Realist strategy has predominated Asia-Pacific security politics since the end of the Cold War, as evidenced by the sustained growth of Chinese nationalism, by the Association of Southeast Asian Nations (ASEAN) member-states' policy of non-interference in their affairs and by the United States' continued strategic role as a regional balancer. Yet liberal initiatives to create and sustain institutions and regimes to deal with security issues have been surprisingly resilient, and most states in the region voice their long-term support for a regional security community.[6] Many regional policy makers recognise that the exclusive pursuit of realism by the great powers (especially the United States and China) is not a viable long-term solution to the achievement of regional stability and cooperation but will merely exacerbate regional security dilemmas. Indeed, the current US bilateral alliance network in the region is already weakened by Washington's tendency to demand strong compliance by its allies to its own policies. China, for its part, has demonstrated it increasingly understands that such bilateral support can only be strengthened by a major regional threat confronting the United States and its allies and it may well seek to avoid behaving in ways that would tend to verify any American argument concerning a 'China threat'. But China remains uncompromising over Taiwan, largely intractable on the Spratly Islands question and determined to pursue formidable military power projection capabilities – all factors that undermine the benevolent image it often wishes to cultivate.

## Defining the Concepts

'Realism' in international relations attempts to deal with human nature as it is and not as it ought to be, and with historical events as they have occurred, not as they should have occurred. 'Realists' argue that states pursue their national interests within an anarchical international system through acquiring and exercising power, and that socio-economic concerns are subordinate to political interests in the pursuit of state power.[7] From this follows that: (1) states (which comprise the primary units in an 'international system') formulate strategic force postures and develop capabilities to pursue their own interests and achieve predictability (that is, 'order') in an anarchic international environment; (2) states cannot be sure of each other's strategic intentions; (3) their strategic capabilities are inherently offensive and thus dangerous to each other; but (4) states act rationally and 'defensively' on the basis of their instincts for survival (preserving their sovereignty).[8]

The opposing 'liberal' school of thought maintains that international relations have moved beyond the stage of states thinking the worst of each other. While not discounting that anarchy may exist in international relations, it believes such a condition can be overcome by states agreeing to pursue absolute gains (where every state gains more than it loses by collaboration) and by cultivating an indifference to relative gains (where one state gains more than another). Liberals posit that states must now recognise they are better off by creating 'regimes' or institutions that encourage shared expectations between states, facilitate inter-state cooperation and provide a basis for deriving mutually acceptable standards of behaviour. The demise of superpower competition and increased global and economic cooperation are viewed as being developments which have the potential to turn the pursuit of national security into an opportunity to cement regional and international amity.[9]

A primary concern of this book is to assess and interpret evolving trends in the Asia-Pacific's strategic environment by examining the applicability of both realist and liberal arguments to such trends. This differentiates it from many other contemporary treatments of the region, which focus on the broader problem of 'Asian security'. These often tend to subject study of the region's evolving strategic dynamics to either theoretical discussions of what 'security' means in a post-Cold War context (with requisite deference to 'constructivist' or 'post-modernist' explanations) or to a comparative analysis of how contemporary Asia resembles or differs from other historical and structural international security episodes.[10] As a result, analysis of Asia-Pacific regional security is often mired by abstract, even obtuse, paradigmatic bickering. Unfortunately, this offers little assistance to Asia-Pacific policy planners and diplomats confronted daily with issues requiring a keen understanding of geopolitics in situations demanding rapid strategic decision-making – they can ill afford to wait for academic consensus.

Most Asian policy makers, only recently liberated from the vestiges of colonialism, revere political sovereignty and survival of the state as the one integral and uncompromising ingredient of security. Governments in the region tend to equate their own political survival with national security. They are more comfortable with traditional definitions in strategic studies than with a security debate clouded by incessant problems of terminology and methodological dispute.[11] To Asia-Pacific policy makers, therefore, theoretical debates emanating from the West over the nature of 'security' are seen to be intellectually elegant but distant from their own immediate interests and agendas.[12] As the group invested with the task of managing highly pressing national and international security issues in a timely and effective fashion, they are likely to decline from even participating in this debate. In making strategic decisions they will instead revert to time-relevant cables dispatched from foreign missions, various intelligence assessments and to their own regional and international contacts and friends. Accordingly, traditional state-centric policy relations are paramount in the region and an integrated realist-liberal framework remains the most relevant approach to discussion of Asia-Pacific security.

It will, nonetheless, be necessary in this study of the Asia-Pacific's complex strategic relationships to deal with selected nuances and corollaries of realism and liberalism. These concepts will be analysed more extensively in chapter 7 as a backdrop to developing the idea of convergent security in greater depth. Brief definitions will be offered here, however, together with the citation of references explaining them in far more detail. Various international relations scholars may well disagree with at least some of these characterisations; they are presented only for the purpose of clarifying their meaning as they may apply to the concerns of this volume.

Several important components of realism including bilateralism, maximal and minimal realism, and power balancing must be described. *Bilateralism* is a security relationship between two states that reflects their relative position within a wider international power balance. Bilateral relationships are usually exclusionary in nature: states enter into bilateral associations because 'they believe the combination of their security interests, their relative capabilities and the systematic context in which they operate is such that relationships inherent to bilateral security politics will be most effective'.[13]

*Maximal realism* is a term initially coined by Christopher Layne to describe a vision of a new world order led by an international hegemon. Also known as a strategy of 'preponderance' or 'primacy', maximal realism promotes a vision of an Asia-Pacific that assimilates that world power's basic politico-economic values. The key to peace and stability, according to this school of thought, is for such a power to maintain military superiority over those who would challenge it and to sustain a willingness to defend the vital interests of its allies. Many advocates of this approach view the United States as the most likely candidate to fill this role.[14]

*Minimal realism* or *neo-isolationism* views the prospect of hegemonic power in the Asia-Pacific as less than beneficial. This school of thought asserts that if a power transition in the Asia-Pacific is inevitable, future Asian conflicts can best be avoided by a downgrading of rival powers' forward military presence in the region (that is, the US-basing presence in Northeast Asia or China's power projection into the South China Sea). Asia's strategic geography – which is predominantly maritime and therefore constrains the prospect of any power undertaking major strategic offensives – combines, in the view of this school, with a continued Asian preoccupation with accruing material wealth to preclude great-power conflict in the region.[15]

Among realists, various forms of *power balancing* have become the most widely discussed scenarios for organising Asia-Pacific security.[16] Power balancing refers to the distribution of military power so as to deny any one regional actor a preponderance of power or hegemony. The objective of power balancing is to ensure that no one actor will prevail over other key actors, short of going to war. Manipulating the distribution of power to one's own advantage through alliance, coalition, concert or other strategies, from the realist perspective, is a legitimate and expected facet of this approach.

Similarly, several aspects of liberalism including multilateralism, neo-liberalism/institutionalism, and greater regional interdependence are integral to the concerns of this text. *Multilateralism* has been adopted by those officials and independent analysts sympathetic to liberalism as a preferred strategy for advancing regional stability. It can be defined as an institutional approach which 'prescribes behavioural roles, constrain(s) activity, and shape(s) expectations' among three or more states.[17] It provides a set of organising principles and rules of conduct that can be used to overcome what John Ruggie has labelled 'particularistic interests and situational exigencies'.[18]

*Neo-liberalism/institutionalism* is concerned with the building and expansion of a 'liberal zone of states' by infusing collective values and norms into Asian societies. Neo-liberal/institutionalists view regional and international institutions (such as ASEAN or the United Nations) as useful for performing a number of functions in international relations that individual states cannot. Most significantly, such organisations are viewed as better suited to define and pursue common objectives for the mutual benefit of all their associates.[19]

Liberals argue that the rationales for sustaining the alliances and coalitions that dominated Asian security politics for most of the postwar era are increasingly challenged by patterns of greater regional interdependence. This can be viewed as a 'condition where states (or peoples) are affected by decisions taken by others. Actors can be affected equally or "symmetrically" or in relative or "asymmetrical" ways'.[20] Advocates of greater Asia-Pacific interdependence argue that states have every incentive to cooperate in building and sustaining regional wealth, guaranteeing future regional access to critical energy supplies, and expanding communication and transportation networks through the pursuit and strengthening of multilateral institutions. By doing so, all of them will gain more over time than by competing with each other for greater prosperity and more resources.[21]

## Argument and Organisation

If Asia-Pacific states are to overcome intra-regional animosities and avoid regional conflicts they must identify and implement policies and mechanisms which combine judicious realism with opportunistic liberalism. Both are applicable to establishing and implementing the means-ends calculations which guide strategic behaviour among states; each can supplement the other in situations where divergent interests might otherwise lead to the escalation of crises into serious regional conflicts.

The concerns of this book relate therefore to the question of how states can modify their traditional search for relative gains without allowing the tensions inherently associated with rapid economic modernisation and political change to overwhelm their willingness to cooperate. The book addresses the question of the probability of competition or cooperation by examining how state policy makers' belief systems which shape their strategic intentions inter-relate with ongoing developments in the Asia-Pacific's overall strategic environment. It also focuses on how effectively these intentions must be communicated.

An underlying assumption of the book is that while analysis of key Asia-Pacific states' national security interests and likely behaviour is useful, significant uncertainty will always pervade any such examination. Convergent security seeks to hedge against uncertain or unexpected policy outcomes by incorporating the strongest aspects of both contending security models. This 'realist-liberal' compromise is not necessarily a great power concert that assumes all powers are satisfied with ongoing trends (China certainly is not). Instead it represents a rational approach to liberalism that satisfies the national security interests of state-centric actors by creating mechanisms (that is, institutions) that minimise the effects of otherwise unconstrained realist behaviour.

In this context, four broad strategic questions relating to realist-liberal debate applicable to the Asia-Pacific region need to be assessed. The first is: to what extent will the evolving national security outlooks of Asia-Pacific states facilitate regional security cooperation or precipitate regional conflict? Second, what are the strategic approaches of China and Japan, Asia's two great powers, to the region? The third question is: how do the other significant strategic actors in the region respond to great power competition and define their own regional security agendas? Finally, to what extent might the strategic interests and behaviour of these powers converge with those of the United States to shape an effective Asia-Pacific security order?

Russia and India are clearly security actors in an Asia-Pacific context. They still, however, remain more tangential to the central focus and thrust of regional power politics than they themselves would admit. Russia's major geostrategic preoccupation remains Europe and the 'China card' is regarded largely as a counterweight for Russian policy makers to apply in that context. India's strategic preoccupations remain primarily directed toward the subcontinent, although China is viewed by New Delhi as a potential rival in that arena. Both states will be assessed where their policies and behaviour have had a major impact on players and issues that will inform the main concerns of this book but both will be treated primarily as 'aspiring powers' on the periphery of the ongoing Asia-Pacific strategic crucible.

Chapters 2 and 3 will review the security interests and outlooks of the two regionally indigenous powers most likely to vie for dominance or 'hegemony' in the Asia-Pacific: China and Japan. The conceptual analysis found in these two chapters raises a key question: will the national security interests and behaviour of the two key Asia-Pacific powers in an increasingly fluid post-Cold War regional security environment precipitate hegemonic rivalries? As they intensify competition, realist policy prescriptions may well prevail. If geopolitical rivalries based on calculations of high relative costs are discouraged, liberal arguments become more salient.

Chapter 4 will assess how two key secondary strategic players in the region, Korea and Taiwan, will react and relate to the strategic initiatives of the three great regional powers. These two states, identified as being the most dangerous flashpoints for regional conflict, most typify realist concerns for Asia-Pacific security. Yet, recent exchanges between South Korea and the North, and North Korea's apparent willingness to engage in dialogue with both the United States and South Korea on the future of the Korean Peninsula, underscore the potential for liberal approaches to modify even the most serious regional security dilemmas. So too does the intensification of social, cultural and economic interaction across the Taiwan Strait, and the cross-Strait dialogue, despite continued bickering and threats by China to assimilate Taiwan by force. A combination of strategic deterrence and diplomatic tenacity may be enough to ensure war avoidance and to avoid incessant crisis escalation if broad principles are identified that provide the basis of future negotiations concerning both inter-Korean relations and the China–Taiwan dispute.

Chapter 5 will review ASEAN and Australia as potential embodiments of convergent security behaviour, and the strategic intentions that have underscored their recent security postures. It will be argued here that the ASEAN member-states constitute a unified regional security actor to the extent that they share a common interest in shaping Southeast Asia's politico-strategic destiny without great power interference. This unity may deteriorate rapidly, however, if multilateral security initiatives such as the ASEAN Regional Forum (the ARF) prove less effective than originally anticipated, if ASEAN itself is weakened by internal strife within individual ASEAN member-states or if realist scenarios dominate security developments over the next ten to fifteen years. At present, both ASEAN and Australia remain sufficiently committed to achieving regional tranquillity in Southeast Asia to collaborate in implementing selective aspects of convergent security.

The last two chapters develop this book's argument more fully: that convergent security can affect future regional stability in Asia. Chapter 6 examines how the United States is responding to emerging Asia-Pacific geopolitics. Earlier chapters provide an understanding of how security is being conceptualised and managed *within* the Asian context; this chapter analyses how Washington may react to evolving Asian security trends. The analysis will take into account that the United States will continue to exercise an active strategic role in the Asia-Pacific as much on the basis of what it does *not* know as for what it does. Budgetary considerations, bureaucratic competition and responses to other actors' strategic behaviour will probably (and unfortunately) influence US policy as much, if not more than, any distinct American grand strategy.

Will other Asia-Pacific states view future American initiatives as nothing more than an anti-China containment posture? Or could the implementation of a new, US-backed multilateral network be managed concurrently with processes of regional transparency and trust-building – a 'building block' approach predicated on initial confidence-building initiated at the bilateral level by China and the United States? The former trend could foreshadow intensified Sino-American tensions leading to regional conflict. The latter development might temper what are disturbing patterns of growing animosity between these two countries in their security relations.

In conclusion, chapter 7 argues that a combination of *ad hoc* bilateral security measures involving established alliances should be applied in combination with the gradual implementation of multilateral architectures. This strategy – integrating bilateral security arrangements with new multilateralist infrastructures – is a key component of the convergent security approach. *Convergent Security*, then, is defined as a managed transition from a regional security system based predominantly on realist-oriented bilateral security arrangements to one based increasingly upon regional multilateral arrangements.

It is acknowledged at the outset of this book that states' security postures cannot be viewed as exclusively self-interested and uncompromising, particularly in an era of intensifying globalisation. Nor is the creation of multilateral structures the only means for attaining greater regional stability and cooperation. Policy pluralism is certainly evident in much of the foreign policy behaviour of the states considered here.

The book's fundamental argument, however, is hardly invalidated by acknowledging pluralism and diversity in Asia-Pacific security politics. Convergent security is neither about reinforcing balancing or hegemonic strategies via alliance reinforcement or expansion, nor building an 'ideal' pluralistic security community where cooperation completely supersedes competition. It is a *process* of gradual community-building by using both bilateral and multilateral instrumentalities that currently exist to cope with rapid structural change, and to maintain sufficient control over key security policy management tasks needed to prevent conflict escalation. If a complementary application can be realised, the question of whether both 'realism' and 'liberalism' can be the right approach becomes less relevant over time.

To be successful in assuring the stability and prosperity of the Asia-Pacific, convergent security requires a dual commitment from the United States. The first part of this commitment is the continuation of a significant American strategic presence in the region. The second part is a simultaneous American willingness to re-orient its security objectives to bring them more into line with the predominant security concerns of its Asian allies. This would involve Washington gradually revising its regional outlook and strategies away from a predominantly defensive posture of checking hegemonic rivals through power balancing, and towards a more positive and active concentration on strengthening Asia-Pacific norms and institutions. Any 'Pacific Community' that emerges during this new century cannot be viable without American influence and resources. Nor can it be sustained without the support of a less realist China playing an active role in a widened regional security network.

A major focus of this book is how Asia-Pacific states can modify their concern with relative gains without allowing the tensions inherently associated with rapid economic modernisation and political change to overwhelm their propensity to cooperate. This book raises some hard questions about the relevance of contending policy approaches to those issues which promise to dominate the security agenda in the Asia-Pacific for years to come.

Indeed, most of this book was completed before the inauguration of George W. Bush as the forty-third President of the United States. Although the new Bush Administration has embarked upon some specific policy courses directly related to problems discussed here (such as accelerating missile defence development and viewing China more as a 'strategic competitor'), the general argument of pursuing extremist policy approaches of either realist or liberal persuasions remains intact. The new Bush Administration has assigned the 'national interest' paramount status in its strategic thinking about the world and the region under consideration here. It is openly sceptical about the utility of liberal prescriptions in serving such interests. To discount the relevance of liberal postulates completely, however, is to risk slipping into a very dangerous form of unilateralism from which the United States cannot lead or influence other international relations effectively.

The unmitigated focus of the Bush Administration on realist politics is better understood if the failed multilateralism of the early Clinton years is taken into account. Having been confronted with the shortcomings of an overly zealous commitment to a liberal or 'Wilsonian' global agenda, the Clinton Administration retreated to a form of 'assertive unilateralism' that was no less extreme a policy than that which preceded it. The 'Clinton Doctrine' justified unilateral American and/or allied intervention where necessary to prevent genocide and other humanitarian catastrophes. In doing so, it signalled a clear disdain for global and regional institutions apart from those led by the United States to manage a global order on an *ad hoc*, even reactionary basis.[22] As one of the key foreign policy advisers for George W. Bush's campaign noted, such policy inconsistency neither strengthened multilateralism nor fulfilled national policy priorities and commitments that were inadequately supported by a shrinking US military capability.[23] George W. Bush thus assumed the presidency with a determination to restore order by prioritising US national security interests to face a seemingly unwieldy and unpredictable world. This determination was sharply tested by the need to exercise careful diplomacy in the aftermath of the spy plane incident where an American surveillance aircraft, damaged by a Chinese military jet, was forced to land without permission on Hainan Island in April 2001.

Subsequently, President Bush was testing a clearly unilateralist version of realism by pressing ahead with the development of a ballistic missile defence system (BMD). Designed to protect American sovereign territory and US forces abroad from nuclear or other weapons of mass destruction (WMD) attacks by so-called 'rogue states', BMD was being perceived by US allies in Europe and Asia with scepticism based on technology barriers and on its strategic rationale. Rejecting the mutually assured destruction of MAD premises of postwar deterrence strategy, BMD emphasised strategic defence rather than a nuclear 'balance of terror' as the best means to protect the United States and its allies against future missile threats. As this book went to press, President Bush was dispatching envoys to Northeast Asia and Australia to explain its reasoning and to placate Japanese, South Korean and Australian anxieties about this shift in US strategic thinking. Daily media reports of the visits in early May 2001 by US Deputy Secretary of State, Richard Armitage, and the US Assistant Secretary of State for East Asia, James Kelly, demonstrated the apparent fluidity of the security environment at this time, the ramifications of which were still being grasped. Preliminary analysis, however, would suggest that the extent to which the Bush Administration could apply a purely realist credo to a world less willing to accept American priorities as its own remained highly questionable. The rationale for applying convergent security to realise greater stability in the Asia-Pacific region, therefore, remained no less salient.

# CHAPTER 2

# Great-Power Strategy I: China

The extent to which the United States will remain a major force in Asia-Pacific security relations is one of the key questions that will determine the stability of the region well into the twenty-first century. The other, equally crucial, question is what kind of power the People's Republic of China (PRC) will become as its economy and military capability grow over the next few decades. This chapter will discuss China's strategic role largely within the context of the realist-liberal debate. It will analyse the PRC's evolving national security interests, postures and behaviour and their implications for future regional stability. This analysis is not intended to replicate the plethora of material assessing Chinese military doctrine and capabilities that has recently emerged from both Chinese and Western sources. The discussion will focus instead on how Chinese military outlooks and capabilities will affect China's future strategic relations with other key Asia-Pacific security actors, and will evaluate China's geopolitics, military thinking and capabilities in the context of its perceived national interests.

How policy makers in China respond to the issue of multilateralism will have an enduring impact on the future of the Asia-Pacific region. The potential gains that would flow from assimilating China into a stable regional security environment – whether this is a balance of power or a regime based on mutual norms and organisational frameworks – are immense. Along with Europe (including Russia) and the United States, China will be one of the three great centres of geopolitical influence and its economic and strategic weight, combined with its vast population and cultural influence, will affect the rest of Asia well into the twenty-first century. As Samuel Kim and Lowell Dittmer have concluded, '[Its] total power in demographic, geopolitical, military and economic terms, coupled with the cultural legacy it has bequeathed to many Asian societies, guarantee that China will be accorded the status of a regional power, even if the extent to which it is prepared to play such a role is debatable'.[1]

Realists argue that China is a dissatisfied power that will try to project decisive force further afield as its military strength grows – that as a result China will threaten the security of other regional states to an extent that they will be forced to form counter-coalitions, or if they do not they will have no choice but to submit to China's will and ambitions.[2] Realists further assert that China's determination to reshape the security landscape in both Asia and the world is underscored by an intense desire to rectify the humiliation suffered by a weak and divided China at the hands of Western powers prior to 1949, and that an equally strong motivation is the desire to translate its impressive economic growth and increased diplomatic clout into an uncompromising quest for predominance. If their argument is correct, efforts by other powers to shape the international agenda by defining transnational norms and by creating regimes to enforce them are only incidental to a China which assigns greater importance to its own national interests than to its image as a responsible – and accountable – major power.

A China perceiving itself as besieged by outside forces will be highly selective regarding the states and policy issues with which it will deal. Such caution will be driven by fear that the Chinese populace and the country's political system would otherwise be 'penetrated' by outside forces. It will adopt a visibly aggressive strategic posture, suspecting the development of anti-China coalitions and the exploitation of China's weaknesses by great-power rivals. By adhering to a 'worst-case' view of how others might be planning to undercut its power and interests, 'China may well be the high church of *realpolitik* in the post-Cold War world'.[3]

If this is an accurate representation of China's thinking, then there is almost no chance that Beijing will support multilateral approaches to resolving Asia-Pacific security issues unless it is able to tailor these approaches to serve its own geopolitical ends. Prospects for stability will steadily decline as a suspicious Chinese leadership consistently resists moves to institutionalise cooperative security norms. Because it views its history as a process of constant exploitation by outsiders, China is predisposed to discount any suggestion that strategic reassurance can supplant great- and middle-power competition in the Asia-Pacific.

In contrast to these sombre realist views, most liberal analysts, while willing to concede that Chinese nationalism is a potentially strong impediment to regional and global stability, argue that such views fail to take into account the certainty that external developments and forces will inevitably influence China's world view. Although Chinese Communist Party (CCP) polemicists continue to issue dire warnings about the need to guard against foreign influences penetrating Chinese society, they also suggest that in working to achieve true 'comprehensive national power', China must come to terms with the limits of its power. It has, for example, had no choice other than to pursue 'open door' marketing and trading strategies which will inevitably make China more economically interdependent. By interacting with external powers the Chinese government is mitigating its self-inflicted internal legitimacy crisis. Perhaps most importantly, Chinese leaders are now pursuing a conflict avoidance strategy that affords China the time it needs to modernise its economy, reconsolidate its political system and develop its military capabilities to a level commensurate with its national ambitions.[4] They can do so because the PRC is less directly threatened by external military forces than at any time since its establishment in 1949. Paradoxically, China's leaders are also compelled to do so because they feel increasingly vulnerable to outside ideological, cultural and technological developments over which they have little control.

According to liberals, a self-confident China may be more inclined to adopt a flexible approach to external developments. It will certainly be more likely to participate in regional and international organisations as a means of generating benefits compatible with its national interests. Beijing has normalised or stabilised relations with most of its neighbouring states in recent years. It has joined and has actively participated in regional and global international organisations and has cultivated a wide array of trading and investment ties to support its quest for economic modernisation. It may not be a 'satisfied power' in the sense that it does not endorse what it sees to be a global status quo dominated by the United States and the West. But it is less prone now to attempt to change the international system by employing violence than it ever was while Mao Zedong was its leader. It no longer actively supports communist insurgencies abroad because it views a stable international environment as a critical precondition for securing its own economic growth and international stature. It negotiates with other great powers by assuming a traditional state-centric identity rather than representing itself as a self-acclaimed 'vanguard' of global revolution. China now views participation in regional and international institutions as a means of gaining acceptance within the international community. It believes that this acceptance can facilitate its own economic modernisation and accord it greater diplomatic influence. Previous Chinese tendencies to draw sharp lines between friends and adversaries have been modified in recent years. This trend may well reflect China's belief that the world is a less threatening place than when the superpowers were vying for influence over Beijing during the Cold War.

Understanding China's fundamental strategic interests should help to clarify the extent to which realist or liberal postures will ultimately prevail in Chinese strategic planning and behaviour. The first step in this process is to identify and evaluate the geopolitical factors that matter the most to China. What most threatens those interests will then be determined. This will be followed by a discussion of how China is responding to those challenges. Finally, implications for regional stability will be assessed.

Realists predict that because China believes that it has not achieved *anquan* or 'complete stability', it will look at the world through competitive lenses and seek to expand its strategic purviews and influence in order to overcome its perceived vulnerabilities. Driven by this motivation, China will show little interest in attaining or preserving a power equilibrium that would satisfy the United States, Japan or other potential geopolitical rivals. This orientation would be consistent with the old Chinese axiom: 'The nation that has no enemy in mind will perish'.[5] Liberals retort that Chinese *realpolitik* will be constrained as China's need to be perceived as a responsible global power intensifies and as its national security interests and outlook become tempered by its need to project a positive image designed to influence its regional neighbours and gain more respect from other global powers.[6] The operative principle could be stated as the 'larger, more authoritative and less divided the multilateral institution or process, the more China will be constrained by image concerns'.[7] If this is true, multilateralism is more likely to curb excessive Chinese belligerence than are strategies of containment.

### China's Geopolitical Calculus

To better understand the national security perspectives of a 'realist' China, it is useful to employ a geopolitical analytical framework. This approach incorporates analysis of concepts like 'strategic frontiers', 'anti-hegemonism', 'border zones', and 'living space'. All of these now appear frequently in Chinese strategic writings. Increasingly, Chinese strategy is preoccupied with establishing not just China's territorial frontiers but 'living space ... contract[ing] with the ebbs and flows of comprehensive national strength' in maritime, technological and economic dimensions.[8] It is important to note, however, that these concepts are narrowly defined in terms of preserving what China deems to be its territorial and sovereign integrity. This includes the recovery of territory and rights of sovereignty that China sees as falling within its *historical* purview.

Chinese strategists note that their country's geostrategic thinking has been less 'global' in its orientation than that of the West. Successive Chinese dynasties have instead focused on protecting China's critical 'Central Plains hinterland', the area between the Yellow and Yangtze Rivers, from northern invaders. This has driven the Chinese to adopt what traditionally has been a 'border-defence oriented geostrategy'. Such an approach has been preoccupied with stabilising domestic opposition and with strengthening China's immediate peripheries through calculated diplomacy or through defensive measures designed to secure the state from invasion. The notion of employing force projection to assure or expand living space has been, until very recently, atypical of the historical Chinese experience.[9]

Currently, China's geopolitical thinking is underscored by Beijing's fear that American diplomacy and high technology will combine to contain Chinese power by pinpointing and exploiting the PRC's strategic vulnerabilities before China can neutralise them.[10] Despite recent efforts to expand its maritime capabilities, China's military power is essentially confined to the Eurasian land mass and adjacent waters. Its exterior lines of communication are highly susceptible to interdiction by sea or air. Despite efforts by Mao Zedong and the People's Liberation Army (PLA) to disperse key industries and resources throughout the Chinese hinterland, the country's politico-economic nerve centres remain concentrated in Manchuria and along its eastern peripheries. Northern and southeast China are vulnerable to concentrated missile and air strikes as well as maritime blockades.

To China's north is Russia, a traditionally hostile and equally landbound state. To the northeast, it confronts an ongoing American military presence on the Korean Peninsula and in Japan. Apart from the American presence on that front, it must also reckon with the increasing indigenous military capabilities of Japan and South Korea. On its western flank, it confronts a resurgent India with a growing nuclear capability and expanding high technology sector. And then there is Pakistan – a nuclear-capable ally that may drag China into the vortex of nuclear conflict on the subcontinent. While China is the only major power with direct land access to Southeast Asia (coupled with a sizeable ethnic representation in the subregion), this advantage is neutralised by its current inability to contest either US naval or collective ASEAN control over key maritime chokepoints and archipelagic waters. If counter-containment is a hallmark of contemporary Chinese strategy, its geopolitical environs provide it with sufficient rationales to perpetuate such a strategic outlook.

Classical geopoliticians vied over how to interpret power in accordance with geographic frontiers and regions. Writing in 1904 Halford J. Mackinder argued that the Eurasian land mass, along with the African continent, should be treated as a single 'World Island', subject to unification by landpower emanating from a 'heartland' situated in the centre and north of the Island, territory commensurate to what is now Russia.[11] Writing towards the end of World War II, Nicholas Spykman contested Mackinder's theory by asserting that any force that could control the 'marginal crescent' stretching from Western Europe through the Middle

East into South Asia and East/Southeast Asia, could neutralise the heart-land's landpower. In the nineteenth century, this role had been assumed by the British Royal Navy; increasingly it would be performed by American sea and air power.[12]

During the Cold War, Chinese commanders faced the very type of geopolitical challenge that Mackinder anticipated: Russian troops occupying outer Mongolia – the 'fist in China's back' – and poised to seize both Manchuria to the east and Xinjiang to the west.[13] Recent Chinese analysis has underscored Beijing's concerns over growing strategic ties between Mongolia and the United States. It is claimed that US military reconnaissance is now directed against the PRC from Mongolian sites, Chinese nuclear installations in Xinjiang are being monitored, and that the United States has established 'an extremely favourable geographic position to keep watch over their [sic] strategic rivals, China and Russia'.[14]

Yet other Chinese analysts posit that Spykman's theory provides an explanation for postwar American containment strategy and for what they view as the current determination on the part of the United States to contain China.[15] These strategists perceive that the Asia-Pacific maritime environment is, for example, a theatre in which there is every possibility of an increasing level of confrontation between China and other regional maritime powers. This is because China is determined to reclaim long-lost space, influence and resources at a time when 'after centuries of bloody struggle, land interests and resources have been divided up and rigidly fixed, while competition over maritime interests [is] still in full swing'.[16] They regard the need to deploy a credible nuclear force as a technological problem directly related to their desire to confirm China's status as a contender for regional and extra-regional influence in the marginal crescent: that such a force may possibly deter US strategic intervention in future contingencies where China may need to confront Taiwan or Japan; that it allows China to cope with the multilateral arms control agenda of Western powers by conducting independent, albeit increasingly discrete, nuclear relations with Pakistan, Iran and other 'rimland' states; and, at the most fundamental level, that it helps to enhance China's 'international status' as a strategic player.[17]

## China's National Security Interests

The preceding analysis offers a rudimentary framework for identifying China's key national security objectives. Despite its recent publication of several defence 'white papers', there is still a relative lack of transparency on the part of the Chinese bureaucratic and policy-making sectors. This impedes efforts by outsiders to synthesise from and discriminate among an increasing wealth of Chinese publications on strategy and military affairs.[18]

Efforts to identify China's core national security interests therefore remain speculative. Nonetheless, it is important to attempt such analysis if responses to Chinese strategic capabilities and behaviour are to be devised and managed. A major school of thought in the West is that China has embraced a posture of 'confident nationalism', that while it would prefer to avoid a major confrontation with hostile external powers like the United States, it is no longer prepared to bow to American power in any future regional confrontation.[19] Confident nationalism is an unmitigated realist national security posture on the part of China to defend its sovereignty, preserve its national unity and project its strategic interests. This view has come to dominate China's approach towards Taiwan. It is reasonable to expect that it will also be increasingly reflected in China's relations with Japan.

There is, however, a different but equally prevalent interpretation of current Chinese security policy. It is that since China believes its involvement in a major war is a remote prospect for several decades, it has prioritised economic reform to such a degree that its traditional 'world view' of competitive ideological camps has been assigned a secondary status to that of pursuing national economic development.[20] Thus, according to this interpretation, 'engagement of China in the international economy, and its incorporation into major multilateral organisations, has enhanced China's cooperative behaviour by providing ideas and incentives for change and shaping the specific nature of policy changes'.[21]

It is argued here that China's 'comprehensive national power' posture (a concept discussed more fully below) has effectively integrated both of these outlooks. China's national economic development has been assigned immediate importance by its leadership, establishing trade, investment and technological relations with the West. However, economic growth is a means to a more fundamental policy end: China plans to assimilate from the West without becoming 'Westernised' and to then use its new-found economic 'muscle' to reshape the international security environment to one more in accord with its own national security interests.

### 'Primary' National Security Interests

China's fundamental security interest is the survival and consolidation of the Chinese state. This objective is multidimensional, involving the survival of the national communist regime; the consolidation of 'lost' and contested territory under firm Chinese control; and avoiding conflicts that it either cannot win or that would impede its campaigns to achieve economic modernisation and greater political influence. None of these objectives has been completely achieved but progress has been visible toward fulfilling all of them since the 1989 Tiananmen Square incident.

The survival of the Chinese Communist Party (CCP)-controlled regime in China is as much a national security problem as one of internal politics because the country's history feeds Chinese perceptions that outside threats are predominantly responsible for China's historical weakness and subjugation. External threat perceptions have been reinforced by the CCP's recent efforts in the aftermath of Tiananmen to strengthen Chinese nationalism, directed against the West, in order to divert questioning of its own legitimacy.[22] The problem with this approach is that China continues to require Western technology and markets to generate credibly what the Chinese term 'comprehensive national power'. This envisions China as a highly developed country with sufficient wealth and technology to become a 'multidimensional regional competitor', capable of challenging US strategic power in East Asia along a broad spectrum of combat scenarios.[23]

The Chinese have dealt with their dependence on Western technology by embracing the approach that the 'best defence is a good offence'. China has attempted to pre-empt Western prescriptions for international security by advancing the PRC's own five principles of peaceful coexistence in international settings, with particular emphasis on 'mutual respect for sovereign and territorial integrity' and 'non-interference with internal affairs'.[24] This approach, in Beijing's view, circumvented the threat to China represented by President George Bush Snr's 'New World Order' concept proposed immediately after the Persian Gulf conflict and thought to be a direct Western assault on the PRC's security. As expressed by China's public security minister in late 1991, hostile outside forces led by the United States and Japan had 'defined China as their key target and have stepped up all kinds of infiltration and sabotage activities'.[25] More recently, Chinese suspicions had focused on the Clinton Administration's 'engagement policy' as a facade for the perpetuation of traditional American containment strategy, previously directed toward the Soviet Union but now targeted against China. Early Chinese press analysis of incoming US President George W. Bush perceived little real difference between his 'actual' China policy and that of his predecessors. Taiwan and missile defence were designated as possible issues where differences could intensify.[26] The new President's decision in April 2001 to sell Taiwan an extensive arms package that included submarines, Kidd-class destroyers and P-3C Orions, and to proceed with developing a ballistic missile defence system, exacerbated such Chinese concerns. In general, Chinese analysts question if US claims that Washington is trying to cultivate better relations with the PRC can be taken seriously. China will remain sceptical so long as it feels that the United States is continuing its traditional anti-Chinese containment strategy by strengthening its bilateral alliance network (particularly the US–Japan alliance).[27]

Under Deng Xiaoping's policy of negotiating irredentist disputes (but on terms inevitably favourable to the PRC), China was successful in winning back control of Hong Kong from Britain (in 1997) and Macau from Portugal (in 1999). The PRC has reserved the right to use force to regain control of Taiwan if growing separatist tendencies among that island's polity eventually lead to the election of a government in Taipei committed to secession from mainland China. Most other territorial disputes, however, have been put on hold. This includes the Spratly Islands controversy and the dispute over control of the five Diaoyutai/Senkaku islands 200 kilometres northeast of Taiwan. Beijing has also accepted existing boundaries as 'a basis for settlement' in recent talks with Russia, India and the Soviet successor states of Central Asia. Over the mid- to long term, however, China could revive a more aggressive posture in any of these disputes, in accord with the strategic frontiers thesis. On the pretext of maintaining territorial security, China may be increasingly inclined to link its growing military power projection capabilities with the need for establishing buffer zones comprised of 'lost territories'.[28]

China is thus determined to build 'comprehensive national power' as a strategy for defending state interests.[29] It intends to assimilate high technology from abroad and develop its economic capabilities at home in order to become an authentic great power during the twenty-first century. The initial, short-term phase of this power-building strategy is based on pursuing an open-door trade policy aligned with a diplomatic posture keyed towards avoiding war with other great powers. The second phase of the strategy (to be implemented sometime between 2020 and 2050), seeks to resurrect traditional goals of defending national sovereignty and enhancing China's major power status by applying its broadening technological, economic and military base. As Michael D. Swaine has noted, the projected shift to a 'second-tier' strategy 'suggests that the Beijing leadership ... once it believes China has attained a relatively advanced level of economic and military development, [will] pursue more assertive nationalist objectives with less regard for the maintenance of a placid and stable regional and global environment'.[30]

The primary risk with this sort of approach is that China may miscalculate the rate of the strategic and military decline of its potential opponents relative to the increase in its own strategic capabilities. Evidence that the Chinese are prone to make this type of mistake has already emerged. China's March 1996 provocation of Taiwan, which incited a more than proportionate American response, stands as a case in point. Nevertheless, this classic misreading of relative power in the region is reinforced in policy assessments currently offered by Chinese analysts. They speculate that the 'inevitable US decline' will affect the global balance of power in favour of China and that this will in turn allow their country to become the dominant Asia-Pacific power.[31] China's strategists will need to be careful in accepting such projections too literally. Many Asia-Pacific states are encouraging the United States to remain fully engaged in the region precisely because of their growing apprehension over Chinese ambitions and strategic capabilities.

### 'Secondary' National Security Interests

Reaching great-power status and redressing historical grievances comprise China's long-term strategic agenda. However, Beijing also has to deal with more immediate regional security concerns. These mesh with the Chinese interest in avoiding regional conflict and pursuing economic modernisation.

In Northeast Asia, China desires a stable Korean Peninsula. The Chinese want to avoid being pulled into a military confrontation with the United States by a belligerent North Korean proxy. At the same time Beijing is struggling to come to terms with the growing prospect that Korea will be unified. It also fears that Pyongyang may turn to Washington out of economic desperation or in an effort to extract counter-leverage at the expense of South Korea.[32] China is also concerned about what it believes is an increasing trend in Japan towards strategic assertiveness.[33] Beijing has noted that Japan is shifting the overall pattern of its military deployments from a 'defensive posture facing the North' (against a now largely extinct Soviet/Russian military threat) to reinforce its security 'to the West' (facing the Korean Peninsula and China).[34] Chinese interest in this subregion has recently involved a selective level of strategic collaboration with Russia, concurrently seeking to acquire advanced weapons technology from the Russians at 'bargain basement' prices.[35] Finally, China worries about the influence of Central Asian ethnic states on its own minority populations; to prevent the spread of restiveness to its own populations China has moved to sign security and cooperation treaties with most of these states.

In Southeast Asia, China wishes to expand its economic relations with the ASEAN states, primarily as a way of easing concerns over China's politico-strategic intentions in that subregion. Economic engagement with the ASEAN states is not, however, considered to be a vital element of Chinese economic modernisation. China would eventually like to see the Asia-Pacific Economic Cooperation (APEC) group replaced by a more indigenous institution as the primary economic organisation in the Asia-Pacific. The 'ASEAN + 3' (initially convened between ASEAN, Japan, China and South Korea in 1997) may provide the framework for such an arrangement. While this would work to China's advantage because the United States would be excluded, there is an attendant risk that the Japanese could assume a dominant role.[36]

China wants to facilitate its access to, and development of, those territories that it has laid claim to in the South China Sea. This would necessitate the ASEAN states eventually accepting a substantial Chinese maritime presence in Southeast Asian waters.[37] As was the case with its campaign of military intimidation launched against Taiwan in early 1996, the Chinese appear to have misjudged ASEAN determination to resist such encroachment. There is little doubt that the Chinese leadership was surprised when Manila reacted as strongly as it did to the PLA's forcible seizure of Mischief Reef in February 1995 (an islet in the Spratly Islands group claimed by both the PRC and the Philippines).[38] Overall, however, China does not aspire to dominate Southeast Asia and the PRC will probably tread carefully. It is reasonable to expect that Beijing will, at least in the short term, seek to avoid inflaming ASEAN sensitivities, including those of its former adversary, Vietnam.[39] Over the long term it will continue to press its sovereign claims in the South China Sea while simultaneously and gradually working to reduce American power and influence in that subregion.[40]

### Threats to Chinese Interests

As acknowledged in its October 2000 defence white paper, China currently faces no imminent strategic or military threat to its national security.[41] It is therefore focusing its defence modernisation efforts on developing force capabilities to cope with mid- to long-term contingencies. China remains politically and geographically united under the current ruling elite, and such control appears guaranteed to endure under the existing political system. In the absence of strong challenges to Chinese sovereignty or elite legitimacy by separatist movements, or by other ethnic and dissident groups, it is difficult to imagine the conditions under which significant change may occur. Over the longer term a Chinese leadership may emerge that, for any number of reasons, is more expansionist-minded or threat-oriented than the current regime and therefore more prone to confront perceived or real opponents with the use of force. As Allen S. Whiting has observed, regime factionalism could lead to heightened threat perceptions based on a belief that foreign interests could more easily exploit China's vulnerabilities at a time of national disunity.[42]

Even during the most sanguine of times, however, Chinese military planners are required to project threatening scenarios in order to justify the continuing claim by the PLA to a substantial portion of the national resource base. This inevitably leads to the questions: where do these officials see China's interest being most seriously challenged and by whom?

China's National Defense Ministry reportedly has identified resurgent Russian nationalism, rising Japanese militarism, and Indian maritime expansionism as the most significant intra-regional threats.[43] Other Chinese concerns include the prospect that unrest in the Soviet successor republics of Central Asia will spill over to infect the minority populations of northwest China; that the dispute over control of the Spratly Islands will intensify; and that Taiwan's growing independence movement will continue to frustrate Beijing's policy agenda.

### The American Threat

There is one threat that China fears more than any other. It is based on the perception that the United States is intent on becoming a global hegemon, disrupting Beijing's irredentist and strategic agendas in the process.[44] In November–December 1993, the Chinese Communist Party Central Committee and the Central Military Commission convened a landmark symposium to consider emerging threats. Although Japan was identified as being China's most likely long-term rival, the United States was classified by a substantial number of the participants as the most pressing threat to China's national security.[45] In a wide-ranging speech delivered to the PLA delegation to the second session of the Ninth National People's Congress in March 1999, Zhang Wannian, Vice Chairman of the Central Military Commission (*Zhongyang Junshi Weiyuanwei*) cited Deng Xiaoping's prediction that China would be the 'next target' of America's 'hegemonic strategy'. He concluded that China must 'fully and comprehensively prepare for the possibility that the United States may launch military aggression against China, manipulate another country into starting a war, or provoke a war by fostering Taiwan independence forces'.[46]

Chinese policy makers are increasingly concerned with Washington's determination to export Western-style democracy to China. This concern has been further exacerbated by an apparent willingness on the part of the United States to compromise the 1972 Shanghai Communique and the 'one China principle'. In Chinese eyes, this has been evidenced by Washington conducting higher profile political relations with Taiwan. The perception of American betrayal has been further reinforced by the United States exporting advanced conventional weapons systems to a number of states in the region, including Taiwan, and by exploring prospects to deploy theatre missile defence (TMD) systems in Northeast Asia that could neutralise Chinese missile systems. Similarly, Chinese analysts accuse the United States of retaining its forces in Japan and South Korea to contain China as much as to protect those long-term treaty allies. Suspicion is also prevalent that the 'China threat' is being fostered by hard-liners in the United States in order to preserve a formidable American military-industrial complex despite the end of the Cold War.[47]

## The TMD Issue

In reality, US missile defence technologies posit the only potential threat to China's own modest but growing nuclear deterrent. Japan, in particular, is collaborating with the US Defense Department and various American defence industries to develop theatre missile defence systems. If actually developed and deployed, TMD could eventually neutralise short- to mid-range Chinese ballistic missiles. The Chinese could respond by: (1) deploying a large number of short-range systems to overwhelm what TMD assets may be in place; (2) deploying missiles with multiple re-entry vehicles or multiple independently targetable re-entry vehicles; (3) by deploying cruise missiles for which no defence technology currently exists; or (4) by adopting various TMD development or procurement options (that is, modified Russian missile defence technology) to neutralise initial military disadvantages they may incur in the region's military balance. To pursue the second option, China has indicated it may need to resume nuclear testing, thereby foresaking its adherence to the Comprehensive Test Ban Treaty (CTBT) while simultaneously affording it the opportunity to develop a completely new generation of nuclear warheads and commensurate delivery systems.[48]

Chinese officials and analysts are genuinely concerned that the United States will succeed in developing the means to neutralise their own country's strategic and theatre nuclear capabilities. In a scathing criticism of the US TMD program levelled in March 1999, for example, Chinese Foreign Minister Tang Jiaxuan warned that the development and research of TMD would exert 'a very unfavourable impact' on the global and regional 'strategic balance and stability in the next century'. He argued it would give the United States and its allies offensive force capabilities 'which will go far beyond ... [their] legitimate defense needs and harm the peace and security of the Asia-Pacific region'.[49]

The prospect of the United States incorporating Taiwan into any Asia-Pacific missile defence system is particularly onerous to Beijing. The Chinese view any such development as an unmitigated infringement of its sovereignty and as a strong indication of American duplicity regarding its pledge to honour the Shanghai Communique as part of the Sino–American normalisation process. The Chinese press cited a 1999 Department of Defense report on TMD feasibility and the possible participation of Japan, South Korea and Taiwan in TMD development as an 'indirect, cover-up roundabout approach' to the issue in an attempt to avoid

China's condemnation of Washington's violation of the Sino–US joint communiques.[50]

It may be that China, in the final analysis, would begrudgingly accept the deployment of US TMD systems to protect South Korea. It is highly unlikely, however, that it would stand by if the United States attempted to employ TMD as a way to deprive Beijing of the means to intimidate Taiwan with its own missile capabilities, should Taiwanese politics evolve unfavourably to Chinese interests. Beijing's acquiescence to the deployment of a highly advanced TMD system involving Japan would also be unlikely.[51]

### Future Conflict Scenarios

The effectiveness of US weapons technology – as it operated during the 1991 Persian Gulf conflict – shocked the PLA and prompted a wholesale revision in Chinese military doctrine towards 'active defence'. While Chinese force planners do not necessarily contemplate a direct American attack on their homeland,[52] they do regard the United States as their most likely antagonist in other threatening scenarios. They project that the United States would contest any Chinese attempt to forcefully assimilate Taiwan or consolidate its territorial claims in the South China Sea. This is because these contingencies would require China to project offshore forces that would constitute both an unacceptable threat to, and too tempting a target for, US naval forces. The Chinese Academy of Military Science war-gaming and contingency planning has reportedly been preoccupied with Sino–American confrontations in the East and South China Seas since the early 1990s.[53]

If the United States were to intervene against Chinese forces in either a Taiwan or South China Sea confrontation, any Chinese surface fleet used to interdict Taiwanese or ASEAN shipping or to transport Chinese troops to key combat zones would be highly vulnerable to air and sea-launched precision-guided weapons and anti-ship missiles. The PLA's modern jet fighter aircraft are still too few in number to redress its lack of air cover, especially in open waters, in the face of any determined American attack against Chinese positions.[54] As was demonstrated during the March 1996 Taiwan crisis, China has little to counter US aircraft carriers that can be deployed along its littorals.[55] In addition, the interoperability of its air, naval and land forces in a combat situation remains suspect. Moreover, the United States and other Western arms suppliers are gradually providing Taiwan and some ASEAN countries (for example, Singapore) with high technology weapons and command and control systems that China cannot match qualitatively in the short term.

*A Japanese Threat?*

In the December 1993 future threats symposium noted above, 60 per cent of the participants identified Japan as being the state that would pose the most serious threat to Chinese security in the year 2020. Japan is viewed as China's major competitor for control over the maritime territory claimed by the PRC and also as the state most likely to block Chinese access to the energy resources under the East and South China Seas. There is little propensity on China's part to view Japan as a potential partner for cultivating regional interdependence and conflict avoidance; instead, Japan is viewed as an increasingly desperate offshore power primed to challenge China's declared strategic frontiers.

When stated publicly, Chinese concerns about Japan's military potential are usually long on rhetoric and lacking in details.[56] China appears to be most concerned about: (1) the potential for Japan to convert its formidable high technology infrastructure into an equally formidable national military capability; (2) the possibility that Japan could spoil China's drive to achieve regional naval superiority by rapidly expanding its own naval and air support strength; and (3) the ability of the Japanese to combine both of these potentialities in order to contain China, with or without allies, once American military power has been withdrawn from the region.

Chinese analysts singularly reject the premise that Japan will fail to develop its military power.[57] They are particularly concerned with Japan's postwar history of efficiently integrating its Civilian and Technology Industrial Base (CTIB) and its Defense Technology and Industrial Base (DTIB). This has given Japan a decisive long-term strategic edge over a China that has developed unsophisticated equivalents, and which now faces the need to emulate Japanese integration of these two sectors.[58] The Chinese argue that Japan is moving away rapidly from its traditional self-defence posture to one that incorporates greater levels of power projection based around the deployment of state-of-the-art weapons systems in future regional contingencies.[59]

In spite of this pronounced and decidedly anti-Japanese stance, the path forward for Chinese policy makers is not really so transparent. A number of countervailing influences must also be taken into consideration. For example, Japan is still seen by China as a potential supplier of economic and technological assistance. More importantly, there is also some speculation that Japan may serve Chinese strategic interests by acting in the future as a counterweight to offset US influence in the region. How China can extract relative gains in its relations with Tokyo while simultaneously (and loudly) disparaging any Japanese efforts to modernise its offshore defences should present Chinese diplomats with one of their greatest policy challenges over the next decade and beyond.

*Russia and India: Residual Threats?*

No two countries were more hostile to China's security objectives during the 1960s and 1970s than the Soviet Union and India (themselves allied by a 1971 Friendship Treaty). By the mid-1990s, China had repaired its ties with both Russia (as the USSR's major successor state) and India, to the point that Moscow had become a quasi-ally while a Sino–Indian *detente* had emerged. Both events surprised many Western security observers. However, it is doubtful if the sale of weapons by Russia to the PRC, or the September 1993 Sino–Indian border agreement, represent the beginnings of genuine and lasting security partnerships.[60] Ultimately, Russia cannot offer China the finance, resources or high technology needed by that state to turn it into a first-class world power. With this in mind, a reconstituted Sino–Soviet alliance would only materialise if Sino–American and Russian–American relations deteriorated beyond all reasonable expectations. Such an eventuality would come as a surprise, not only to Beijing, but also to Washington and Moscow. Future Sino–Indian relations will hinge decisively on whether Indo–Pakistani animosities escalate. China probably would not stand by and watch passively if India sought to neutralise Pakistan through military action. This would, after all, be ceding to New Delhi complete hegemony over the subcontinent.[61]

Recent trends in Sino–Russian relations have been largely positive, especially in the realm of security relations. In fact, liberals can point to a number of developments in Sino–Russian relations that testify to the continued utility of regional bilateral security cooperation. Some of these developments have been represented by bilateral confidence-building agreements covering issues like border demarcation and disarmament, no first-use of nuclear weapons, and no nuclear targeting against each other's territory. Realists can counter that China is extracting far more than it is contributing as its relationship with Moscow deepens. They point to the fact that improving relations with Russia will allow China to shift the bulk of its military power away from its traditional role of defending its northern borders against Eurasian threats. These forces will then be available to support the PRC's campaign to reunite Taiwan with the Chinese mainland. It will also facilitate Chinese attempts to develop a capacity to project offshore power far into Southeast Asia. Greater Chinese access to Russian armaments at bargain-basement prices can only be perceived by China's leaders as an added strategic bonus.

Globally, China is relying increasingly on playing the 'Russian card' in an effort to counterbalance the expansion of American influence into the former Eastern Europe via an enlarged North Atlantic Treaty Organization (NATO).[62] When China reportedly floated a proposal to forge a military alliance with Russia in late 1996 it was probably designed as a countermeasure to offset expanding American strategic influence in

Europe. But this initiative was rejected by the Yeltsin Government, partly because Russia desperately needed (and still needs) to sustain inflows of Western capital, but also because Russian policy makers believed that it would be unwise to superficially dismiss the reasons behind centuries of historical Sino–Russian animosity simply to orchestrate an expeditious temporary geopolitical 'balancing' act. This was especially true when neither Russia nor China could hope to provide the economic resources and technological knowledge that the West has on offer for both.[63]

Several factors may undermine the recent progress that China believes it has made towards neutralising 'the Russian problem'. One is that the Russians remain apprehensive that increasing Chinese commercial predominance in the Russian Far East could presage moves by China to regain areas currently under Russian control that China considers to be 'lost territories'.[64] Russia has also been slow in fulfilling its various commitments to scale back its nuclear weapons systems (the Duma only ratified the START II Treaty in April 2000, more than seven years after its original signing in January 1993). Russian shipbuilding programs, and especially the construction of nuclear attack submarines, continue apace and Russia's largest naval exercise in ten years was conducted in the Pacific during April 1996.[65] These trends serve notice to China, to other Russian neighbours and to the West that a 'feeble but stable' Russia should not be assumed to be a permanent fixture in international relations.[66]

China has no real interest in cultivating a permanently weakened Russia. In a Chinese Foreign Ministry policy paper assessing Russian politics, reportedly submitted to China's State Council in May 1995, the Foreign Ministry argued that Yeltsin's retention of power was in Beijing's best interests because it would probably avert a Russian civil war, avert separatist tendencies among the Siberian republics that lie adjacent to a number of minority populations in northwestern China, and help counter 'hegemonic' behaviour being displayed by the United States throughout the Asia-Pacific region. Beijing believes that the Five Power 'Agreement on Strengthening Trust in the Military Sphere in the Border Region' (signed by China, Russia, Kazakhstan, Kyrgyzstan and Tajikistan in July 1996 and expanded to the 'Shanghai Six' with Uzbekistan's entry in June 2001) strengthens the Commonwealth of Independent States.[67] It also insists that the 'Beijing Declaration', issued by President Jiang Zemin and President Vladimir Putin during the latter's visit to China in July 2000, forcefully promotes 'a multipolar world and the building of a just and fair new international order'. Collectively the PRC's leadership views such agreements as 'dealing a blow to hegemonists playing power politics' in Eurasia. More fundamentally, by keeping the Eurasian heartland 'stable and friendly' (rather than 'stable and feeble'), China is hedging against incurring the hostility of a Russia that may re-emerge as a great power.[68]

The crushing defeat of the Indian Army by the PLA at Aksai Chin in 1962 infused a deep and enduring scar on India's national psyche and has fuelled an intense determination in New Delhi to avoid being humiliated by the Chinese again.[69] Beijing is well aware that its military success in the Himalayas has created an enduring and increasingly complex security dilemma on its southwest border. In the aftermath of the Cold War, Sino–Indian rivalry promises to intensify as China and India vie for influence in the Northern Tier, the Indian Ocean and Southeast Asia. Beijing's support for the internationally despised Burmese military junta, its transfers of nuclear and missile technology to Pakistan and its sustained political hardline over Tibet can all be attributed to its need to contain Indian regional aspirations. India may or may not rank just behind the United States and Japan as China's 'most pressing security concern'.[70] However, their respective geopolitical ambitions and strategic vulnerabilities make China and India natural rivals. The end of the Cold War has sharply underscored that rivalry on such questions as Tibetan nationalism, Indo–Pakistani confrontation, and Burma's future role in both Southeast Asian and Indian Ocean politics.[71]

A basic Chinese concern regarding 'the India problem' relates to its protracted territorial dispute with New Delhi. Although no real military skirmishes have occurred on the Sino–Indian border since the mid-1980s, the inability of the two Asian giants to resolve their conflicting interpretations of where their mutual boundary lies reflects a larger problem: a fundamental mistrust of each other's willingness to refrain from encroaching on the other's strategic buffer zones which otherwise would insulate them. In September 1993 China and India signed an agreement formalising a 'Line of Actual Control' between the Sino–Indian border established during the late 1980s. This accord was designed to maintain the status quo until a final border settlement was negotiated, but a permanent solution is yet to emerge, despite many rounds of talks that have spanned nearly a decade.

The primary strategic goal governing Chinese actions on their side of the border dispute is the need to prevent the Indian influence in Tibet, traditionally quite strong, from gathering momentum. There is no question that such a development would greatly complicate Beijing's efforts to maintain control over that vital but restive province. China views Tibet as a potential staging post for the spread of ethnic and social disunity throughout the rest of Central and Inner Asia. So long as Beijing controls Tibet, the PRC will remain largely insulated against these subversive forces.[72] As a measure of its determination to retain such control, China has prioritised the deployment of tactical nuclear weapons. This is specifically designed to deter regional opponents like India from intervening in any future uprising in Tibet, or from seeking to exploit Chinese strategic weakness should other forms of separatism sufficiently distract the central government. To that end, China reportedly simulated tactical nuclear warfare scenarios in military exercises conducted near Tibet in 1988.

Since that time it has also targeted land-based intermediate-range ballistic missiles (IRBMs) against Indian cities. It has developed the solid-fuelled CSS-5 to replace the liquid-fuelled CSS-2, thought to be the primary 'India-targeted' component of the PRC's nuclear force. The main Indian nuclear threat to China is the *Agni* IRBM which, when fully developed, will be able to target key Chinese sites.[73] This development fits logically into Beijing's adoption of a 'limited nuclear deterrence' strategy designed to achieve escalation control against regional adversaries in any future regional dispute.[74]

Less understandable, in a deterrence context, is why China has assisted Pakistan to develop its nuclear capability by transferring nuclear technology and potential delivery systems to that state. Why did some Chinese officials support this policy when it can only serve to aggravate China's security dilemma *vis-à-vis* India? After all, India has expanded and diversified its nuclear potential in response to threats from both China and Pakistan. Such behaviour by the PRC does not coincide with the institutionalist approach it has adopted on many weapons of mass destruction (WMD) issues in recent years such as signing the Nuclear Non-Proliferation Treaty, the Comprehensive Nuclear Test Ban Treaty, the Biological Weapons Convention and the Chemical Weapons Convention. Nor does it reflect a traditional realist strategy which would call for pragmatic power balancing over the perpetuation of an open-ended arms race.

The answer seems to lie with the Chinese leadership placing sovereign prerogatives such as the conduct of arms sales and the WMD-related relationships *above* its international arms control obligations when dealing in a South Asian context. China continues to favour Pakistani efforts to match Indian military power. During the 1990s it sold several nuclear reactors to Pakistan, transferred numerous high performance A-5 Fantan A and F-7 jet fighter aircraft to that country and is continuing with its efforts to help modernise the Pakistani Army's tank force.[75] These procurement initiatives are viewed by India as strengthening Pakistan's ability to conduct forward defence operations. China is also thought to be helping the Pakistanis narrow the military technology gap that exists between India and Pakistan. This gap may close further as future Chinese weapons become as sophisticated as their Russian counterparts as a result of the ongoing and substantial Sino–Russian arms sales relationship.[76]

It seems unlikely that India and China will overcome their widely divergent attitudes to how China should relate to Pakistan and other South Asian countries. Beijing will continue to assume that the right to establish and expand comprehensive ties, including military sales, with South Asian states is compatible with the normal course of conducting bilateral relations with other countries. India will regard such actions as an encroachment on its 'special interests' in South Asia and attempt to limit Chinese strategic influence in the subcontinent. Developments that are illustrative of the continuing South Asian security dilemma that is fuelled by New Delhi's insistence that China respects its 'sphere of influence' include: (1) efforts to cut Chinese–Sri Lankan military ties prior to India intervening there with its own 'peacekeeping' forces in 1987; (2) India's decision to apply economic pressures and sanctions against Nepal until the latter country cut off its military sales relationship with China's NORINCO defence corporation; and (3) Indian concerns over Chinese involvement in Burma's construction of naval and electronic tracking facilities in the Bay of Bengal adjacent to India's Andaman Islands territory.[77]

Unlike India's obsession with the Chinese nuclear threat, China views India as a local or regional conventional military threat but not necessarily as a substantial nuclear threat.[78] Recent Indian advances in the development of the *Agni*, and India's refusal to sign the Comprehensive Test Ban Treaty, have not yet been directly linked by Chinese analysts to the emergence of a major Indian strategic threat to Chinese security. This seemingly benign outlook appears to be consistent with China's limited deterrence strategy. China *demonstrates* its nuclear resolve to India by deploying tactical nuclear weapons on the Qinghai and Tibetan plateaus and by maintaining what is at least an implicit program of nuclear and missile assistance to Pakistan. In doing so, it expects that India will be deterred from challenging Chinese power in Tibet or in Central and Inner Asia. However, as independent observers have noted, this constitutes a 'high risk' strategy on China's part because it rests upon the premise that India will never attempt to match China's nuclear supremacy. If this proves to be a miscalculation, the Sino–Indian nuclear relationship could develop into a fully-fledged nuclear arms race with clearly adverse implications for regional stability.[79]

Of greater short-term concern to China's strategic planners is how Beijing's strategy to use Burma as a launching point for expanding Chinese strategic access to the Indian Ocean and to Southeast Asia may be complicated by the Sino–Indian rivalry. China has cultivated Burma's military junta by supplying it with massive quantities of conventional armaments (fighter aircraft, naval patrol boats, artillery, tanks and anti-aircraft systems). In return, China has been granted access to the Burmese naval facilities at Hianggyi Island and in the Coco Islands.[80] This not only effectively positions China to monitor Indian naval activities in the Bay of Bengal but it also provides it with the ability to circumvent the Malacca Strait in the event of any future conflict occurring in the

South China Sea. Indian strategists regard a Chinese-controlled Burma as a potential Chinese invasion route to India. This can only work to China's long-term detriment as it will reinforce the very anti-China containment coalitions that Chinese strategists insist are unwarranted in the absence of a genuine 'China threat'.[81]

## China's Evolving Military Doctrine

The PRC released its first comprehensive defence white paper in July 1998 and followed up with the second version in October 2000.[82] While representing marked progress over China's inaugural white paper issued in 1995, these two posture statements still fell short in adequately explaining the primary tasks set for its defence planners. Both papers dwelled instead on the need to refute 'hegemonism and power politics' and to move toward a multipolar world, based on 'mutual security and common trust' and one devoid of security alliances. The documents qualified China's acceptance of institutionalist prescriptions, however, by arguing that participation in regional and multilateral organisations is not the same as a commitment to be bound by the policies emanating from such groups. In this context, the PLA's key mission was to hedge against strategic uncertainty through streamlining force redundancies, and pursuing weapons modernisation. National defence would thus be consolidated, aggression would be resisted, national unification would be sought (particularly in the case of Taiwan) and China's territorial integrity and security would be preserved. The October 2000 document stipulated that these goals would be realised through: (1) consolidating national defence 'independently' and through 'self-reliance'; (2) implementing a posture of 'active defence' by seizing the initiative in combat after an enemy has struck; and (3) building a lean and strong military force 'the Chinese way'. All of these measures would be subordinated to the nation's 'overall economic construction'.[83] The white paper did not stipulate, however, what specific doctrinal or strategic approach would be adopted to achieve these objectives.

In trying to fill this analytical vacuum, analyses of military issues in various Chinese journals are of some use. They are becoming increasingly sophisticated and collectively they provide a general understanding of how Chinese defence planners are grappling with contemporary security problems. However, in isolation these sources are inadequate because the ideological rhetoric often shades the most important points raised. This prevents external analysts from reaching objective conclusions about China's strategic intentions and encourages them to make and accept distorted assessments of China's force structure.[84] From a Western perspective, such obfuscation also reinforces the conclusion that Chinese policy makers have yet to reach consensus over a 'unified' national security posture. This interpretation is further strengthened because the roots of Chinese military thinking are largely at odds with the 'intentions/capabilities' matrix that so often drives Western military planning.[85]

### The Primacy of Realism

Of most relevance to this section is the point raised at the outset of this chapter: for now, China adheres to a largely unqualified realist world view. China's primary national security interest is 'government stability' (or, more literally, 'government preservation'), through the uncompromising pursuit of national sovereignty and territorial integrity.

In his excellent assessment of China's national security outlook, David Shambaugh has described how these objectives shape its military posture and external security behaviour.[86] Chinese strategists believe that national power is always relative among states as the world is in constant flux: state-to-state security relations are constantly changing; military power is only one aspect of overall national power; and states are destined to experience cycles of prominence and decline. These assumptions reflect conditions of impermanence, comprehensiveness and determinism respectively. A strong and unified Chinese state can overcome China's historical tendency to be dominated by foreigners. But to do so Chinese culture needs to be protected from 'creeping capitalism' and other forms of foreign penetration.

Other analysts have expanded on Shambaugh's observations by noting that China's policies of realism have resulted in a gradual supplanting of the Maoist 'grand design' strategy of international relations (as applied during the Cold War) with an 'inside-out' regional strategy. During the first four decades of the PRC's existence, Mao Zedong and his successors attempted to blend class theory with geopolitics. Initially, China sided with the USSR and communist forces in the developing world against the US-led capitalist camp. Later Mao forged an expedient coalition with the West so as to neutralise the even greater threat of 'Soviet revisionism'. His successors have pursued Chinese strategic interests somewhat differently. They have concentrated mainly on achieving China's economic and military modernisation through an increased assimilation of foreign technology and by avoiding obvious 'tilts' or alignment with various great powers.[87]

China's postwar strategy has remained consistent in Beijing's adherence to *realpolitik*. This has emphasised the need to vindicate territorial claims, establish regional hegemony (albeit not openly), increase China's global status and alter the rules of the 'international system' to its own advantage.[88] Most Chinese elites have viewed multilateralism largely as a guise for others to manipulate China and to prevent it from achieving its national interests. They harbour suspicions of international organisations because such entities are perceived as potential instruments for unwarranted intervention in China's sovereignty and internal affairs. The PRC is wary of what it views as recent US efforts to link regional interdependence and multilateral security dialogues with reinforcing the American leadership role.[89]

Chinese analysts have acknowledged that ongoing and historical structural changes, both globally and in the Asia-Pacific region, necessitate a strategic reassessment of policy approaches. The demise of superpower bipolarity took place far more rapidly than many of them anticipated. This triggered an intensive debate within China over how the world should be viewed in the 1990s. Many Chinese analysts argued against the evolution of a simple 'multipolar' framework in place of bipolarity. They concluded instead that international power would be diffused into various functional sectors: that is, the United States, Japan and the European Community would dominate the international political economy while the United States and Russia would still largely control strategic nuclear politics.[90] Others, however, feared that the United States could evolve into a unilateral global hegemon, aggressively challenging China's national interests on such issues as Taiwan.[91] As the decade evolved, a rough consensus developed within Chinese policy-making circles that a type of regional interdependence could emerge, but one still dominated by regional great powers operating firmly along realist lines.[92]

Recent Chinese policy documents underscore one important point. 'Multipolarity' from a Chinese perspective would *not* be synonymous with 'multilateralism', as envisioned by liberals, because China's *realpolitik* does not allow for the possibility that genuine 'diffuse reciprocity' (the long-term, approximately equal, realisation of national interests) can actually occur. Cooperation or conciliation is only adopted as a short-term, expedient tactic rather than as an enduring principle or commitment; otherwise the United States, Japan or Taiwan could use Chinese concessions to realise absolute gains, increasing their own power at China's expense or, even worse, China's own interests could become unacceptably intertwined with those of foreign powers.[93]

China's thinking on this issue consolidated toward the latter part of 1997 when the PLA's newspaper published a definitive article on what was termed a 'New Security Concept'. Arguing that the old 'Cold War mentality' has been swept away by the tides of history, the article integrated realist and liberal postulates to force a comprehensive Chinese view of the world. The most fundamental of these were: (1) the preservation of sovereign authority within a state with no outside intervention;

(2) the avoidance of exercising leverage or sanctions in economic and trading relations between the states; (3) the harnessing of science and technology for peaceful purposes rather than to seek strategic advantage; and (4) the adoption of 'purely' defensive military strategies by rejecting alliances and preventing crises through the pursuit of common and comprehensive security.[94]

The 'New Security Concept' was further refined by China's 1998 defence white paper and by subsequent documents.[95] It was becoming clear, Chinese press reports noted, that the Asia-Pacific region and the world-at-large is moving inexorably towards multipolarity and that strengthening of multilateral dialogues and cooperation is the best means to guarantee peace and security. NATO's recent geographic expansion and politics of military intervention and the United States' recent efforts to strengthen its Asia-Pacific alliances were negative developments that must be countered.[96] China envisions itself as an increasingly significant global actor, invested with the responsibility for leading the Asia-Pacific region into a new era of peace and prosperity. Contrary to its traditional scepticism of multilateralism, China came to embrace some of its key components by the end of the century. Developing multilateralism in Asia through intensifying security dialogues and solidifying economic ties in lieu of outdated alliance politics is the key to achieving greater regional stability.[97]

China has implemented the New Security Concept by pursuing a multidimensional strategy: (1) smoothing relations with its immediate neighbours through border agreements and related confidence-building measures; (2) collaborating with Russia to counterbalance US international security postures related to arms control and peace enforcement; and (3) implementing a regional diplomacy of 'anti-hegemony' designed to shape a regional security environment where US alliance systems will no longer be relevant or necessary.[98]

Therefore, China could decide to embrace multilateralism as a long-term strategy to extricate remaining US forward deployed forces in the Asia-Pacific which Beijing believes mar China's relations with Japan, South Korea and Taiwan.[99] Signs also emerged by the late 1990s that the Chinese concluded it was in their interest to build strategic nuclear arms control and nuclear non-proliferation regimes. It is thought that these could improve China's long-term security by enhancing its image as a responsible world power; that they would help to constrain US technological breakthroughs that might otherwise render China's own nuclear weapons systems redundant; and that such mechanisms may inhibit potential nuclear competitors like India from attempting to match China's own capabilities.[100] Any relentless American pursuit of missile defence technology, however, could lead to China again revising such calculations and adopting a harder line towards institutional mechanisms of strategic reassurance.

### Active Defence and 'Local War'

China's national defence posture has shifted significantly since Mao Zedong's 'People's War' (PW) doctrine held sway over the PLA during much of the Cold War. The PW doctrine evolved from the successful postwar revolutionary experience of the CCP. It emphasised the primacy of politics, the superiority of men over weapons, the judicious application of weak forces against stronger opponents and the waging of protracted war by the masses.[101] During the late 1970s People's War was replaced by 'People's War Under Modern Conditions' (PWUMC). This emphasised positional over protracted guerilla warfare; the systematic defense of Chinese cities over counter-attacking more powerful opponents in the countryside; the development of a Chinese nuclear force to deter nuclear war; and denial of nuclear supremacy to an opponent by surviving any nuclear attack so that the PLA would ultimately prevail through protracted conventional warfare.[102]

In 1985 another major change occurred in Chinese military planning. China's Central Military Commission concluded that the nation's military doctrine should be revised to one of 'active defence' (*jiji fangyu*).[103] Active defence/local war strategy envisions China waging small-scale conflicts along its 'peripheries'. It also places a greater emphasis on rapid force projection than did PWUMC along with the application of high technology and intense firepower, and the achievement of military objectives over a relatively short period of time. These aspects were deemed even more important by Chinese military commanders after they observed the relative ineffectiveness of the PLA's performance in the 1979 Sino–Vietnamese conflict.[104] The Central Military Commission concluded that the PLA should prepare to fight and win 'local wars' rather than major nuclear conflicts against the Soviet Union or the United States. It decided that China would need to strengthen its capacity to fight along its own border and peripheries, where it could operate within 'controlled space and time'. To realise this type of strategy, however, China would be required to streamline its armies to ensure that the PLA embodied a greater level of lethality and increased mobility subject to efficient command and control.

China's active defence/local war strategy was thus designed to be 'integrative and comprehensive', requiring the PLA to be prepared for a variety of regional contingencies. Chinese strategists still insist, however, upon applying a realist perspective to regional security matters coupled with Mao Zedong's traditional concept of 'stretch' or 'mismatch'. This is a strategy that calls for the employment of all available Chinese resources to gradually shift the military balance away from an adversary and into China's favour. But active defence/local war strategy departs from PW and PWUMC by emphasising that there are increased prospects for a greater number of smaller regional conflicts in the post-Cold War era. 'Border defence' entails both internal security threats in minority areas such as Xinjiang and Tibet and armed conflicts against foreign invaders. The latter might include a future US military intervention to defend Taiwan, although Chinese defence analysts have not specifically demarcated this contingency under the border war category.

In mid-1993 the PLA conducted a series of military exercises emphasising combined operations in the Guangdong province that were clearly designed to test China's rapid reaction capabilities in the South China Sea.[105] Preparation for amphibious operations against Taiwan is also preoccupying Chinese military planners.

China's military modernisation programs should ultimately benefit from the PRC's adoption of an active defence/local war strategy. It provides a more systematic and coherent doctrinal guideline for strengthening Chinese military power than did its predecessors and it relies less upon ideological bromides to rationalise away the strategic weaknesses of the PLA. It acknowledges the advantages of employing highly trained personnel in coordinated military operations with limited strategic objectives. By emphasising border defence, Chinese strategists are also being forced to revise their traditional defensive bias – luring the enemy into the deep before counter-attacking, a strategic approach that anticipated high casualty rates among, and occupation of, China's urban populations. Mao's famous quote of tolerating several hundred million deaths is recalled in this context.

There are several reservations to consider with this updating of defence strategies. First, there is the danger that China's military leaders may apply the new doctrine before the PRC achieves the necessary force levels and diversity of capability needed to make it credible, or they may apply it ambiguously. This concern seems particularly applicable to China's nuclear strategy of 'limited deterrence'. Active defence emphasises the value of pre-emptive strikes as an essential tactic enabling the 'weak to overpower the strong'. 'Limited deterrence' relies instead on China maintaining a sufficient nuclear force structure to avoid nuclear pre-emption. Certainly, ongoing analysis in the Chinese or pro-Chinese Hong Kong press tends to portray China's nuclear force as accruing ever greater lethality and size, at both the strategic and tactical level of operations.[106] Yet there appears to be genuine confusion within Chinese nuclear planning circles on how these forces, traditionally designed for second-strike counter-value or city-busting missions (China still observes a 'no first-use' nuclear weapons posture) really 'fit' into the narrower and more precise conceptual framework of offensive counter-strikes and related active defence components.[107] Without resolving this problem, China cannot really determine how its nuclear retaliatory capability will relate to overcoming future adversaries in limited war scenarios.

This problem was graphically demonstrated when the United States deployed two aircraft carriers in March 1996 in response to China's military exercises leading up to the presidential election in Taiwan. Prior to March 1996 it was thought that even the few nuclear weapons China targeted against the United States would be sufficient to deter significant US military intervention in a China–Taiwan confrontation.[108] Beijing was clearly surprised when the Clinton Administration deployed American aircraft carriers in or near the East China Sea just prior to Taiwan's presidential election. It clearly declined to test US resolve or to escalate the crisis despite reports that at least some Chinese hardliners were prepared to test the 'Los Angeles option' if the Americans opted to interdict PLA units firing test missiles off Taiwan's shores. Until it develops a more imposing nuclear force, Beijing cannot be sure that the United States will allow it to launch a full-scale invasion against Taiwan.[109]

A second problem with the active defence/local war approach is that the resource 'stretch/mismatch' axiom is still part of the strategy. The idea that 'inferior forces can defeat superior forces' and that a 'people's war' is still the foundation of active defence undercuts the new strategy's utility. This is because it concedes that a high-technology war started by a major adversary could still overwhelm Chinese border defences forcing the PLA to apply the old PW/PWUMC defensive tactics within China's own borders.[110] Active defence strategy therefore presents the risk that Chinese force planners could become too preoccupied with what *type* of wars China may be fighting over the near-term at the risk of under-assessing how China can *prevail* in local war situations if the other side initially applies active defence better than the PLA. Therefore, if a future regional conflict involving China emerges as something other than a replay of the Persian Gulf conflict, the only real recourse for Chinese commanders would appear to be returning to fighting the very type of indecisive wars of attrition that the active defence strategy is supposed to avoid. China is prepared to respond conceptually to 'the last war fought' but may not be prepared to adjust to the inevitably unique challenges of future warfighting scenarios.

### Merging Force Capabilities With Security Intentions

China's security planning has been influenced more by perceptions of how technological change will affect warfighting capabilities than it has been by threat assessments or strategic priorities. China wants to project greater military power beyond its borders but it cannot oppose simultaneously every other potential military rival. However, China's preoccupation with infusing high technology into its defence systems does indicate that the country's policy elites have little inclination to modify their regional security interests to assuage their neighbours' threat perceptions.

The Chinese tendency to link force capabilities to uncompromising relative gains maximisation has become even more pronounced following Deng Xiaoping's death in February 1997 as the PLA exerts greater influence over China's national security posture.[111] Regardless of what type of leadership rules China, however, greater Chinese defence policy transparency will become critical if future regional security dilemmas are to be avoided. China's defence modernisation must be convincingly represented as part of a larger and natural process of great-power evolution. Any future Chinese leadership will need to become as sensitive to the policy benefits of strategic restraint as to those emanating from the acquisition of strategic power. A Chinese quest to strengthen its naval offshore defence and power projection capabilities (by adopting, for instance, a 'green-water active defence' strategy) will need to be credibly represented as something less threatening than an instrument to enforce Chinese territorial claims.[112] The 'defensive motivations' for China purchasing or co-producing advanced Russian jet fighter aircraft also need to be better postulated by Chinese policy makers. A 'limited nuclear deterrent' will need to be justified in terms other than those of preventing US intervention against China in any future regional conflict. If Beijing cannot justify these programs more effectively than it has to date as being 'defensive' in their orientation, they may well become catalysts for an intensified and destructive Asian arms race.[113]

Ascertaining the extent to which the Chinese leadership can temper its recent enthusiasm for accruing and deploying military high technology as a policy end unto itself will be critical in any future assessment of China's overall force capabilities. How does this 'obsession' complicate China's requirement to integrate its force capabilities with its national security priorities? A key problem is that the 'Persian Gulf factor' that has underwritten much of the active defence/local war doctrinal approach does not really fit in with the types of warfighting scenarios that China is likely to encounter in the Asia-Pacific. China is less likely to be fighting on its own homeland than it is elsewhere. For example, China may find itself applying military pressure against an increasingly independent Taiwan, against ASEAN rivals for control of the Spratly Islands, or engaged in defending its North Korean ally against South Korean and American forces in a renewed Korean conflict. If these Asian 'flashpoints' were to erupt and evolve in ways which drew the PRC into war, the conditions would be very different from those which unfolded in Kuwait. They would certainly vary from the border conflict scenarios which dominate

China's active defence posture. None of these contingencies would find China defending its own population or industrial centres.

Nor would China be applying massive firepower against an inferior military opponent as was the case in the Persian Gulf conflict. The strategy of limited nuclear deterrence would apply only in the unlikely event that the United States decided to risk escalating the defence of South Korea or Taiwan up to the level of general nuclear war – an improbable scenario. It is also improbable that China would wish to destroy Taiwan in order to annex it, thus eliminating the very technological, economic and industrial infrastructure so coveted by Beijing. Similarly, it is unlikely that China would employ its nuclear capabilities or even a significant portion of its conventional force structure simply to preserve Kim Jong-il's regime.

Active defence anticipates that the Chinese would take pre-emptive military action against an adversary intent on invading China. Yet the current absence of any such threat undercuts the doctrine's immediate applicability to China's 'defence' and intensifies regional suspicions that active defence is nothing more than a crude front for Chinese expansionism. China's plans to accrue and deploy high technology weapons systems are therefore at risk of being perceived by other regional security actors as nothing less than an affirmation of Beijing's ambitions to achieve unmitigated great power status.

This is particularly true with regard to its nuclear force modernisation.[114] The PLA is moving to reinforce its strategic nuclear deterrent and complicate American calculations about how to neutralise it by developing a wide range of delivery systems and by concentrating upon the survivability of its nuclear force.[115] In 1999 disclosures surfaced in US Congressional hearings of possible Chinese espionage directed at gaining advanced nuclear weapons technology as well as China's acquisition of exported satellite technology relevant to improving its nuclear targeting capabilities. Although contested, those assertions made by the Cox Committee Report underscored Beijing's marked determination to acquire very advanced nuclear warheads.[116] During the 1990s Chinese missile systems did not have the ability to threaten American or Russian 'hard targets' (military command centres, missile silos, etc.) and so they were, according to now declassified Chinese sources, directed against 'soft targets' (big cities in potentially hostile countries) in order to serve as a credible limited deterrent.[117] In late May 1995 China first tested the *Dong-feng* 31, a solid-fuel ballistic missile that will eventually be deployed on fast-moving trucks or nuclear missile submarines, giving China a secure second-strike capability.[118] Respected Western defence analysts have estimated that the PRC will possess a credible intercontinental nuclear strike force by 2010, supplementing its already formidable range of theatre nuclear forces which could be applied along China's peripheries.[119]

Such a capability will widen the strategic options available to Chinese defence planners with respect to escalation control. It will also give China's nuclear capacity an unquestionably offensive dimension that moves far beyond a 'local war' context.

### Conclusion: China and Regional Stability

China's ultimate willingness to shift from a strategy of *realpolitik* towards a strategic posture more compatible with liberal prescriptions depends on several key factors: how successful China's economic and defense modernisation programs prove to be; whether or not the Chinese leadership views stable economic and diplomatic ties with other Asia-Pacific states as being vital to that process; the extent to which China may come to view regional multilateralism as a viable and cost-effective alternative to the US–Japan alliance for curbing future Japanese military power if US force withdrawals accelerate in the region; and finally, how useful Beijing finds the ongoing precedents for interdependent or multilateral security behaviour with which it is already involved, that is, the Comprehensive Nuclear Test Ban Treaty and the ARF.

The first factor has several critical dimensions but none more vital than the future evolution of Sino–American and Sino–Japanese bilateral relations and their effect on China's ability to import knowledge, technology and capital. The relevant 'multilateral' aspect flowing from these bilateral ties is how China can employ its membership in Asia-Pacific Economic Cooperation (APEC), its involvement in the Asia–Europe Meeting (ASEM) process and its status as an ASEAN dialogue partner to accrue greater leverage to be applied against both Washington and Tokyo in order to secure trading and investment arrangements more favourable to China.[120] How the United States might respond to such a Chinese strategy of 'calculated multilateralism' will be assessed in chapter 6.

More generally, China can – and has – used APEC as a dialogue mechanism for negotiating with the United States, Japan and the European Union over the terms of the PRC's anticipated accession into the World Trade Organization (WTO). The multilateral context of such bargaining inherently complicates Chinese strategy. It provides a counterweight to China's historical tendency to view 'self-reliance' as an indispensable national attribute. Further blurring of dyadic trade and politico-security ties by intensified multilateral bargaining and diplomacy may gradually modify the Chinese view that its economic and defence modernisation programs must take automatic precedence over what Beijing often sees as multilateral-based efforts by strong states to collaborate with weak partners against other large powers such as China.[121] Beijing's recent conciliatory postures on the Spratly Islands question (without, to be sure, relinquishing its sovereign claims to these islets) provides some encouragement. It has agreed with the ASEAN claimants that the United Nations Convention on the Law of the Sea (UNCLOS) should be the governing criterion for resolving the territorial dispute and it has agreed to negotiate the issue multilaterally. China has also actively participated in the ARF's multilateral discussions on regional confidence-building measures and its cooperation in furthering the Korean peace process is indisputable.[122] China appears to be becoming increasingly comfortable with multilateral settings, although it is still unwilling to bring what it regards as 'core' security issues such as Taiwan and nuclear force reductions to such forums.

Despite its criticisms, China retains a stake in the US bilateral alliance system to the extent that US military power contains Japanese remilitarisation and still deters a North Korean invasion of China's new-found trading ally, South Korea (and prevents the Chinese need to intervene militarily on Pyongyang's behalf). Although hardly ever stated in public speeches or writings but often relayed in private discussions with Western officials and analysts, the 'Japan factor' is related to China's concern that with the demise of US bilateral alliance system in the Asia-Pacific, China would be confronted with a Japanese strategic rival that could become a match for China in a very short space of time. Japan could also attempt to forge an anti-China coalition in the region, involving Vietnam, the Malay member-states of ASEAN, and possibly India and/or Australia. China's ambition to become a dominant regional power would be undermined by the reality that a regional power vacuum could precipitate the very conditions precluding its fulfilment. Convincing China that the only alternative to greater cooperative security in the region is a higher prospect of war will be a major challenge, given Beijing's sense of cultural and historical destiny and the CCP's continuing tendency to employ nationalism to shore up its internal credibility and legitimacy.

China's rise as a global power and its dissatisfaction with the international system as it stands clash with efforts to induce Beijing into endorsing and following norms and rules aimed at constraining its behaviour. China is determined to end American strategic involvement in the Taiwan Strait and to gradually minimise the United States' strategic influence throughout the Asia-Pacific region. To avoid future regional crisis and conflicts, Washington and its regional allies must demonstrate to the post-Deng generation of Chinese leaders that their country's interests are not inherently irreconcilable with every Western objective and that China can gain long-term advantages by cooperating with other regional powers in an institutional context. Building a strong track record of successful economic and security exchanges within the context of those arrangements and organisations in which China already takes part is the best means for demonstrating the utility of cooperative security postures and behaviour to Beijing.

China already shares special responsibilities with the world's other great powers to pursue responsible and broadly-based security politics that transcend irredentism and expansionism and to honour its existing regional and international security commitments. Underlying this axiom of great-power politics is the fundamental reality that if China chooses not to play, there is no real prospect that multilateral security regimes and regional confidence-building norms will become an integral part of Asia-Pacific security politics. Because power balancing and other alternatives to shaping a future regional security order are laden with risk and miscalculation, it is incumbent on Chinese and other regional policy makers to sustain and build upon existing multilateral precedents and architectures.

CHAPTER 3

# Great-Power Strategy II: Japan

As international structural changes intensified throughout the early 1990s arguments postulated by both the realist and liberal approaches anticipated that the US–Japan alliance would be substantially transformed. Realists argued that the end of the Soviet military threat in Asia – the most obvious raison d'être for American–Japanese postwar security cooperation – would inevitably result in both Washington and Tokyo relating to each other more as rivals than as allies.[1] Liberals, in contrast, predicted that the processes of 'complex interdependence' would eventually lead Japan and other American Cold War allies in the region to support the strengthening of multilateral security institutions in a quest to realise the 'sense of certainty and confidence that [the American] hegemon formerly provided'.[2]

Interestingly, neither hypothesis has been entirely confirmed and, as with most things, reality is to be found somewhere in the middle ground. Indeed, the US–Japan Mutual Security Treaty (MST) was enhanced throughout the 1990s as continuing geopolitical uncertainties in Northeast Asia infused both American and Japanese policy planners with determination to maintain and strengthen their security alliance. Realist fears that an intensification of economic rivalry between the United States and Japan would spill over to undermine strategic relations between the two countries have given way to a consensus that their sustained alliance affiliation may actually help the gradual development of effective multilateral security institutions in the region.[3] But such institutions are not likely to supersede the MST as the fundamental basis for Japan's national security policy and for US regional strategy at any time in the near future. They would, at best, supplement the traditional extended deterrence and power balancing functions of the alliance with dialogue and confidence-building measures. They would engender modest levels of strate-

44

gic reassurance and insure that Japan will evolve as a peaceful and constructive security actor in any emerging Asia-Pacific security order. This chapter will initially provide an assessment of Japan's national security postures as they have evolved in a postwar context. This will be followed by an examination of Japanese threat perceptions, including analysis of how the US alliance relates to these concerns. The discussion will then focus on two specific issue-areas that will be integral in fashioning Japan's future security interests and behaviour: (1) its role in helping the United States shape future alliance strategy, particularly in regard to the Korean Peninsula, China and Southeast Asia (consistent with realist strategy); and (2) its involvement in broader regional initiatives for security cooperation (more compatible with the liberal approach). The analysis will conclude with an assessment of how Japan might reconcile these two policy directions as it becomes a more significant player in Asia-Pacific security politics.

## Japan's Evolving Security Posture

For nearly half a century, two fundamental principles have guided Japanese defence thinking: (1) interpretation of the 1947 Constitution's Article 9 (the so-called 'peace clause') means Japan can only deploy minimum force levels for self-defence; and (2) as a consequence of this, a militarily weak Japan must rely upon US security guarantees embodied in the US–Japan MST to deter external threats to Japan's own security. At different intervals throughout the Cold War, Japan's security outlook has been challenged or slightly modified but these two premises have persevered. Indeed, on taking Japan's top political office in April 2001, Prime Minister Junichiro Koizumi suggested that the Japanese Constitution should be revised to better recognise Japan's Self Defense Force (SDF) as a regular military organisation.[4] Subsequently, however, his rhetoric was toned down in his speech to the National Parliament days later, not surprisingly since past short bursts of postwar-Japanese nationalist sentiment have been tempered by the dominant strategically moderate views of Japan's contemporary polity. They reflect what John Endicott has identified as the primacy of 'internationalism' over self-reliance in Japan's world view: that the country's development and prosperity is best pursued through interdependence with the outside world, and particularly with the United States.[5]

Early in the Cold War, Prime Minister Yoshida Shigeru entrenched a Japanese security outlook inextricably tied to dependence on the United States by establishing the 'anti-war' component of the Japanese Constitution as the bedrock of the country's political identity. He conditioned Japanese public opinion to reject the idea that the SDF was meant to function as a normal military force. Instead, the SDF was to conduct missions comparable to that of the United States Coast Guard (that is, search and rescue or disaster relief).[6] Japanese bureaucracies – quickly evolving as the predominant domestic political power in the country following the purge of military and political leaders by the Allied Occupation authorities – filled the void left by Japan's lack of a powerful military-industrial complex. They seized upon the US alliance as a surrogate for indigenous national security planning and as a means for underwriting Japan's postwar economic recovery, growth and power.[7] This legacy contains both realist and liberal elements: Japan pursued relative gains in the non-military sectors of international politics (primarily trade) but has happily institutionalised strategic dependence.

The October 1976 'National Defense Program Outline' (NDPO) or *Taiko*, which remained Japan's core national security document for two decades, assumed that Japan would not be subject to major armed aggression and that the US security treaty would be sufficient to prevent other Northeast Asian conflicts from spreading to the Japanese mainland. Accordingly, significant constraints were built into Japan's defence posture. These were directed towards satisfying a pacifist domestic electorate and alleviating concerns by other Asian states that Japan would revert to its prewar strategies of power projection. These constraints included observing three non-nuclear principles – Japan would not possess, produce, or allow the transit of nuclear weapons within its territory – and limiting the improvement of its defence capabilities to enhancing surveillance and dealing with 'small-scale aggression' without US assistance or intervention.[8]

Successive postwar Japanese leaders have been preoccupied with reconciling the dichotomy of a deeply anti-militarist public sentiment (emanating from the country's defeat in World War II) with the imperative of addressing the country's essential security needs while lacking indigenous power projection capabilities. The NDPO force posture, which evolved from these anomalous, even contradictory, priorities, was inevitably ambiguous. The NDPO mandated a defence capability for Japan aimed at preventing or defeating 'limited and small-scale aggression' but one that could not be interpreted as possessing capabilities normally associated with power projection. While permitting the SDF to make qualitative and quantitative improvements in its weapons inventory, Japan's military human resource targets were never met and heavy dependence upon the United States was accepted as a strategic imperative.

Norm Levin has identified three specific factors underlying Japan's failure to achieve any real strategic cohesion in its defence posture: (1) a tendency to deny collective responsibility for Japan's pre-World War II strategic behaviour by singling out the military as being exclusively culpable, therefore impeding the development of a healthy defence establishment; (2) a reluctance to conceptualise modern conflict in Northeast Asia as anything other than an appendage of global conflict in which the SDF would defend itself as best it could until US reinforcements arrived; and (3) a determination to minimise defence spending.[9] The overall effect of these factors has been to encourage successive Japanese governments to view the SDF as a military necessity designed only to supplement US power in Northeast Asia in the event Japanese territory was directly involved in a conflict.

Despite maintaining the SDF's capabilities with a defence budget that has grown to rank among the world's top five, Japan has resisted converting any significant part of its substantial economic infrastructure into commensurate military power. Indeed, it still spends around 1 per cent of its gross national product on defence in spite of the self-imposed 1 per cent limitation being lifted in 1986. Most realists either insist that this postwar trend is a temporary anomaly to be rectified when the US security umbrella is eventually withdrawn or that Japan's wartime experience has simply rendered immediate successor generations reluctant to pursue national security through normal avenues. Liberals counter that the United States has actually encouraged the growth of Japan's military establishment as it has insisted that Japan share the West's 'defence-burden'.[10]

### Comprehensive Security

Japan's quest to find an acceptable balance between domestic pacifism and strategic independence entered a new phase in 1980 with the introduction of a new national security strategy labelled 'comprehensive security'. The Prime Ministerial Study Group on Comprehensive Security was created to resolve the issue.[11] Prime Minister Ohira's premature death, and his successor's difficulties in transforming the recommendations of the Study Group into government policy, may well have rendered the creation of a strong central agency to coordinate the development of a comprehensive security approach infeasible.[12] However, this concept was sufficiently important in the evolution of the country's doctrinal outlook to merit further examination.

Several important objectives affecting Japan's national security posture were designated by the Prime Minister's Study Group. While not intending to transform the MST, those promoting comprehensive security argued that bilateral alliance relations with Washington could be reinforced if the Japanese were more willing to develop self-defence capabilities without their country necessarily becoming an offensive military power. At the same time, the Study Group recommended that Japan should pursue an 'omni-directional' foreign policy in the region, designed to improve relations with the Soviet Union and China as well as with those Southeast Asian states that remained suspicious of Japanese intentions on the basis of their wartime experience.

The credibility of the comprehensive security strategy was seriously questioned when the Soviet Union increased its military deployments to Northeast Asia in the mid-1970s. Realist critics like Okazaki Hisahiko, one of Japan's most prominent security analysts, argued that this development precluded Japan from regarding either the Soviet Union or China as being susceptible to any comprehensive security-style diplomatic offensive. Okazaki contended that a Japanese military build-up undertaken within the framework of the US alliance would be the best way to prevent any further deterioration (as he perceived it) in the balance of power in East Asia.[13] Comprehensive security was also undercut as US–Japanese trade relations became more linked, however tacitly, to American exhortations for its ally to assume a greater share of the West's defence burden.

The strategy was successful in allowing Japan to capitalise on Sino–Soviet tensions and on a commensurate warming of Sino–American relations. Comprehensive security's emphasis on Japanese economic growth as a contributing factor to regional stability was particularly relevant in encouraging Japan's pre-eminence as a financier of China's economic development. The Sino–Japanese Treaty of Peace and Amity (signed in August 1978) was viewed in Tokyo as a necessary diplomatic counterweight, for example, to growing Soviet power and entirely consistent with the logic of comprehensive security. So too were Japan's overseas development assistance (ODA) initiatives directed predominantly towards Southeast Asia. These were driven by a Japanese belief that a lowering of tensions in Indochina, combined with the strengthening of the economic prosperity and political stability of the ASEAN member-states, could only reinforce Japan's economic influence in that subregion.

### Reconsiderations

Structural changes resulting from the end of the Cold War have led Japan to reconsider its security interests and postures. The Soviet threat no longer exists and the end of bipolarity has forced Tokyo to reassess its politico-strategic identity. As Barry Buzan has noted, 'there can be no doubt that Japan had a good Cold War' because it was able to sustain unimpeded economic growth and enjoy uninterrupted socio-political stability under the American strategic guarantee.[14] The key question facing Japan after the Soviet Union's demise is to what extent the US–Japan MST will continue to facilitate Japan's interest in maintaining regional and global stability without it needing to move away from its preferred image as a pacifist state.[15]

The 1991 Persian Gulf War provided a catalyst for re-evaluation as Tokyo found itself the subject of immense resentment in Western electorates that were dispatching and sacrificing their own troops to salvage access to oil fields which provide Japan with approximately 70 per cent of its energy supplies. Japan abstained from both direct and indirect military involvement in that conflict while fighting was actually taking place (it rejected American requests for use of its transport planes and supply ships). It also bickered with Washington over how large a financial contribution it should make to the UN-supported military operation although an allocation of $US13 billion was finally negotiated. It did dispatch an Overseas Minesweeping Force of six ships to the Persian Gulf, but only well after hostilities had ceased. Even this modest deployment generated widespread debate in Japan over its possible violation of Article 9 while generating shame in other quarters because Japanese military personnel were not involved in the actual defence of the oil resources so critical to the country's survival and economic well-being.[16]

The Persian Gulf episode underscored Japan's need to develop a more credible and forthright policy for future peacekeeping operations other than merely promising 'appropriate international contributions' on a case-by-case basis. It was clear from that event that its aspirations to become a global political power commensurate with its economic weight would remain unfulfilled if it continued to labour under its existing security policy frameworks. Furthermore, there was the prospect that the strains in its security relations with the United States over defence burden-sharing could intensify. Although support for a Japanese SDF role in future peacekeeping operations gradually increased (by early January 1994, nearly 49 per cent of the Japanese polled supported such operations), Japan also made it clear that it would only participate in non-military contingencies.[17] Although not precisely defining 'non-military', the Japanese Foreign Ministry stated explicitly that it did not consider the 'activities of the kind of multinational force that was organised at the time of the Gulf crisis' as falling under the category of UN peacekeeping operations.[18] According to this posture, the future defence of Middle Eastern oil fields was still not Japan's responsibility.

In the meantime, Japan began to review the NDPO with a view to adjusting its overall defence planning in accordance with a changing international environment. In 1994 Prime Minister Hosokawa Morihiro appointed a nine-member Roundtable on Defense Issues to review Japan's future security problems and policies. The Roundtable adopted a strategic outlook reminiscent of comprehensive security and it recommended economic and political, as well as military changes, in the NDPO.[19] It argued that an invasion of Japan as part of a global war, which had been the dominant contingency in postwar Japanese planning, was no longer a valid scenario. Consequently, the country's defence posture would need to pay more attention to an emerging regional and international security environment that would be dominated and shaped by US-managed military alliances and by multilateral security regimes working to underwrite global stability.[20]

In looking at the future, the Roundtable predicted that the US–Japan MST would constitute the core security structure for the Asia-Pacific, but that it would also be supplemented by regional or UN peacekeeping operations and by security dialogues and other regionally indigenous confidence-building measures. These would be designed to build greater transparency and to ensure conflict prevention. The Roundtable endorsed SDF involvement in future UN collective security operations while still preserving the restraints embodied in the Japanese Constitution. As was the case in the comprehensive security approach some fifteen years previously, this committee envisioned an integration of realist and liberal approaches to security politics as the most effective means for achieving national security interests and regional stability.

Pacifist critics of the Roundtable's findings argued that they did not apply Article 9 explicitly enough to the problem of specifying the conditions under which the SDF would be permitted to participate in any future UN collective security action. The costs of proposed defence modernisation programs such as purchasing airborne warning and control systems (AWACs) and of developing theatre missile defences were also disparaged.[21] So too was the Roundtable's ranking of post-Cold War threats. Hard-line pro-defence factions, by way of contrast, questioned the advisory group's focus on the potential escalation of regional disputes. They believed that threat identification should be more focused on Japan's individual national security circumstances. The North Korean nuclear threat, dormant territorial disputes with Russia, and China's long-term military capabilities, they argued, should have been assigned a much higher priority.[22]

The revised NDPO was approved by the cabinet of Prime Minister Murayama Tomoichi in late November 1995 and an updated 'Mid-Term Defense Buildup Plan' was passed by the Parliament.[23] Most of the advisory group's strategic guidelines were adopted but the authorised force strength levels were lowered (from 180 000 SDF personnel to 145 000) while the numbers of destroyers, combat aircraft and anti-submarine aircraft were also reduced substantially. Alliance politics applied in a regional context was therefore integrated with the reality of budgetary constraints. The logic of comprehensive security was revived by mandating the SDF's capability for responding to and effectively operating in an array of contingencies other than those precipitated by external military threats to Japan, that is, large-scale disasters, terrorism and UN peacekeeping missions. As one Japanese political columnist concluded, the 1976 NDPO emphasis on Japan building up sufficient military power to prevent a foreign invasion had been replaced by a more subdued national security posture, emphasising more intense collaboration with and, by implication, greater dependence upon, its American ally.[24] The calculus of the Yoshida Doctrine appeared to prevail, and the primacy of the MST's Article 5, authorising joint US–Japan action against an invasion remained unquestioned.

*The Okinawa Crisis and Its Impact*

This outcome proved to be transitory. Even while the final version of the revised NDPO was working its way through Japan's substantial bureaucracy, the rape of a Japanese schoolgirl by three US military personnel stationed in Okinawa (during September 1995) triggered a major review of the US basing presence in Japan. The credibility of the 47 000-strong US force presence was at stake as a significant portion of the Okinawan populace openly demonstrated against the American military presence on their island. Elsewhere, Japanese public opinion began to swing against a continued US basing presence anywhere in Japan (up from 23 per cent in August 1995 to 40 per cent by mid-October).[25]

Tokyo's defence planners were caught in a serious policy bind. They were well aware that the Japanese electorate would oppose any substantial redeployment of American forces to the Japanese mainland (US bases complexes also operate in Honshu and Kyushu, but three-quarters of US military facilities in Japan were concentrated on Okinawa, covering nearly 20 per cent of that prefecture's main island). At the same time, however, Japanese policy makers could risk the perception that they were doing nothing to resolve tensions on the island. Following the publication of some polls that showed a rise within Japan in public opposition to US basing arrangements, the *Asahi Shimbun* speculated that 'the seriousness of this problem [the Okinawan basing issue] could shake the very foundations of the Japanese–US security arrangement'.[26]

President Clinton's April 1996 visit to Tokyo provided the occasion for a compromise which included a considerable reduction in land used for US facilities. It also proved to be the catalyst for a more far-reaching reassessment of US–Japan alliance relations that ultimately led to a revision of the 1978 Defense Guidelines. A Joint Declaration on Security was signed by Clinton and Prime Minister Hashimoto reaffirming 'their strong determination' to build on their two countries' legacy of security cooperation.[27] The US pledged to maintain approximately 100 000 military personnel in the Asia-Pacific region (including some 47 000 personnel in Japan) and to enhance intelligence and logistical cooperation with its Japanese ally. The latter commitment was embodied in an Acquisition and Cross-Servicing Agreement (ACSA) designed to give the US forces operating in Japan greater access to Japanese supplies and services during times of crisis and to facilitate coordination of future SDF participation in regional or global peacekeeping operations.[28] It was also aimed at strengthening Article 6 of the MST, which calls for Japan to assist US forces in 'Far Eastern contingencies'.

By assuming this commitment, the Hashimoto Government risked alienating the pacifist sectors of the Japanese electorate. Japanese pacifists were already in a nervous state as a result of President Clinton's introduction of aircraft carriers to the East China Sea during the Taiwan Strait crisis, an event that had occurred less than a month prior to Clinton's visit to Tokyo.[29] The Hashimoto Government's willingness to explore the revised defence guidelines for the US–Japan alliance sent a strong signal to Washington that Japan was prepared to broaden the extent of its strategic collaboration with the United States in both a military and politico-diplomatic context. It was, moreover, an inevitable quid pro quo for Japan continuing to benefit from a reconstituted, but still substantial, US force presence on Okinawa.

American concessions on Okinawa underscored the Clinton Administration's growing recognition that the United States would have to exercise greater sensitivity towards Japanese public concerns about the US military presence in Japan. Alliance revitalisation could only succeed if both US and Japanese policy planners took into account several key factors. Intermittent cases of misbehaviour by US troops and environmental issues raised by Okinawan landowners were important catalysts for intensified local resentment. Indeed, in January 2001 these feelings of resentment were only exacerbated when further alleged attacks were perpetrated by American soldiers within a week of a six-month curfew being lifted. But it also had to be acknowledged that Japanese mainlanders were highly reluctant to assimilate an increased American military deployment in lieu of that on Okinawa. Japanese critics of the US force presence in Japan tend to cite their country's $US 4 billion annual 'contribution' to the cost of stationing US forces in that country, far more than that expended by any other American ally, despite the fact that the US Congress consistently rails against Japan's protectionist trade policies.[30]

*Regional Collective Defence: A Japanese Role?*

With Northeast Asia's geopolitical environment shifting dramatically, Japan has been compelled to reassess its strategic identity and postures. Forging security coalitions with other regional security actors to pursue its own regional balancing strategy (a purely realist approach) was still problematic because it would require levels of remilitarisation that would be unacceptable to both the Japanese public and to Japan's neighbours. At the same time, relying exclusively upon institution-building would expose the gap between Japan's economic power and its lack of military capabilities. It would underline Japan's inability to protect its wealth against other forces in the region inclined to either reject or defect from multilateralism.

In recent years, several policy jolts have swayed Japan to initiate a comprehensive examination of its security identity and to critically reassess its alliance relationship with America. These included the Persian Gulf War threatening Japanese oil supplies, the end of the Soviet Union and global bipolarity, the latent threat imbedded in China's new assertiveness and the policy challenge presented by North Korea's missile program. The major issue that emerged from this process was how Japan could finesse its continued adherence to the Constitution's Article 9 at a time when it was becoming more evident that the Yoshida Doctrine and the US security umbrella were becoming outmoded.

In September 1997 the final draft of the revised US–Japan Defense Guidelines was approved by the US–Japan Security Consultative Committee meeting in New York.[31] Its basic aspects are summarised in table 3.1. Like the earlier 1978 version, the intent of this document was to outline a 'comprehensive planning mechanism' but more emphasis was placed on bilateral cooperation aimed at enhancing regional security rather than focusing exclusively on the defence of Japan. Accordingly, the trend originally set by the November 1969 Nixon–Sato communiqué of gradually shifting the focus of the MST towards Article 6 (which anticipates Japanese support for US forces engaged in Far Eastern contingencies) and away from Article 5 (which commits the United States to defend the Japanese homeland from a 'bolt out of the blue' military strike) was reaffirmed.[32]

The MST's transition from a component of US global deterrence strategy to one more focused on regional balancing did not mean that the US commitment to Japan's defence had declined. The *context* of that commitment changed so that the United States reaffirmed its support for a more strategically capable Japan that pledged to develop a more symmetrical alliance relationship with more substantial Japanese input. In return, Japan benefited from a continued US force presence neutralising China's rising military power, access to advanced US military technology and continued low levels of defence spending in relative terms.

US military planning may indeed be shifting away from its heavy reliance on Northeast Asian basing complexes during the Cold War to be a more fluid and diverse set of operational and training arrangements. This development, however, is hardly synonymous with any American disinclination to defend the world's second largest economy and Asia's most established postwar democratic state if its survival were threatened. Japan continues to play a vital economic and increasingly critical political role in the Asia-Pacific region for the United States to be anything other than an engaging security partner. It should be remembered that the Defense Guidelines were intended to consolidate that commitment rather than detract from it.[33]

Like its predecessor, the revised Guidelines addressed mutual steps to be taken by Washington and Tokyo if 'an armed attack against Japan is imminent', including an intensification of information and intelligence sharing. But it varied from the original document by underscoring Japan's responsibility as the *primary* defender in such a contingency – acknowledging that the likelihood of a major 'Soviet-threat' style attack against that country was remote and that even a smaller SDF than that maintained during the Cold War could cope with those few local conflicts and crises which might involve Japan. Hypothetical contingencies cited in the revised Guidelines included an air attack against Japanese territory, the defence of surrounding waters and sea lanes of communication, airborne or seaborne invasions, and 'other threats' such as guerilla-commando type attacks or ballistic missile attacks. While no specific source of threat was identified, it seems clear that North Korean missile strikes against Japanese military installations, airfields and ports were the primary reason why the latter category was formulated. A Chinese navy capable of projecting offensive power against key oil lifelines, or blockading Japan, in the event of future territorial disputes would similarly fit the control of surrounding waters or sea lanes of communication scenario.

The more controversial part of the revised Guidelines related to how Japan would cooperate with the United States in regional contingencies not directly involving Japanese territory. This was particularly problematic in relation to Taiwan. Article 5 of the Guidelines effectively broadens Japan's regional security purview by allowing the SDF to participate in relief and refugee operations, search and rescue operations in non-combat areas, non-combatant evacuation operations using Japanese vessels, and rear-area support activities in international waters and airspace outside of combat zones. In August 2000 a government manual was released to the Japanese media that addressed specific procedures for SDF rescue operations for Japanese caught abroad during future crises: the Japanese government would establish a liaison office to discuss rescue methods after being alerted by the Foreign Ministry and a taskforce reporting to the Japanese prime minister would be established; following Cabinet approval, SDF transport planes, ships and helicopters could supplement or replace chartered flights or civilian aircraft as modes of evacuation if initial rescue efforts were impeded.[34]

**Table 3.1**    Guidelines for US–Japan Defense Cooperation, September 1997

| Functions and Fields | | Examples of Items of Cooperation |
|---|---|---|
| Cooperation in activities initiated by either Government | Relief activities and measures to deal with refugees | Transportation of personnel and supplies to the affected area<br>Medical services, communications and transportation in the affected area<br>Relief and transfer operations for refugees, and provision of emergency materials to refugees |
| | Search and rescue | Search and rescue operations in Japanese territory and at sea around Japan and information sharing related to such operations |
| | Noncombatant evacuation operations | Information sharing, and communication with and assembly and transportation of noncombatants<br>Use of SDF facilities and civilian airports and ports by US aircraft and vessels for transportation of noncombatants<br>Customs, immigration and quarantine of noncombatants upon entry into Japan<br>Assistance to noncombatants in such matters as temporary accommodations, transportation and medical services in Japan |
| | Activities for ensuring the effectiveness of economic sanctions for the maintenance of international peace and stability | Inspection of ships based on UN Security Council resolutions for ensuring the effectiveness of economic sanctions and activities related to such inspections<br>Information sharing |

**Table 3.1**   Guidelines for US–Japan Defense Cooperation, September 1997 (*continued*)

| Functions and Fields | | | Examples of Items of Cooperation |
|---|---|---|---|
| Japan's support for US Forces activities | Use of facilities | | Use of SDF facilities and civilian airports and ports for supplies and other purposes by US aircraft and vessels |
| | | | Reservation of spaces for loading/unloading of personnel and materials by the United States and of storage areas at SDF facilities and civilian airports and ports |
| | | | Extension of operating hours for SDF facilities and civilian airports and ports for the use by US aircraft and vessels |
| | | | Use of SDF airfields by US aircraft |
| | | | Provision of training and exercise areas |
| | | | Construction of offices, accommodations, etc., inside US facilities and areas |
| | Rear area support | *Supply* | Provision of materials (except weapons and ammunition) and petroleum, oil and lubricants (POL) to US aircraft and vessels at SDF facilities and civilian airports and ports |
| | | | Provision of materials (except weapons and ammunition) and POL to US facilities and areas |
| | | *Transportation* | Land, sea and air transportation inside Japan of personnel, materials and POL |
| | | | Sea transportation to US vessels on the high seas of personnel, materials and POL |
| | | | Use of vehicles and cranes for transportation of personnel, materials and POL |

**Table 3.1**   Guidelines for US–Japan Defense Cooperation, September 1997
*(continued)*

| Functions and Fields | Examples of Items of Cooperation |
|---|---|
| *Maintenance* | Repair and maintenance of US aircraft, vessels and vehicles<br>Provision of repair parts<br>Temporary provision of tools and materials for maintenance |
| *Medical services* | Medical treatment of casualties inside Japan<br>Transportation of casualties inside Japan<br>Provision of medical supplies |
| *Security* | Security of US facilities and areas<br>Sea surveillance around US facilities and areas<br>Security of transportation routes inside Japan<br>Information and intelligence sharing |
| *Communications* | Provision of frequencies (including for satellite communications) and equipment for communications among relevant US and Japanese agencies |
| *Others* | Support for port entry/exit by US vessels<br>Loading/unloading of materials at SDF facilities and civilian airports and ports<br>Sewage disposal, water supply, and electricity inside US facilities and areas<br>Temporary increase of workers at US facilities and areas |

**Table 3.1**   Guidelines for US–Japan Defense Cooperation, September 1997
*(continued)*

| Functions and Fields | | Examples of Items of Cooperation |
|---|---|---|
| US–Japan operational cooperation | Surveillance Minesweeping | Intelligence sharing Minesweeping operations in Japanese territory and on the high seas around Japan, and information and intelligence sharing on mines |
| | Sea and airspace management | Maritime traffic coordination in and around Japan in response to increased sea traffic Air traffic control and airspace management in and around Japan |

*Source*: US Secretary of Defense, 'The United States Security Strategy for the East Asia-Pacific Region', (Washington, DC: USGPO, 1998), pp. 21–2.

In mid-1999 a joint naval exercise focusing on search and rescue operations was conducted between three Japanese Maritime Self Defense Force (MSDF) destroyers, two South Korean destroyers and 1000 soldiers. This set a precedent for Japanese–South Korean military cooperation and represented a significant effort to apply the type of operations envisaged by the Defense Guidelines to actual Japanese military planning and operations.[35] Other functions, however, have been left deliberately ambiguous. For example, would Japanese forces be authorised to return hostile fire in the process of evacuating Japanese citizens from a South Korea under siege? Would escort units of the Japanese MSDF be able to open fire if its minesweepers were attacked in international waters?

Notwithstanding consistent denials and 'clarifications' by Japanese politicians and bureaucrats, the credibility of Japan's postwar self-defence posture was sharply tested when the Guidelines' potential collective defence implications were evaluated. The new document was quite explicit, for example, in calling for a 'bilateral coordination mechanism' to organise responses to 'situations in areas surrounding Japan that will have an important influence on Japanese peace and security'.[36] Any such entity inherently entails allied 'mutual' or collective assistance. According to one interpretation of international law a state can legitimately seek to enter into an alliance arrangement in order to defend itself and still be considered to be operating within a 'self-defence' frame-work provided that the country concerned is incapable of defending itself with purely domestic resources. This is known as the principle of *droit naturel*.[37] This self-defence criterion becomes increasingly murky when and if Japanese pilots at the controls of airborne warning and control systems aircraft convey targeting information to US combat forces engaging North Korean troops. The same ambiguity applies to when or if Japanese minesweepers operate in international waters to facilitate American naval operations in the East China Sea. A stage is reached in joint military operations when the term 'self-defence' must inevitably become euphemistic. An American defence official involved in a preliminary analysis of the Guidelines stated what had become obvious to most regional policy analysts, 'the alliance has essentially been transformed from one oriented primarily to Article 5 of the Mutual Security Treaty (MST) – the narrow self-defence of Japan – toward one more balanced between Articles 5 and 6 – regional security' thus achieving one of its aims noted above.[38]

It is uncertain to what extent Japanese initiatives to merge their country's postwar self-defence posture with a low-key 'quasi-collective defence' doctrine will facilitate or undermine regional stability. The initial responses of Japan's neighbours to the release of the Defense Guidelines reflected their long-standing concerns about Tokyo's strategic intentions.[39] American and Japanese officials were dispatched to Beijing, Seoul and other Asian capitals to explain that the revised Guidelines were designed neither to contain specific countries nor to rationalise a buildup of Japanese military power. However, their reassurances were often met with scepticism. Although the South Korean government issued a qualified endorsement, observing that the Guidelines appeared to meet the prerequisites of international law, officials from President Kim Young-sam's own New Korea Party (NKP) condemned them as 'virtually paving the way for a heightened Japanese military influence in the region'. Independent Korean political observers argued that the NKP statement unquestionably reflected concerns shared by the majority of the Korean people.[40] China's leadership was openly incensed, particularly when Japan's Chief Cabinet Secretary Kajiyama Seiroku and other Japanese officials observed in August 1997 (a month before the final Guidelines draft was released) that the Taiwan Strait would be included within their geographic purview on the basis that this would be consistent with the MST's post-1960 definition of the 'Far East Region'. Chinese Prime Minister Li Peng labelled this interpretation as 'utterly unacceptable'.[41]

Subsequent diplomatic efforts by Prime Minister Hashimoto and other Japanese officials to reassure China that the SDF would not be found anywhere near the Taiwan Straits in the event of a crisis and that Japan would not be projecting regional military power in any other capacity failed to placate Beijing. One of the reasons for this is that the Chinese government is reportedly concerned that Japan may already have drawn up plans to evacuate Japanese residents in Taiwan along with Japanese tourists if a China–Taiwan military confrontation erupts.[42] Japanese claims that SDF forces will not be operating near the island in such a situation appear, therefore, to be more than a little disingenuous. In the meantime, Japanese policy analysts have continued to express genuine surprise over Chinese and Korean apprehensions regarding the SDF's future development and missions. They argue that there is little understanding in China or Korea about how strong the self-imposed constraints on Japanese military behaviour really are. According to their view, conducting humanitarian missions and responding to refugee problems that may arise in areas proximate to Japanese territory cannot be reasonably viewed as threatening the national security of any other state.[43]

A second major problem emanating from the revised Guidelines was that alliance transparency was sure to be complicated by political debate within Japan over how the Guidelines would withstand constitutional scrutiny and legislative opposition. As debate intensified over what would be Japan's security identity in the early twenty-first century, it was unclear just how far the Japanese government would be able to go in persuading key domestic political sectors in the Parliament and in the electorate to accept the premises advanced and tasks identified by the Guidelines, ACSA and other related alliance agreements.

Questions lingered about the meaning and implications of the revised Guidelines, notwithstanding the crucial Lower House of the Japanese Parliament approving legislation for authorisation of the new version of the Defense Guidelines to become law in late April 1999 (final passage of the Guidelines occurred in May).[44] Japanese parliamentarians supporting the bill acknowledged its ambiguity, and admitted that they did not know if Japan would even support the United States if Okinawa or other parts of Japan were to be targeted by a North Korean missile or pulled into a future Sino–American conflict over Taiwan. The Deputy Chief of the Liberal Democratic Party's Policy Affairs Council could only surmise that the Japanese government would judge the situation at the time, based on whether it would severely affect Japan's peace and security.[45]

Moreover, constraints on what the SDF could do remained stringent. Japan's navy was still not authorised to board international ships on the high seas to enforce international sanctions unless it had approval to do so from the flag nation. The future use of the MSDF in a naval blockade against a regional adversary was left undetermined and subject to further parliamentary debate. Although the SDF could act with the Prime Minister's consent to support US forces in a genuine emergency where Japan's own security was at stake, the Japanese government would need to secure 'later approval' of any such action from the Parliament for it to be deemed constitutional. American forces' use of Japanese civilian facilities and bases as part of an operation directed against a regional adversary such as North Korea would be authorised. But how the SDF was used in such a contingency could be subsequently questioned by the Parliament.[46]

The best and most immediate policy course for Japan appeared to be for Japanese policy planners to work with their American counterparts towards gradually identifying solutions to the 'grey zone' areas of their defence collaboration. Any such process would need to be low-key and could not be allowed to confuse broader Japanese strategic policy aims. It is possible, but unlikely, that a full-scale defence debate will transform Japan's propensity to collaborate with its American ally in the near future. Japan has concluded that its neighbours are even less prone to trust it and to work with it than Washington. Both Japan and the United States need to lobby to allay domestic Japanese and wider regional concerns over Japan's possible future role in collective regional defence. The best way of moving forward in this regard would be to concentrate on refining collective defence within an alliance context so that Japanese constraints pertaining to specific military operations are clearly established and observed. At the same time, however, Japan and the United States would need to continue their current posture of 'double ambiguity' regarding those specific regional conflicts that would trigger a jointly coordinated response. If China and South Korea (for different reasons) were to be allowed to dictate the MST's future collective defence agenda by imposing conditions of geographic purview, a core rationale for the United States and Japan to engage in mutual defence collaboration will have been lost.

Without directly confronting the collective self-defence issue, the revised Guidelines delayed what seemed to be inevitable – Japan gradually undertaking more comprehensive steps to support the rapid projection of American military power in a future regional contingency by directly assisting US forces in their combat missions. Such a contingency may have to occur before the Japanese domestic political constraints, which inhibit this type of force planning, will be overcome. A review of contemporary Japanese threat perceptions and how they relate to this problem will allow for a greater understanding of why Japan's current defence posture needs to undergo just such a change.

### Japanese Threat Perceptions

In order to understand the relative effectiveness of bilateralism and multilateralism as future policy options for Japan it is necessary to first identify the forces most threatening to Japanese interests. As the Cold

War has receded into history, official Japanese threat assessments have tended to focus on two broad geopolitical problems: (1) what Kent Calder has labelled 'the Northeast Asian arc of crisis', encompassing a divided Korea, an increasingly dangerous Taiwan Strait and an uncertain Sino–Russian entente; and (2) the 'troubled seas' of East and Southeast Asia through which flow much of Japan's energy supplies and its international trade lifelines.[47] The Japan Defense Agency has observed that unresolved flashpoints dominate the security environment of both subregions. Any progress that Europe has made in applying multilateral security politics to address its traditional points of tension (notwithstanding its conflict zones in south-eastern Europe) is not likely to be replicated in the Asia-Pacific at any time in the near future. In the absence of such progress, the Defense Agency concludes, Japan will need to work with the United States to avoid episodes of crisis escalation.[48]

## *The Koreas*

The prospect of a renewed Korean War, although possibly less likely in view of recent efforts at rapprochement between the two Koreas, remains a pressing Japanese security concern. It was clearly the contingency most responsible for many of the aforementioned changes in the US–Japan Defense Guidelines. At the height of the Korean 'nuclear crisis' in mid-1994 the North Korean government publicly warned Tokyo that it would 'devastate' Japan if that country were to assist the United States in a war effort against the North or if it were to impose widespread economic sanctions on Pyongyang. The sanctions issue was particularly sensitive because, until the onset of the Asian financial crisis, Japanese sources provided ¥60 billion flow of remittances annually to North Korea (mostly from North Korean descendants residing in Japan). Japan was one of the North Korean regime's most important sources of foreign exchange.[49] By mid-1997 much of Japan reportedly could be targeted by existing North Korean *No-dong-1* missiles (derived from *Scud* technology similar to that used by Saddam Hussein against Israel in the Persian Gulf War). This threat intensified on 31 August 1998 when North Korea tested a *Taepo-dong-1* missile, which flew over Japanese territory.[50] Japan subsequently withdrew food aid to the North and temporarily discontinued its funding contributions to the Korean Peninsula Energy Development Organisation (KEDO). Any future North Korean missile strike could well involve the delivery of biological or chemical warheads against 'soft' Japanese targets (population and industrial centres) as well as against US bases.[51]

Western estimates usually project North Korea's eventual destruction if any such scenario were to unfold. The military effectiveness (accuracy or reliability in weather conditions) of North Korean missile delivery systems is also questionable. The *No-dong* and *Taepo-dong* missile systems are sufficiently lethal, however, to be regarded as formidable weapons of terror that could be applied against Japan to extract significant strategic concessions. The extent to which a highly urbanised and densely industrialised Japan could withstand a surprise attack involving weapons of mass destruction is unclear. In addition to its limited ballistic missile capabilities, North Korea can also deploy and deliver low-flying, anti-ship cruise missiles and possibly chemical weapons (it retains a formidable chemical weapons stockpile but has no effective low-range delivery systems for targeting them).[52] If not successfully interdicted, these could wreak havoc on Japanese shipping lanes. However, the logic for initiating such an attack is weak. North Korean officials have acknowledged that the more than half a million North Koreans living in Japan provide 'indispensable' support and revenue to the existing North Korean regime. Future Japanese investment will also be critical to Kim Jong-il's long-term survival.[53]

The October 1994 Agreed Framework between the United States and North Korea appears to have at least temporarily modified the North Korean nuclear threat. The nuclear problem will be manageable from Tokyo's perspective so long as North Korea complies with its agreement to refrain from developing an independent nuclear weapons capability in exchange for Western and Japanese technical and financial help in modernising its nuclear reactors. Until the *Taepo-dong* test firing, Japan was an active participant in KEDO since its inception in March 1995. While it continues to honour its current KEDO commitments, Japan is well aware that North Korea's nuclear program is merely 'frozen' until 2003, contingent upon its satisfaction with KEDO's efforts to install light-water reactors less capable of producing nuclear weapons-grade fuel. Negotiations lifting the Japanese food assistance ban imposed after the *Taepo-dong* missile launch recommenced in late 1999 and Japanese assistance was resumed in March 2000 with limited rice shipments after the North accelerated its 'smile diplomacy' in the region and agreed to join the ARF.[54]

A third, longer-term problem concerns Japan's future relations with a unified Korea. Despite their extensive trade ties and their mutual strategic alignment with the United States, relations between Japan and South Korea remain tense. They are especially complicated by territorial disputes and by lingering South Korean historical grievances that readily translate into apprehensions over Japan's future regional identity and behaviour.

Japanese–South Korean relations deteriorated in February 1996 when their long-standing territorial dispute over a group of small islands in the Sea of Japan known as Takeshima (in Japanese) or Tokdo (in Korean) intensified. Both Tokyo and Seoul declared overlapping 200 nautical mile exclusive economic zones (EEZs) which included the islands. The South Korean government accused Japan of reverting to its 'old colonial habits' while Japan blamed South Korean fisherman for over-exploiting the waters around the contested islets.[55] In November 1997 Japan's Vice-Minister for Foreign Affairs summoned South Korea's ambassador to Japan and expressed his country's 'strong regret' over South Korea's continued occupation and development of the contested islets.[56]

In 1998 both countries took several measures that promised to temper such concerns. In February newly elected South Korean President Kim Dae-jung pledged to strengthen his country's relations with Japan and moved quickly to resolve the fisheries dispute. In late September, Japanese Prime Minister Obuchi Keizo intervened directly in negotiations and achieved a settlement on both fishing boundaries and quotas, which Kim endorsed in early October. A summit between the two political leaders was convened in that same month which produced a remarkable Japanese statement of apology for transgressions during its colonial occupation of Korea and a Korean statement of appreciation for postwar Japan's contributions to the international community. By the end of the summit, it appeared that significant progress had been made toward achieving genuine Japanese–South Korean normalisation.

Collectively, these developments constitute an impressive break in the overall postwar trend of Japanese–South Korean animosity. It remains unclear to what extent the two countries will be able to sustain their momentum and overcome the entrenched forces of nationalism and hostility that permeate their perceptions. Furthermore, the two countries' major territorial disputes remain unresolved, South Korea's economy remains fundamentally dependent on Japanese prosperity and China could exploit its generally good relations with Seoul as a means to minimise Japanese influence on a divided or unified Korean Peninsula.[57] Korean unification could exacerbate Japanese hostilities toward a newly created economic and geopolitical competitor, particularly if a unified Korea coalesced with China on key security issues. Continued US strategic involvement in Northeast Asia would appear to be the best guarantee for precluding this destabilising scenario from materialising.

The June 2000 North–South Korea Summit between North Korean leader Kim Jong-il and South Korean President Kim Dae-jung thus reconstituted Japanese policy calculations towards the Korean Peninsula in several important ways. Most significantly, it provided critical momentum for thawing the Japanese–North Korean impasse that had hardened most dimensions of that bilateral relationship after North Korea's 1998 *Taepo-dong* missile test. Tokyo could not be seen as being out in front of a liberal South Korean leader in reaching out to the North but could afford to resume negotiations for normalisation of Japanese–North Korean ties once the Summit had taken place (the tenth round of such talks commenced in August 2000). Secondly, Kim Jong-il's admission during his talks with his South Korean counterpart that a continued US force presence in Northeast Asia was constructive as a balancing and stabilising component in that subregion's power equilibrium was also notable. It signalled that North Korea shared long-term interest of Japan: to modify regional security dilemmas as the best means to guarantee the current North Korean regime's survival until a Korean reunification formula could be derived and implemented, that would not leave any of Northeast Asia's great powers strategically disadvantaged.

Various barriers to improved Japanese–Korean relations remain. How might Japan precisely 'compensate' North Korea for historical transgressions? How can the North be locked into more enduring arms control measures (especially in regard to cutting or eliminating its ballistic missile capability)? Most substantially, how would Japan cope with a unified and powerful Korean state over the long term, especially if the United States uses such a development as a rationale for reducing or withdrawing its own force presence from both Korea and Japan? Japanese liberals view such prospects as mandating the imperative to create a 'community of nations' in Northeast Asia. Realists perceive them as the catalysts for greater regional instability and conflict if the uncertainties surrounding North Korea's future are not confronted more objectively through adhering to a myopic commitment to engagement.[58]

## Japan and the TMD

Because the potential lethality of North Korea's missile threat to Japan cannot be ignored, Japanese policy planners have discussed with the United States prospects for collaboration in the development of a TMD system. President Clinton initially proposed that Japan collaborate with the United States on TMD in June 1993. From that time until late 1997 Japanese negotiators conducted nine 'working level' talks with US officials on such a project, while nearly ¥500 million was spent on feasibility studies to assess the TMD's relevance to Japanese defence problems.[59]

In August 1997 the Japanese government announced it was 'postponing' a final commitment to work with the United States in developing a TMD. The Japan Defense Agency did request ¥80 million to continue research on Lightweight Exoatmosphere Projectile (LEAP) missile technology to be loaded on to the *Aegis* missile system already fitted to major Japanese surface warships – a technology in which Japan felt it excelled relative to the United States. Cost factors were cited publicly as the key reason for the postponement. It was surmised that the minimum cost of development would be ¥1 trillion and this was unacceptable at a time when the Japan Defense Agency was being asked by the Finance Ministry to slash ¥920 billion from its 1996–2000 mid-term defence buildup program.[60]

But other concerns besides project expenses also influenced Japan's position. These covered a wide range of issues, including weapons system viability, intelligence management, and political constraints. The speed of *No-dong-1*'s re-entry trajectory appears too great for the interception capabilities of existing TMD components – including the theatre high altitude area defence (THAAD) missile, the Patriot PAC2 extended range interceptor (ERINT), and LEAP. Moreover, the TMD would be coordinated by US satellite systems, leaving Japan as a completely 'passive player' in terms of command and control. That problem was partly addressed when Japan announced in December 1998 that it would launch four reconnaissance satellites of its own by 2002 to assist the United States with future 'crisis management' and to avoid future strategic surprises such as that provided by the August 1998 North Korean missile launch. The Japanese moved ahead with developing an independent satellite surveillance capability, notwithstanding American objections to the project.[61]

Japan may also need to develop a more politically credible set of rationales to justify its working with the United States in building anti-missile systems. There is continued uncertainty as to whether or not Japan's participation in any TMD project may be a violation of Japan's long-standing ban against exporting arms, although there are precedents for defence *technology* collaboration with the United States. Launching TMD interceptors into space would also seem to violate a 1968 parliamentary resolution that Japan would only participate in peaceful extra-terrestrial ventures.[62] If Japan were to help coordinate a TMD operation with US and South Korean TMD components to defeat a missile attack launched exclusively against South Korea or US military positions on South Korean territory, its opposition to participation in collective defence organisations would be undermined. Another Japanese analyst surmised that the North Korean missile threat had become a *political* weapon that was capable of destroying the US–Japan alliance if it was not carefully managed. He posited that Japan found itself 'between the devil and the deep blue sea', with the United States pressing hard to win formal Japanese TMD research collaboration while North Korea, Russia and China were warning that any such collaboration would bring to the fore the regionally destabilising 'containment' aspects of the US–Japan alliance.[63]

Despite these concerns, Japan and the United States eventually announced their joint collaboration on TMD at the 'two-plus-two' ministerial security meeting held in New York during September 1998. Japanese diplomats attending this summit cited North Korea's *Taepo-dong* missile test as pushing Japan into formal collaboration with the United

States on TMD development.[64] As any TMD deployment would be only 'defensive' in nature and conducted within the context of the US alliance, the Japan Defense Agency argued that it would not violate Japan's Constitution or other legislative constraints. In August 1999, a more comprehensive agreement for joint US–Japanese research on TMD was signed in response to continuing fears regarding North Korea's long-range ballistic missile program.[65] However these decisions remain controversial since China, in particular, views TMD as an integral part of a new US–Japan containment policy directed primarily against itself.[66]

### A 'China Threat'?

While extensive analysis has been offered on Sino–Japanese relations, the discussion which follows is intended to focus more specifically on the extent and the ways in which Japan may feel its national security is jeopardised by a more powerful China. Most Western analysts contend that there has been a perceptible shift in Japanese thinking since the mid-1990s (and particularly since the 1996 Taiwan Strait crisis) about what Chinese power projection capabilities mean to Japan's own security.[67] Japanese policy makers do not regard China as an imminent danger, and are amenable to working with the current Chinese leadership to prevent or defuse regional crises that may arise from intensified Sino–American tensions or as a hedge against the decline of American strategic power and commitment to Asia.[68]

At least three key factors could substantially intensify Japanese apprehensions about a 'China threat': (1) excessive Chinese nationalism precipitating unacceptably high levels of risky Chinese behaviour in the region, such as a military confrontation in the Taiwan Strait or interdiction of critical sea lanes of communication in the South China Sea; (2) Chinese development of high technology weapons systems capable of neutralising or overwhelming current Japanese defence capabilities; or (3) sustained Chinese economic growth creating a desire on the part of China to secure energy resources through military power projection at the expense of Japan. The next section will focus on the possible ramifications of intensified Chinese nationalism and how substantial Chinese defence modernisation may influence Japan's national security outlook.

Japan's pre-Cold War legacy of militarism and colonial occupation, coupled with China's history of exploitation by Japan and other foreign powers, has led to the development of a security culture in Beijing that projects a 'worse case' interpretation on to current Japanese regional security policies. China is accustomed to reminding Japan about its wartime transgressions as a means of gaining negotiating leverage. Chinese Premier Zhu Rongji recently declared the Chinese government would not demand a written apology from Japan for its invasion of China during World War II. However, continued visits by Japanese government officials to Yasukuni Shrine and Japan's linking of yen loans to China's nuclear and maritime behaviour still rankle with Chinese leaders.[69] Beijing often links (and justifies) a highly nationalistic regional posture to real or contrived apprehensions about future Japanese strategic intentions. In their bilateral relations this has complicated Sino–Japanese efforts to address a territorial dispute over the Diaoyutai/Senkaku Islands in the East China Sea. In a broader context, China has recently sought to portray the US–Japan alliance as a tool for frustrating China's quest to reassimilate Taiwan – a form of 'internal interference'. Moreover, it argues that Japan is acting as a US proxy in seeking to 'contain' a fictitious 'China threat'. Japan, on the other hand, is becoming more inclined to adopt a hard-line stance on Chinese behaviour in the East China Sea and, as a result, to view the 'China threat' more seriously. The Senkaku (in Japanese) or Diaoyutai (in Chinese) Islands are located 200 kilometres northeast of Taiwan and consist of five uninhabited islands and three barren rocks with a total area of approximately 6.5 square kilometres. These islands were included in the 'Okinawa reversion' engineered by President Nixon and Prime Minister Sato in 1969. Chinese officials found their inclusion in the reversion to be 'highly disturbing' because of their proximity to Taiwan (which also claims ownership of the islands), and made them a focal point of their 1970 campaign against 'Japanese militarisation'. However, Chinese officials valued normalisation of relations with Japan much more highly and opted to shelve the dispute on the condition that Japan would negotiate general navigation and fishery agreements with the PRC.[70]

Intermittent Sino–Japanese confrontations have flared up over the islands since that time. The expectation that oil reserves are located under the sea in the vicinity of Diaoyutai/Senkaku Islands is a key reason why both China and Japan have adopted such a hard line over who exercises sovereign control. Both countries are net importers, and control of the islands would cede exploration rights to approximately 30 000 square kilometres of continental shelf.[71] But even more fundamental issues relating to Chinese perceptions of Japan are involved. In 1996 Chinese Premier Li Peng infused Chinese nationalism into the Diaoyutai/Senkaku issue by warning Japan to control its 'militarist' right-wing political groups which intermittently travel to the islands and plant Japanese flags or refurbish lighthouses there. Li admonished the Japanese for 'hurting the feelings of the Chinese people'.[72] Chinese Foreign Ministry spokesman Shen Guofeng inserted what, from a Japanese perspective, has become an all too familiar historical spin. Calling on Tokyo to be 'sensible' regarding the dispute, Shen observed that 'from a historical perspective, what constitutes a threat of war in the region, I'm afraid, is no other country than Japan'.[73]

This was a message strongly repeated by Chinese President Jiang Zemin during the highly controversial China–Japan Summit held in Tokyo during late November 1998. In a speech delivered to Waseda University students, Jiang insisted that 'it is imperative to face squarely the unfortunate episode in the history of Sino–Japanese relations and draw lessons', and that Japan needed to take special care to avoid pursuing militarism.[74] Yet China had its own reasons for avoiding an escalation of the dispute, including the need to avoid a direct confrontation with Japanese naval forces which were quite capable of defeating the outmoded Chinese naval assets that could be deployed in the East China Sea.[75]

China's efforts to introduce nationalist grievances into its opposition to the revised US–Japan Defense Guidelines, which address emergency situations in areas surrounding Japan, are illustrative of this trend. After the March 1996 Taiwan Strait crisis and the April 1996 US–Japan Joint Security Declaration, China stepped up its criticism of the alliance on the grounds that it was manifestly an instrument of anti-China containment.[76] During his September 1997 visit to China, Prime Minister Hashimoto attempted unsuccessfully to convince Chinese leaders that this criterion was not 'geographical' but would be applicable on a case-by-case basis in accordance with how Japan might be threatened by a particularly contingency.[77]

By pursuing a nationalistic policy line so relentlessly in their security relations with Japan, Chinese leaders may well have generated a self-fulfilling prophecy – conditioning Japanese perceptions so that the 'China threat' thesis is now gaining more acceptance in Japan. Japanese envoys to Washington have conveyed their determination to monitor Chinese military developments more closely. Japan temporarily suspended approximately ¥96 million worth of loans to China (about one-sixteenth of Japan's total assistance to the PRC) after China had conducted a nuclear weapons test in August 1995 in defiance of the international community's quest for a comprehensive ban on any such testing.[78] Both houses of the Japanese Parliament subsequently passed resolutions condemning such tests.

Based on this recent history, experts and the general public in Japan are beginning to grapple with the concept that China may indeed be a looming threat to Japanese security interests. In a survey of Japanese defence experts undertaken for this study, the majority of respondents (55 per cent), characterised China as 'hegemonic; wanting and pushing for more influence in the region'. Yet most of those surveyed also felt that containment was *not* the proper strategy for Japan or its allies to adopt in dealing with Chinese power, belying past Chinese claims that Tokyo was intent in applying the revised Defense Guidelines toward such a posture (see table 3.2). In March 1997, the majority of those surveyed for a *Mainichi Shimbun* poll said that they were worried about what they perceived as a potentially threatening Chinese military buildup, as opposed to 20 per cent who were not concerned. The same poll revealed that well over half of those surveyed supported the US alliance while only 14 per cent opposed it.[79] These results underscore an evolving Japanese concern about future Chinese intentions and power, but one that is not immediately preoccupied with China as directly threatening Japan so long as the American alliance remains operative.

### China's Defence Modernisation: Japanese Perceptions

One of the clearest findings from the survey of Japanese national security experts presented in table 3.2 is the concern expressed about China's growing military capabilities. Japan has traditionally downplayed its need to develop state-of-the-art weapons technology and high performance weapons systems in favour of developing 'dual use' technologies that could give it an edge in the commercial marketplace.[80] It has opted to rely mostly on the US military presence in Northeast Asia, and on American weapons systems, to counter Soviet/Russian offensive power in that subregion. Furthermore, it has not been overly pre-occupied with Chinese military power projection because China lacked a broad-based industrial development program capable of producing competitive high technology weapons systems.

With China's decision in the early 1980s to shift its focus toward developing a more comprehensive defence technology and production base, Japanese policy planners are now reconsidering their position. They are beginning to question what aspects of Beijing's defence modernisation program will threaten Japan's security. To date, they have concluded that no substantial shift has occurred in the East Asian military balance as a result of recent Chinese efforts to modernise their defence forces and that Japan's continued access to US advanced military technology has actually improved Japan's overall strategic position. They remain worried, however, that China's sheer size, its potential for economic growth, and its proven willingness to use force in the pursuit of its strategic interests are all factors that need to be constantly assessed.

Official Japanese assessments of Chinese military capabilities have been careful to avoid extensive speculation about how they may affect Japan's national security.[81] Since the mid-1990s, however, a lively debate has ensued in the Japanese media, involving academics, journalists and some government analysts. Areas of special concern are: (1) the quantity and quality of weapons China is just beginning to introduce into its force

**Table 3.2**   Survey of Japanese defence experts

| Questions and Responses | % |
|---|---|
| *Q: A threat to national security is, in your view, associated with which of the following:* | |
| A.  A potentially hostile country's military capabilities | 60 |
| B.  Diplomatic influence on specific issues which is employed in ways adverse to your country's interests | 30 |
| C.  Economic leverage directed against your country's interests | 5 |
| D.  Territorial claims which contradict your country's own sovereign interests | 5 |
| E.  Alliance politics perceived as working against your country's interests | 0 |
| *Q: Which of the following statements best describes how you perceive China:* | |
| A.  Friendly and growth oriented, busy 'catching up' with the more developed nations | 0 |
| B.  Neutral, but developing constructive ties with other countries in and beyond the region | 5 |
| C.  Influential in some regional matters, but generally kept busy sorting out its own numerous problems | 35 |
| D.  Hegemonic; wanting and pushing for more influence in the region | 55 |
| E.  Hostile, often aggressive; wanting to become an influential global superpower | 5 |
| *Q: For China to be a positive force in regional/global security politics, which of the following factors do you consider to be most important:* | |
| A.  China continuing its economic development leading to expanded economic ties | 15 |
| B.  New laws and regulations on trade and legal issues which work towards making China's political system similar to those of other industrialised democracies | 50 |
| C.  China's future success in developing multilateral ties with many of its neighbours | 5 |
| D.  China playing an increasingly important role as mediator in regional conflicts | 0 |
| E.  China's success in avoiding and defusing conflicts with other nations in the region | 30 |
| *Q: For China to be considered a potential threat, which of the following statements is, in your opinion, most true:* | |
| A.  China modernises and strengthens its military | 45 |
| B.  China's economic and technological capabilities catch up with those of the OECD states | 15 |
| C.  China becomes increasingly aggressive over territorial claims | 35 |
| D.  China's government intensifies human rights oppression | 5 |

**Table 3.2**   Survey of Japanese defence experts *(continued)*

| Questions and Responses | % |
|---|---|
| *Q: In your opinion, which of the following reactions would be most constructive in response to any 'China threat':* | |
| A.  Deterrence | 20 |
| B.  Counter-alliance | 0 |
| C.  Containment | 5 |
| D.  Engagement | 55 |
| E.  Collective Security | 20 |
| *Q: Assuming China is or becomes a threat, is it possible to bargain with China:* | |
| A.  Yes, although China can appear threatening, the leadership is generally pragmatic and open to compromise | 10 |
| B.  Yes, if treated as at least an equal the Chinese leadership will prefer dialogue to conflict | 15 |
| C.  Yes, but only from a position of strength – in order to convince the Chinese that bargaining is their best option | 45 |
| D.  No, the Chinese will inevitably read any attempt at a compromise as a sign of weakness and push harder | 0 |
| E.  No, China is determined to rectify what it views as historical grievances and will only bargain at the tactical level without compromising its long-term strategic objectives | 30 |

*Source*: Author's survey of twenty Japanese defence experts in 1998. Identities must remain anonymous as a pre-stated condition of survey participation. Analysts polled included government officials and academics.

inventories; (2) the lack of transparency in China's defence budget; and (3) the PLA's ability to sustain offensive military capabilities against Taiwan and in other localities proximate to Japan's own defence perimeters. While some analysts are more prepared than others to give China credit for both enhancing its force strengths and reporting them more accurately than others, a general consensus has developed among Japanese defence observers regarding the following points:

- The gap in quality between US, Japanese and most Chinese conventional weapons systems remains significant, with many of the Chinese surface ships, submarines and combat aircraft remaining in its dwindling force inventories reaching the end of their combat usefulness;
- China tends to under-report what it is spending on defence even though it still adheres to a strategy designed to produce and deploy weapons systems based on relatively simple technologies;
- Because it is the beneficiary of continued US extended deterrence guarantees, Japan is not immediately threatened by China's nuclear capability, although there is growing concern about Chinese tests of

mobile missile delivery systems that would be harder to target or defend against with a TMD system; and

• The most 'threatening' aspect of China's military modernisation is its *psychological* dimension, sharpened by China's stated intentions to project maritime power throughout the region and its potential ability to convert its massive economy-of-scale into military power.[82]

North Korea's destiny may be Japan's most urgent security concern but the emergence of China as an economic and long-term strategic rival to Tokyo for shaping Asia's new regional order is of vital importance. How well Japan can meet this challenge will be determined as much by China's reading of the US–Japan security alliance, and by Washington's bilateral relations with Beijing, as by how China and Japan relate to each other. If the alliance proves, in the words of one American official, to be 'the Asian corollary of a NATO expansion', China will conclude that it is an instrument of containment, rendering systematic 'trialogues' between the three powers more difficult and raising the stakes over existing regional flashpoints.[83] There is little sustainable evidence to date that China is ready to view the revised Defense Guidelines as anything other than an overtly realist-oriented example of power politics. Without a change of heart in Beijing, Tokyo may ultimately be forced into making the one strategic choice it would prefer to avoid at all costs: relinquishing the American alliance to satisfy China or remaining allied to Washington as its only option to avoid remilitarising on its own in order to counter-balance Chinese power.

### Declining Concerns Over Russia

Japanese security diplomacy towards the Russian Federation has been encumbered by Tokyo entertaining unrealistically high expectations for achieving progress in resolving traditional differences, and by Russia's inability to sustain a cohesive strategic posture towards Japan. However, Japan's willingness to strengthen its trade, investment and diplomatic standing with the Russians will influence how Russia evolves as a future regional security actor. This evolution matters because Russian cooperation is especially needed if multilateral solutions are to be successfully applied to the problems of controlling the pace and scope of regional arms sales, effectively securing nuclear installations and fissile material, and responding cohesively to the growth of Chinese power.[84]

The ability of Japanese policy makers to deal with Russia constructively remains encumbered by two predominant constraints. These are: (1) the continuing inability by Moscow and Tokyo to resolve the lingering 'Northern Territories' question; and (2) Japan's failure to posit to Russia that the changing dynamics of the US–Japan MST are directed towards Tokyo's emergence as an influential Asia-Pacific state as opposed to a global strategic power. Until their deeply ingrained suspicions of each other are addressed more comprehensively and consistently, the Russian–Japanese relationship will remain as one of the Asia-Pacific region's intractable security dilemmas.

Japan's territorial claim to a group of small islands in the southern Kuriles – Etorufu, Kunashiri, Shikotan and the Habomai – has been a major impediment to the normalisation of Soviet/Russian–Japanese relations since the end of World War II.[85] While formal diplomatic ties were established between the Soviet Union and Japan in 1956, Moscow has not signed or ratified the 1951 San Francisco peace treaty nor has it negotiated a separate peace treaty to end the technical state of war that has existed between the USSR/Russia and Japan since 1945. Prior to the Soviet Union's collapse, Russian leader Boris Yeltsin and the USSR's last leader, Mikhail Gorbachev, had offered plans for gradually settling the dispute and reverting the islands to Japanese control. However, in the face of intensifying Russian nationalism, these proposals were jettisoned by the end of 1991. Understandably frustrated, Japan subsequently attempted to link its support for Russian membership in the G-7 group, and the future of Japanese economic assistance, to Moscow with the return of at least two of the islands (Shikotan and the Habomai). This formula conformed roughly to a Soviet proposal for a peace treaty between the two countries advanced in 1956 which quickly dissipated when neither side pursued it aggressively at that time. Japan's linkage diplomacy tactics were opposed by Japan's other allies (the United States, France and Germany) which were concerned that President Yeltsin's political survival was vital for Russian democratisation. Tokyo subsequently softened its position at the July 1993 G-7 summit, proceeding to extend a $US1.8 million aid package to Russia through multilateral channels but still withholding strictly bilateral assistance.

President Yeltsin finally visited Japan in October 1993 (after two postponements) and signed the Tokyo Declaration with Japanese Prime Minister Hosokawa Morihiro. It committed Russia and Japan to the pursuit of a settlement of the Northern Territories dispute based on 'historical and legal facts'. The Japanese Ministry of Foreign Affairs' description of this agreement represents it as establishing 'the basis for an early conclusion to a peace treaty through solution of the territorial issue'.[86] Two subsequent meetings between President Yeltsin and Prime Minister Hashimoto during another G-7 summit in Denver in June 1997, and in Krasnoyarsk in early November 1997, gave this objective further impetus by establishing the year 2000 as a deadline for the successful negotiation of a peace treaty and by setting out a more specific timetable for Northern Territories reversion. Hashimoto also announced a three-phase Japanese approach for strengthening Japanese–Russian ties: (1) the consistent pursuit of trust-building; (2) the identification and pursuit of mutual interests; and (3) the establishment of a long-term constructive approach on the Northern Territories issue and economic ties.[87] These criteria were acceptable to Yelstin, who was increasingly interested in pursuing an 'omni-directional' foreign policy with Japan and China as a means of countering American global influence.

However, as one analyst has astutely observed, Russia and Japan 'continue to disagree about whether economics (trade, investment and credits) or politics (the territorial dispute and the signing of a peace treaty) should be the pace-setter in the relationship'.[88] A high percentage of Russian military officials and strong nationalists still regard the Northern Territories as strategically significant and as symbolic of Russia's determination to defend its territorial integrity in an era in which Moscow is confronted by major security problems in its 'Near Abroad'. Forming part of the Kurile island chain, which encloses the Sea of Okhotsk, the contested islands sit astride what was a major transit route used by Soviet nuclear powered ballistic missile submarines. Yet the importance attached to maintaining this strategic advantage is declining as the Russian Navy has developed alternative tactics that reduce overall reliance on deployments in the Sea of Okhotsk. Essentially, by deploying *Delta* III/IV or *Typhoon* class submarines in the Arctic with the Northern Fleet the Russian navy can now be assured of achieving adequate target coverage across both the Atlantic and Pacific Oceans.[89]

Japanese strategists are aware of these developments. This knowledge has led them to puzzle over why various Russian military elites continue to engage in worst-case strategic planning and advocate levels of strategic readiness that reflect such assessments.[90] The Russian military planners appear to be oblivious to the lowering of Russian–Japanese strategic tensions that has been achieved to date and is further promised by their political masters' pursuit of a policy of multilateral diplomacy designed to reduce points of conflict with all of the other great powers. It would be reasonable to conclude that these contradictory Russian postures are a manifestation of intense policy disputes that are occurring between conservative military elements and residual civilian-reformist sectors within Russia's leadership.

What is more certain is that Moscow's unstable domestic political situation and its persistent economic problems have precluded the Northern Territories dispute from being resolved smoothly and the prospects for this happening in the near future are declining. A summit convened between Yeltsin's successor, Vladimir Putin, and Japanese Prime Minister Mori Yoshiro in Tokyo during September 2000 made little progress in resolving the Northern Territories dispute or reaching terms for a peace treaty. Putin stopped in Sakhalin on his way to Tokyo where he reassured that province's ardently nationalist governor, Ivor Farkhutdimov, that he would not hand over the southern Kurile Islands to Japan. This effectively blocked any aspirations Mori may have entertained about realising the Krasnoyarsk vision of agreeing on a reversion process by the year 2000. Indeed, Putin had already denied the viability of any such commitment some months prior to his summit with Mori, 'absolutely ruling out' transferring the disputed territory. The Russian Duma's Deputy Speaker reinforced his president's decision labelling the setting of a deadline for signing any such agreement 'one of the biggest mistakes' of early post-Cold War Russian foreign policy. Putin and Mori met again at the end of March 2001 on the shores of Lake Baikal. While the Russian leader officially recognised Japanese claims to Habomai and Shikotan (in conjunction with the 1956 joint declaration), no real progress was made. Mori was crippled politically and could only reiterate Japan's traditional demands that all four islands should be returned.[91]

In the absence of a stable Russia, inevitably Japan's strategic options for dealing with future Russian governments will be qualified. Before important bilateral or multilateral initiatives are undertaken they will need to be discussed carefully with the United States, China and other regional security actors.

*Japan and Multilateral Security: Regional Dimensions*

A consensus presently exists among Japanese policy makers and most independent Japanese analysts that their country should pursue multilateral security politics in the Asia-Pacific as a 'supplement' to the US bilateral security treaty rather than as its replacement.[92] At the same time, however, Tokyo has concluded that a liberal approach to Asia-Pacific security will succeed only if the region's two strategic giants – the United States and China – which project both substantial economic and military power become more committed to embracing this process over that of power balancing. As this has not yet happened (nor is it likely to occur anytime soon), Japanese liberals must still search for ways to facilitate consensus on key regional security issues.

It is notable that other Asian states initially reacted coolly when Japan attempted to introduce modest multilateral security initiatives independently of Washington. They were sceptical of Tokyo for two main reasons. The first is because Japan had refused to fully come to terms with its wartime behaviour. The second is that it had declined to support post-World War II collective security ventures with real political will and strategic assets as opposed to merely paying out financial subsidies. Japanese critics, moreover, posit that their country was simply shirking behind the 1947 Constitution to escape its responsibilities in a post-Cold War international environment.[93]

Japan's legacy of limiting military operations in deference to Article 9 is clearly ingrained in Japan's aforementioned peacekeeping operations law passed in 1992: 'minimally armed' and neutral Japanese forces would only operate in non-combat (or cease-fire) areas; the belligerents would need to endorse a Japanese presence; and any such presence would be terminated if conflict resumed, leaving what was left of the peacekeeping component to the mercy of the belligerents or initiating an unseemly scramble for replacements. This position can hardly be seen as a major participation in collective security management. Japan's passiveness in the face of the December 1996 hostage-taking crisis at its embassy in Lima, Peru, further underscored the reality that the Japanese public is unwilling to incur risks in return for building a secure international order.

Notwithstanding these difficulties, the premise that multilateral security politics can serve as an effective means for strengthening regional stability is still entertained positively within some Japanese policy circles and by an increasing number of independent analysts.[94] Foreign Minister Nakayama Taro's proposal, advanced at the 1991 ASEAN Post-Ministerial Council meeting in Kuala Lumpur, for ASEAN to organise a regional security dialogue was not initially embraced by the Southeast Asian countries since they were preparing their own dialogue blueprint for introduction the following year. But Japanese diplomats remember it as a major innovation and as having been instrumental in convincing the United States to take a more positive view of the multilateral approach. In this instance, they argue, Japan's 'intellectual style' of Asia-Pacific regime building acted as a catalyst for the eventual creation of the ARF.[95]

Emboldened by the ASEAN experience, Prime Minister Miyazawa Kiichi quickly seconded Australian Prime Minister Paul Keating's 1992 proposal for a heads-of-state summit to be convened annually at the APEC forum. Keating was convinced that such a summit could be transformed into an institutionalised vehicle for regional political and security cooperation along the lines of the Conference on Security and Cooperation in Europe. Miyazawa advanced this vision in a major foreign policy speech delivered in Washington in October 1992. He also appointed a panel of scholars to study how the US–Japan bilateral alliance could coexist with the proliferation of regional multilateral security dialogues. In January 1993 he announced that it was Japan's intention to participate actively in such dialogues, a posture that was subsequently labelled the 'Miyazawa Doctrine'.

Implicit in his remarks, however, was sensitivity to the need for others in Asia to take the initial lead so as not to inflame suspicions that Japan was overstepping its limited prerogatives for defining any type of regional security order.[96] In a similar vein successive Japanese prime ministers have expressed 'remorse and deep reconsideration' (Kaifu), 'deep reflection and regret' (Murayama) and 'profound remorse and apologies for Japan's wartime "aggression" and colonial legacies' (Hosokawa). But such confessionals have been increasingly criticised by conservative Japanese political factions and analysts as unnecessarily deferential. They argue that Japanese national security interests can no longer be shackled by waning historical legacies that are all too often manipulated against their country.[97]

Japanese foreign policy experts and officials acting in private capacities have entered into a number of 'Track Two' dialogues with American, Russian, Chinese and South Korean counterparts to discuss Korean security issues. However, they responded tentatively to a 1994 South Korean proposal for creating a separate Northeast Asia Security Dialogue, viewing it as premature.[98] They were more enthusiastic about the joint American–South Korean proposal for the commencement of Four Power Talks on a Korean peace treaty, involving the United States, China and the two Koreas realising that neither Korea would tolerate an initial Japanese presence at such a forum.

The pace of *ad hoc* multilateral security dialogues quickened following the 1996 Taiwan Strait crisis, with Japan becoming more intent on integrating China into a framework of regional preventive diplomacy. With the Clinton Administration's full support, Japanese diplomats organised a series of trilateral meetings with Chinese, American and Japanese participants in late 1997 and early 1998 to engage with each other about the changing context and implications of the US–Japan alliance and other regional security issues.[99]

In January 1997 Japan's prime minister embarked on a five-nation tour of the ASEAN subregion and enunciated what became known as the 'Hashimoto Doctrine': proposing an annual summit with ASEAN leaders, and regular bilateral talks between Japan and individual ASEAN states on security issues. But Japan's efforts to integrate China into regional security deliberations appeared to backfire in this instance. ASEAN officials responded coolly to Hashimoto for fear of alienating Beijing at a time when China was assuming a more active and positive role in Asia-Pacific multilateral security politics. This judgement seemed to be confirmed by China's moderate and positive role in supporting regional and international measures to cope with the Asian financial crisis. The ASEAN states have since moved to adopt an initiative similar to the dialogue mechanism that the Americans and Japanese were pursuing with China in Northeast Asia. This avoided creating the impression that Japan and ASEAN were colluding against Chinese interests in exclusive talks.[100] The upshot of this policy direction has been for ASEAN to incorporate Japan into regional multilateral settings on its terms, gradually inculcating the Japanese into a more substantial diplomatic and security role in Asia-Pacific affairs but not to the extent that either the US–Japan alliance is disrupted or Chinese and Korean sensitivities over any latent or potential Japanese 'imperialist' tendencies are intensified. The 'ASEAN + 3' initiative typifies this approach. It entails the 'deepening' of economic ties in areas of regional trade and financial management – sectors in which Japan is comfortable and can make a major contribution. Long-term security connotations may flow from the pursuit of such 'functional' arrangements but they can be reconciled with more traditional security policy concerns through the ARF and other mechanisms where Japan and South Korea would be expected to defer to US interests.

### The Realist-Liberal Debate Revisited

Japan's difficulties in pressing its multilateral diplomacy initiatives throughout the region are indicative of a wider problem in that country's post-Cold War security policy that directly relates to the realist-liberal debate. How could defence relations with the United States be adjusted in response to a newly emergent regional balance of power? This is particularly difficult at a time when the Japanese electorate is still largely apprehensive about Japan's becoming a 'normal power'. Moreover, Japan's neighbours are directly opposed to any such prospect and Japan's bureaucrats are more comfortable exercising regional and international influence only through diplomatic and economic means and via established institutional venues. Realists argue that military power flows from economic predominance and that Japan is confronting this historical inevitability as the United States intensifies its pressure on Japan to assume a greater level of responsibility for securing global oil supplies and for assisting US defence efforts in Northeast Asia. Yet it has become more difficult, not less, for the Japanese government to justify a continued American basing presence in Japan, or to generate defence funding, at a time of increased economic uncertainty.[101]

Realists in Japan maintain that their country has no other choice, as the twenty-first century begins, than to reinforce the American alliance and the Yoshida Doctrine, even at the risk of compromising the Constitution.[102] From this perspective, power balancing remains the proven response to international structural change and the American alliance remains the core element of any such strategy.[103] The Defense Guidelines will need to be further consolidated to define Japanese alliance responsibilities and prerogatives more clearly. Japan's leaders must be more effective in building public support for the alliance in their country while becoming more sensitive to projecting a favourable diplomatic-economic image in the United States. They must also be adroit in precluding Japan from becoming caught between American and Chinese strategic agendas wherever possible while maintaining strong security ties with the United States. These imperatives can only be achieved by working to enhance bilateral consultations with US policy counterparts on a more regular and systematic basis and to address forthrightly and comprehensively hard issues such as TMD, defence burden-sharing and Korea.[104] By fulfilling these conditions, many realists would argue, Japan's transition to becoming a more 'normal power' would be facilitated.

Liberals are less prominent than their realist counterparts in Japan because very few influential politicians or independent analysts have opposed the MST. However, debate is now intensifying as to the merit of the traditional rationales put forward to justify continuing Japanese security relations with the United States. Most Japanese observers who question various aspects of the alliance still concede that the MST must be retained at least until it is clear that multilateral security approaches can succeed in the region. They regard the treaty not so much as a regional power balancing mechanism but as an instrument of strategic reassurance that facilitates the development of greater Japanese diplomatic and strategic self-confidence.[105] In this context, they view the 1996 Joint Declaration on Security as an initial step towards implementing 'extended bilateralism' – that the MST will remain the primary structure for US–Japanese security relations, but it must also be supplemented by multilateral forums such as a Northeast Asian security dialogue or the ARF.[106]

Liberals in Japan, and those abroad who study Japanese foreign policy, are also more concerned than their realist counterparts with the linkages between their country's domestic politics and its security behaviour. They therefore do not restrict their analysis to the 'international system' and how multilateral security institutions may 'supplement' regional power balancing. Instead they argue that Japan's strategic culture, history and political institutions are all relevant to its contemporary security postures. Soeya Yoshihide, for example, has introduced the concept that Japan's 'dual identity' interacting with Asia's 'dual structure' is a key factor in both Japanese and regional security politics. Japan views itself as behaving like a 'small country', dependent upon the MST for its security but viewed by other regional security actors as a traditional great power.[107]

Realists counter that Japan's strategic culture and its legacy of pre-World War II imperialism undermine its ability to work with either the region's other great powers or with small states to identify common norms and to implement security regimes. Japan remains a potential structural leader that could become a power balancer if it were to become more strategically independent of the United States.[108] But liberals are increasingly backing Soeya's general line of reasoning, claiming that Japan's self-restraint in developing military capabilities, along with its diplomatic initiatives to support the ARF and a Northeast Asian security dialogue, classify it as an entrepreneurial and intellectual leader, intent upon regime-building.

In fact, Soeya's dual identity/dual structure model appears to partly transcend both the realist and liberal camps. It recognises that Japan's 'dual identity' allows it to retain the US security tie as a dependent participant in regional power balancing (a realist posture) while simultaneously allowing it to work with ASEAN in reducing prospects for conflict in maritime East and Southeast Asia, and with the United States, China, both Koreas and eventually Russia to defuse tensions in Northeast Asia (a liberal approach). But it is weighted toward the liberal paradigm because it envisions Japan as an entrepreneurial or intellectual player using predominantly non-coercive leadership attributes to create a new Asia-Pacific security order. The key to this model's eventual relevance seems to be how much the United States and China will allow Japan to define an agenda for security in the Asia-Pacific without exercising their great-power veto out of a fear that Tokyo will accrue too much influence.[109]

## Conclusion

Japan believes it deserves to become a more influential power in Asia-Pacific politics. Its failure to develop and project a clear consensus on how it will assume the responsibilities commensurate to attaining that status has prevented Tokyo from fulfilling this aspiration. Policy makers and their critics within Japan still tend to argue over constitutional prerogatives and constraints and how best to supplement US defence efforts in the region. Its modest diplomatic forays into multilateral security politics have been reactive and tepid, leaving ASEAN to spearhead liberal initiatives in the region. Because Japanese decision-making tends to be consensus-oriented, incremental and dilatory, prospects are remote that Japan will adopt a security doctrine that explicitly posits the country's national security interests in a truly independent context.[110]

Any future efforts by American officials to link US–Japan trade relations with US security relations are likely to be deflected by the Japanese. Any serious impairment in those security ties would leave Japan with no acceptable alternative security ally at a time when its economic competitiveness may be under serious challenge, a situation no Japanese government would wish to confront.[111] Indeed, some evidence suggests that American officials are keen to re-prioritise the relationship. In October 2000 a definitive report on America's relations with Japan was presented by a special bipartisan study group including Joseph Nye, and Richard

Armitage, who subsequently became George W. Bush's Deputy Secretary of State. The report argued that the Clinton Administration had assigned far too much emphasis on the Sino–American relationship at the expense of the US–Japan alliance. Japan, the group concluded, needed to return to the forefront of US strategy in the Asia-Pacific if American security interests in the region were to be sustained and strengthened.[112] In early May 2001 Armitage visited Tokyo in his official capacity and urged Japanese leaders to move towards a relationship with the United States that would be more like the alliance between Britain and the United States, 'in that it is taken for granted that of course we will consult on all matters, and of course we have a very in-depth, warm and personal relationship regardless of which [political] party comes to power'.[113]

Japan's search for acceptable multilateral security postures has been challenged by the need to establish some level of compatibility between potentially conflicting interests. Tokyo must reconcile US–Japan defence and security cooperation with rising Asian market economies that do not necessarily share Japan's political values or its national security interests. The search has also been complicated by the lack of a 'pan-Asian' strategic legacy equivalent to the NATO mandate to deter Soviet military power in Europe.

As Hashimoto Ryutaro discovered after floating one of several Japanese 'doctrines' in Southeast Asia, the ASEAN states seem more interested in manoeuvring between Japan and China to neutralise the power of both rather than collaborating with them to find a common basis for regional order. For its part, Japan tends to view Southeast Asia as a geopolitical hinterland which happens to sit astride its own critical oil and resource lifelines. Nothing resembling the Atlantic Charter is on the horizon in such an environment. Indeed, the most positive feature of Japan's alliance politics, as viewed by that country's neighbours, is that a US strategic presence constrains Japan's military capabilities.

In these circumstances, Japan has embarked on a multi-layered strategy to establish its politico-strategic legitimacy in a multipolar world. It is attempting to fuse bilateral (the US alliance) and multilateral (ARF and APEC) policy mechanisms to cope with ongoing structural change in the region. For this approach to work, Japan will need to overcome both the excessive pacifist strains within its domestic polity and to become more effective in trust-building with its neighbours and other key powers. It will need to be more creative than it has been so far in reconciling its own ambition to become a more influential multilateral entrepreneur with the need to adopt a sufficiently conciliatory set of policies to win support for its agenda. Reaching a *modus vivendi* with China on territorial disputes, alliance perceptions and regional crisis management is the first pre-requisite; coming to terms with its own past in ways that finally convince its neighbours that it can peacefully relate to their own histories and cultures is the second; and interacting with ASEAN states effectively on issues other than those of finance and development is the third. If these pre-requisites are not met, it is certain that Japan will remain a frustrated player in regional security politics and will have failed to achieve its aspiration to become a more 'normal power'. The US alliance remains the best stopgap currently available to Japan for gradually reconciling these policy objectives.

# CHAPTER 4

# Other Key Players I: Korea and Taiwan

A major feature of contemporary Asia-Pacific security politics is the pervasive sense of strategic uncertainty shared by its middle and small powers. The recent structural shift from the tight bipolarity of Soviet–American geopolitical competition to a loosely defined and more complex multipolar security environment has left these smaller players clearly more independent but also more vulnerable. The challenges now facing these states may be more ambiguous but are no less formidable than those confronted during the Cold War.

The Korean Peninsula provides the most telling example of this trend. Here we find two regimes separated by that country's demilitarised zone maintaining Cold War force levels and implacably opposed ideologies, even as one struggles to feed its population and the other confronts its most serious postwar economic crisis. The Taiwan Strait confrontation is a no less indomitable affair; Taiwan is one of the region's most liberal political societies and successful economies yet China continues to insist it has the right to reassimilate that island by force if it declares its formal independence from the mainland. Most ASEAN member-states face the twenty-first century with their domestic political systems fragile, their long-standing territorial disputes unresolved, their ethnic and nationalist tensions intensifying and their economic futures increasingly uncertain. Australia, the Southwest Pacific's dominant power, is struggling to gain acceptance among the region's states as a fully-fledged 'Asian' nation while strategic ties to past, extra-regional 'great and powerful friends' are still being maintained.

Despite their varying historical and cultural legacies and different strategic concerns, the Korean Peninsula, Taiwan, ASEAN and Australia are currently bound together as second-tier politico-security units by their common status as the Asia-Pacific's 'other key powers'. This terminology is controversial and may be conceptually vague without explanation. For the purposes of this study, the most fitting criteria would appear to be a combination of those specified for 'security powers' by Australian Foreign Minister H. V. Evatt (in an April 1945 BBC radio broadcast) and those for significant 'minor powers' stipulated by the eminent international relations theorist Martin Wight. These would include:

- certain powers, which by reason of their resources and geographic position, will prove to be of key importance for the maintenance of security in different parts of the world (Evatt)
- a [middle] power with such military strength, resources and strategic position that in peacetime the great powers bid for its support and in wartime, while it has no hope of winning a war against a great power, it can hope to inflict costs on a great power out of proportion to what the great power can hope to gain by attacking it ... [or] a [minor] power which has the means of defending only limited interests (Wight)

Taken together, other key powers – whether a single political unit (such as Australia or Taiwan), a unit comprised of contending regimes (a divided Korea) or multiple units adhering to a common set of foreign policy interests and principles (ASEAN) – have sufficient influence and impact on regional security to be key actors in the Asia-Pacific strategic environment.[1]

Several characteristics underscore the relevance of these 'other key powers'.[2] One is their continuing pursuit of military modernisation. A second is their increasing tendency to seek diversity in their politico-security relations, driven by a common desire to enhance their manoeuvrability within a rapidly changing global security environment. A third feature has flowed from this shared aspiration: a propensity to explore various formal and informal multilateral security frameworks to supplement but not to replace their traditional bilateral security ties with various great powers.

All three of these trends link these states to the realist-liberal debate. Their sustained defence modernisation efforts, realists would argue, illustrate the intensification of the security dilemmas in which a number of these states are involved and their lack of faith in liberal prescriptions for regional confidence-building and stability. Nor, realists argue, are their pursuits of new security relationships, in either a bilateral or multilateral context, indicative of anything more than their desire to preclude any one great power from dominating the Asia-Pacific region by collaborating tacitly either among themselves or with other great powers to avoid regional hegemony.[3] Liberals assert that the trend towards new forms of multilateral security relationships with the larger powers will gain momentum as the other key powers realise the advantages of seeking security through these relationships.[4] Liberals further argue that if multilateral security cooperation prevails, the prospects increase commensurately for 'lesser powers' to maintain strategic autonomy.[5]

This chapter will focus discussion on the Korean Peninsula and Taiwan – 'key powers' that must manage what are perhaps East Asia's two most dangerous flashpoints. Chapter 5 will examine ASEAN and Australia which together comprise a large part of the Asia-Pacific's 'southern rim'. As 'units', of course, the two Koreas and ASEAN are constituted by more than one state but they are considered as collective entities here because: (1) their foreign policy agendas are highly inter-connected; and (2) they are identified as such by other regional and global actors. In the case of the Koreas, this joint identification focuses on national identity and unification and, in the case of ASEAN, on how Southeast Asia's integration must proceed apart from great power interference. Taiwan's security preoccupations evolve around a single major issue: avoiding assimilation by China on Beijing's terms, while Australia clearly pursues its own interests as a distinctly independent regional security actor. The two chapters are further differentiated along 'subregional' lines. The Korean Peninsula and Taiwan are both aspects of 'Northeast Asian' security. Their strategic destinies will ultimately effect the future security of the two major Northeast Asian powers that this study is concerned with, China and Japan. In contrast to this, Southeast Asia and Australia together represent the maritime or 'offshore' dimension of regional security.

This chapter has been organised into two major sections covering both Koreas and then Taiwan. These sections have been further divided into three separate subsections. The initial subsection provides a brief overview of the Korean and Taiwanese security environments and how military strategies have evolved in response to perceived threats. This is followed by a discussion of how these 'other key powers' have dealt with great-power security politics. In this context, both of the Koreas and, to a lesser degree, Taiwan have recently attempted to diversify their traditional security postures of great-power dependence. The concluding subsections explore whether these diversification strategies will strengthen multilateral regional security cooperation or reinforce realist patterns of power politics. While these trends may not be uniform in all four instances under review in this chapter and the next, taken collectively they provide an understanding of how the Asia-Pacific second-tier powers are adapting to the region's changing security dynamics and how their policies and postures will influence the type of regional security order that takes shape.

### The Korean Security Environment and Military Strategies

Korea's fate is the most immediate security issue in Northeast Asia. Although there is only a relatively small risk of the Democratic People's

Republic of North Korea (DPRK) invading the Republic of Korea (ROK), it cannot be discounted entirely, even as its leadership has begun to open up to the outside world.[6] Previous speculation about that regime's imminent demise has proven to be premature. The continued resilience of North Korea's political institutions, despite Kim Il-sung's death in 1994, the pre-eminence of its military structure and the effectiveness of its diplomacy in extracting food aid and related concessions are developments that have all worked to underscore the complexity of dealing with the North and of projecting future developments there.[7]

The North Korean policy labyrinth intensified even more during the year 2000. An historic summit was convened for 13 to 15 June in Pyongyang between South Korean President Kim Dae-jung and Kim Jong-il, Chairman of the Democratic People's Republic of Korea's National Defence Commission and the leader of North Korea. The meeting produced the 'Five-Point South-North Joint Declaration' that pledged the two erstwhile rivals to jointly resolve the issue of reunification through a combination of the confederation formula (gradually narrowing the two sides' differences) favoured by the South and the 'Koryo Federation' approach (unifying first but with both governments retaining significant powers) traditionally favoured by the North. Clause Two of the June 2000 Joint Declaration pledged both sides to pursue common elements of confederation and federation and to observe an interim period of coexistence before reaching final unification. Regular and systematic dialogue between key officials from the two sides would be held and economic cooperation would be expanded significantly.[8] Speculation arose that a similar trip by Kim Jong-il to Seoul could lead to a diplomatic breakthrough whereby the armistice governing the 1950–53 Korean War cease-fire could be replaced by a formal peace treaty. The liberal vision of community-building in Northeast Asia seemed to be alive and well, with Kim Dae-jung speculating that diplomatic events could lead to greater regional economic opportunities and to the expedited formation of a Northeast Asian security community. Underlining this vision was Kim Jong-il's newfound public acknowledgment that US troops needed to remain deployed on the Korean Peninsula to provide the stability and balance of power required in Northeast Asia for the two Koreas to complete the Korean unification process peacefully.[9]

Realists contend that Korean reconciliation is by no means assured and that a unified Korea would present a whole new set of strategic problems that could destabilise Asian security. Greater democratisation in both Koreas would subject each government's foreign policies to greater pressure from domestic public opinion that would be highly susceptible to new forms of nationalism precipitated by the euphoria of achieving Korean unification. Far from reinforcing that American balancing role, a resolution of inter-Korean rivalry would increase pressure on American policy makers to withdraw troops from the Peninsula. That pressure would come from Korea, where 67 per cent of the public now favour a 'gradual' US military withdrawal, and in the United States where the lack of a clear deterrence mission in Korea would make current levels of US force commitments less sustainable. Regionally, any substantial US retraction could well leave Japan feeling isolated and highly threatened; China believing it could incorporate a united Korea into its own regional sphere of influence; and Russia increasingly keen to assume America's current balancing role on the Peninsula – a quest which would clearly put Moscow at odds with both China and Japan.[10]

Moreover, realists assert, it is far from clear that the momentum for Korean rapprochement generated by the summit will be sustainable. While Pyongyang has softened its stance on insisting that federation is the only way to pursue unification, it has yet to designate specifically how its revised outlook correlates with the South Korean approach. North Korea's military conducted what Western analysts have described as 'robust' military exercises throughout the year 2000. US–North Korea discussions on terrorism and on North Korea's missile program have continued to languish despite recent initiatives by Washington to reduce US trade and investment sanctions directed toward the DPRK. Ultimately, plans by the United States to deploy a TMD system in Northeast Asia and North Korea's propensity to use what nuclear weapons and missile delivery capabilities it has as bargaining chips to secure economic and strategic concessions from Washington may jettison prospects for long-term progress in stabilising the Korean Peninsula.[11] The momentum of this peace-building process was slowed during early 2001 as President George W. Bush demonstrated greater reluctance than his predecessor to embrace détente with the North Koreans. To ascertain the comparative prospects for liberal and realist agendas prevailing in Korea, a brief assessment of some key factors shaping its security outlook is provided below.

*Strategic Outlook*

Several key factors have shaped the national security outlooks of both Koreas throughout their postwar division. These include: (1) the Korean Peninsula's geography, strategically located between Northeast Asia's major powers; (2) escaping the Korean people's legacy of *sadae* ('serving the great'); and (3) a preoccupation with how, not if, Korea would once again become a unified state.[12]

Geopolitically, the mostly mountainous Korean Peninsula conjoins southward from the Northeast Asian mainland for approximately 1000 kilometres, separating the Yellow Sea from the Sea of Japan. During the Cold War it constituted the easternmost appendage of a highly volatile arc of conflict that divided the American and Soviet global geostrategic spheres of influence. That arc of conflict included such buffer states as Greece in the Balkans, Turkey, Iran, Afghanistan, Thailand and the Indochinese countries and Korea. Secretary of State Dean Acheson omitted the Peninsula from the US defence perimeter in what proved to be an ill-fated February 1950 speech on US foreign policy. So although not immediately recognised as critical to Western defences, Korea's Demilitarized Zone (DMZ) nevertheless emerged as a very sharp boundary between the American and Soviet strategic orbits. Don Oberdorfer's seminal study of the Peninsula has captured the essence of Korea's geopolitical quandary:

> Korea has been a country of the wrong size in the wrong place: large and well located enough to be of substantial value to those around it and thus worth fighting and scheming over, yet too small to merit priority attention by more powerful nations on all but a few occasions. Korea's fate was often to be an afterthought, subordinated to more immediate or compelling requirements of larger powers, rather than a subject of full consideration in its own right.[13]

### Precedents

Inter-Korean strategic competition has fluctuated widely over the past half century. Although South Korea's population was double that of the North's, it suffered fewer casualties than did the DPRK during the Korean War. It also enjoyed a comparatively greater and more reliable access to its allies' economic assistance and markets during the Cold War than was evident in North Korea's relations with the Soviet Union and China. Nevertheless, the North initially appeared to be prevailing in this rivalry. The North Korean leadership put immense faith in its prescribed 'socialist transformation' strategy, clearly outstripping South Korea's economic performance during much of the 1950s while primarily relying on a consistent inflow of Soviet weapons systems and on nearly 200 000 Chinese forces deployed within its boundaries throughout most of the 1950s to deter any South Korean and/or American invasion. Moreover, South Korean President Syngman Rhee was in no position to escalate hostilities after the Korean War's armistice was put into effect in 1953. Although entering into a Mutual Defense Treaty with South Korea in August 1953, the United States vigorously opposed Rhee's consistent 'March to the North' rhetoric as overly provocative and doomed to fail if put into practice since South Korea's army was no match for North Korea's New People's Army, even if the latter were to be unsupported by Chinese troops.

Several trends unfolded during the ensuing decades that generally worked to reverse the relative fortunes of the two Koreas. Collectively, these trends have elevated South Korea to an ascendant strategic position on the Peninsula. Important features were Kim Il-sung's misguided decision to emphasise national self-reliance in economic development and defence modernisation; changes in South Korea's leadership which transformed that state into an economic and military power; and the North's failure to precipitate a revolution south of the DMZ either by applying tactics of unconventional warfare or by engaging in selective dialogue with the ROK.

A military coup in May 1961, led by General Park Chung Hee, removed Syngman Rhee from power and permanently changed the thrust of South Korean economic and military policy. General Park emphasised 'export-oriented' economic development, complemented by rapid industrialisation. Prior to his assassination in September 1979, Park had instituted a significant number of reforms. Collectively they allowed the ROK to reach approximate military parity with the North, while the South Korean economy was enjoying spectacular growth (by 1989 the South Korean economy was seven times larger than the North's). The ROK, like North Korea, also introduced a 'defence self-reliance' policy at this time. However, in contrast to the North Korean case, this doctrine was embraced only *after* the country's war-damaged economy had mostly been repaired and it was largely based on the military performing specific functional tasks rather than being directed towards fulfilling ideological criteria. By 1977 South Korea was producing nearly 50 per cent of its own defence equipment and was primed to expand its defence industrial base still further when the United States agreed to provide $US1.5 billion in foreign military sales credits to help fund force improvement programs.[14]

The United States initially moved in 1977 to withdraw the remaining 32 000 US ground forces based in Korea. Apart from intelligence estimates, President Carter had another, more personal incentive for reducing military assistance to the ROK: he found many of the Park regime's human rights standards to be morally and politically repugnant.[15] However, miscalculations of North Korean military strength by the US Central Intelligence Agency and US Defense Intelligence Agency were disclosed publicly in Congressional hearings during June and July 1979. These reports revealed that the North Koreans had deployed far greater levels of ground forces near the DMZ than had previously been suggested. As early as 1971–72 the North Korean force structure had grown to around 700 manoeuvre battalions, almost double the size of its southern counterpart and clearly representing an offensive force strategy designed to decimate ROK defenses. The Carter Administration was forced to reverse its decision to withdraw US ground forces.

At the end of the twentieth century it became apparent that given the extremely small and highly populated combat radius projected for any renewed Korean conflict, wreaking havoc on successive Korea People's Army (KPA) echelons, through pinpoint targeting utilising powerful conventional weapons systems, would be a more effective and more rational strategy with which to defend South Korea. This strategy was preferable to relying exclusively and immediately on US tactical nuclear weapons deployed in the ROK as the ultimate rung of conflict escalation. In any case, such weapons had been removed following President George Bush Snr's decision in September 1991 to withdraw all American ground-launched tactical nuclear systems. The nuclear escalation option may well have precipitated Chinese military intervention and even North Korean nuclear responses against US positions in Korea, Japan or elsewhere in the East Asian theatre of operations. Nor would strategies relying upon the massive application of conventional or nuclear firepower be optimal given South Korea's terrain and lack of strategic depth. Buying time to regroup and to counterattack successive KPA echelons is most critical to defeating North Korea's *blitzkrieg* strategy.

*Military Strategy and Modernisation: Current Trends*

Two historical 'constants' underscore the Korean confrontation as it has evolved to the present time. First, even if the ability of South Korea and the United States to counter it has become more proficient in recent years, the North Korean military threat remains unquestionably formidable, despite the euphoria that followed the first inter-Korean leaders summit in June 2000. The second constant is a residual American discomfort in deploying high levels of ground forces in South Korea. In 1990 the East Asia Strategic Initiative (EASI) projected a phased withdrawal of these forces over a ten-year period. This decision was retracted in November the following year when concerns intensified over North Korea's nuclear intentions.[16] But tensions have still surfaced between South Korean and US policy officials due to efforts by Kim Dae-jung's government to cut the ROK's defence budget (a 4 per cent cut was proposed for 1998), the ROK's apprehensions over the possible decline of the US security role in Japan and continuing differences between Washington and Seoul over defence technology transfers.[17]

South Korean and American strategic analysts generally agree that North Korea still represents a significant threat to South Korean and East Asian security. A South Korea defence white paper published in December 2000 largely concurred with a US Defense Department report, released three months previously, that little evidence had surfaced of any reduction in North Korean power directed towards the South and that the DPRK's force capabilities reflected a 'dogged adherence' to a military-first policy, notwithstanding that country's severe economic and social problems.[18] The continuing deployment of the bulk of Pyongyang's ground forces within 80 kilometres of the DMZ, its persistence in conducting frequent military exercises in that vicinity, its refusal to modify its doctrine of military revolution and its failure to seriously reform those policies that have led to the wholesale destruction of its domestic economy and food production and distribution systems are all inherently destabilising factors that continue to affect security trends adversely both on the Peninsula and in the region more generally. In this environment US and South Korean deterrence strategy remains a key insurance factor in restraining any remaining North Korean ambitions to reunite the Peninsula by force.

At the same time, successful deterrence, combined with recent diplomatic events, is also raising the prospect that the issue of Korean unification will ultimately end in a so-called 'soft landing', that is, conditions will be created through diplomatic and economic engagement 'which will allow North Korea to stabilise and reform its economy, enhance its integration into the Northeast Asian community, and thereby lessen its presence as a security threat'.[19] Engagement has been embraced, in particular, by the US State Department, but it is anathematic to many in the West that consider the North Korean regime to be morally repugnant. The 'soft landing' strategy seeks to avoid either an 'explosion' of military conflict on the Peninsula or an 'implosion' of North Korea's internal stability brought about by food shortages, massive refugee flows and destructive infighting among elements of the North Korean government that could lead to crisis escalation in Korea and throughout Northeast Asia. There are several potential benefits of engagement strategy. These include giving North Korea a greater stake in the status quo, affording it every opportunity to cooperate prior to isolating it more effectively from other states if such opportunities are rejected and endeavouring to 'open up' the North Korean regime to greater internal policy debates that lead to more reasonable policy behaviour. American military experts, however, have tended to discount either scenario. As the commander of US forces in South Korea observed in April 1997, 'While North Korea's population is grievously suffering, due to its economic collapse, its military remains strong and capable. Let there be no mistake – this military force poses a real threat to the peace and stability here'.[20]

Despite the DPRK's continuing projection of a formidable military threat, South Korea's defence modernisation efforts have allowed it to increase its qualitative advantage over its North Korean counterpart. Those who argue that this advantage is what counts the most in assessing the Peninsula's military balance employ the concept of 'force multipliers'.

These are operational or environmental factors that increase combat advantages for one or both combatants. Weather, terrain, command and control, logistics and units' relative firepower accounting for higher enemy attrition rates are all force multipliers in various combat scenarios. South Korean military weaknesses, of course, are still evident. ROK forces have only a modest capability to defend themselves against a concentrated chemical weapons attack and they are short of multiple rocket launchers and artillery fire control systems. They are hardly able to defend themselves against the DPRK's ballistic missile threat, even with Patriot missile batteries the effectiveness of which is increasingly debatable.[21] TMD systems may be eventually deployed to neutralise North Korean *Scud, No-dong* and *Taepo-dong* ballistic missiles carrying WMD warheads; however credible TMD capabilities remain years away and billions of dollars short.[22]

Over the short term, the South Koreans will bolster their missile deterrence capability. In January 2001 the South Korean Foreign Ministry announced it would develop and deploy missiles with a range of 300 kilometres that could hit any North Korean target to strengthen South Korea's 'independent security'. This superseded a previous self-imposed limit on ROK missile ranges of 180 kilometres which had been supported by the United States as a means of preventing an accelerated proliferation of missile systems on the Peninsula.[23]

*Warfighting Scenarios*

Extensive analysis has been been published recently in unclassified Western sources assessing the probable outcome of any renewed Korean war. Several dominant conclusions have emerged from this literature.[24] Nearly all of these assessments discount the possibility that the KPA would be able to achieve strategic surprise during an initial attack. It follows that it is unlikely that the North could break through the linear defences along the DMZ and capture Seoul before the United States effectively reinforced the South's initial lines of defence. Indeed, some of the most optimistic estimates even project that a full-scale North Korean military invasion (as traditionally envisioned in 'unification-by-force scenarios') must be ruled out completely. Given the deteriorating economic circumstances in the DPRK, they conclude that the KPA would be incapable of sustaining a full-scale assault for more than a few days.[25]

Is such optimism warranted? A still definitive assessment by the Joint Intelligence Center at the United States Pacific Command (JICPAC) conducted in late 1993 surmised that while any North Korean attack on South Korea would be a 'very difficult operation', it was unprepared to predict an American–South Korean Combined Forces Council (CFC) victory under all circumstances.[26] Several other recent studies have also cautioned against predicting a positive outcome for the US–ROK defenders given the uncertainty surrounding a number of key issues.

None of these issues, singularly or collectively, may warrant challenging the fundamental premise that South Korea and the United States would ultimately prevail provided they had the political will to do so. However, what they do suggest is that it is prudent to avoid overconfidence against a North Korean opponent that has always valued strategic surprise and has maintained an *esprit de corps* within the DPRK's armed forces.

With the military balance shifting increasingly in favour of the South, it is unlikely that the North will ever realise its traditional aspirations to unify the Peninsula on its own terms unless there is some prospect that it will receive decisive outside military support. China's participation in the 'Four Power Talks' on reaching a permanent peace agreement and Korean unification that commenced in Geneva during late 1997, and its hosting of direct bilateral talks between the DPRK and ROK in Beijing which were held in April 1998, would appear to preclude, at least over the short-term, any such support from materialising. Russia is likewise attempting to strengthen its political influence on the Peninsula but more as a strategy to balance US power throughout Northeast Asia rather than as a direct investment in North Korea's survival and security. The ongoing inter-Korean dialogues may ultimately reduce the likelihood that the South must defend itself against a renewed North Korean assault. Great-power involvement in and miscalculations about such negotiations could yet complicate bilateral efforts by Seoul and Pyongyang to forge their own national destinies. Given this prospect, the Koreas' relations with key external parties need to be assessed.

## The Koreas' Great Power Politics

### *Alliance Diversification?*

Although Cold War structures of alignment and enmity are receding into history across the globe, the Korean Peninsula is often described as a 'last outpost' of that conflict. However, this is a misleading characterisation belying the growing complexity of both Koreas' security diplomacy. While South Korea has retained its alliance with the United States as the cornerstone of its strategic defence policy, the days when Seoul was no more than a strategic supplicant of Washington are long since past. South Korea's spectacular rise to economic prosperity during the 1980s allowed President Roh Tae-woo to implement his *Nordpolitik* initiatives towards the Soviet Union and China. These moves culminated in South Korea being able to achieve the normalisation of diplomatic relations with these two countries – North Korea's two primary Cold War allies – in the early 1990s.[27] Later in the decade, moreover, visible strains developed between the ROK and the United States over managing the North Korean nuclear question. Tensions also emerged over South Korea's determination to isolate its rice supply from the liberalisation of its agricultural market, the intensification of South Korean nationalism with a visible anti-American orientation among segments of the ROK's populace and Seoul's frustration with what it views as an increasingly unilateralist tendency in US alliance policies.[28] All of these developments prompted Seoul to explore ways of supplementing its security relationship with the United States by talking to other players in the region, although cautiously, so as not to jeopardise the primacy of the ROK–US relationship.

Lacking the ROK's economic resources, North Korea sought to play its 'nuclear card' in order to extract significant economic concessions from the United States and Japan, allowing Pyongyang to establish a grudging independent and comprehensive political relationship with Washington. In doing so, it sought to gain leverage and legitimacy at South Korea's expense and the chances of the DPRK's long-term survival have unquestionably been bolstered in the process. To balance its 'American initiative' Kim Jong-il's regime has also sought to maintain its traditional ties with China and, to a lesser extent, Russia (as will be discussed below). It has also continued to collaborate selectively with other states such as Pakistan and Iran on weapons development, underscoring its independence from Western-driven security regime politics.

The pursuit of 'independent security' diplomacy by both Koreas has made the management of Northeast Asian security politics a far more difficult task for the major powers, specifically China and the United States. Seoul and Pyongyang are both troubled by serious American policy inconsistencies (at least that is how they are perceived). For the DPRK, these relate to the 1994 Agreed Framework and, for South Korea, to the general direction of US regional security politics. Recent anti-US protests in South Korea, and a tendency for at least some South Koreans to be excessively optimistic about inter-Korean relations, could endanger the continuity of the US–ROK alliance. As one respected South Korean analyst has recently argued, 'in order for South Korea and the United States to maintain their alliance, both governments must attend to it urgently … the relationship is entering a time of complex and difficult challenges and requires enhanced nurturing and protection'.[29]

Furthermore, both Koreas are also currently labouring under immense economic burdens. North Korea's economic infrastructure is incapable of providing for the basic needs of its population. This pressure could lead to a violent implosion of the DPRK. In order to vent that pressure, it is still conceivable that a desperate DPRK might precipitate a major conflict on the Peninsula if current inter-Korean efforts to cement and sustain economic ties prove to be unsuccessful. Cruise ship tours to North Korea's Mt Kumgang, a rise in inter-Korean trade during 1999 and South Korean investment in North Korean manufacturing enterprises all proceed steadily. All of these trends, as well, withstood a June 1999 North–South Korean naval clash in the West Sea precipitated by North Korean fishing boats failing to observe the Northern Limit Line, the extension of the DMZ into adjacent Yellow Sea waters.[30]

Another possible approach to eventual integration would be, of course, for the South to use the North's economic weakness as a lever by which it might open the door to a peaceful assimilation of that state.[31] Unfortunately, Seoul has no overwhelming short-term motivation for taking on the costs of such a policy as its own economy has come under serious threat since the 1997–98 Asian financial crisis. With these conflicting forces at work it is not surprising to find that the atmospherics over the Peninsula remain charged. There seems every reason to suspect that security politics in the subregion will continue to ricochet between wide and often unanticipated extremes of diplomatic breakthroughs and renewed crises. By default, this effect cannot help but spiral outwards and impact on the fundamental strategic calculations of the great powers.

### A Broadening of South Korean Security Diplomacy

Roh Tae-woo's *Nordpolitik* initiative, resulting in the Soviet Union/Russia and China significantly modifying their previously strong politico-strategic ties with North Korea, set an important precedent for South Korean diplomacy. As intimated above, South Korea has shown a marked tendency in recent times to explore potential avenues for attaining diplomatic leverage beyond its security relationship with the United States. In this respect the ROK is increasingly positing itself as an independent regional 'middle power'. The ROK views this broadening of its security dialogue as a vital counter-move designed to check Pyongyang's strategy of seeking to distance Washington from Seoul by applying divide and rule tactics.

In terms of its importance to South Korea, no single bilateral relationship or set of bilateral ties can replace the American alliance as long as the Korean Peninsula remains divided. However, there is an increasing level of recognition in both Seoul and Washington that the ROK–US Cold War alliance, emphasising deterrence and solidarity, must be replaced by a more complex and fluid post-Cold War alliance.[32] In general, it is agreed that this new alliance would focus on maintaining an acceptable Northeast Asian and Asia-Pacific power balance until it can be superseded by appropriate and enduring multilateral security instruments. During this 'consolidation stage' South Korean and American vital strategic interests will continue to converge: ensuring South Korea's survival and deterring hegemonic aspirants in the region.

In January 1998 then President-elect Kim Dae-jung articulated a new national security policy. Kim issued three basic principles for dealing with the North: (1) the South has no intention of undermining or assimilating North Korea; (2) the South would actively pursue a policy of reconciliation and cooperation with the North; and (3) this posture of strategic reassurance would, nonetheless, be balanced by the South 'not tolerating' armed provocation. This so-called 'Sunshine Policy' of engagement was, of course, eventually rewarded by the June 2000 inter-Korean summit and by Kim Dae-jung's subsequent receipt of the Nobel Peace Prize. In keeping with this broad agenda for reconciliation, the 'Sunshine Policy' also moved to decouple private economic exchanges from national security considerations when it came to financial dealings involving the DPRK.[33]

### North Korea: Diversified Diplomacy as a 'Survival Strategy'

Pyongyang played its 'nuclear card' directly and successfully as a strategic bargaining chip relative to the United States, establishing a de facto bilateral relationship with that great power when it became evident that Russia and China were no longer tied to defending North Korea except under the most obvious circumstances of self-defence. Several bilateral agreements were signed that constituted the basic framework of this revised North Korean policy approach. This included the US–North Korea Agreed Framework (October 1994), the Berlin Agreement in September 1999 and the October 2000 US–DPRK Communiqué committing both countries to replace the 1953 Armistice Agreement with 'permanent peace arrangements'.

Under the terms of the Agreed Framework the DPRK was to refrain from developing or deploying its own nuclear weapons. In return, the West would provide the DPRK with light-water nuclear reactors and alternate energy sources like heavy fuel oil. In addition, the Americans pledged themselves to work towards the normalisation of diplomatic relations. The continuing viability of the KEDO that was established to implement the Agreement has come to be seen in North Korea as a critical measure of US commitment to this process.[34]

Since then policy makers in Pyongyang have closely scrutinised the US Congress to ascertain its willingness to underwrite the relatively modest expense of supplying the North with heavy fuels in preference to paying the mounting bill for maintaining the substantial US military investment in Northeast Asia (estimated to be at least $US3 billion annually).[35] Initial signs were hardly promising in this regard. Two highly critical reports on North Korea were released by the US House of Representatives International Relations Committee in early 1999. One report, prepared by the US General Accounting Office speculated that North Korea diverted some of the heavy fuel oil it imports from the United States for purposes not specified in the Agreed Framework. The other complained that North Korea's nuclear weapons and nuclear strike capabilities threatened the United States more at the turn of the century than was the case when the Agreed Framework was signed in 1994.[36] The extent to which an unsympathetic Congress will underwrite President George W. Bush's initial hard line against Pyongyang is one of the critical political issues shaping US–DPRK security relations. So too are continuing disagreements between the DPRK and the United States over missile issues. The October 2000 Communiqué resulted from a visit to Washington by North Korean Vice-Marshal Cho Myong-rok, the highest ranking DPRK official ever to visit the United States. After conferring with President Bill Clinton, US Secretary of State Madeleine Albright and other US officials, Cho agreed with his hosts that the North Korean moratorium on the testing of long-range ballistic missiles undertaken with the Berlin Agreement should stay in place and that the North–South dialogue process toward unification should be accelerated.[37] The momentum towards the full normalisation of relations between the DPRK and United States, however, appeared to be stymied by a lack of progress on committing North Korea to stop all long-range missile development. Indeed, American reticence to extend assurances about recognising North Korean sovereignty appeared to be directly linked to lack of North Korean transparency regarding the DPRK's missile program and its exports of missile technology. Continued differences on these issues foreclosed President Clinton visiting North Korea before his term of office expired, although Secretary of State Albright did travel to the DPRK in late October 2000 to meet North Korean leader Kim Jong-il.[38]

There are limits as to how far North Korea can pursue better ties with the United States to ensure its own survival. The DPRK cannot risk alienating China, its one remaining strategic ally and one that has no interest in sustaining an enduring American strategic presence and influence on the Peninsula.[39] The North Koreans are therefore engaged in a delicate balancing act. They are conditioning the United States to deal with them independently while they simultaneously try to maintain a level of tension in that relationship that will assuage Beijing's concerns that Chinese influence is declining.

The DPRK's relations with Moscow, its other traditional postwar ally, are undergoing a limited revival as part of Vladimir Putin's resuscitated 'East Asia Strategy'. This is designed to challenge US strategic interests in that region as part of a general Russian strategy to contest US global supremacy. Soviet/Russian–North Korean relations have previously become strained when the DPRK openly supported the unsuccessful coup attempt by communist hardliners against the established power structure in Moscow during August 1991. This alienated both the crippled Soviet Union and the ascendant Russian state in the process.[40] The fundamental Russian policy rationale for sustaining even limited ties with North Korea was subsequently driven more by reactive rather than pro-active reasoning. Moscow's concern was that it would be prevented from exercising strategic influence on the Peninsula and this far outweighed the immediate advantages that it hoped to accrue through its bilateral relationship with Kim Jong-il's regime.[41] Russia also resented its exclusion from the Four Power Talks and KEDO but afforded token support to the former, primarily out of its fear that Japan could quickly remilitarise and 'go nuclear' if the Agreed Framework broke down.

Soon after Vladimir Putin formally succeeded Boris Yeltsin as President of Russia in May 2000, he moved to solidify ties with Pyongyang that his predecessor had allowed to languish. Within two months, he had visited the North Korean capital and successfully linked Russian–North Korean ties to his campaign against the United States' proposed National Missile Defence (NMD) system. During his visit he assumed that North Korea would discontinue its own ballistic missile defence program if North Korea was allowed to use space launch vehicles (SLVs) of 'other nations' to launch one or two satellites per year.[42] By accepting such a formula, the United States would be tacitly conceding that the rationale for NMD would no longer exist in North Korea's case since that country's ballistic missile force would cease to exist.

The United States responded by asking for clarification: if the international community provided North Korea with SLVs, it would only enhance Pyongyang's development of its own missile systems. Putin's Foreign Minister, Ivan Ivanov, responded by insisting that any SLV carrying North Korean satellites would only be launched from other countries and entail peaceful space exploration. United States diplomats proceeded to explore seriously the Russian–North Korean initiatives and discussed it extensively with North Korean negotiators in bilateral talks conducted at Kuala Lumpur in November 2000.[43] The Russian leader's emboldened geopolitical style served notice that Russia would become a greater factor in the Peninsula's strategic evolution.

This trend was further reinforced by the Russian State Duma's expedited and decisive ratification of a new Treaty of Friendship, Neighborliness and Cooperation with North Korea in July 2000 after months of delay. Although extending a much more qualified commitment to North Korea's defence than the 1961 treaty between the Soviet Union and the DPRK that it replaced, the new agreement was characterised by Ivanov as

an instrument that would clearly reduce North Korea's international isolation and facilitate unification on the Peninsula by opening up opportunities for more systematic Russian cooperation with both Koreas.[44]

It is probable that North Korea will continue to apply the tactics of
diplomatic ambiguity to compensate for its strategic and economic vulnerabilities: oscillating between preferences for inter-Korean negotiations and multilateral discussions in order to minimise any prospect that
the region's great powers could reach a consensus on the 'Korean problem' that does not serve its own interests. It is unclear, however, whether
this politico-strategic balancing act will be able to overcome the latent
threat posed to the DPRK's long-term survival by its internal problems.

### Prospects for Multilateral Security on the Peninsula

The outcome of the realist-liberal debate as it applies to the Korean
Peninsula hinges on the propensity of both Seoul and Pyongyang to
modify their long-standing security dilemma and on support of the
major powers, especially China and the United States, in any solutions
which may be proposed. Any liberal-oriented outcome would be predicated on the fulfilment of two preconditions: (1) that bilateral and multilateral security instruments can be made to complement rather than
conflict with the few Northeast Asian mechanisms of strategic reassurance that are currently operating; and (2) that existing alliance relationships (that is, the US–ROK alliance and the PRC–DPRK alliance) are
revised so that they can serve as the 'building blocks' of a Northeast Asian
security regime. While remaining elusive in the Cold War's immediate
aftermath, these criteria are attainable if fundamental strategic miscalculations can be minimised or avoided.

*Promoting Strategic Reassurance*

Security instruments on the Korean Peninsula are existing arrangements
that are designed to prevent or deter conflict there. Existing instruments
relevant to Korea include the UN armistice which ended the combat
phase of the Korean War in July 1953, the United States–South Korea
Mutual Defense Treaty signed in September 1953, the Sino–North
Korean Treaty of Friendship, Cooperation and Mutual Assistance signed
in September 1961, the October 1994 American–North Korean Agreed
Framework, the September 1999 Berlin Agreement, and most recently,
Russia's Treaty of Friendship, Neighborliness and Cooperation with
North Korea. North Korea no longer recognises the legitimacy of the
1953 armistice. Multilateral instruments include the KEDO, created to
implement the Agreed Framework commitments to North Korea, and

multilateral dialogue groups like the ARF and Council for Security Co-operation in the Asia-Pacific (CSCAP) where China, both Koreas and the United States consider regional and international approaches for enhancing Korean stability.[45] The Berlin Agreement is a bilateral 'under-standing' reached between North Korean and US diplomats that North Korea would suspend its missile program in return for the United States lifting most of its economic and trade sanctions in place against the North since the Korean War. This agreement is fully supported by Japan and South Korea, thus giving it a multilateral dimension.[46]

Mechanisms of strategic reassurance are the specific steps taken by various parties that are designed to prevent misunderstandings or back-sliding with respect to prior commitments where those obligations were designed to reduce tensions. In the Korean Peninsula, these include the specific rules in effect for force deployment and military conduct in the DMZ (still observed by North Korean and CFC forces despite North Korea's renunciation of the armistice); the convening of negotiations at various levels concerning specific issue areas which if left unaddressed could intensify tensions (that is, inter-Korean and the Four Power Talks regarding Korean peace and unification and US–North Korean bilateral discussions on North Korean ballistic missile production and exports); and both North and South Korean adherence to specific international security regimes such as the nuclear non-proliferation treaty.

The liberal approach to advancing strategic reassurance and collabo-ration involves encouraging the further establishment of multilateral arrangements directly relevant to Northeast Asia. However, bilateral security treaties have been the cornerstone of great power strategy in the Peninsula and remain so notwithstanding Chinese and American partic-ipation in the ARF and their willingness to at least engage in the informal Northeast Asian Cooperation Dialogue (NEACD).[47] Even the Agreed Framework, arguably the most successful product of multilateral negoti-ations on a Northeast Asian security problem to date, is still shadowed by 'the vague threat that [its] non-implementation ... will return both sides to a confrontational path ... [and that] the mechanisms necessary to pre-vent misunderstanding have not been clearly defined thus far'.[48] The degree to which these mechanisms can be transformed to instruments which clearly reinforce strategic reassurance is a key measure of how effective strategies of cooperation and engagement will be in resolving the Korean problem.

To some extent both liberals and the isolationist factions of the Amer-ican realist camp posit the same general argument about alliance rele-vance: that the old Cold War alliances maintained by the great powers with the two Koreas can no longer be justified as credible instruments of extended deterrence. Liberals argue that the US–Korea alliance will remain viable only if it becomes a component of overall US global strategy as it should operate in a post-Cold War environment. The neo-isolationists argue that North Korea does not constitute a direct threat to American vital interests because there is no longer any contending hegemon (with the Soviet Union's demise) challenging American global predominance and that South Korea is more than capable of assuming responsibility for its own defence.[49] More 'orthodox' realists reject this isolationist position, however, by insisting that global pre-eminence can only be maintained by creating local power balances that preclude the emergence of regional hegemons that may, in turn, force inter-regional alliances capable of challenging American global dominance.[50]

### Creating Building Blocks through 'Expansive Bilateralism'

What specific steps or mechanisms do liberals envisage as appropriate to affect a transition of Korea from a residual Cold War flashpoint to an integral component of a Northeast Asian security regime? Two types of mechanisms are most prominent in their arguments: (1) revised bilateral security relationships that can serve as intermediate catalysts for strengthening multilateral security architectures; and (2) enhanced arms control measures negotiated within existing frameworks of conflict reduction.

In the Korean case, the ROK has found it advantageous to ensure that its regional security interests are not projected *exclusively* through the US–ROK bilateral alliance, even though that relationship remains the key component of its overall security posture. For example, in July 1994 at the inaugural meeting in Bangkok, South Korean Foreign Minister Han Sung-Joo proposed the creation of a Northeast Asian Security Dialogue or NEASED (not to be confused with the aforementioned informal or 'Track Two' Northeast Asian Cooperation Dialogue or NEACD). Offshoots of the NEASED have been proposed by various Korean strategic analysts.[51] Moreover, North Korea has gradually accepted the inevitability that US–South Korean and US–Japanese alliance consultations about the Agreed Framework facilitate the ability of all three states to meet their respective commitments to KEDO, even at the cost of that organisation managing 'a scope of activities [that] will increasingly impact on what the North Korean regime has seen as sovereignty and security concerns'.[52] It allows this to occur because it knows that China is the only other real source of food and fuel assistance that the DPRK can rely upon. Too much dependence on Beijing would violate the *juche* or 'self-reliance' ethos so carefully nurtured by Kim Il-sung and his current successors.

It is clear that a more comprehensive and systematic arms control agenda needs to be pursued if the Peninsula's security dilemma is to be modified significantly. To help achieve this end the Basic Agreement on

Reconciliation, Nonaggression and Exchanges and Cooperation (signed by both the ROK and DPRK in December 1991 in the twilight of the Cold War) could be activated and serve as the basis for implementing credible arms control negotiations on the Peninsula. This treaty was negotiated during one of the few lulls in North–South hostility, the temporary 'thaw' having been created by the Bush Administration's decision in 1991 to remove American tactical nuclear weapons from the Peninsula. It has been allowed to stagnate, however, because the North Korean nuclear threat intensified and the two sides failed to reach an understanding on the governance of a Joint Military Commission.[53] A great deal of the minimum requirements demanded by the two Koreas for establishing strategic reassurance between them are encapsulated in its stipulations. The most critical requirements include:

- The formal recognition by each Korea of the other's sovereign legitimacy as a critical intermediate step to confidence-building and ultimate unification;
- A resumption of the High Level Talks that originally produced the Basic Agreement (but which have been discontinued since September 1992);
- Linking inter-Korean dialogue more closely to the Four Power Talks by reaffirming the adherence of the Geneva discussions to chapter 1 of the Basic Agreement that calls for the 'transformation of the state of armistice into a state of peace'. This would require the United States to allow at least hypothetical discussions to occur regarding the status of US forces in South Korea;
- Military confidence-building measures designed to limit prospects for surprise attack, to achieve crisis prevention/crisis management and to limit and reduce specific types of weapons systems need to be considered extensively. This includes restricting the types of weapons systems deployed in certain areas of the DMZ ('limited deployment zones' or LDZs); notification of military manoeuvres coupled to a gradual reduction in their scope and frequency; the establishment of hot lines and crisis management centres and various inspection/verification measures.[54]

It is noteworthy that most of these measures could be implemented bilaterally, independent of the US–ROK and DPRK–Russian or PRC–Russian bilateral alliances. But ultimately their development would be dependent, on strengthening the building blocks inherent to multilateral participation. North Korean officials' involvement in arms control-related discussions with their American counterparts pertaining to nuclear weapons and delivery systems can serve as a useful foundation for subsequent inter-Korean as well as regional and international arms control talks. The US–DPRK ballistic missile talks have, in particular, allowed North Korean negotiators to gain experience and to broaden their frame of reference while providing US officials invaluable insights on negotiating with a formidable adversary.

North Korea's interaction with the International Atomic Energy Agency (IAEA) leading up to the October 1994 Agreed Framework is another useful precedent, liberals would argue, for conditioning that state to the benefits of cooperative security. Indeed, IAEA inspections of DPRK nuclear facilities during the 1994 nuclear crisis were politically 'more palatable' to the North Koreans than the next best alternative which was to allow its 'rival sovereign', South Korea, or its US ally monitoring access. The norm of nonproliferation as it had been developed within the context of international regime politics (at the UN and IAEA) is powerful testimony according to liberal analysts for the utility of epistemic community involvement in situations of crisis defusion.[55] Various Track Two mechanisms could be used to integrate North Korea more fully into the regional and international arms control communities. These mechanisms would include workshops, dialogues and related information networks conducted outside official channels but involving both government officials acting in an informal capacity and independent experts from academic and policy research institutions.

*Pursuing Multilateral Security Dialogues*

Multilateral security dialogues are confidence-building mechanisms but, by themselves, they cannot resolve differences as enduring and intense as the dispute between North and South Korea. They can, however, facilitate and support the type of inter-Korean dialogue that may eventually lead to conflict resolution on the Peninsula and possibly even peaceful national unification.[56] Gaining full North Korean participation in such dialogues is the key to achieving these outcomes and to ensuring that they mature as alternatives to the alliance and deterrence mechanisms of the Cold War. This will only be possible if Pyongyang becomes truly convinced that power balancing strategies are giving way to cooperative security as the dominant means of organising international security in Northeast Asia. Otherwise, the North will continue its traditional strategy of manoeuvring among the region's great powers and making its substantive participation in multilateral security dialogues conditional on its ability to extract relative gains at the expense of South Korea.

North Korea's current insistence that it will only join the six-state Northeast Asian Security Dialogue after the United States and Japan normalise relations with it is illustrative. Well aware of North Korea's effort to shift its traditional *juche* strategy from a Sino–Soviet focus to dividing the United States and South Korea, Han Sung-Joo advanced the NEASED concept in order to frustrate this move. The NEASED would link the ARF more closely to core security problems on the Peninsula and in Northeast Asia by enlisting direct great power support for systematic subregional dialogue on threat reduction. The ARF's orientation towards cooperative security means that it could be employed as a potential counterweight to North Korean 'zero-sum' diplomacy aimed at isolating the South. For this reason, the DPRK resisted affiliation with any NEASED (often labelling the idea an American or Japanese plot to exercise hegemony over Northeast Asia) and in the NEACD, its 'Track Two' counterpart, which has involved informal and private discussions between government officials and security policy experts from China, Japan, Russia, South Korea and the United States since October 1993.[57] But Pyongyang joined the ARF in July 2000 as a means to expand its diplomatic linkages with developing nations in the region and as a symbolic acknowledgment of its sovereign legitimacy in the eyes of its neighbours, even in the absence of *de jure* recognition from the United States and Japan.[58]

North Korea's outlook toward multilateralism is thus gradually softening as it seeks alternative outlets for recognition, legitimacy and assistance in order to apply its hedging strategy (an updated version of *juche)* against the United States predominantly, and both Russia and China more subtly. This approach is congruent with a greater North Korean willingness to engage the South in *formal* diplomatic settings, thereby at least tacitly acknowledging a need to bargain with the ROK even if it still denies that state's right to exercise independent autonomy. Like China, North Korea is endeavouring to play a realist game in institutionalist settings.[59] Unlike the Chinese, however, the North Koreans confront the region's increasingly sophisticated multilateral instrumentalities from a position of crippling economic weaknesses and with a largely unproven diplomatic *modus operandi* beyond their proven acumen of extracting concessions from Washington in an atmosphere of nuclear brinkmanship. Until recently, the ARF refrained from taking a more direct interest in the Peninsula's intermittent crises because there was little real prospect that the North Koreans, the Americans or Chinese would allow multilateralism to supplement, much less supplant, the realist-oriented politics of alliance formation and coalition-building in that part of the world. In July 2000, however, the ARF provided the venue for substantive bilateral US–North Korean discussions on the issue of North Korean ballistic missiles between Secretary of State Albright and her DPRK counterpart, Paek Nam-sum. In this context, a formula of 'security pluralism' – the supplementation of bilateral security interaction with multilateral frameworks that can facilitate and coexist with bilateral negotiations –

was tested and found to be a highly appropriate policy approach for pursuing regional security.[60]

*Ad hoc* multilateralism has now become ensconced in Korea at sufficient levels and in enough issue-areas to infuse liberals with a greater hope that their approach may prevail in determining the nature of the emerging Northeast Asian security environment. Bilateral confidence-building measures negotiated between the Koreas during the early 1990s were problematic because they tended to underscore North Korean vulnerabilities and post-Cold War isolation in direct juxtaposition to South Korean economic strength and its continued support from the United States. Incentives for Pyongyang to strengthen these arrangements therefore remained weak. By contrast, *ad hoc* multilateral measures such as food assistance and KEDO required the great powers to demonstrate their stake in a stable Peninsula and, by extension, acknowledge the current North Korean regime's legitimacy as a negotiating agent. They signalled a gradual acceptance in the broader international community that Kim Jong-il's government must be engaged to secure against an outbreak of North Korean aggression and to manage any wholesale political changes that may occur in the North, whether they be the result of a 'soft landing', 'implosion' or 'explosion'.[61]

## Taiwan

Taiwan may be considered by Chinese leaders as a mere 'renegade province' but its economic prosperity, ongoing political dynamism and 'pragmatic diplomacy' all work to confer it with the status of a significant regional middle power. This fact was underscored by the Asian financial crisis, with Taiwan considered to be one of the Asian economies most equipped to withstand its reverberations based on its current account surplus, abundant foreign currency reserves, small foreign debt, mostly reputable business practices and still growing economy.[62] By the mid-1990s Taiwan had taken its place among the world's twenty largest trading nations, ranking as the third largest capital exporter and one of Asia's biggest investors. Although cross-strait tensions in early 1996 precipitated a sharp drop in trade with China, overall economic interaction with the PRC has grown so rapidly that the Taiwanese and Chinese economies are now inextricably interdependent.[63]

In many ways, Taiwan's economic modernisation and political development have made it a 'role model' for newly industrialised economies. Yet its ability to sustain this success will very much depend upon its ability to project a sufficient level of military power and to preserve its security relations with the United States.[64] Chinese President Jiang Zemin delivered a lunar new year's eve speech in late January 1995 that included a comprehensive eight-point proposal designed to ensure the PRC's 'respect for Taiwanese compatriots' way of life and desires to remain masters of their own affairs'.[65] A little more than a year later, however, Chinese military exercises which included short-range missile tests proximate to Taiwan's two largest harbours, Keelung and Kaoshiung, were carried out as Taiwan was holding its first free presidential election in March 1996.[66] Mainland China continues to adhere to what it views is its right to assimilate Taiwan by force if other approaches fail. 'Plans of action' have reportedly been drawn up by various PLA military strategists that include various scenarios for 'liberating' Taiwan. These may be at least partially regarded, however, as posturing by the PLA to solidify the positions of commanders and strategists within a highly nationalistic Chinese regime prone to use the Taiwan crisis as a means to solidify its own legitimacy.[67]

To forestall Chinese military action, Taiwan has pursued a multidimensional strategy, incorporating revisions of its military doctrine to maximise the costs of any such Chinese invasion, a foreign policy of 'pragmatic diplomacy' to build bilateral and multilateral networks of support for its survival, and a concerted posture of multilateralism to accrue regional and international political status commensurate with its economic strength. Each of these initiatives will be assessed below in the context of arguing that Taiwanese policy makers are pursuing a complex strategy that incorporates both a realist and liberal dimension. Taiwan pursues realist strategy by adhering to a posture of 'self-help' when it comes to military modernisation. It is compelled to do so by constraints imposed on its military relationship with the United States resulting from the strategic imperatives underwriting overall Sino–American relations. Simultaneously the Taiwanese are following liberal prescriptions of cooperative security through their efforts to rejoin the United Nations and to become more integrated with the international community through various institutional affiliations. This sets Taiwan's policy apart from that of China because the latter is a far more discriminating participant in security forums and regimes and traditionally wary of the tendency of these to compromise its own irredentist and strategic agendas.[68]

*Evolution of the Taiwanese Security Environment and Military Capabilities*

Like South Korea, Taiwan's postwar national security posture has been dominated by a single and pervasive threat perception: deterring a military attack by mainland China. Beijing refuses to recognise Taiwan as the Republic of China (ROC) but merely views it as a breakaway province. From mid-1950 to 1979 Taiwan fell under the umbrella of US extended deterrence strategy and the possibility of a Chinese invasion could be largely discounted. In April 1979 this changed when the US Congress passed the Taiwan Relations Act (TRA) in keeping with its decision to normalise relations with the PRC. Under this legislation, Washington moved to a position of sustaining US–Taiwan security relations on a 'case-by-case' basis in preference to offering blanket security. This American stance has since been characterised as a posture of 'strategic ambiguity'.[69] President George W. Bush briefly and inadvertently sharpened this US posture in late April 2001 when he asserted in a television interview that the United States would do 'whatever it takes' to defend Taiwan in response to the PRC initiating measures to assimilate that island by force. Subsequent statements were offered by the new President over the ensuing days, however, to restore Washington's traditional balancing of its one-China posture with its defence commitment to Taiwan.[70]

Since the normalisation of Sino–American relations in 1979, but particularly since the end of the Cold War, Taiwan has conducted a substantial military modernisation program. Initially, this was designed to counter inherent Chinese quantitative military superiority but in recent times it has also had to try to offset qualitative improvements being made by the PLA.[71] It has gradually reoriented its military strategy from an offensive posture, in effect throughout the 1950s and much of the 1960s, towards a predominantly defensive posture. This reorientation has reflected a fundamental change in Taiwan's aspirations. It has shifted from seeking to overthrow the communists on the mainland via a resumption of the Chinese civil war to the limited goal of ensuring Taiwan's survival as a self-declared sovereign polity. Taipei's leaders have been constrained from carrying out this strategy by Chinese attempts to prevent the sale of *any* defensive weapons systems to Taiwan by successive American governments and other Western powers. The PRC argues that such sales violate the 'one-China policy' and that the United States and other Western arms suppliers that have recognised the PRC should gradually reduce and, ultimately, eliminate any such sales in keeping with that policy.

Realists argue that this stance reflects Beijing's determination to apply an uncompromising relative gains strategy against Taiwan, pursuing an irredentist agenda that can only be checked by power equal or greater than its own. During the 1996 Taiwan Strait crisis, they argued that Chinese military exercises and missile tests 'turned interdependence arguments on their head'.[72] They further assert that growing Sino–Taiwanese interdependence is not synonymous with greater Chinese leverage over Taiwan's own economic development. Taiwanese investors tend to establish labour-intensive industries on the mainland rather than more competitive knowledge-intensive enterprises. Any Chinese strategy to restrict Taiwanese access to the Chinese market via sanctions during a future crisis would thus affect the PRC more negatively than Taiwan because the latter has the greater ability to diversify its interests and finances in an era of globalisation.[73] Given these circumstances, the United States should seek opportunities to perpetuate Taiwan's 'economic miracle' and democratic political system to counter Chinese power in East Asia. The Taiwan Security Enhancement Act (TSEA) proposed by various members of the US Congress is a stronger version of the American commitment to Taiwan's defence than is the 1979 TRA and is one proposed means to do this.[74] Approved by the US House of Representatives in February 2000, but postponed for deliberation by the US Senate, George W. Bush declared his support for the TSEA during the 2000 US Presidential Campaign.

Liberals counter that China cannot afford to fan regional fears of a 'China threat' by over-reacting on Taiwan at a time when its own economic development is at an historical crossroads and Taiwan's prosperity can make a critical difference to the PRC realising its own economic ambitions. Only a subsequent and concentrated diplomatic effort by both the American and Chinese sides to strengthen their dialogue on the Taiwan issue led to defusion of the issue, culminating in the 1997 and 1998 Jiang–Clinton summits and President Clinton's reiteration in Shanghai (30 June 1998) that the United States did not support Taiwan's independence, did not have a two-China policy and did not support Taiwan's independence in international organisations (the 'three nos' speech).[75] Liberals insist, however, that the only way to overcome the residual 'awkward dilemma' of the United States supporting a one-China policy while simultaneously remaining committed to defend Taiwan, is to convince China to pledge it will not attack Taiwan while compelling Taiwan to forgo any option of declaring its independence from China.[76] They also have proposed a trilateral dialogue between China, Taiwan and the United States to develop confidence-building measures. The Clinton Administration rejected this approach, insisting that China and Taiwan needed to reach a political solution on what was an 'internal Chinese problem'.[77] Liberals contend these factors rendered China's use of coercive diplomacy against Taiwan and the United States during the Taiwan Strait confrontation a risk-laden Chinese strategy of coercive diplomacy. It worked in jarring the United States to resume a strong 'one-China policy'. However, it also intensified the Sino–American security dilemma in the East China Sea rather than contributing to overall regional stability. The realist-liberal debate over Taiwan may be resolved only when unification is achieved either by mainland China eventually assimilating Taiwan by force, Taiwan voluntarily integrating with a more democratic China, or Taiwan achieving its independence without Chinese dissent. That the first prospect appears increasingly likely at this stage in history requires an assessment of how Taiwan's military strategy and capabilities as an Asia-Pacific middle power relate to those projected by its Chinese opponent.

## The Current Military Balance

Prior to the 1996 Taiwan Strait crisis, public opinion in Taiwan over China's readiness to invade that island was often divided between those who argued that such an act was likely if Taiwan either declared its independence or fragmented into irreconcilable pro-China and anti-China divisions and those who discounted both China's political will and military ability to conduct any such invasion.[78] The cross-Strait crisis galvanised the Taiwanese electorate to demand the clarification and strengthening of Taiwan's national security strategy in ways that reinforced the island's defence and deterrence capabilities. The most critical elements in a credible Taiwanese deterrence posture include: achieving a judicious combination of 'warfighting' (offensive-oriented) and defence/deterrence postures against PLA forces; retaining air superiority over the PLA air force by achieving high kill ratios; engaging PLA navy units with long-range anti-ship missiles (that is, the *Harpoon*) and lethal short-range fire-control systems; quelling any Chinese effort to complete an amphibious crossing of the Taiwan Strait; maintaining a high state of combat readiness; and ensuring the continuation of a credible American extended deterrence commitment to intervene on Taiwan's behalf in the event that China does resort to force.[79] If these components are met by Taiwanese armed forces, the odds of Taiwan incurring an outright invasion by the Chinese mainland will be low. This will be true notwithstanding the bellicose rhetoric employed by PLA commanders and the 'worst case analysis' applied by intermittent US Defense Department estimates as a means to prod successive American presidents into sustaining an arms sales relationship with Taipei. Other conflict scenarios apart from a full-scale PLA invasion must be considered. Those most commonly cited are a ballistic missile attack against key Taiwanese ports, airfields or selected civilian population centres or a naval blockade designed to strangle Taiwan's economy. Other possibilities which work to undermine the strategic value of the 'sub-invasion' options for coercing Taipei into submission include: the threat of disproportionate retaliation by Taiwanese and US strike forces; the questionable accuracy of Chinese ballistic missiles deployed near Taiwan; and evolving developments in military technology that make it more difficult over time to render China's ships, helicopters and transport aircraft capable of following-up its missile salvos or naval pre-emption against Taiwan with an amphibious-airborne assault.[80]

If Taiwan adheres to these general strategic guidelines most conducive to realising an effective deterrence posture against China, specific requirements must be fulfilled to implement them. These include the development and deployment of state-of-the-art defensive weapons systems such as precision guided air-to-air and air-to-ground missile systems, more modern surveillance aircraft (P-3 *Orions*), and diesel electric submarines; maintaining appropriately high levels of defence spending to maintain them; and strengthening Taiwan's early warning capabilities through procurement of advanced radar and airborne surveillance.[81] Taiwan's military modernisation program accelerated noticeably after 1990. This effort has been complicated by the PRC's own defence modernisation efforts in recent years which have threatened to overcome Taiwan's traditional qualitative advantages in combat aircraft, intra-Strait sea control (via shipborne air defence, mine and amphibious warfare), and ground/air fire support (that is, ground force mobility and surface-to-surface missiles).[82] To deal with this situation Taiwan has had to rely increasingly on acquiring sophisticated foreign military equipment, a sales process substantially inhibited by China's threats to downgrade ties with any state that transfers military systems to the Taiwanese. President George W. Bush's April 2001 decision to sell a comprehensive package of destroyers, diesel submarines, surveillance aircraft and other military items at least partly reversed this trend of China exercising such a de facto veto.

Extensive literature exists covering Taiwan's prospects for successfully defending itself against China in a future contingency. Most independent Western and a number of Taiwanese analysts believe that 'China's relative power with respect to Taiwan is [still] insufficient to ensure battlefield success but is sufficient to threaten Taiwan with the possibility of battlefield defeat'.[83] In other words, the 'fog of war' or combat ambiguity of so much concern to classical strategists is very much in evidence when different Taiwan Strait scenarios are reviewed: factors of timing, politico-strategic will and allied intervention are all integral to calculating their outcome and they are all subject to a high degree of uncertainty. With this caveat offered, it can be reasonably surmised that China's ability to harass Taiwan proper in ways reminiscent of its incessant shelling of the offshore islands during the Cold War has increased due to improvements in its naval and short-range ballistic missile systems. This may eventually force Taiwan to implore Washington to sell it more advanced weapons systems or to allow Taiwan to collaborate with the United States in developing TMD technologies.[84] There has been much speculation about the sale of *Aegis* but as one analyst has argued, Taiwan does not need *Aegis* destroyers since the expense of the system outweighs the benefits of its limited coverage. It remains highly uncertain that China will be in a position to exercise control over the air or the sea to the extent needed if it wanted to be assured of certain victory in launching a fully-fledged invasion against Taiwan before 2010. This is because

China lacks a number of important capabilities including integrated command and control systems, carrier forces and precision-guided munitions capabilities. China's current advantage in submarine capabilities is applicable to enforcing at least a partially successful blockade in the absence of US intervention on Taiwan's behalf.[85]

### Great-Power Politics – The US Intervention Factor

The above conclusions underscore the important role that the United States will play in any future military confrontation over the Taiwan Strait, even if that role is unsolicited. As one American intelligence analyst has observed: 'the Chinese clearly understand that Taiwan is the place where the seismic plates of Chinese and US national interests collide'.[86] Accordingly, as the respected China analyst Chas Freeman has noted, 'China is working to build the capacity not only to take Taiwan but to sink American aircraft carrier battle groups … As Chinese power grows … the United States can either prepare for war with China over Taiwan or it can promote political accommodation'.[87]

At first glance, these comments may appear to be overly dramatic; however, Sino–American behaviour in the Taiwan Strait since the 1990s validates them. In December 1995 the US aircraft carrier *Nimitz* and its escort battle group traversed the Strait in a clear demonstration that the United States was unwilling to tolerate any further escalation in military provocation by China. At the time the Chinese were 'protesting' against Lee Teng-hui's visit to Cornell University the previous June and American diplomatic efforts to soothe Chinese ire had been rather unsuccessful. In response to the incursion by the *Nimitz* battle group, the Chinese reportedly warned the Americans that if American warships traversed the Strait again they would be contested by the PLA.[88]

The US deterrence posture intensified during the 1996 cross-Strait crisis and reports have since surfaced that American security officials were drawing up war scenarios in the weeks leading up to breakthrough talks in Virginia between US National Security Adviser Anthony Lake and his Chinese counterpart Liu Huaqin. Liu was forced to deny remarks attributed to the PLA's Deputy Chief of General Staff Xiong Guangkai that China was prepared to conduct a nuclear strike against Los Angeles if the United States intervened against a Chinese invasion of Taiwan. In response, US Secretary of Defense William Perry and US Secretary of State Warren Christopher reportedly warned him that China would face 'grave consequences' if such an invasion occurred. These comments were prompted, in part, by reports that China's military exercise off Taiwan's coast was the most aggressive in years. One M-9 ballistic missile tested by the Chinese had apparently flown directly over Taipei before splashing down in the Strait.[89] Further provocative statements were issued by both sides just prior to President Clinton's trip to China in June–July 1998. While Chinese President Jiang Zemin convened a three-day meeting with his top advisers to derive strategies for 'speeding up reunification of the motherland', the US House of Representatives voted 411-0 on Congressional Resolution 270 urging China to renounce its option to use force against Taiwan.[90]

Despite Clinton's affirmation during his mid-1998 China visit of the so-called 'three nos' policy, these trends indicate that the disturbing gap between Chinese and American perspectives regarding Taiwan is unlikely to close in the near future. These same trends strengthen realist arguments that insist a Sino–American security dilemma over Taiwan remains intact. Fundamentally, the Americans regard Taiwan as a separate de facto state, an important regional 'middle power', a major trading partner of the United States and an Asian showcase for Western democracy in Asia. China, on the other hand, may be prepared to tolerate Taiwan's separate political system in the short term in order to reap immediate economic benefits but it is unlikely that it will ever compromise on the principle that Taiwan is a part of China. Unless the United States substantially adjusts its own posture to accommodate Beijing, an explosion in the Taiwan Strait cannot be discounted.[91]

This last point is illustrated in particular by Chinese sensitivity to various US studies speculating about Taiwan's inclusion in any future US TMD system. In a wide-ranging interview conducted during early March 1999, Xu Shiqian, Director of the PRC's Chinese Academy of Social Science's Taiwan Institute, expressed doubts that the United States would actually transfer TMD-related technology directly to the Taiwanese. But including Taiwan in any American 'TMD blanket', Xu warned, would constitute 'serious interference in China's internal affairs'. He concluded that the United States would be well advised to weigh the ramifications of any such move 'conscientiously and solemnly', instead of letting China–US relations deteriorate over the TMD issue.[92] The Pentagon study on Asia-Pacific TMDs concluded that Taiwan could be defended against Chinese ballistic missile attacks through 'upper-tier exo' land-based or sea-based (that is, Navy Theatre Wide-like tracking radar and missile interceptor TMD) systems.[93] It made no mention, however, of how the PLA could circumvent TMD through launching salvos of cruise missiles or through other offensive strategies that would render TMD much less relevant in a future Strait contingency.

If it proves impossible to resolve the Taiwan question through diplomacy, some form of US military action may become inevitable. However, the PRC's ability to sustain constant military pressure on Taiwan may have the effect of tempering, if not completely neutralising, US public support. While the United States' regional interests are at stake in the outcome of the Taiwan dispute, vital American national security interests are not. Unless the PRC is prepared to do the very unlikely – escalate a conflict to the point of threatening a nuclear exchange – there is no prospect of the US homeland coming under threat from the PRC. The geopolitical imperative of accommodating 1.3 billion mainland Chinese into a post-Cold War international security framework remains paramount in American calculations. Barring future miscalculations in either Chinese or Taiwanese policy behaviour which precipitate a conflict in the Strait which no party really wants, the probability of US military intervention in this part of the world should remain relatively low *vis-à-vis* China and Taiwan, hopefully, reaching an eventual political settlement on their differences. Alternatively, China might force Taiwan into the PRC based on an eventual Taiwanese recognition that effective US support will not be available in the event of such conflict. The latter prospect appeared unlikely as George W. Bush, having assumed the American presidency in January 2001, went on record as supporting the United States defending Taiwan if China were to attempt to assimilate that island by force, a position, as noted above, that was reiterated most explicitly three months later.[94]

## Taiwan's Strategic Diversification

### Pragmatic Diplomacy

The election of Chen Shui-bien as President of Taiwan in March 2000 was initially viewed by many regional policy makers and independent analysts as a destabilising watershed in Sino–Taiwanese relations. Chen was the first opposition politician elected to lead Taiwan since the Guomindang fled the mainland in 1949. His Democratic People's Party (DPP) was historically on record as favouring Taiwanese independence from China, although this posture has been recently modified to avoid alienating Taiwan's 'mainstream' voters who favour a gradual and tacit evolution of that island's political identity relative to the unification question. Since he was voted into power, Chen has extended a concessionary line to Beijing on that issue: there will be no statement of independence, no referendum on Taiwan's preferred political status; no pursuit of his predecessor's (President Lee Teng-hui) 'special state-to-state relations' vision; and no abrogation of the National Unification Council which conducts intermittent negotiations between Chinese mainland officials and their Taiwanese counterparts on Sino–Taiwanese relations.[95]

Chen's moderate approach was unexpected by the PRC and led Beijing to respond inconsistently to his performance, sometimes with restraint in the hope of extracting further concessions from the new Taiwanese leader but at other times with condemnation that Chen is unable to swing other DPP factions more towards his own position. Chen also opted to pursue a temperate international diplomatic posture by shifting away from buying support from other countries with economic assistance and instead preserving and consolidating what friends and ties Taiwan retains in the international community. A brief review of how Taiwanese diplomacy has recently evolved should illuminate the significance of this shift.

Throughout the 1990s Taiwan projected its 'pragmatic diplomacy' to overcome Chinese efforts to isolate it from the international community. Pragmatic diplomacy was designed to translate Taiwan's economic assets into international acceptance of its existence and perpetuation as a legitimate political entity separate to the PRC. It was not a strategy for gaining Taiwan's independence but for establishing Taiwan's 'equal footing' with the PRC before substantial negotiations to unify the two sides into one China are undertaken. The policy was initiated soon after then Vice-President Lee Teng-hui was sworn into office as acting president in January 1988 following Chiang Ching-kuo's death. The new president called for an effort to sustain existing formal diplomatic relations with those states still recognising the Republic of China, to develop more substantive relations with those countries not maintaining formal diplomatic ties with Taiwan and, most substantively, to push for Taiwan's admission (or readmission) into international organisations.[96]

Pragmatic diplomacy initially enjoyed visible success in strengthening Taiwan's influence in international financial circles. As discussed below, however, it failed to make significant inroads towards improving Taiwan's official international diplomatic status. Most fundamentally, the strategy reinforced Taiwan's ability to exist as a de facto, independently functioning force within the post-Cold War international system. It therefore successfully undermined the image that the PRC has cultivated so assiduously over the years of Taiwan as a 'pariah state'. This is extraordinary for a political entity whose *de jure* national sovereignty is questioned or officially denied by most of its trading partners. It also reflected a conscious strategy by Taiwan's political leadership to neutralise the more radical sentiments expressed by secessionists on that island that are aimed at exploiting the frustrations of many Taiwanese who would otherwise call for Taipei to declare its complete independence from China.

The creation of unofficial bodies to initiate cross-Strait communications in 1991 and the inauguration of informal cross-Strait talks in Singapore in 1993 could be regarded as the most significant achievement of pragmatic diplomacy. The founding of the Straits Exchange Foundation in Taipei and the Association for Relations Across the Taiwan Strait in Beijing did not signify any narrowing of differences between Taiwan and the PRC over the reunification issue. However, it did underscore China's increased concern that the unification issue could become superseded by the evolution and intensification of perceptions within the international community associated with an 'independent Taiwan'. This apprehension had already been reinforced by the ascension of a Taiwanese-born president and by the Guomindang's gradual acknowledgment that contemporary Taiwanese society has few direct links to the ROC's mainland legacy.[97] Cross-Strait talks were frequently interrupted by intermittent strains and deteriorations in Sino–Taiwanese relations. But they served a useful function for Taiwan by allowing its leadership to argue to its Chinese counterpart that an effort is being made to preserve the ethos of unification in the face of rising separatist pressure within Taiwan's own electorate.

Momentum in expanding cross-Strait ties was undermined in July 1999, however, following an interview conducted by Taiwan's then President, Lee Teng-hui, with the German broadcasting network, *Deutsche Welle*. Lee insisted that 'the legitimacy of the rule of the country [of Taiwan] comes from the mandate of the Taiwanese people and has nothing to do with the mainland' and that constitutional amendments in Taiwan 'have placed cross-Strait relations as a state-to-state relationship or at least a special state-to-state relationship'.[98] Lee's postulate severely tested China's 'one country, two systems' approach towards Taiwan and incensed Chinese leaders who perceived it as commensurate to a virtual Taiwanese declaration of independence. China accelerated its deployment of missile sites opposite Taiwan and intimated that it would 'not rule out' applying force against the island if it concluded that a peaceful resolution of the China–Taiwan dispute on its own terms would not be forthcoming. The crisis peaked in early August when the Clinton Administration warned of 'grave consequences' if China took military action against Taiwan in response to informal probes by Chinese officials visiting Washington on US intentions if China attacked the island.[99]

By mid-September it was clear that China would not opt for military action against Taiwan. Two major factors worked to restrain Beijing. Favourable relations with the United States needed to be preserved at a time when the Chinese Government was desperate to enter the WTO. Moreover, uncertainty continued to prevail among PLA planners over how successful any military operation would be apart from missile strikes that would symbolically verify that China did not consider the Taiwanese population to be 'Chinese'. In late December the CCP leadership reportedly met in Beijing and recommended that high-level contacts be restored with the Taiwanese leadership anticipating that a newly elected Taiwanese president (with an election due in March 2000) would be easier to deal with than Lee Teng-hui.[100] Chinese leaders were surprised by

Chen Shui-bien's election and have remained uncertain on how to deal with his initiative to convert pragmatic diplomacy to what might be termed the 'diplomacy of conciliation'.

### Multilateral Security and Taiwan

Taiwan has maintained relations with and joined a few multilateral institutions, including APEC and the Asian Development Bank, by representing itself as something other than a sovereign entity. Multilateral security politics have not taken hold in the Taiwan Strait situation because of China's insistence that resolving its problems with Taiwan is strictly an intra-Chinese affair mandating 'non-interference' by outside parties. The PRC's actual motivation to exclude Taiwan from multilateral security deliberations has been aptly described by Peter Lewis Young as 'what concerns Beijing is that if a de facto diplomatic identity is accorded to Taiwan in international forums, then this identity may be used by some later Taiwanese nationalist government as a basis for claiming *de jure* diplomatic identity'.[101]

Beijing's position can be contested by arguing that it is essential the Taiwan Strait issue be incorporated into the ARF and other credible security dialogue processes and that this could be initiated at an informal level of discussion. Emphasis could be placed on selected issues of development politics and human security and on economic trends for the entire region where Taiwan's economic muscle would have direct and uncontested relevance.[102] Taiwanese officials have indeed offered to apply their country's 'economic muscle' to support Asia-Pacific security regimes so that regional disputes can be resolved more easily through regional dialogue. Such economic clout did prove decisive in eventually wearing down China's resistance to Taiwanese full membership in APEC and to 'observer status' in the WTO and other regional and international economic organisations. Taiwan has had to assume the nomenclature 'Chinese Taipei' or similar labels to placate Chinese insistence that Taiwan is not a participating sovereign power.[103]

The legitimacy of the so-called 'Track Two diplomacy' approach comes into question, however, if mainland China remains unwilling to participate in a multiparty setting.[104] Track Two diplomacy is the unofficial or informal interaction between states or groups to develop strategies for resolving conflicts at the official level. This resistance has been most evident in the PRC's rejection of Taiwan's drive to re-enter the United Nations that began in mid-1993. It was expelled from that body in October 1971 by UNGA Resolution 2758 which authorised a shift in representation for China from the Republic of China (Taiwan) to the People's Republic of China (China). Between 1993 and 1996 Taiwan's drive for UN reinstatement gained momentum, as the initial total of three countries supporting the revocation of UNGA 2758 grew to seventeen by mid-1996 (all of these being small Latin American and African countries which formally recognise Taiwan in return for substantial Taiwanese economic assistance). Sentiment for some type of UN role for Taiwan had visibly intensified.[105] In July 1996 the European Parliament passed a resolution urging the UN to set up a special task force to study the feasibility of Taiwan taking part in UN-affiliated organisations and the US House of Representatives followed up with a concurrent resolution supporting the European Parliament's declaration.[106] A poll gauging American public opinion on the Taiwan UN question released in March 1997 found that 72 per cent of the 1015 American adults surveyed backed Taiwan's membership to the UN and 80 per cent of those supporting this position indicated they would still do so even if such a development angered the PRC.[107]

Mainland China, of course, has rejected any initiative for Taiwan to participate in the UN in whatever form. It argues that Taiwan has no inherent right to participate in the international community through the UN or through other international organisations and it has since adhered to this position consistently.[108] It has also increased diplomatic pressure on those states still recognising Taiwan as the Republic of China and has projected the issue as a key test for future Sino–American relations. President Clinton's 'unilateral statement' when visiting China in mid-1998 that the United States does not believe that Taiwan should be a member of any organisation for which statehood is required rewarded Beijing's hardline approach to this question.[109] Apart from conforming to the 'one China principle' established by three previous joint China–US policy declarations governing the two countries' *de jure* relations, American rationales for applying its policy of not recognising Taiwan's right to UN membership were explicitly stipulated by Assistant Secretary of State Winston Lord in testimony delivered before the US Congress in September 1994. Unlike the German and Korean cases where there was agreement between the two competing political entities that both could enter the UN, no such agreement exists between the PRC and Taiwan. In the absence of any such agreement, the United States would be inconsistent in observing a 'one-China policy' if it supported Taiwanese UN membership while Taiwan's sovereign status was designated by Beijing's leadership as the basis for its opposition to such membership.[110]

Nevertheless, the PRC is still confronted with a serious policy challenge regarding how it will manage the Taiwan question as part of its overall multilateral regional security politics. On one hand, it cannot afford to alienate its Asian neighbours by appearing to portray Taiwan as the major impediment to efforts for building such a framework at a time when Taiwanese prosperity and political stability is increasingly viewed as a role model for overcoming the Asian financial crisis and surviving the forces of globalisation. On the other hand, the PRC fears that it would lose control of the Taiwan issue if Taipei is able to convert its economic acumen into diplomatic payoffs. Incessant efforts by China to exclude one of the region's economic powerhouses, Taiwan, from assuming a larger role in the region's formulation of both new cooperative security arrangements and fresh economic architectures could undercut Beijing's own diplomatic influence and economic aspirations in the region. But if the avowed pro-independence Taiwanese political factions were some day to form a government, mainland China's worst expectations would materialise.

### Future Directions

The Taiwan Strait issue remains one of the Asia-Pacific's most crucial flashpoints at a time when strategic competition in the region is competing with economic preoccupations for political primacy. As the situation stands now, the PRC has boxed the Taiwanese government into two rather narrow premises for justifying its own continued existence. It may contend that the Chinese communist regime is destined to topple from within and thereby rationalise its own existence on the grounds that, as a legitimate heir, it has every right to await the turn of events and the possible future extension of a mandate from the people of the mainland to reunify the nation. Or it may argue that it has governed a separate, de facto Taiwanese sovereignty for nearly half a century and that Beijing must accept this reality.

The first premise is not viable. The global diplomatic community has not proven amenable to it; South Korea's 1992 switch to recognising the PRC as the one legitimate government of China, and Taiwan's failure even to advance the issue of UN participation on to the UN General Assembly's agenda, drive home the painful point that the PRC is a powerful state with enough leverage to frustrate any Taiwanese claim. As noted above, only a few small and weak states in developing regions outside of Asia still acknowledge Taiwan as a sovereign China. Moreover, the PRC has survived the Tiananmen Square incident and the subsequent American human rights assault with greater tenacity than most democrats would care to admit. For Taiwan to remain adamant that the Chinese communist regime's demise is imminent is merely to court perceptions of its own increasing irrelevance in a diverse and dynamically changing region. In retrospect, Taiwan's decision to end the 'Period of Mobilization for the Suppression of Communist Rebellion' in May 1991 seems to have been a wise one.

The second approach – that Taiwan is an independent sovereignty apart from China – may, over time, gain increasing sympathy with broad sectors of the international community largely convinced that Taipei has done everything asked of it, and more, to earn *de jure* recognition. However, this development remains inhibited by the PRC's power and resources. Taiwan will be required to stand up to mainland China's 'carrot and stick' strategy of intermittently coercing and inducing it into political capitulation for some time to come. Cross-Strait negotiations are merely one such 'carrot' and the PRC's development of its military power projection capabilities the latest 'stick' that Beijing has sought to apply to the end-game. China's diplomacy has become more sophisticated as the Cold War recedes but the PRC's basic objective has changed little: to realise a single, 'unified' China under CCP rule.

Continued US adherence to and support for the TRA remains the most meaningful and obvious counterweight at Taiwan's disposal for buying it time to 'expand its living space internationally' and for gradually wearing down the PRC's resistance to the Taiwanese assuming an international political role more commensurate to their economic status. The TSEA, by contrast, appears to risk provoking China at levels disproportionate to the risk undertaken by the United States in implementing it. The United States will clearly need to maintain its support for the TRA, at levels necessary to prevent a PRC *fait accompli* on the Taiwan Strait issue, in order to preserve its own regional influence into the next century. However, as Bernice Lee argues, a continuation of the posture of strategic ambiguity will only be effective 'if neither China nor Taiwan is inclined to upset the status quo'.[111]

Because of this factor, inter-regional pressure to allow Taiwan to join multilateral economic and security dialogues must become an increasingly important component of Asia-Pacific diplomacy. The PRC cannot afford to pursue irredentism regarding Taiwan so rigidly as to compromise prospects for enhancing its long-term regional influence. Its careful management of the Hong Kong transition process is evidence that Beijing is aware of this constraint. Multilateralism's emphasis on collaborative diplomacy and norm creation underscore China's need to pursue its objectives toward Taiwan in a balanced manner. In this sense, China is forced to at least acknowledge liberalism's relevance and possible impact on its Taiwan strategy. Taiwan's prospects of survival have also improved with its recent policy shifts away from observing an exclusively realist or zero-sum outlook towards the 'China threat', to cultivating a more diversified and increasingly sophisticated set of diplomatic, economic and strategic postures toward Beijing. Yet Taipei's long-term fate depends on the United States' willingness to sustain credible deterrence commitments on its behalf while simultaneously supporting a long-term diplomatic solution to the PRC–Taiwan security dilemma. This approach conforms to the general postulates underlying the convergent security strategy proposed in the concluding chapter.

## Conclusion

The above analysis yields several broad observations pertaining to both Koreas and to Taiwan as 'middle powers' in the contemporary Asia-Pacific security environment. These, in turn, can be applied to the generalisations about middle-power diplomacy introduced at this chapter's outset.

First, great-power dependence remains acute in the security policies of both South Korea and Taiwan but less so in North Korea's case. South Korea's efforts to diversify its security relationships at both the bilateral and multilateral levels have not generated sufficient options for it to gain significant strategic independence from the United States or to be, in its own right, a major determinant of any emerging regional power balance. The North Korean threat remains the most prevalent factor in Seoul's security thinking despite incessant analysis and optimistic signals about Korean reunification or speculation about a re-emergence of a politico-cultural intimacy with China. The United States, arguably, remains the one power investing the resources needed to neutralise Pyongyang's more bellicose tendencies. Korea's continuing animosities towards Japan resurfaced in May 2001 when South Korea cancelled a planned military rescue exercise with Japan while demanding 'corrections to distortions' in Japan's officially sanctioned history textbooks, a constant source of tension between Japan and its Northeast Asian neighbours.[112]

Although no less prosperous than South Korea, Taiwan remains more dependent. Its almost total reliance on intermittent US weapons sales to maintain a rough military balance in the Taiwan Strait and its nearly complete diplomatic isolation from major international organisations attest to China's success in neutralising Taiwan's pragmatic diplomacy. It also exemplifies the difficulty that any middle power has in deflecting a great-power strategy that is totally dedicated to eliminating it as an independent player in the international system. Taiwan's difficulties in this regard are compounded by its own great-power guarantor's inability to project a consistent and coherent policy toward the Taiwan Strait. America's 'strategic ambiguity' is a product of policy-making fragmentation between Washington's executive branch, which tends to defer to Beijing for very realist reasons, and the US Congress and public opinion, both of which project high levels of support for Taipei's economic and democratic achievements. This situation creates mixed signals that Beijing has learned to mostly ignore and which Taiwan has been unable to sufficiently manipulate to its geopolitical advantage. At best, the Taiwanese enjoy only partial linkage to the American domestic polity and this may not be sufficient to ensure that it can outlast the mainland's communist regime. As a presidential candidate during 2000, George W. Bush called for a more transparent American strategic commitment to Taiwan; it is far from certain that George W. Bush, as President, will be any more capable than his predecessors on delivering such a posture.

North Korea has been the most strategically independent middle power assessed in this chapter. This has nothing to do with its leadership's inherent ability but rather is related to the rapid structural changes accompanying the end of the Cold War and the effective removal of its traditional great power patron, the Soviet Union, from the international scene. If the North Korean economy was ever able to function effectively, the USSR's demise and the end of its massive subsidies to Kim Il-sung exposed it as incapable of operating in a world of intensified globalisation and interdependence. Both Kim and his son, however, discovered that the diplomacy of nuclear brinkmanship afforded North Korea new opportunities for relating to the United States, the major power that counts the most in the Peninsula's security equation. The Chinese were also willing to assume an indirect role in this high stakes game, leveraging their still significant influence over their intermittently troublesome and always unpredictable North Korean ally to extract various concessions on trade, high technology access and strategic dialogue from the United States within the overall context of 'strategic engagement'.

Limited by its obvious preference for preserving the status quo in regional and international security politics, that is, limiting the spread of nuclear weapons and preserving its access to the Asian marketplace, Washington gradually succumbed to North Korean demands for extraordinary economic and strategic concessions. The depth and scope of American benevolence would have, under most circumstances, undermined its Northeast Asian security alliances beyond repair, but neither Japan nor South Korea had any other allies-in-waiting. For a state predicated on uncompromising socialist ideology, North Korea proved to be an unmitigated practitioner of realism. It extracted substantial relative gains at Washington's expense without any tangible support from the American body politic.

The final observation of this chapter is that stability and peace on the Korean Peninsula and between China and Taiwan may ultimately be linked to domestic political and economic transitions occurring on both sides of Korea's DMZ and the Taiwan Strait. This prospect does not invalidate the realist-liberal debate, but enriches it by linking it to the need to better understand those socio-cultural and political factors now driving the forces of structural change in the Asia-Pacific region. This conceptual task is no less relevant in assessing middle-power strategic behaviour in Southeast Asia. It is especially critical in the Northeast Asian subregion, however, because the immediate potential for conflict escalation is far greater. Both realists and liberals must come to terms with factors of nationalism, ethnicity and culture that can otherwise blur both of their paradigms and render their policy explanations irrelevant. The challenge is to link these factors in ways that provide an analytical framework capable of reconciling these diverse factors and interests and thus achieving conflict avoidance at the state-centric level.

CHAPTER 5

# Other Key Players II:
# ASEAN and Australia

If liberal strategies for attaining regional security were to emerge as predominant in any sector of the Asia-Pacific region, until very recently Southeast Asia and the Southwest Pacific would have been nominated by many observers as the most likely venues.[1] Rapid decolonisation occurred throughout Southeast Asia following World War II. The emergent states tended to emphasise nation-building over inter-state competition. At the same time, Australia and New Zealand became increasingly preoccupied with shifting their strategic, diplomatic and commercial orientations away from Europe (as former British dominions) towards their northern Asian neighbours.

One effect of this development was a shared preference for fashioning increasingly regional outlooks and postures. This provided the founding member-states of ASEAN, and Australia in particular, with a common framework for greater strategic interdependence at the end of the Cold War. In Canberra and the various ASEAN capitals there existed a sense of optimism that anarchy in this part of the world could be overcome by applying 'constructive engagement' strategies, multilateral dialogues and confidence-building measures. It was anticipated these would be major steps towards achieving a genuine regional security community.[2] However, the Asian financial crisis, intra-organisational tensions, unstable governments within ASEAN and revived great-power strategic interest in Southeast Asia all worked to undermine liberalism in the sub-region during the late 1990s.

The realist explanation for this setback is that liberal strategies failed to anticipate and cope with the substantial tensions and contradictions that may arise when multilateralism, based on 'universal' values, norms and ideas (such as democracy, legalism, and human rights) confronts state-specific interests (that is, the primacy of sovereign interests and state identities).[3] Events have confirmed this explanation: inter-state differences over territorial and resource disputes, market competition, lingering historical animosities, nationalist and ethnic tensions and great power relations all account for ASEAN being more conflict-prone than advocates of the 'ASEAN Way' would ever concede.[4]

If the realist paradigm ultimately prevails in Southeast Asia, it will be largely due to the inability of an enlarged ASEAN to reconcile and integrate multilateralism with the emerging strategic challenges generated by an intensifying regional multipolarity. If the great powers do not support multilateralism in the region there is every chance that the ASEAN states and Australia will gravitate by default towards rival Chinese and American strategic orbits. Alternatively, if the United States were to adopt a more isolationist posture towards the region, a situation could emerge where China, Japan and, over the longer term, perhaps even India would all be vying for influence throughout Southeast Asia. Under either scenario, power balancing, security dilemmas and a return to bipolarity or hegemonic competition would be assured.

Along with Taiwan and the Korean Peninsula, ASEAN and Australia have become polities that, while not shaping the Asia-Pacific's emerging strategic environment, can greatly influence its stability. ASEAN's future cohesion and its ability to translate multilateral diplomacy into regional stability will strengthen Asia-Pacific security politics; its lethargy, fragmentation or demise will render ASEAN ineffectual and precipitate regional anarchy. At present, as will be argued in this chapter, Southeast Asia's nation-states are at an historical crossroads. Two alternate futures now present themselves. The group could survive with a mandate to facilitate the building of a subregional security regime compatible with liberal approaches and responding to countervailing great-power behaviour in ways which clearly work to the ASEAN member-states' collective self-interest. Or, it could implode, leaving fragile Southeast Asian regimes vulnerable to coping with external threats and internal legitimacy crises in a manner reflecting realist postulates.

It can be argued that Australia's strategic concerns are more diverse than in the past. For much of its history Australia was consumed with the need to engage the support of powerful allies to deter invasion from potential Asian adversaries. Indeed, it is only during the past two decades that Australia has consciously sought to define itself as part of the 'region'. Nevertheless, it has now become a major proponent of regional interdependence and liberalism, and has provided both entrepreneurial and intellectual leadership for multilateral security politics, both within Southeast Asia and throughout the wider Asia-Pacific.[5] Its spearheading of the International Emergency Force in East Timor (INTERFET) is the latest and perhaps most graphic example. Such leadership has been selective and pragmatic, balanced by continued, long-standing defence ties with the United States. Its multilateral diplomacy has been largely designed to preclude its isolation from the region it once feared.

Adopting a similar format to that used in chapter 4, ASEAN and Australia will be examined successively here. Initially, various problems underlying the strategic outlooks and postures of the various ASEAN states will be briefly discussed and Australian strategic perceptions and doctrine will then be reviewed. The chapter will close with a brief discussion of how salient emerging multilateral security initiatives in Southeast Asia relate to the realist approaches that remain prevalent in the subregion. Both the ASEAN and Australian experiences since the 1980s have shown that realist postulates can be at least partially combined with liberal strategies. However, such integration will remain unimportant unless the Asia-Pacific's great powers are willing to support it. How they might do so will be discussed in the concluding chapter of this study.

### ASEAN: Strategic Problems and Postures

Both continental Southeast Asia (Cambodia, Laos, Thailand, Vietnam, and Burma) and its maritime counterpart (Brunei, Indonesia, Malaysia, the Philippines, and Singapore) confront fundamental challenges of strategic geography which transcend intermittent changes in regional power configurations.[6] A brief review of these challenges can provide understanding of contemporary threat perceptions and force planning in specific ASEAN states and the factors that multilateral security architectures such as the ARF must incorporate into any framework intended to effect strategic restraint.

Southeast Asia has been and remains a geopolitical 'shatterbelt', that is, a 'politically fragmented area of competition between maritime and continental regimes'.[7] Thailand, for example, has oriented its economy towards Japan and the United States and has therefore become part of a pan-Pacific maritime sector dominated by those two states. Yet its strategic orientation is gravitating more towards the Asia-Pacific's major continental power in China. Vietnam is likely to follow the same pattern as its economy develops, although it will accommodate Chinese interests less easily than has Thailand. The strategic relations between Malaysia, Indonesia and Singapore rest on the ability of the first two polities to coexist effectively with the latter, more economically dynamic and strategically cohesive, Chinese island-state. Burma's isolation, Cambodia's endemic instability, Laos' lack of economic infrastructure and political deference to Vietnam, Brunei's lack of size and the Philippines' distance from Southeast Asia's core render these countries less critical to Southeast Asia's contemporary power balance. The Philippines' intensifying resistance to China's envelopment of the South China Sea and Burma's growing strategic relationship with Beijing, however, are both trends that could significantly affect Southeast Asia's future security environment.

ASEAN can be broken down further into three 'geostrategic domains'.[8] Two of these domains are exclusively maritime: (1) the area from the Gulf of Thailand in the West towards the East China Sea; and (2) the area emanating from the Bay of Bengal and Andaman Sea projecting towards the northern approaches of the Strait of Malacca. The third area is a 'continental edge' that includes Indochina, Thailand and Burma. These states are conceptually unified by their proximity to China. The difference in maritime and continental edge strategic orientation is reflected in their defence force structures and the geopolitical advantages and limitations they enjoy or incur as a result of their locations.

Southeast Asia's geostrategic significance is primarily based on its location: some of the world's most important sea lanes of communication (SLOCs) and trade routes cross the subregion. Consequently, some ASEAN states have concluded that their strategic interests are best served by strengthening their capabilities to project naval and air power to control these routes. Their defence budgets rose sharply during the early 1990s as their naval and air forces prepared to defend offshore territorial claims, EEZs and long coastlines. The importance of this orientation increased further when the EEZs controlled by a number of ASEAN states expanded substantially after UNCLOS came into force during November 1994. China's naval expansion has been another significant catalyst for ASEAN maritime states to upgrade their own maritime strike capabilities.[9] The Asian financial crisis caused some ASEAN states to reduce their defence spending substantially but by 1999 regional defence spending had increased in real terms by 6.2 per cent (see table 5.1).[10]

*The Continental Edge: Vietnam, Thailand and Burma*

Most Southeast Asian states have prioritised fighting at sea and in the air at the expense of preparing for protracted warfare against rival ground forces. However, this has not been universally accompanied by a relative decline of the military's influence over day-to-day politics and defence postures. It is true that the process of political reform occurring within at least some of these states has entailed a 'return to the barracks' by their military sectors and a commensurate increase in the power exercised by civilian policy makers. Thailand and the Philippines have been perhaps the most obvious cases.[11] Other military organisations in this subregion retain what many democrats would regard as disproportionate levels of influence. Burma is the clearest example, with its military junta exercising total power over state mechanisms, and Vietnam also remains a 'soldier-state'.

**Table 5.1**   ASEAN and Chinese Defence Spending 1996–1999 (in US$m)

|  | 1996 | 1997 | 1998 | 1999 | % of GNP in 1998 | % of GNP in 1999 |
|---|---|---|---|---|---|---|
| Brunei | 344 | 353 | 386 | 402 | 6.7 | 6.7 |
| Burma | 2 012 | 2 067 | 2 142 | 1 995 | 5.0 | 5.0 |
| Cambodia | 185 | 254 | 155 | 176 | 5.1 | 5.1 |
| Indonesia | 4 797 | 4 812 | 967 | 1 502 | 0.8 | 1.1 |
| Laos | 79 | 63 | 34 | 22 | 2.6 | 2.3 |
| Malaysia | 3 695 | 3 377 | 1 891 | 3 158 | 2.6 | 4.0 |
| Philippines | 1 520 | 1 422 | 1 521 | 1 627 | 2.3 | 2.1 |
| Singapore | 4 129 | 4 122 | 4 936 | 4 696 | 5.6 | 5.6 |
| Thailand | 4 393 | 3 248 | 2 124 | 2 638 | 1.7 | 1.9 |
| Vietnam | 970 | 990 | 943 | 890 | 3.5 | 3.1 |
| China |  |  | 38 191 | 39 889 | 5.3 | 5.4 |

*Sources:* International Institute for Strategic Studies, *The Military Balance, 2000/2001; The Military Balance 1998/99;* Tim Huxley and Susan Willett, *Arming East Asia* (London: Oxford University Press for the IISS, 1999), p. 16; Australian Defence Intelligence Organisation, *Defence Economic Trends in the Asia-Pacific* 1998.

Indonesia's military remains influential in that country's domestic politics despite recent trends to end the military's 'dual function role' (*dwi fungsi*) there and to curb its previous near monopoly over state organs.

Continental Southeast Asia remains wedded to the realist paradigm. Vietnam and Burma have strongly resisted internal liberalisation on the grounds that national security requires a state's political and military organs to be tightly integrated. Both emphasise their need to sustain vigilance against potential external foes within or beyond Southeast Asia. The Vietnamese government, for example, released a defence white paper in July 1998 which highlighted the need for that country's army to wage a credible 'people's war' strategy 'on diverse terrain, and in different weather'.[12] Burma remains under the authoritarian yoke of its generals who have suppressed legitimate political opposition in the country, while cultivating low-key strategic ties with Beijing.[13]

### Vietnam

Vietnam's strategic situation has transformed radically since the 1980s. Following its military victory over South Vietnam and national unification in the mid-1970s, the Vietnamese Communist Party adopted what appeared to its ASEAN neighbours to be an explicitly aggressive and expansionist regional posture. Vietnam initially rejected ASEAN's proposal for a regional neutrality zone and prepared to confront what it viewed as a de facto Sino–American–ASEAN coalition. It forged an alliance with the USSR in November 1978 prior to invading Cambodia in January of the following year. This action supplanted Pol Pot's Chinese-backed regime with one subservient to Hanoi. It then successfully withstood a retaliatory Chinese invasion in February 1979 aimed at preventing Vietnamese hegemony in Indochina.

Nearly a quarter of a century later, Vietnam's strategic interests have undergone a substantial revision. It now enjoys a tenuous detente with China, full membership in ASEAN and a steadily improving relationship with the United States. The Russian strategic presence is all but gone. Vietnam is intent on modernising its economy without altering its hardline Marxist political system. Its army has become a skeleton of its once formidable self and Hanoi's primary security concerns are to stabilise its Indochinese neighbours. There is little apprehension in Thailand or in other ASEAN states concerning reinvigoration of Vietnam's hegemonic aspirations. More attention is being paid to Vietnam's economic modernisation efforts and its integration into ASEAN.

Along with most other ASEAN states (Burma is the major exception), Vietnam shares suspicion about China's long-term geopolitical intentions. Unlike the latter stages of the Cold War when it had formidable Soviet strategic support, Vietnam cannot count on any outside power to provide deterrence against Chinese military action in the South China Sea or along the Sino–Vietnamese border. At present, if invaded by a large outside power, the Vietnamese Army could do little more than retreat to mountainous interiors if a militarily superior opponent were to cut off links between Hanoi and Ho Chi Minh City, Vietnam's two key population centres. The retraction of external military assistance to Vietnam over the past few years has meant that Vietnamese weapons systems are deteriorating at an ever-increasing rate. In order to address this growing deficiency, Vietnam's best option may be to solidify its bilateral defence ties with those other ASEAN states that also view China as the subregion's most serious long-term threat.[14] Vietnam could initially defend itself credibly if Chinese forces attacked Vietnamese border positions, but even here the force balance is shifting perceptibly against the Vietnamese.[15] Neutralising this potential Chinese threat was a major reason why Vietnam signed a border demarcation agreement with China in December 2000 after more than eight years of negotiations.[16]

Given this ongoing concern with China's power projection capacities, Vietnam has begun to pay some attention to developing its naval power. This transition has been inspired largely by Vietnam's claim to the Spratly Islands and recent Vietnamese skirmishes with Chinese units in the South China Sea. In 1994 Vietnam acquired two Type 124-1RA missile boats and a corvette from Russia, and it purchased two mini-submarines from North

Korea in 1997. In October 1998 Hanoi secured a Russian commitment to sell naval vessels and *Su-27* air superiority/ground attack fighters to Vietnam.[17] Yet Vietnam's ability to project itself as a maritime power remains minuscule compared to that of China and most of its ASEAN counterparts despite its control over Cam Ranh Bay, one of the region's major naval installations. Its maritime weakness neutralises whatever advantage Vietnam might enjoy as a result of its geographic proximity to contested offshore areas.

Vietnam still exercises de facto strategic hegemony over most of Indochina and could extend its power into 'continental Thailand' in a future subregional conflict if unimpeded by the Chinese. It is capable of accessing and controlling the strategically susceptible mountain areas of east-central Burma, Laos and northeastern Thailand. It is therefore able to apply 'coercive power' against these neighbours.[18] Laos, in particular, remains Vietnam's closest ally, with leaders in both countries continuing to emphasise politico-economic ties while downplaying the military implications of their 1977 'friendship treaty'.[19] With the demise of the Khmer Rouge, relations between Cambodia and Vietnam have improved but they remain far from cordial. Anti-Vietnamese sentiment in Cambodia remains intense. Border areas remain contested and Thai influence among various Cambodian economic and political factions is regarded with deep suspicion by Hanoi.

*Thailand*

Like Vietnam, Thailand's strategic postures are now shaped predominantly by three factors: concerns about internal land threats; responding to ground warfare-oriented external threats; and most recently, the need to secure commercial and maritime approaches. Up until the later stages of the Cold War, communist insurgency forces, ethnic separatist movements, uncontrolled refugee flows and other 'national stability' concerns ranked ahead of external threat perceptions in the estimates of Thai military planners. This orientation has now visibly changed.

Vietnam's occupation of Cambodia throughout much of the 1980s, along with recent poor performances by the Royal Thai Army against Laotian and Burmese elements in border skirmishes, have clearly heightened Thai sensitivity to external threats.[20] The northeast and eastern parts of Thailand contiguous to the trans-Mekong areas along the Thai–Cambodian river, and the Vientiane plain which extends from the Laotian lowland area, are normally considered to be the most vulnerable areas of Thai defence. No real natural barriers stand between these sectors and key Thai industrial and communications centres around Bangkok.[21] The Thai–Burma border, where Thai forces have coped with Karen insurgency groups, Burmese refugees and drug traffickers, is also a significant concern.[22] Malay ethnic groups living in Thailand's four southern provinces have also been the source of intermittent tensions between Thailand and Malaysia, although less so in recent years.[23] Vietnam's military withdrawal from Cambodia and its normalisation of ties with ASEAN have partially modified Thai concerns over land threats.

Finally, economic and maritime dimensions comprise increasingly important considerations which shape Thai threat perceptions and policy responses. One authoritative observer has described the revised Thai calculus in the following terms: 'the main concern is no longer an overwhelming threat posed by a Vietnam seeking hegemony, but instead, the promotion of Thai economic interests in the region'.[24] Thai strategic thinking has normally been oriented towards creating favourable local and regional power balances in which it is aligned with a preponderant coalition. Its strategic gravitation towards China since the early 1990s manifests this historical tendency. Yet Thailand has also sought to maintain its alliance ties with the United States in order to protect its growing maritime trading interests. This has been reinforced by the realisation that developing maritime assets to protect its 'blue water interests' and 2300 kilometres of coastline have spiralled beyond its budgetary means.

The prospect of future Indian maritime encroachment into the Andaman Sea and the approaches to Thailand's west coast is clearly a matter of concern. However, Burmese naval activities off the Isthmus of Kra are increasingly regarded as Thailand's most pressing maritime contingency. In December 1998 and January 1999 several naval skirmishes took place between Thai and Burmese naval vessels in disputed fishing waters along the Isthmus. Thai and Burmese diplomats subsequently smoothed over the incidents but they reflected the potential for the escalation of a long-standing territorial dispute.

In general, the Gulf of Thailand is of less immediate strategic concern. Thailand and Malaysia, for example, have successfully negotiated a number of issues related to resource access and patrol areas. However, countervailing EEZ claims are still held by Thailand, Malaysia and Vietnam in the Gulf and these may become a source of future security tensions between these ASEAN states.[25] Moreover, the Gulf could be blockaded with relative ease by a hostile maritime power intent on cutting off Bangkok from vital SLOCs, given that over 90 per cent of Thailand's exports are seaborne.

Unfortunately, Thailand's ability to prepare for such future contingencies has been severely affected by the Asian financial crisis. The Thai government slashed the country's defence budget by over 40 per cent in early 1998 (to 80.9 billion baht, over $US2 billion), the largest cut of any ASEAN defence budget. The country's armed forces were compelled to cancel or postpone most major weapons purchases.

Because Thailand's National Security Council is now dominated by civilians, the government was able to insist on these cutbacks despite pressure from the military. The military may well have resisted them much more vigorously if its influence in Thai politics had not declined so precipitously following the pro-democracy demonstrations of May 1992. However, the military's current subservience to civilian authority should not necessarily be regarded as a permanent condition, given that it remains politically active in rural areas and relatively cohesive while the civilian political factions have become less credible due to deterioration of the national economy and a marked increase in political corruption.[26]

*Burma (Myanmar)*

Burma's ruling military junta (the State Peace and Development Council or SPDC) believes that its own political survival is totally integral to the survival of the Burmese state. The current regime's preoccupation is to maintain its political power base in the face of rampant domestic opposition and widespread international condemnation by suppressing the former and deflecting the latter. It is intent on developing close bilateral economic relations with China and the ASEAN states, all of whom have adopted a 'constructive engagement' approach toward Rangoon (Yangon). This strategy has succeeded to the extent that Burma became a full member of ASEAN in July 1997.

The SPDC has balanced its 'soft' regional economic diplomacy with a 'hard' strategic posture. This has included increasing the manpower levels of its army at a time when most other regional states have reduced theirs in response to the Asian financial crisis. Since the mid-1990s Burma has purchased F-7 jet fighters, modified *Jianghu* missile frigates, Type-69 battle tanks and other armaments from China. It has also been supplied with helicopters and various small arms from Russian and East European sources.[27] Most of these systems allegedly have little to do with projecting power in the region but are presumably directed towards quelling ethnic minorities or nationalist insurgents. The Burmese Army is now the second largest force in Southeast Asia (after the Vietnamese Army), totalling nearly 300 000 personnel. Burma faces no real external threat, a condition that has existed since Thailand relinquished its traditional strategy of supporting Burmese rebels in 'buffer zones' in March 1996. Throughout much of the late 1990s Thailand pursued a 'constructive engagement' policy towards Yangon in order to cultivate economic ties. While Western support for SPDC opponents such as Aung San Suu Kyi is resented as unwarranted interference in internal Burmese affairs (support which intensifies China's affinity with the current Burmese regime), such political pressure is not a military or strategic threat.

*Maritime Southeast Asia: The Malayan Peninsula,*
*Indonesia and the Philippines*

Whereas Indochina captured the world's attention during much of the Cold War, the South China Sea and contiguous strategic areas of contention are now Southeast Asia's most volatile flashpoints. Maritime ASEAN states are highly conscious of their vulnerability to growing Chinese military power undermining their own capabilities to defend contested territorial claims. The gravity of this situation is compounded by Indonesia's intensifying political instability, by the Philippines' growing political uncertainty, and by ethnic and political tensions sharpening in other ASEAN countries.

The Asian financial crisis and its internal political ramifications have effectively slowed the defence modernisation programs of the two key Malay states, Malaysia and Indonesia. However, if China's ongoing defence modernisation leads to it deploying a greater naval presence in the South China Sea, or to Beijing adopting a more aggressive posture in Southeast Asian waters, it is unlikely that this 'cooling off' period will last. The peninsular ASEAN states will either have to find new resources for military expenditures or they will have to seek more support from the United States to balance Chinese capabilities. Either scenario involves greater risks for conflict than a comprehensive security strategy that emphasises regional collaboration. Both Jakarta and Kuala Lumpur have embraced the comprehensive security ethos (along with most other ASEAN member-states) but this step by itself is not enough. In Indonesia's case, the preservation of domestic sovereignty is rapidly becoming an all-consuming preoccupation. The key for ASEAN states is to find an acceptable balance between focusing on domestic stability and preserving external security interests over the next decade. The latter task concerns a rising and more assertive China or other external actors that may emerge to contest China's interests in ways that directly relate to the ASEAN states' own sovereign or territorial prerogatives.

*Malaysia*

Malaysia in recent years has shifted from a counter-insurgency defence posture to one directed more towards external contingencies. Much of Malaysia's latest round of defence spending was completed before the onset of the Asian financial crisis. It is unclear to what extent that crisis will affect Malaysian defence capabilities over the long-term.[28] The country experienced a precipitate drop in defence spending during 1998 but still rebounded strongly in 1999 (see table 5.1). It is clear, however, that the financial crisis had significant ramifications for short-term Malay strategic force planning. The government postponed procurement of helicopters, additional offshore patrol vessels (only six out of a scheduled twenty-seven to be purchased) and cancelled a submarine purchase (Malaysia currently lacks any such capability). A large naval base at Kota Kinabalu in the eastern state of Sabah, planned to be built as a complement for the major western installation adjacent to the Strait of Malacca, may not become operational in the near future.[29]

All of Malaysia's force acquisitions since the early 1990s underscore a substantial change in its military doctrine. It has moved away from emphasising counter insurgency operations to establishing power projection capabilities on land, in the air and on the sea. This change advances the Malaysian concept of 'comprehensive security' – balancing the development of military power with the 'strengthening of national resilience' and regional confidence-building.[30]

Malaysia's force modernisation initiatives address the comprehensive security concept. Efforts have been made to establish Malaysia's 11th Division as a Rapid Deployment Force (RDF) for the defence of border areas (although such efforts have been at least somewhat impeded by the lack of strategic transport and attack helicopters).[31] Naval modernisation is directly linked with perceived needs to defend EEZs, the Sabah or adjacent sea lanes of communication deemed vulnerable to external interdiction or harassment. Air power is to be integrated into RDF and sea defence missions, and will constitute a backup to air defence systems protecting key Malaysian command centres and basing installations. However, Malaysia's geography (mountain ranges along the Malay Peninsula that would make detection of incoming hostile aircraft more difficult), combined with its difficulty in fielding sophisticated early warning assets, leave the country vulnerable to an opponent using sophisticated jet fighters and missile systems. A relatively weak defence technology industrial base extends little hope for Malaysia improving this situation in the near future.[32]

Malaysia's defence postures and planning, therefore, are not designed to transform that country into a formidable military power. They are intended to build and maintain a small but relatively effective military force relative to those of its regional neighbours and capable of coping with limited external aggression. The problem with this posture is that Malaysia may find it extremely difficult to achieve this capability. Some Western analysts, for example, have argued that the objective of deterring 'limited external aggression' may amount to nothing more than Malaysian ability to deter future Singaporean military action against Malay interests.

Malaysia's and Singapore's leaders know that their ongoing tensions over border control locales, water rights and other minor issues cannot be allowed to prevail in their overall strategic relationship. Yet both states appear reluctant to initiate long-term confidence-building measures needed to modify their differences. Tensions between them intensified during 1998, especially as it became apparent to Malaysia's leaders that Singapore's defence capabilities were not affected adversely by the Asian financial crisis. Singapore's military aircraft were denied access to Malaysian airspace and both sides' armed forces were put briefly on higher alert status.[33] In August 1999 Malaysia's Deputy Defence Minister cited Singapore's purchase of Israeli anti-tank guided missiles as proof of an 'insensitivity' to Malaysia's Islamic orientation (Malaysia does not formally recognise the state of Israel). Independent observers speculated that the real source of Malaysian concern was that this weapon system enhances Singapore's deterrence capability against future Malay efforts to coerce that city-state into political or strategic concessions.[34]

*Singapore*

Singapore is a vulnerable, highly trade-dependent, microstate nestled between a very large Malay power (Indonesia) and a middle one (Malaysia). Some analysts have argued that Singapore's relative economic prosperity, advanced technology and growing military capability classifies it as a middle power as well.[35] It is doubtful that Singapore would play any meaningful defence role in states or regions other than its own (the acknowledged criterion for reaching middle-power status) as its defence posture is directed completely towards defending its own sovereignty against its larger Malay neighbours (notwithstanding their common ASEAN membership).[36]

Neither Malaysia nor Indonesia have been favourably disposed towards this prosperous Chinese enclave (Singapore's population is 76 per cent Chinese) operating in their midst.[37] Singapore's lifeblood is access to the subregion's straits and sea lanes; both Indonesia and Malaysia have adopted the 'archipelago' concept of international sea law which entails rigorous enforcement of broad interpretations of their EEZs.[38] The two Malay states control most of Singapore's potable water and much of its food supply.

How vulnerable Singapore is to Malaysia's intermittent posturing was underscored when Malaysia rejected Singapore's offer, extended in 1998, to raise revenue for the Malaysian economy in return for continued water supply access rights when the current agreement expires in 2061. The Malaysian government put Singapore on notice that the water supply question would henceforth be linked to other bilateral disputes between the two countries.[39]

Most observers concur that Singapore's concepts of national security and strategic planning are realist, with the principles of self-help and power balancing evident throughout its 'total defence' doctrine.[40] The total defence doctrine emphasises that modern security policies entail states' entire populations and resources rather than mere confrontations between their armed forces. Domestic stability and national will are paramount to deter aggression as is the effective mobilisation of civil resources to supplement military power. Efforts to achieve defence self-reliance partially compensate for Singapore's lack of size and natural resources.

Notwithstanding how efficient and unified Singapore might be, it cannot hope to defeat a major regional adversary. Total defence is therefore supplemented by a diplomatic strategy designed to win friends and allies, not just among Singapore's neighbours but with those friends and allies willing to collaborate with it. This has paid dividends by allowing the Singapore Armed Forces (SAF) to conduct much of its training offshore to compensate for its own space constraints. Until recently, Taiwan provided training facilities and storage space for much of Singapore's tank force. Australia has provided facilities both for the deployment and training of its jet fighters and for the training of ground forces at Shoalwater Bay in Queensland. The United States also hosts various air squadrons. The Taiwan connection has recently diminished for both political and logistical reasons; Australia's involvement is increasing.[41]

Given that political relations with Malaysia have been especially tense since the mid-1990s, Singapore made a special effort to maintain cordial relations with Indonesia, particularly after the ascension of the Habibie government in May 1998. Throughout the post-Cold War period, however, the strategic collaborator that has mattered most to Singapore has been the United States. This is true for no other reason than the United States is viewed as the only acceptable balancer to Chinese power in the region. More than any other ASEAN state, Singapore's national deterrence strategy coincides with American determination to retain its bilateral alliance network in Southeast Asia. Providing US forces access to basing systems and cultivating training relationships that enable the SAF to train at US sites are important aspects of this bilateral defence arrangement.[42]

Singapore's economic viability was less affected by the Asian financial crisis than that of most other Asian states. Although the city-state was not immune from the effects of the crisis, it actually spent more on defence in real terms during 1998 than it did the previous year, resulting in its defence budget becoming the largest in ASEAN (around $US5 billion).[43]

The city-state's defence modernisation programs are thus proceeding with little real interruption. The Singapore Army's order of battle was revised substantially in 1994 to create a rapid deployment force that could operate interdependently with naval and air force units.[44] New weapons systems purchased since 1995 include advanced F-16C/D jet fighter aircraft with precision guided munitions, three submarines from

Sweden, armoured personnel carriers, *Chinook* helicopters and landing ships for tanks.[45] Additionally, the quality and comprehensiveness of Singapore's indigenous defence industry and technology base is unrivalled in the ASEAN region.[46]

Singapore's key strategic challenge is simultaneously its major policy dilemma: how to avoid alienating its Malay neighbours while still adhering to a deterrence strategy that cannot be reasonably perceived as directed against any other threat. Its participation in the Five Power Defence Arrangements (FPDA) and in other joint military exercises is one of the few confidence-building mechanisms available for Singaporean defence officials to clarify their strategic intentions to their Malaysian counterparts.[47] Singapore is also searching for an effective means by which to reassure Jakarta that it is not merely a Chinese proxy situated and operating in the middle of the Malay world. It must also display a convincing sensitivity to Malaysian and Indonesian apprehensions over encouraging the United States to deploy and operate its forces too closely and too frequently, undermining Malaysia's and Indonesia's postures of regional resilience and non-alignment.[48]

Singapore's total defence concept – a posture which envisions the entire nation being prepared to fight a war within 6 to 8 hours – can be perceived as a pre-emptive strategy rather than one of true deterrence. This leads to the question of how Singapore's national security doctrine really fits with ASEAN's stated security objectives of non-interference in each other's affairs, neutrality and region-wide amity and cooperation. Thus far, Singapore has been unsuccessful in integrating realist military planning with multilateral security diplomacy.

*Indonesia*

In many ways, Indonesia is ASEAN's most prominent state; its destiny will largely determine ASEAN's future viability. It has nearly half of ASEAN's land space, nearly half of its people and sits astride most of the sea lanes of communication that link the Indian and Pacific oceans.

Indonesia also embodies a postwar national development experience venerated by its Southeast Asian neighbours: achieving independence through a largely 'self-reliant' revolution; gaining international distinction as a leader in the Cold War non-alignment movement; achieving substantial economic growth for several decades prior to the Asian financial crisis by reinforcing 'national resilience'; and serving as an informal mediator during the Indochina crisis in the 1980s and, more recently, for the South China Sea dispute. It has opted to attract Western financial support and investment while still championing regional neutrality. In the post-Sukarno era (after 1965) it has generally eschewed the pursuit of hegemonic ambitions to fill a maritime or region-wide Southeast Asian power vacuum, instead choosing to cultivate a judicious balance of power between local and extra-regional powers. By doing so, it incurred minimum ASEAN opposition to its occupation of East Timor and, for a while, modified extra-regional pressure on that issue. It has encouraged a continued American 'over-the-horizon' strategic presence in maritime Southeast Asia as a check against Soviet and Chinese expansionism and has maintained its access to and influence within regional and international economic institutions.[49]

As the ASEAN state most affected by the Asian financial crisis, it is uncertain to what extent Indonesia's long-standing strategic posture remains applicable to its rapidly evolving domestic political situation. The Indonesian military and its Golkar political party dominated President Soeharto's New Order since he assumed power in October 1965. The military for many years thereafter rationalised the creation of a 'territorial defence' system which allowed it to suppress indigenous political opposition in East Timor, Irian Jaya, Aceh and other flashpoints.[50] The end of the Soeharto regime in May 1998 marked a watershed in the military's socio-political role, with substantial reassessment and reorganisation of the military taking place throughout late 1998 and early 1999.[51] This was not accompanied by a much needed modernisation of true defence capabilities or sufficient expenditures on rank and file military personnel to modify the *Tentara Nasional Indonesia's* (TNI) (Indonesia's armed forces, formerly *Anskatan Bersenjata Republik Indonesia* (ABRI)) engagement in corrupt business practices.[52]

The government of President Abdurrahman Wahid, after assuming office in October 1999, has been preoccupied with holding Indonesia together as a unified nation-state. Indonesia acquiesced to the demands of the East Timorese independence movement after its own preferred formula for granting East Timor more autonomy was rejected in the referendum held on 30 August 1999 in that province. Given the ensuing violence in East Timor following the vote that led to the establishment of a UN peacekeeping operation there, the new Indonesian government was confronted with a plethora of secessionist movements and ethnic disputes in Aceh, the Moluccan Islands, Irian Jaya and in other parts of the country. Intensifying religious animosities between Muslims and Christians, particularly in Ambon but in other locales as well, likewise present a major challenge to Jakarta's elites intent on maintaining Indonesia's long-term political cohesion. Fighting intensified in Aceh during late 1999 and early 2000 after the Wahid government rejected the option of holding a referendum on its independence. A ceasefire negotiated with the Free Aceh Movement in May 2000 has barely quelled separatist tendencies in that province. Ambon, the capital of the

Moluccan Islands, has experienced severe internecine warfare between Christians and Muslims.[53]

The military's future status and role will be central to how these issues are resolved. Allegations of army complicity in pro-Indonesia militia activity within East Timor following the independence referendum, coupled with Jakarta's subsequent reluctance to enforce the protection of United Nations peacekeepers in the province, suggest that the Indonesian military will continue to resist any political reforms that threaten national integrity. The murder of three relief workers from the United Nations High Commission for Refugees in West Timor by local militias in September 2000 incensed Western governments and prompted US officials to threaten imposing sanctions against Indonesia.[54] It is improbable that Indonesia's political culture will transform into a liberal democracy so rapidly as to foreclose continued tensions between Jakarta and its traditional Western supporters and benefactors.

Indonesia's nation-building is further complicated by the sheer diversity of religious and cultural factions within the country, creating for the government and particularly for the military 'a deep-seated sense of insecurity, constantly fearing the effects of disintegration and general political instability which could be exploited or exacerbated by outside forces'.[55] To overcome this prospect, the 'Archipelagic Outlook' was introduced into Indonesian strategic doctrine in December 1957, and was substantially refined for incorporation into ABRI doctrine nine years later. The concept is designed to ensure that the geographic unity of the Indonesian nation is enforced through rigid vigilance in its territorial waters, and by relating to both Indonesia's neighbours and to extra-regional powers with an effective posture of national resilience and consolidation. In this sense, Indonesia relates to the outside world from an introspective frame of reference: dividing it into three concentric circles with Indonesia at the centre. The first circle includes ASEAN; the second the Southwest and South Pacific; and the third is that part of the world of most interest to ASEAN, especially Northeast Asia and South Asia.[56] Indonesia's intent is to build effective and enduring 'spider webs' of regional security cooperation within these three circles but particularly with the ASEAN states to help protect its own archipelago.[57] It is also determined to insulate its waters from foreign encroachment by building up its indigenous military capabilities and by promoting 'cooperative security' among its neighbours.

In this sense, Indonesia's strategy dovetails with those stipulations embodied in the UNCLOS framework which recognises that surrounding seas and straits are an integral component of sovereign statehood. The Indonesian navy's closure of the Sunda and Lombok Straits in September 1988, ostensibly to conduct military manoeuvres there, was intended to demonstrate Indonesian resolve to enforce its interpretation of Archipelagic Outlook applicability.[58] Yet the Soeharto government adopted a generally liberal approach to embedding the Archipelago Concept into its regional diplomacy. It negotiated no fewer than fifteen agreements and treaties with its neighbours on seabed boundary delineation including Malaysia, Singapore, Thailand, Australia and Papua New Guinea. Indonesia did so 'in the belief that "good fences make good neighbours" and the success in these boundary negotiations have been helpful in restoring confidence on the part of Indonesia's neighbours in her (sic) peaceful intentions'.[59] This philosophy has also extended to the 'traffic separation scheme' in the Strait of Malacca jointly administered by Indonesia, Malaysia and Singapore. With Soeharto's departure, the Wahid Government appeared to be emphasising a more nationalist approach to the pursuit of national maritime interests by restructuring and strengthening its naval and air support capabilities to patrol and protect the Indonesian archipelago of some 13 000 islands.[60]

The Soeharto government released two defence white papers (in 1995 and 1997) which were primarily efforts to achieve greater transparency by conveying and justifying Indonesia's national security approaches to that country's regional neighbours.[61] Apart from occasional elliptical references to the Korean Peninsula and the Spratly Islands as potential 'influences' on the Asia-Pacific security environment, neither document identifies any specific external threats that would justify Indonesian defence postures and expenditures.

At present, Indonesia is not confronting the prospect of invasion by a foreign power and is most concerned about external influences that may threaten internal 'harmony'.[62] Of particular concern are intensified expectations for Indonesia to improve its human rights practices and the influence exerted by the international financial community. Australia, for example, is regarded in many Indonesian political quarters as an irritating initiator of such pressures and a state that tends to represent US preferences for human rights reform in the region.[63] Nonetheless, at a time when the Asia-Pacific's balance of power is undergoing rapid structural change, Indonesian policy makers are paying greater attention to how regional developments will affect their own strategic thinking. The most pressing issue is ASEAN's continued ability to play a meaningful role in its strategic environment and the prospect that its inability to do so will precipitate a new Southeast Asian power vacuum. A corollary to this is a concern over what China's long-term strategic intentions in the South China Sea are and how its maritime power projection capabilities are developing.

In the interest of maintaining policy balance and avoiding excessive strategic alignment with the world's remaining superpower, Jakarta continues to emphasise that it is not the United States' strategic ally. It has refuted press rumours that the United States wanted to build military bases in Irian Jaya or Natuna to compensate for the loss of access to bases in the Philippines.[64] In deference to a strong Malaysian viewpoint, it reaffirmed its support for regional neutrality (what ASEAN has termed the Zone of Peace, Freedom and Neutrality or ZOPFAN) when Singapore offered to host selected US military operations in August 1989.[65]

In any case, various tensions continue to strain American–Indonesian relations. These include Washington's opposition to the Indonesian government's perceived recalcitrance in controlling elements of the military and pro-integrationist militias from wreaking destruction in East Timor; various human rights and intellectual copyright issues; and the perceived severity of the International Monetary Fund (IMF) reform measures US financiers drew up for sustaining Indonesia's financial liquidity during the Asian financial crisis.

All of these irritants remain a source of frustration for American military commanders. They are acutely conscious of Indonesia's geostrategic location.[66] But the US decision to suspend all military links with Indonesia on the basis of Jakarta's failure to quell militia violence in East Timor in the aftermath of the independence referendum highlights the frailty of strategic cooperation between two very different cultures experiencing difficulties with each other's respective value systems. Indonesia remains unwilling to negotiate formal alliances that involve any of the Asia-Pacific's major powers.

Jakarta did enter into a formal security agreement with Australia in December 1995. The Agreement on Maintaining Security (AMS) signed with Australia was the first formal security commitment which any Indonesian government has undertaken since gaining independence in 1948. Although not entailing an automatic obligation to defend each other from external threats, the two countries agreed 'to consult each other in the case of adverse challenges to either party or to their common security interests'.[67] From Jakarta's initial perspective, the accord with Australia was a constructive development in the country's foreign policy for several key reasons: (1) it provided an alternative outlet for Indonesia to widen the scope of its foreign and security policy beyond traditional ASEAN confines without becoming directly entwined in great power competition; (2) it sent a signal to China that Indonesia could, and would, intensify its maritime security networks to deter what Jakarta regarded to be potentially hegemonic behaviour in Southeast Asia's major sea lanes and archipelagos; and (3) it served as a confidence-building measure by reassuring Australia that Indonesia does not represent an expansionist threat in Southeast Asia or the Southwest Pacific (that is, against Papua New Guinea); and (4) by affiliating with one of the United States' closest security allies in the Asia-Pacific, it gravitated Indonesia more closely towards US security networks without requiring it to enter into a formal strategic affiliation with the United States.[68]

Ultimately, however, the AMS proved incapable of withstanding the pressures of the East Timor crisis and in September 1999, less than four years later, Indonesia's Coordinating Minister for Political and Security Affairs, Feisal Tanjung, announced that Indonesia would abrogate the AMS 'in consideration of Canberra's attitude and actions, especially those leading up to the United Nations decision to dispatch a multinational force into East Timor'. Tanjung asserted that Australia's posture was 'no longer consistent with the spirit and letter of the agreement'.[69] Although Australia's Prime Minister Howard derogated the utility of the AMS and belittled his Labor Party political opponents' consternation over its demise, Indonesia's action reflected a deep sense of Indonesian antipathy toward Australian posturing and lack of sensitivity towards Indonesia's political instability.

Indonesia's internal political stability has been further undermined by the savage effects of the Asian financial crisis on its national economy. The Indonesian rupiah was the currency most seriously affected by Asia's economic downturn in the second part of 1997, depreciating 80 per cent against the US dollar (from approximately R10500: $US1 to R17000: $US1). Although the defence budget had been increased by 17 per cent for 1998, currency depreciation and domestic inflation eroded its real increase to a level of between 30 and 40 per cent less than the amount expended in the previous year. This caused Jakarta to curtail most of its planned arms purchases and much of its military training. Shipments of Russian jet aircraft and helicopters and German submarines were postponed indefinitely or cancelled.[70]

This trend has rendered Indonesia's task of enforcing its Archipelago Outlook with its own resources over the short-term almost impossible. The country's internal political problems are now consuming the military's attention and resources, and the lack of air and naval coverage around Indonesia's critical straits emits the unintended signal that it cannot be a major strategic player in its own area of maritime interest, one that more than half of the world's merchant fleet vessels transverse. The volume of Indonesian trade that passed through Southeast Asia's major sea lanes (the straits of Malacca, Sunda and Lombok and the South China Sea) reached nearly $US64 billion in 1994; ASEAN's volume was a half trillion dollars and the total trade volume was double that of ASEAN.[71] Indonesia will remain dependent on external forces to safeguard its own trade and resource access for some time to come while it struggles to implement a new political system. Moreover, Indonesia's intra-ASEAN leadership, evident throughout the Soeharto era, is likely to continue to erode and, unless this role is assumed by other Southeast Asian states, this will further undermine the institutional capacities of this organisation.[72]

## The Philippines

Many contemporary assessments of the Philippines' national security start with the fundamental assumption that addressing external threats is less central to maintaining its security than are the tasks of resolving internal socio-political conflicts and completing a tenuous process of nation-building. Two experts on Philippines security politics have summarised this proposition: 'Internal security has remained the priority down to the 1990s, and it is precisely because the "enemy" has been within, rather than an external "other" that conflict has arisen between the security needs of state and populace'.[73] Accordingly, this argument concludes that real security in the Philippines can only be realised when the ruling oligarchy is supplanted by the 'institutionalised participation' of the country's populace. Until then, insurgency movements, rampant poverty, overall social alienation and domestic political instability will dominate the Philippines' politico-security landscape. The toppling of President Joseph Estrada in January 2001 following charges of widespread corruption and graft and his replacement by Gloria Macapagal-Arroyo, a member of yet another Philippines family political dynasty, is illustrative. This 'silent coup' only became possible when the Philippines armed forces shifted its support from one to the other, underscoring how fragile the country's democratic institutions remain well after half a century of independence.

Yet several developments are now challenging the Philippines' preoccupation with its own political identity and are sensitising Filipino leaders and the country's overall populace to their country's vulnerability to regional security trends. First, the Asian financial crisis completely undermined plans to build a credible defence program. Apart from the procurement of two logistical support ships from the United States, a few trainer jets, and some forty armoured personnel vehicles, the Philippines armed forces have experienced little force modernisation and prospects are bleak that this trend will be reversed in the near future.[74]

Second, paralysis in the Philippines' military modernisation has occurred at the same time that China has constructed installations and airstrips in the Mischief Reef area of the Spratly Islands, an area which is also claimed by the Philippines. This Chinese initiative has galvanised the Philippines into sounding the alarm over what it perceives are expansionist Chinese ambitions in the South China Sea. Apart from violating the Philippines' territorial claim to the reef, the Chinese presence represents, in the words of former Philippine Defense Secretary Orlando Mercado, 'a dagger at our underbelly'. While the reef is only 300 kilometres from the northern Philippines island of Palawan and well within the Philippines' 200 nautical mile EEZ, it is more than 1000 kilometres from China's coastline.[75]

Third, recent efforts by the Estrada Government to link the Spratly Islands dispute to the 1951 US–Philippines Mutual Defense Treaty (MDT) failed to garner support from the American policy-making community. It seemed clear that the United States is far more preoccupied with crises in Southeastern Europe, the Middle East and Northeast Asia. In addition, the negative sentiment created by the Philippines Senate's rejection of the 1991 basing renewal agreement to retain US forces at Subic Bay still lingers. While the Secretary of State in the George W. Bush Administration, Colin Powell, specifically cited Japan, South Korea and Australia during his Senate confirmation hearing, he said nothing to highlight the US–Philippines MDT, preferring instead to put it rather innocuously in terms of the United States wanting to work with its 'other allies in the region'.[76]

Without substantial US military assistance, it is unlikely that the Philippines will be able to enhance its strategic capabilities and credibility. Lacking modern fighter aircraft, naval vessels or a joint reaction force, the country has virtually no ability to project meaningful military power to defend its outer islands or EEZs. Nor are there any prospects that such components will be in place within the foreseeable future. This situation undermines the Philippines' long-held objective to avoid excessive dependence on external allies and weapons suppliers. Its Self-Reliant Defense Posture (SRDP) Program, originating in March 1994, has been riddled with special interests in the country's defence sector undermining the ability of the Armed Forces of the Philippines (AFP) to provide for even its most basic material requirements.[77] It also renders superfluous the 1998 'Six Point Defence and Security Program', emphasising crisis response and a Philippines contribution to regional peace and security.[78]

In fact, Philippines' military planners lament what they deem to be a lack of support for military modernisation by both their government and the public at large. Even as its dispute with China over Mischief Reef intensifies, the Estrada government insisted that external threats confronting the country constitute a 'potential' rather than imminent danger to national security. The question of how long the Philippines can wait to confront a 'clear and present danger' of aggression before strengthening its defences and alliances appears to be less than pressing to those special interests that currently control much of the country's purse strings and politics. Without a major change in policy direction, Manila's ability to control its own strategic destiny will remain sharply constrained for the indefinite future.

### The Future of ASEAN and Southeast Asian Security

The diversity of individual ASEAN states' security problems underscores the need for that organisation to focus less on perpetuating cosmetic unanimity and more on the security challenges faced by its various member-states. ASEAN's enlargement in April 1999 to include all ten Southeast Asian countries was designed to enhance its diplomatic and strategic influence and to allow the subregion to speak as one voice on key security issues. Coupled with the 1997 economic crisis, it actually highlighted the diversity of political systems and strategic interests within that grouping and threatened its overall cohesion.[79]

Three key challenges – each directly related to the realist-liberal debate – will be critical to ASEAN's survival and relevance as it advances into the new century. First, a new generation of Southeast Asian elites will need to be convinced that ASEAN can be responsive to their particular national interests. Second, that organisation's future viability will depend upon those elites' consideration of the transfer of at least some of their sovereign prerogatives to a stronger, transnational ASEAN. Third, any such transfer will only occur if ASEAN members are willing to monitor and influence each other's domestic approaches to political and economic stability. This would be a stark departure from normal ASEAN adherence to the principle of non-interference in each other's domestic affairs but one that is increasingly necessary if ASEAN's ministerial and committee decisions are to be translated into the national policies of its member-states.[80]

The first requirement entails ASEAN moving beyond the 'broadening' of its membership to 'deepening' its security agenda, thereby highlighting its relevance to the strategic concerns of its individual members. This means adjusting its traditional organisational identity to one more amenable to confronting problems and encouraging transparency, even at the risk of generating controversy rather than papering over very real differences in political systems, economic priorities and socio-cultural outlooks. Thailand's effort to promote 'flexible engagement' within ASEAN circles was designed to address this problem. Although rebuffed by most other member-states, the organisation did adopt a compromise approach – labelled as 'enhanced interaction' – to safeguard its time-honoured practice of 'non-interference in others' internal affairs' while authorising greater transparency and regional involvement in the economic and financial practices of each ASEAN economy.[81] This represents

**Table 5.2** Selected military capabilities in the ASEAN region

| | Total (Active) Armed Forces | Fighter Aircraft | Submarines | Main Battle Tanks (MBTs) or Light Tanks (LTs) | Surface and Patrol/Coastal Combatants |
|---|---|---|---|---|---|
| Brunei | 5 000 | — | — | 16 LTs | 3 missile craft and 6 other patrol craft |
| Cambodia | 90 000 | 19 Mig-21s | — | 150 MBTs/20+ LTs | 4 inshore/riverine patrol craft |
| Indonesia | 297 000 (25 000 in the army) | 104 including 12 F-15s & 21 A-4 Skyhawks | 2 | 355 LTs | 17 frigates (most with *Harpoon* or *Exocet* surface-to-surface missiles [SSMs]); 4 additional missile craft; 16 corvettes; 4 torpedo craft; 36 patrol craft, and coastal combatants |
| Laos | 29 100 | 12 Mig 21s | — | 30 MBTs/20 LTs | 16 Riverine patrol boats |
| Malaysia | 96 000 | 84 combat aircraft (assorted F-5E/F-5F, MiG-29s and *Hawk* ground-attack fighters) | — | 26 LTs | 4 frigates with *Exocets* or Melara SSMs; 41 patrol/coastal combatants |
| Burma | 429 000 | 47 F-7/FT-7 & 36 A-5M combat aircraft | — | 100 MBTs/105 LTs | 2 corvettes; 6 missile craft (with Chinese SSMs); approx. 60 coastal/patrol combatants |
| Philippines | 106 000 | 11 F-5A/5B combat aircraft | — | 40 LTs | 1 frigate; 60 patrol/coastal combatants (no missiles) |
| Singapore | 60 500 (incl. 39 800 conscripts) | approx. 90 F-16s 37 F-5Es/F-5Fs | 1 | 63 MBTs/350 LTs | 24 patrol/coastal combatants (6 corvettes and 6 missile craft and 12 patrol craft) |
| Thailand | 301 000 | 34 F-16s 33 F-5As/F-5Es | — | 282 MBTs/510 LTs | 1 aircraft carrier; 14 frigates; 88 patrol and coastal combatants |
| Vietnam | 484 000 | 189 combat aircraft incl. 53 Su-22s and 12 Su-27s | 2 midget subs | 1315 MBTs, approx. 620 LTs | 6 frigates; 42 patrol and coastal combatants (incl. 12 missile craft) |

*Source:* IISS, *The Military Balance 2000/2001.*

a modest but significant first step in updating the 'ASEAN Way'. The participation of ASEAN force contingents in INTERFET and its successor, the UN Transitional Administration in East Timor (UNTAET) is also encouraging.

Among the most obvious imperatives for a more 'strategically germane' ASEAN is supporting Indonesia's quest to re-establish 'national resilience' and stability. It might also endeavour to define and enforce concrete rules of non-aggression applicable to contested territory and to ethno-nationalist insurgency groups operating across borders. Working together, ASEAN elites might also aspire to defining distinctly 'Asian' models of civil society. These would be distinct from those versions they believe are often unjustifiably imposed upon them by various Western governments, non-governmental organisations (NGOs) and other self-appointed extra-regional guardians of 'human security' values.[82]

Given Southeast Asian states' sensitivity to preserving their sovereign identity and prerogatives, the second challenge to ASEAN's future relevance appears even more daunting. As intimated in chapter 1, realists argue the politics of integration has no precedent and has no chance of succeeding in the ASEAN sector or throughout Asia.[83] Liberals consider its realisation to be a critical prerequisite for the Asia-Pacific's continued regional prosperity and stability. Greater regional integration involves a restructuring of ASEAN to attain more coordination between that organisation's secretariat in Jakarta and national decision-making bodies. It also entails an agenda to integrate various ASEAN member-states' postures on regional security problems rather than merely relying upon protracted consultation and consensus-building. Substantial political barriers remain, especially for ASEAN's newer members that have yet to experience the levels of political liberalisation that are in various stages of development within the founding member-states.[84] But to opt for 'more of the same' diplomatic style is to risk defaulting ASEAN's future to the vagaries of a regional negotiation style that has thus far yielded inadequate results relative to the time and resources devoted to it.

The third and related challenge – ASEAN member-states monitoring each other's security situations and offering timely advice and selective policy intervention to those in trouble – is a highly contentious issue that has only begun to be considered within ASEAN forums.[85] This notion directly contradicts the realist notion of 'self-help' and the ASEAN legacy of non-interference in domestic affairs. These axioms, however, have become increasingly fragile as a more interdependent world evolves, complete with economic, environmental and strategic issues that defy indigenous solutions. The Asian financial crisis had a transnational 'domino effect' on regional economies that spared no ASEAN state. Indonesian forest fires and the inability or unwillingness of authorities in

Jakarta to contain their effects within their country's sovereign boundaries became a human security blight throughout peninsular Southeast Asia. The Spratly Islands dispute remains impossible for any single ASEAN state to resolve through the traditional application of force.

How Southeast Asian military outlooks and capabilities should relate to these emerging challenges is still unclear more than a decade after the end of the Cold War. More certain, however, is that ASEAN states have yet to make the conceptual transition from viewing defence as a means for defending the national interest to regarding it as a possible attribute for advancing genuine collective gains in the region. Indeed, the realist ethos of measuring perceived power balances and power vacuums remains firmly in place within the security politics of this subregion. The preferred strategic approach for most ASEAN states is to manoeuvre among those great regional and extra-regional powers that they regard as critical to shaping structural changes in the Asia-Pacific, calculating their own force levels and force doctrines within this context.

The ARF provides an obvious basis for pursuing an approach more compatible with liberalism whilst, simultaneously, affording the ASEAN states the opportunity to gauge great-power regional perceptions and intentions on a regular and systematic basis.[86] The ARF has yet to elevate the ASEAN states to the specific status of active arbiters of great power disputes, but it has gradually become the venue for more significant bilateral security negotiations between regional disputants such as that when the United States and North Korea utilised its mechanisms in Bangkok in July 2000 (see chapter 4). Although the ARF remains a cooperative security arrangement rather than a collective security or collective defence mechanism, it can encourage common codes of conduct based on ideas of cooperative security but lacks the ties to bind its affiliates to a common security outlook.[87] This book's concluding chapter advocates convergent security as a promising means to compensate for, or to overcome, these limitations.

### Australia: Strategic Perceptions and Doctrines

Australian strategic outlooks are influenced predominantly by realist calculations about size, distance, resources and orientations. These calculations have translated into this 'middle power' seeking or maintaining selective alliances to overcome its perceived vulnerabilities and to develop as a maritime trading state. Throughout the postwar era Australia has also adopted variants of 'forward defence' postures to create a shield of friendly regional powers directed towards capitalising on its great distance from most industrial power centres that could otherwise threaten it.[88] The three postwar Labor Governments (Whitlam, Hawke and Keating) implemented what could be viewed by many as a distinctly liberal security agenda, seeking to 'engage' Southeast Asia and China.[89] A small dissenting group of critical theorists argue that the forces of international change, including emerging offensive weapons technologies and unpredictable interests of traditional allies, require Australia to consider alternative geopolitical strategies such as armed neutrality, nonprovocative defence, social defence or civilian defence.[90] To date, the Australian policy establishment has rejected these alternative frameworks, insisting that Australia's area of direct military interest is inherently too extensive; that a consensus over what constitutes 'offensive' versus 'defensive' weapons is too elusive; and that alliance ties with regional security partners, particularly the United States, are essential to Australia's strategic interests.[91]

How Australia eventually resolves these contending approaches is important to overall Asia-Pacific security because this country, with the world's sixteenth largest economy and ranked among its top five commodity exporters, tends to be an activist in regional security politics and to play 'beyond its weight' by influencing the strategic perceptions of both Japan and the maritime ASEAN states. Moreover, Australia cannot escape its geography; indeed, this factor is destined to largely shape its strategic orientations. The latest Defence White Paper (released in December 2000) designates three geographic zones that determine the relative intensity of defence efforts and allocation of its strategic resources.[92] Australian policy makers are particularly aware of how political instability in Indonesia could trigger unprecedented political volatility in the Malay world to their immediate north. Yet they must 'continue their edgy walk around a disaster area closer to home than the current generation of Australians have ever known'.[93]

The prospects of Australia confronting a direct military invasion remain very low, but a destabilised Indonesia and Malayan Peninsula would generate intense economic pressures at a time when Australia is considering what the eminent geopolitical analyst Saul B. Cohen has deemed one of the most important questions in its history, 'not whether Australia *is* Asian but how it can best adjust to *being* Asian'.[94] This remains true notwithstanding Prime Minister Howard's politically motivated claim that Asians must accept Australia's heritage and its Western culture.[95]

Strategically, this adjustment towards Asia will entail Australian defence planners reconciling their traditional preferences for buffer zones and American security guarantees with region-centric defence postures, balancing both approaches. What will be required is a judicious integration of realist and liberal postulates into a strategically coherent doctrine that will allow Australia to become 'more Asian' without losing its politico-cultural identity. The major risk that Australia runs is that it will become geopolitically subservient to the larger Asia-Pacific powers in the process. How Australia has faced this challenge over the past decade and how it might do so over the next ten to fifteen years will be discussed below.

## Background

As the strategic hub of the Southwest Pacific or 'Australasian' subregion, Australia views greater Asia both opportunistically and apprehensively.[96] It has embraced the Asian marketplace over the past three decades as the key to its own economic future.[97] To underwrite this economic process, the Hawke and Keating Governments, with the tutelage of Foreign Minister Gareth Evans, embraced a foreign policy of 'comprehensive engagement'. This posture enmeshed Australia's regional future with that of the ASEAN member-states.[98]

Yet Australia remains prone to view the region through a realist lens. Its first foreign policy white paper released in 1997, entitled *In the National Interest*, noted that rapid regional growth enabled many Asian states to increase their military expenditure and to focus on protecting offshore territories and natural resources. If regional instability and conflict were to intensify over arms races and resulting security dilemmas, conditions might arise where Australia could thus become subject to acts of 'external coercion' designed to compromise its independent decision-making or to exploit its substantial resources.[99]

Even with the Asian financial crisis at least temporarily slowing the rate of defence spending in most Asian countries, Australia maintains substantial defence for a country with approximately 19.2 million inhabitants. In 1999 it spent approximately $US7.775 billion on defence and plans to increase defence spending by an average of about 3 per cent per annum over the next decade. By comparison, Singapore, ASEAN's biggest defence spender, spent $US4.696 billion in 1999, slightly above the levels it spent in 1997 and 1998.[100] Apart from Singapore, none of the ASEAN states approach the technological standards of the Australian Defence Force's (ADF) defence systems and none can begin to field the ADF's diversity of force assets.[101] Australia's defence capabilities provide what one naval analyst has aptly labelled as an 'adjacent force projection' capability: an ability to operate effectively in intense combat situations at long distances against a moderate regional threat.[102] Furthermore Australia relies on substantial land-based air defence capabilities deployed in the north and northwest sectors of the country to defend the maritime passages which are critical in providing the strategic depth needed to protect its major population centres.[103]

If Australia wishes to defend all of its vast territory effectively it has little choice other than to deploy this type of force. If its contiguous EEZs are included, Australia is responsible for defending approximately 10 per cent of the earth's surface. This includes the distance between the Cocos Islands which are located approximately 1750 kilometres north-west of Perth to the Great Barrier Reef and down to the Tasman Sea in the east – a total land area of 7.68 million square kilometres and 1.85 million square nautical miles.[104]

This formidable geographic purview raises the obvious question of where the strategic priorities for the ADF lie, given that no modern military establishment is able to allocate unlimited funding support for every desirable mission. The Australian Defence Department's 2000 Defence White Paper stipulates the following hierarchy:

• Ensure the defence of Australia and its direct approaches;
• Foster the security of Australia's immediate neighbourhood;
• Promote stability and cooperation in Southeast Asia;
• Support strategic stability in the wider Asia-Pacific region;
• Support global security.[105]

These criteria collectively signalled a conceptual departure from the 'defence-in-depth' posture of Paul Dibb's *Review of Australia's Defence Capabilities* prepared for the Hawke Government in 1986, and the subsequent *Defence of Australia 1987* White Paper. In that posture, an adversary would be confronted with increasingly formidable defence layers the closer it came to Australia's shores – from intelligence and surveillance through naval and air patrols far out to sea to highly mobile rapid deployment ground forces backed by air support if the enemy actually reached Australian shores.[106] By the turn of the century Australia's defence planners had pushed Australia's defence lines beyond the 'air–sea gap' defined by these two documents to include the arc of islands to Australia's north and east that otherwise could serve as bases from which either a major attack on Australia or limited incursions against that country could be launched.[107]

This gradual shift from defence-in-depth to a more 'proactive' strategic posture signalled the ascendancy of a realist posture favoured by the Department of Defence over the institutionalist orientation of comprehensive engagement favoured by the Department of Foreign Affairs and Trade. The Department of Defence was increasingly concerned by what it viewed as a possible 'China threat', by the possible emergence of a region more strategically hostile to Australia and by what it regarded as a need to revive the US alliance if Australia were to ensure its access to emerging defence technologies.[108]

After taking power in March 1996 the Howard Government moved quickly to convey its belief that 'Australia's defence does not begin at [the] coastline'. Thousands of Australian personnel subsequently trained with substantial elements of the American Pacific Command in the March 1997 *Tandem Thrust* joint amphibious exercise, an operation described by the Defence Minister as being directed towards 'contingency response operations in the Pacific area'.[109] Australia also continued to conduct a substantial number of military exercises with other regional security partners (see table 5.3). Although the Defence Department subsequently denied that Australia was returning to the forward defence posture prominent in Australian strategic thinking and planning throughout the Cold War, its 1997 Strategic Review confirmed that Australia's strategic focus had 'expanded to cover the whole Asia-Pacific' and that China's growing military power would be an 'important new factor in our strategic environment'.[110]

The 2000 Defence White Paper attempted to restore a sense of geographic balance to what had become by 1996–97 a de facto Australian commitment to pursue forward defence missions on the tenuous assumption that any US strategic behaviour in the region was fundamentally in line with its own strategic interests. A more cautious Australian posture emerged in this document, prioritising 'strategic stability' in the wider Asia-Pacific region through the avoidance of great-power confrontation. As one of Australia's most respected journalists noted, the White Paper 'probably terminated' the old debate about 'forward versus continental defence' by embracing a dual strategy of high technology acquisition and maintenance via alliance affiliation with the United States combined with a mobile landforce for military operations in its own neighbourhood.[111]

Southeast Asia was viewed with a somewhat uncharacteristic liberal tendency for the Howard Government as a potential 'resilient regional community that can cooperate to prevent the intrusion of hostile external powers and resolve peacefully any problems that may arise between the region'.[112] Translated more literally, Australia had supplanted the unabashed forward defence posture that it had championed only three to four years earlier with a local defence strategy that depended upon China and the United States avoiding direct conflict on a region-wide basis for its own credibility.

Early indications were that at least part of this outlook coincided with that held by the incoming Bush Administration as Secretary of State Colin Powell expressed a desire to avoid conflict with the Chinese over Taiwan 'to encourage others who [have] the capacity to act' in defusing local contingencies and to 'coordinate' the United States' own policies towards Indonesia in conjunction with Australia's.[113] Concerns lingered among various Australian observers about the United States' insistence to move abroad with development of its ballistic missile defence programs, alienating China in the process and over US expectations that the

**Table 5.3** Australian Defence Force: combined exercise partners, 1992–93 to 1996–97

| | 1992–93 | | 1993–94 | | 1994–95 | | 1995–96 | | 1996–97 | |
| | No. | % | No. | % | No. | % | No. | % | No. | % |
|---|---|---|---|---|---|---|---|---|---|---|
| ASEAN | 17 | 24.6 | 26 | 32.9 | 37 | 38.1 | 45 | 41.7 | 47 | 42.7 |
| United States | 22 | 31.9 | 33 | 41.8 | 28 | 28.9 | 24 | 22.2 | 22 | 20 |
| New Zealand | 21 | 30.4 | 12 | 15.2 | 24 | 24.7 | 23 | 21.3 | 25 | 22.7 |
| Papua New Guinea/ Southwest Pacific | 2 | 2.9 | 4 | 5.1 | 2 | 2.1 | 3 | 2.7 | 5 | 4.6 |
| Other | 7 | 10.2 | 4 | 5.0 (approx.) | 6 | 6.2 | 13 | 12.1 | 11 | 10 |
| Total | 69 | 100 | 79 | 100 | 97 | 100 | 108 | 100 | 110 | 100 |

*Source*: Adapted from Department of Defence Supplementary Submission to the Joint Standing Committee on Foreign Affairs, Defence and Trade, *Australia and ASEAN: Managing Change* (1998), p. 194.

Australians remain a loyal and 'involved' ally in supporting distinctly American national security interests in the Asia-Pacific region. These apprehensions were underlined with reports that the United States was reinforcing its intelligence presence at the Pine Gap joint installation to watch Chinese naval developments and that this base would be a key nerve centre for any US NMD.[114] By mid-2001 Australia's Labor Party, anticipating an election win by the end of that year, was seriously questioning American missile defence strategy and Australia's future role in supporting it. Labor policy analysts were deeply concerned that the Bush Administration's preoccupation with such a defence system could destabilise regional security by alienating China and undercutting international arms control precedents.[115]

### Reconciling Realist and Liberal Approaches in Australian Security Policy: Key Factors

The predominant reasoning and tone of the Howard Government's strategic thinking as it assumed power was unmistakably realist. This was modified somewhat by the growing realisation during its first term of office that Australia's regional security is also shaped favourably by its participation in the various multilateralist agendas and venues emerging in the Asia-Pacific. With the outbreak of the East Timor crisis, however, Howard appeared to revert to his original realist disposition. In the interview for *The Bulletin* noted above, he propagated what became subsequently (and perhaps unfairly) labelled 'The Howard Doctrine' – envisioning Australia as a 'deputy' peacekeeping agent in the Asia-Pacific region for underwriting the United States' preferred vision of a global order. As a Western country with Western interests located in Asia, the Prime Minister surmised, Australia should be less conscious of cultivating 'special relationships' with its Asian neighbours 'at all costs' and more intent on pursuing its own interests and values.[116] This view was, moreover, basically compatible with traditional alliance rationales: the United States expects its allies to take the lead in regional conflicts where 'major American interests are not involved',[117] a notion reiterated by Colin Powell's testimony more than a year later.

Howard was nevertheless forced to modify his new 'doctrine' within days of enunciating it. Denying that he had actually used the term 'deputy' during his interview with the journalist, the Prime Minister insisted that his government remained 'deeply committed' to the development and democratisation of Indonesia and of other Southeast Asian states. He further indicated that Australia sought to 'act in concert with friendly nations within our region' to achieve common strategic objectives. But he remained steadfast in the view that Australia must deal with

Asia on its own terms, although it should not 'impose our views on other countries'. Opponents accused Howard of using the East Timor crisis to vindicate a sense of Australian triumphalism and to back up its own, unique regional identity with a more robust national defence capability. Nor, they concluded, did the Prime Minister link Australia's new-found East Timor peacekeeping commitment to any larger foreign or strategic policy 'grand design'. According to these critics, the danger of this posture is that if Asians are confronted with the image of a more assertive, realist Australia, they will turn against that country.[118]

The evolution of Sino–Australian relations during 1996–97 is illustrative. China was successful in tempering Canberra's rhetoric on the 'reinvigoration' of the Australian–American alliance by lashing out at what it characterised as Australia's pursuit of an outmoded Cold War alliance strategy designed to contain Beijing. It argued that if Australia remained the United States' 'southern anchor' in the region, Australia could not be regarded as a legitimate Asian state.[119] This policy line was directed toward what China knew would be relatively sympathetic ASEAN ears; if Australia was pursuing what the Southeast Asians regarded as abrasive realist strategies at the expense of their own multilateral regional initiatives, how could it expect to be regarded as supporting the 'ASEAN Way' or even as a 'genuine' Asian country?

Chinese pressure was instrumental in compelling Australian diplomacy to revisit comprehensive engagement. Part of this adjustment was to establish Canberra's independence from traditional non-Asian allies. It thus demurred from supporting the American and British boycott of the new China-appointed legislature in Hong Kong during the 1 July 1997 changeover from British to Chinese rule. Australia also dissented from US and West European condemnation of China's human rights practices at the UN Human Rights Commission. Beijing 'rewarded' Australia with increased imports of Australian wool and iron ore.

From China's perspective, the point had been made effectively: Australia could not expect to have the best of both worlds – a closer alliance with America based on containing Chinese power trends possibly inimical to its own long-term strategic interests while simultaneously cultivating Chinese trade and favours under the guise of constructive engagement or regional interdependence. As the Clinton Administration moved towards solidifying its own engagement posture towards China during 1997–98, the pressure on Australia to make hard choices between realist and liberal postures waned temporarily. But the issue is bound to be revisited on a future occasion when Sino–American tensions intensify over a particular regional security issue. Future differences between Washington and Beijing over the political status of Taiwan present the most likely example of Australia's foreign policy dilemma in this regard.[120] Australia's political and logistical support (via Pine Gap) for an American national missile defence system also ranks high among those factors that could exacerbate Sino–Australian relations. Canberra's backing of the NMD could negate whatever confidence-building value the 2000 Defence White Paper had that Australian troops would not be committed to military ventures beyond its own neighbourhood except in peacekeeping operations. Australia would be viewed by Beijing as contributing directly to US regional and global capabilities targeted against Chinese strategic deterrence assets.[121]

Ultimately, Australia's future strategic influence will be determined by how well it reads major power strategic interests and postures – most importantly Chinese and American – and how it tailors creative and relevant policy responses. If constructive engagement is to be pursued successfully, China will need to be convinced that its interests are best served by moving towards greater multilateral cooperation with other regional actors. If close alliance relations with the United States are to be maintained, Australia must be sensitive to appearing too intimately aligned with American interests and strategies. However, it must balance preservation of its strategic independence with a sustained and consistent encouragement of the United States to continue its security presence in the region. By doing so, it will underwrite ASEAN's support for such a US role and facilitate the prospect that China may eventually accept multilateral security politics as a better means for achieving regional stability than great power competition.

Over the short term (2001–05), Australia is likely to confront its most pressing strategic challenges in Southeast Asia and the Southwest Pacific. The need to maintain a stable relationship with Indonesia looms as the most immediate problem. The dispatch of an Australian-led peace-enforcement operation, INTERFET, to East Timor after sustained pro-Indonesia militia violence there confirmed that Canberra would play a key role in monitoring the ongoing transition of that former Indonesian province to an independent state. This same sense of responsibility was cultivated among Australian policy makers after Indonesia declined to allow 'an extended period of conciliation-building autonomy' between pro-independence and pro-Indonesian factions in East Timor. Indonesian President Habibie insisted that a referendum be held almost immediately after rejecting Prime Minister Howard's suggestion (made in a December 1998 letter to Habibie) that the former option be pursued. But Australia was prepared to intervene militarily in the situation only with Indonesia's acquiescence and with UN authorisation. Doing otherwise would have been 'tantamount to declaring war' against Indonesia during East Timor's transition to an independent state: 'an option no responsible [Australian] government could have contemplated'.[122]

It is expected that Australia will need to allocate substantial economic and military resources to ensure that reliable infrastructures are put into place for East Timor's national governance and development.[123] While Indonesia belatedly authorised the presence of the peacekeeping force, the ensuing nationalistic rhetoric emanating from Jakarta suggests that increasingly the foundations of the bilateral relationship are being questioned by key sectors of the Indonesian polity. Indonesia's continuing resentment of Western 'interference' in its domestic affairs coupled with a variety of internal political struggles have combined to make the East Timor issue a potent source of anti-Australian sentiment within Jakarta.[124]

Illustrative was the aforementioned Indonesian renunciation of the 1995 Australia–Indonesia AMS in September 1999.[125] This agreement arguably provided a potential framework for developing bilateral relations within a liberal context via regular consultations, increased transparency and expanded confidence-building. Its collapse highlighted the nascent tensions in Australia's policy towards Indonesia: the need to accommodate the latter's longer-term economic growth and rising political influence in Southeast Asia through strategic cooperation while simultaneously projecting the need for substantive democratic reform within that state. Australia's ability to manage these tensions in the wake of the East Timor crisis will be crucial in determining the future stability of its relationship with Jakarta and other ASEAN member-states.

Over the longer term (to the year 2015), Australia faces two related, major strategic challenges: (1) relating to Northeast Asia as an effective 'middle power'; and (2) maintaining sufficient military and strategic influence to play a meaningful security role in the Asia-Pacific region. The first objective is primarily a diplomatic mission; the second involves problems of military high technology and sustaining viable alliance relations with the United States.

*Australia's Middle-Power Strategy In Northeast Asia*

As an important diplomatic actor and 'middle power' in the region, Australia may be well positioned to facilitate strategic stability in Northeast Asia. Several factors relating to the realist-liberal debate underlie this proposition.

Australia has cultivated strong and enduring bilateral relations and common interests with both Japan and South Korea for a number of years. In a 'realist' context, Australia and Japan share a postwar legacy as the United States' two closest allies in the northern and southern parts of the Pacific theatre of operations. Their 1976 Basic Treaty of Friendship and Cooperation set the context for their extensive bilateral political ties. In August 1997 the two countries forged a 'Partnership Agenda' further underwriting their relationship.[126] Both are highly dependent upon international trade and are vulnerable to shifting patterns of the international political economy. Both Australian and Japanese policy makers, however, have elected to keep their trade problems with the United States separate from their strategic relations with their most important ally.

In regard to Australia–ROK strategic relations, South Koreans retain warm memories of Australians due to Australia's participation in the defence of their country during the Korean War. More recently, Australia has lobbied extensively for North Korean compliance with the Nuclear Non-Proliferation Treaty and it resumed normalised ties with the DPRK in May 2000. It contributed $A3 million in 1994 and $A5 million in 1996 via the KEDO to costs of the construction of two light-water nuclear reactors in the DPRK. That contribution had totalled $A17.9 million by November 2000.[127] In July 1996 inaugural joint Australian–ROK political-military talks were conducted in Seoul, the same year in which a similar dialogue commenced between Australia and Japan.

Increasingly, a second factor has impacted these heretofore realist by-products of the US Pacific alliance network. Australia views these bilateral dialogues as instruments of institutionalist diplomacy that complement rather than compete against emerging multilateral security venues in the region.[128] Australian policy makers therefore recognise that a case can be made that the realist and liberal paradigms must complement each other if the full advantages of these evolving relationships are to be realised. The most important security-related stipulation found in the Australia–Japan Partnership Agenda, for example, is Article 14, dealing with 'Regional Strategic and Security Cooperation'. The concepts stipulated in the first section of Article 14 reflect the core of the initiative's strategic significance and merits citation in full:

> 14 (a): The Governments of Australia and Japan, in light of the recent re-affirmation of their respective security relationships with the United States, and in joint recognition of the vital contribution the United States makes to underpinning the security of the Asia-Pacific region, will work together to sustain the United States' important regional role. This will be achieved through each country's alliance with the United States and by supporting the constructive participation of the United States in multilateral security dialogues.

Australian and Japanese policy makers are thus mutually committed to two major policy approaches concerning Asia-Pacific regional security: (1) a continuing US presence is vital if regional security is to be realised and sustained; and (2) in each instance alliance viability is directly related to the necessary strengthening of multilateral security as a key component of the Asia-Pacific regional security framework. Indeed, the remainder of Article 14 links the process of multilateral-directed alliance politics with the strengthening of the ARF in areas of confidence-building, preventive diplomacy and arms control.

The third factor emanates from the two already discussed – Australia's realist bilateral legacy in Northeast Asia and the convergence of the realist-liberal paradigms there as a precondition for successful multilateralism. This factor relates to how the Australian–Japanese security dyad could play an increasingly decisive role in sustaining American strategic engagement in Asia. In this sense, Australia may be able to apply its experience with structuring bilateral dialogues as instruments of strategic reassurance, rather than of alliance or deterrence, to contribute to positive regime-building efforts. More specifically, Australia has a long-established and well-earned reputation as a credible player in diplomacy. In this role, Australian energy and resources might be directed towards supporting such Japanese initiatives as the Tokyo Forum, which convened in 1998 to explore prospects for complete nuclear disarmament.[129] The findings of the Canberra Commission, a group of independent experts convened by the Keating Government in 1995 to explore the same question, could be employed as a precedent for addressing Northeast Asian-specific military issues.[130]

### The High Technology Dimension[131]

The 'Revolution in Military Affairs' (RMA) is assuming an increasingly important role in shaping contemporary alliance politics. As Paul Dibb has argued in his seminal article on the subject as it applies to the Asia-Pacific region, sophisticated RMA remains well beyond the reach of most regional defence establishments.[132] Australia must be a partial exception to this precept for at least three reasons. First, as a middle power, it must be able to pursue 'proactive' strategies designed to shorten conflicts and to compensate for the force imbalance that a future regional adversary could establish against Australia. Second, it must, with such a force imbalance, achieve high levels of joint force integration and inter-operability. Third, it must exploit information technologies to use its limited force capabilities with maximum effectiveness.[133]

Despite its often acclaimed objective of achieving 'defence self-reliance' against most tangible regional contingencies, Australia lacks the economies of scale and a sufficiently formidable, indigenous, high technology base to fulfil these three objectives on its own. Indeed, the Australian government conducted a major review during 2000 to identify a 'new mix' for its defence force structure after concluding that the country could not afford to maintain its present level of high capability strike systems well into this century.[134] The American alliance provides Canberra with a conduit through which these objectives can be largely met.[135] A key consideration is to what extent will ongoing US force doctrine and capabilities allow the US to export RMA to Australia between now and 2015?

Different warfighting styles and priorities adopted by US and Australian military doctrines complicate this RMA transfer process. The Americans prefer to apply overwhelming force through firepower and strategic manoeuvre while Australia tends to achieve military objectives through economy of effort over longer periods of time. It is most likely that Australia will focus on assimilating those RMA capabilities that will allow the ADF to participate in a medium-intensity to high-intensity conflict as part of an international coalition force led by the United States, and to facilitate the ADF's inter-operability with US forces under such circumstances. The ADF will also absorb those technologies most relevant to defending the 'sea–air gap' dividing Australia from Indonesia and other northern neighbours. Major priority will thus be assigned to developing surveillance, reconnaissance, and intelligence capabilities that enhance overall command and control systems directing 'highly mobile, dispersed, joint operations'. Specific force multipliers would include satellite and advanced AWACs, and technical intelligence systems (including signals intelligence and high-resolution satellite imaging, electronic warfare systems and advanced radar and sonar systems).[136]

Although by no means inclusive, three additional 'high military technology' components appear critical to future operations by the Australian–American alliance in Asia-Pacific theatres of operation. In the absence of region-wide arms control breakthroughs in controlling the spread of weapons of mass destruction (WMDs), TMD systems will become increasingly relevant to defending against state-controlled WMD and various ballistic or cruise missile capabilities emanating from Northeast Asia (China and North Korea) and South Asia (India and Pakistan).[137] The Pine Gap Joint Defence Facility has already been cited as a key link in any NMD system developed by the George W. Bush Administration between 2005 and 2015. The Howard Government has reportedly budgeted funding to establish a US space-based ground station for a new infrared satellite detection system (SBIRS) to support NMD. Australia's Defence Science and Technology Organisation (DSTO) has been participating in NMD/TMD-related research with the US Defense Department's Ballistic Missile Defense Organization since 1997. At the time of writing, however, the United States has not formally asked Australia to be a full-fledged NMD collaborator. As noted previously, the Australian Labor Party has expressed serious reservations about NMD's value as a contributing element to Asia-Pacific peace and stability and about its implications for precipitating nuclear proliferation in the region. Opinion is divided over the actual effects a rejection to assist American NMD efforts would have on the alliance.[138]

A second component, more directly related to RMA, is enhanced and time-relevant intelligence and operational capabilities that can be applied over a broad geographic circumference. As intimated above, defending Australia's maritime and air approaches against hostile forces at distant points in the Indian Ocean (proximate to its offshore territories) or in the South Pacific may well be dependent upon its ability to apply these types of capabilities at the outset of crisis.[139] Its access to such technology also allows Australia to operate more effectively in a regional strategic framework extending beyond strictly bilateral alliance functions. Australian forces conduct regular and extensive joint military exercises with New Zealand, Indonesia, Malaysia, Singapore and Thailand and more intermittent ones with Brunei and the Philippines.[140] They also drill with Japanese and South Korean forces under American command during the biennial Rim of the Pacific (RIMPAC) maritime exercises in Hawaii and the Cope Thunder joint air exercise in Alaska.

But the quality and quantity of the Australian–American bilateral strategic planning, intelligence sharing, and consultative mechanisms far exceeds any commensurate set of relationships which Australia has with its regional neighbours. As the Australian Defence Department's 1997 *Australia's Strategic Policy* bluntly concluded: 'our alliance with the United States is by any measure our most important strategic relationship ... a complex strategic relationship which operates at many levels and in many ways'.[141]

The third element, again reflecting Australia's growing concern with RMA, is more secure military communication operations. The prospect of crippling even the most sensitive US computer systems as a precursor to launching a strike against the United States has been discussed extensively in recent years.[142] Much less discussion has been directed towards securing Australia against such a contingency; one classified government report (the Dudgeon Report) has presumably explored options for strengthening protection of its national information infrastructure.[143] Until mid-1998 there was little evidence that extensive ANZUS coordination in these RMA areas had occurred.

This planning gap was addressed by US Secretary of Defense William Cohen and his counterpart, Australian Defence Minister Ian McLachlan, during the July 1998 Australia–United States Ministerial Talks (AUSMIN) in Sydney. An alliance Defence Acquisitions Committee was created to coordinate interoperability in areas such as submarine warfare, airborne early warning and control and combat aircraft operations. The AUSMIN communique underscored the centrality of the 'knowledge edge' to future alliance military operations.[144]

*Debate About Future Alliance Policy and Regional Security Approaches*

Despite ANZUS enjoying a wide consensus of support among both American and Australian policy planners, defence policy debates in Australia have recently intensified relative to alliance relations. The major concern is how Australia's strategic interests should be identified and projected at a time of increasing tensions between China and the United States. Related to this issue is how Australia should project its security interests in Southeast Asia at a time when China is exerting greater influence in that subregion and in light of the recent political turmoil experienced by Indonesia. The Australian Defence Department has adhered to the criterion that the 'lead time' for Australia to identify a serious regional threat is between ten and fifteen years.[145] Issues that challenge Australian strategic planners and portend a more vigorous public discussion of Australia's defence priorities and strategies include: how Australia is to manage the possibility of being drawn into a conflict between China and the United States over Taiwan; how to respond to further internal instability in its near northern 'arc of crisis' (Indonesia, Papua New Guinea and the fragile states of the Southwest Pacific); and how to deal with so-called 'wild card' threats such as massive refugee influxes, and the growing Islamic influence of politics in the Malay states. A major question increasingly confronting Australian policy makers is the extent to which they can succeed in 'bridging' their Asian policy priorities with the American alliance. Australians can take some comfort that Washington has been willing to work with both Indonesia and Australia to resolve the Asian financial crisis and to restore economic growth to this part of the world. Opinions may vary on the tactics underscoring the International Monetary Fund (IMF) approach; however, as long as the principals agree on the overall policy objectives, there are strong prospects that the goodwill shared by these two allies did contribute substantially to a resolution of the region's economic crisis.

It would be useful to reflect upon how the Howard Government's announced determination to 'reinvigorate' the American alliance had affected that arrangement. The alliance agenda appears to have remained fairly consistent, despite the rapid forces of change transpiring in the region. It is not clear, therefore, that it is in actual need of fundamental repair. The two allies' geostrategic compatibilities as Pacific maritime powers are self-evident; what incompatibilities there are appear more related to each country's strategic circumstances than to any obvious problems in the bilateral relationship. For example, while the United States was initially reluctant to contribute substantial resources to support the Australian peacekeeping operation in East Timor, Washington explicitly expressed the need for the Indonesian military to respect the independence vote and endorsed Australia's leadership role in the multinational force.

Washington's reluctance to contribute direct military assistance to the East Timor operation is understandable when it is recalled that the bulk of the United States' energy and resource investment in the Asia-Pacific is directed towards Northeast Asia's industrial powers (Japan and South Korea) rather than towards the sparsely populated and relatively distant Southwest Pacific littorals. Australia could never be designated as one of the world's central chokepoints, and yet Australia's level of access to American decision-making channels, technological infrastructures and social structures is remarkable for a country of its size. Along with Britain and Canada, it may be confidently asserted that Australia truly does enjoy the status of being among the United States' closest – if not necessarily the most geostrategically crucial – allies. While the Whitlam Government may have reviewed the need for the alliance in the early 1970s and the Keating Government may have attempted to balance it by carving out a 'role' for Australia in Asia during the early 1990s, the centrality of the alliance has persevered. If Australia is increasingly an Asia-Pacific 'middle power' – and there are many good arguments that support this assertion – it is doubtful that any bilateral relationship it develops with a particular Asian partner will surpass the cultural affinity and deeply embedded heritage of mutual interest and collaboration which remain the hallmarks of Australian–American relations.[146] This fundamental reality was what John Howard was endeavouring to underscore in justifying Australia's military intervention in East Timor. Unfortunately, the style adopted to make the point unnecessarily undermined the equally important policy principle that Australia needs to assimilate and respect Asian viewpoints as these are integral to the formulation and projection of its overall foreign policy interests and behaviour.

Perhaps if there is any 'crisis' in Australian–US security relations, it is that much of what is deemed to be worthwhile about that alliance is assumed but is hardly ever explicated in the wider public domain. Until the East Timor crisis, only those people implacably and obviously committed to the alliance, or those incessantly opposed to it, tended to discuss its ongoing relevance and even then these protagonists could only expect to attract a very small audience of policy elites and observers. This created a misleading image of bland indifference at best or, more seriously, one of banal irrelevance. Events leading up to Australia's peacekeeping commitment to its immediate north, however, have prompted wider public discussion in Australia on the meaning and continued utility of the alliance – a development that should augur well for its continuation over the long term.

In reality, Australia is hardly the compliant or completely dependent American ally that alliance detractors have traditionally suggested has been the case. It could be better characterised as a state that works assiduously and with some effectiveness towards achieving mutual Australian–American security interests. ANZUS contributes to strategic reassurance in an Asia-Pacific region that lacks an immediate, overarching regional threat but which also understandably seeks a long-term consensus on a future regional security order. For Australia, it is a relationship where the benefits still clearly outweigh the potential risks and actual costs. For America, Australia offers a similar, albeit dynamically evolving, culture with a common frame of geopolitical reference. The two countries share a heritage of communion in war and an affinity for promoting democratic institutions in peace. Collectively, these factors make the alliance largely immune to the relatively minor policy differences that often impede relations between other states less trusting of each other. In the present geopolitical climate of international uncertainty, Washington could ask for no more, but Australia must work harder to make the Americans understand why Australia should expect no less.

### Conclusion: The Viability of Multilateral Strategies

Recent initiatives by ASEAN and Australia to implement cooperative security policies represent a viable test case for assessing the future of multilateralism as an instrument for managing Asia-Pacific security. ASEAN by itself, or in its ARF context, hardly resembles a fully fledged 'security community'.[147] War between ASEAN member-states is not totally unthinkable; military build-ups, although temporarily impeded by economic crisis, are still planned; ASEAN's 'code of conduct' for respecting each other's domestic political systems falls short of constituting a formal and compelling framework for institutional allegiance; and ASEAN's attempts to engineer Southeast Asian economic integration have been visibly tepid. It has had little real effect in realising economic interdependence or in solidifying political amalgamation. ASEAN has, at best (to paraphrase Sheldon Simon), become 'an anarchy of friends but no more than an anarchy'.[148]

Asia's larger powers are moving quickly to fill the void by pressing their own agendas in the subregion. China has complemented its aggressive South China Sea posture with exercising restraint in devaluing the renminbi during the Asian financial crisis. The latter move has helped foster an image of a more mature China underwriting regional stability. Japan countered with the Miyazawa Plan, intended to extend $US30 billion of financial assistance and trade benefits to the ASEAN region. Both moves compared favourably to the American hardline policies underlying the stringent IMF reform packages; they signalled a determination by Beijing and Tokyo to compete in a very realist fashion for influence throughout Southeast Asia.[149]

Australia's sense of affinity with ASEAN has likewise become increasingly ambiguous. The 'Western' aspects of its political culture favour a legalistic approach to diplomacy. Accordingly, Australia is less comfortable than are Southeast Asian societies with deriving obligation through informal consultations and practices, that is, the 'ASEAN Way'. Australia has sought depth and relevance in its own approach to multilateralism that remains dissynchronous to the ASEAN approach, frustrating nominal liberal-institutionalists in Canberra. Australian analysts have come to see the 'ASEAN Way' as nothing more than an alternative style for imposing agendas indecipherable from traditional realist preoccupations with power and narrow interests.

By the mid-1990s this Australian sense of disillusionment translated into Canberra's gravitation back towards bilateralism as its preferred *modus operandi* for security interests in the region. As Michael Leifer has observed, the 1995 Australian–Indonesian security treaty could be interpreted as a tacit lack of faith in ASEAN's strategic relevance by two of ARF's most important founding members. Indonesia found ASEAN's informal code of conduct to be too constraining for its own sense of status and weight, and ARF too inclusive to allow it much leverage relative to that grouping's larger powers. Australia had become disillusioned over ASEAN's tendency to shape ARF's diplomatic identity and agendas. The Indonesian treaty, along with a reiteration of Australia's strategic ties with the United States (also frustrated with ASEAN's centrality within the ARF and with ARF's lack of formal infrastructures) was the predictable response.[150] Now that the realist calculations that instigated that particular bilateral security have proven to be no more resilient, ASEAN's future relevance appears less bleak. It may, however, rest upon whether its member-states and their 'Western' affiliates can find a middle ground between the former's consensus not to commit to institutionalised norms and the latter's insistence on focusing upon concrete objectives and on specific processes to fulfil them.

Furthermore, developments in East Timor have led to a probable long-term Australian military commitment to a protracted multilateral peacekeeping operation fraught with potential strategic drawbacks. Australia's prospects of becoming accepted as a full member of any Asian 'community' have become almost nil for some time to come because it has alienated Southeast Asia's largest and most influential state to the extent that the AMS has now been abrogated. Its current diplomatic weakness and its inability to fund the levels of military capability it would need to compensate for this situation leave it with no other option but to rely ultimately on the US alliance and its extended deterrence guarantees. This condition affords Canberra scarce leverage to promote multilateralism throughout the region until positive linkages with its northern neighbour can be renewed.

The abrogation of the AMS has barely made a dent in what is still a prevalent trend of bilateral power balancing in Southeast Asia, tending to validate the realist prognosis for the subregion's strategic destiny. China's attempts to enhance its strategic ties with some ASEAN states (particularly Burma and Thailand), combined with its efforts to isolate others on key issues (for example, the Philippines in the Spratly Islands dispute), reaffirms Beijing's preference to deal bilaterally with Southeast Asian actors on key issues while using multilateral fora to renounce lingering American collective defence postures in the area. In these circumstances, realists can assert with confidence that Beijing is unlikely to embrace institutionalist agendas over the foreseeable future. The realist end-game of an uneasy power equilibrium is hardly appealing. If the liberal approach is to ultimately prevail in Southeast Asia and to be revived within Australian policy-making circles, multilateral options must be made more relevant.

Three key challenges need to be met if this is to transpire.[151] First, bilateral security arrangements need to be implemented less as power balancing exercises and more as steps designed to achieve greater security and cooperation among both the bilateral participants and other subregional actors. Australia, in particular, must sell its continued alliance affiliation with the United States in this manner or continue to endure the criticism of Malaysia, and the tacit scepticism of other ASEAN powers, that it is perpetuating 'Western' influence and interests in Southeast Asia at their expense. It must continue to pursue and strengthen its comprehensive set of low-key but critically transparent bilateral political-military dialogues with ASEAN states and other Asia-Pacific sovereignties.

Second, if multilateralism is to succeed in Southeast Asia, the ASEAN states must devise a basis for Northeast Asian concerns to be represented within the ARF. At present, ASEAN diplomats have failed to cope with the core strategic issues shaping Northeast Asia's security environment.[152] These issues include but are not limited to Korean reunification, a possible Sino–Japanese security rivalry, and prospects of a new arms race involving WMDs and the deployment of new offensive and defensive missile systems. According to one analyst, ASEAN needs 'to cede a measure of control over the ARF to devote more attention to Northeast Asia's security concerns, which are the most intractable and serious in the region. Otherwise the Forum runs the risk of losing its institutional pre-eminence and its relevance for the larger powers of the Asia-Pacific'.[153]

Third, multilateralism is not synonymous with the politics of multipolarity. It is important not to assign short-term power balancing strategies, however essential, greater weight than long-term multilateral objectives. Three issues illustrate the tendency by the region's great powers to assign greater emphasis to the politics of power balancing than to promote regionalism and multilateralism. These are: America's insistence that its regional bilateral alliances take precedence over multilateral security approaches, China's employment of ARF to promote 'equal security' with respect to those alliances, and Russia's grudging support of but lingering ambivalence towards the Four Power Talks on Korean Unification. Until this tendency is confronted and modified, multilateralism will be extremely difficult to achieve.

The case of ASEAN reflects a general strategic trend prevalent throughout the entire Asia-Pacific region: a reluctance to trade off significant levels of national sovereignty in the interest of community-building. Australia was willing to do just this at the outset of the post-Cold War era but a more conservative government came to power in that country in the mid-1990s that was much less comfortable with multilateralism than with alliance reaffirmation. However, the propensity to assign national security paramount status is hardly as 'safe' as its proponents would suggest. The risk is always present that the region's great powers will default from balancing the threats of most concern to these middle powers or will balance in ways that prove even more inimical to their survival and security than if they declined to balance at all. Other approaches that traverse a middle ground between realism and liberalism need to be implemented in a region that has thus far failed to embrace either as a preferred posture. The final chapter will offer 'convergent security' as a possible remedy.

CHAPTER 6

# The Super-Power Respondent:
# The United States

American policy planners view the contemporary 'international system' as transitional and amorphous. States are perceived as acting in their own interests ('realist' actors) but as constrained both by multinational institutions and the forces of globalisation (trends consistent with the 'liberal' worldview). Lacking widespread consensus on political values and truly robust collective security mechanisms, however, Asia-Pacific states are regarded by Washington as forming a 'classical' multipolar system, potentially susceptible to geopolitical competition and serious regional conflict.[1]

The risk of widespread regional competition exists notwithstanding that the world's remaining superpower currently enjoys an unrivalled power base in the region. It continues to exploit the Asia-Pacific's growing levels of wealth through its control of global trading and investment practices. It maintains technological supremacy in a world where both Asian allies and Asian adversaries covet American software, telecommunications and artificial intelligence for both commercial and military use. Yet such influence is bought at a very low strategic cost: approximately 100 000 US military personnel are deployed in the region and usually subsidised substantially by host countries.

Even so, Washington is clearly shifting its strategic orientation from its traditional 'Eurocentric' focus to one increasingly directed towards the Asia-Pacific. Greater US commitments to offshore deployments in the arc spanning the Persian Gulf to Northeast Asia are now the rule rather than the exception.[2] China increasingly looks likely to fill what analysts label America's 'enemy deprivation syndrome': the need to have an enemy around which a more cohesive (and realist) foreign policy can be shaped. As George W. Bush assumed the presidency in January 2001, concerns throughout the region intensified over the new Administration's willingness to differentiate between policy pragmatism that incorporates both realist and liberal elements and the outdated politics of the Cold War. To understand the relative prospects of future US policy in the region, that country's recent strategic thinking and behaviour in an Asia-Pacific context needs to be assessed.

The strategic thinking of the United States, an 'eastern rim' Asia-Pacific security actor, has reflected that of a revolutionary state – isolated from global power centres by two vast bodies of water and caught between countervailing instincts of idealism and pragmatism: developing commercial links in both Europe and Asia while avoiding entangling alliances or involvement in foreign wars (the pragmatic dimension), exporting the democratic values of the American body politic to other societies as a means of conflict avoidance (the idealistic component). Over time, American national security thinking has conformed to what Michael Howard has termed the 'social dimension' of Clausewitzian strategy – a trinity of political objectives (realist), operational instruments (pragmatist) and the 'popular passions [or] social forces' which the American people going to war express (idealist).[3] It cannot be said, however, that American grand strategy has moved smoothly along a 'Clausewitzian continuum', especially since the end of the Cold War. No great geopolitical threat or hostile ideology has yet emerged to succeed Soviet power, focusing and mobilising America's public opinion and its formidable national resource base around a central strategic design commensurate to the containment strategy that US policy planners embraced during most of the postwar era.[4]

Americans have never been comfortable pursuing power as an end unto itself. When Ronald Reagan justified larger US military budgets during his presidency, he appealed to what he instinctively knew to be his electorate's apprehension about the intentions and capabilities of the Soviet Union as a totalitarian state. He did this by labelling the USSR an 'evil empire'. The 'Reagan Doctrine' expanded the President's highly idealistic foreign policy beyond the Soviet confrontation to justify the promotion of 'American-style' democracy and human rights in the world's developing regions.[5] Most notably, it embodied a historical tendency of American policy makers to reject expressing policy as a bare manifestation of the national interest. As John Mearsheimer has cogently observed, realists fight wars and accrue power without making value judgements about their adversaries, whereas Americans like to think they enter conflicts to defend 'lofty moral goals' and to defeat 'bad states'.[6]

With the Soviet Union's demise, Washington's adoption of an 'enlargement' strategy to advance the forces of democracy was very much in character with this historical propensity to embrace and project an idealistic foreign policy.[7] Realist critics accused the Clinton Administration of merely emulating President Reagan's enthusiasm for intervening in limited third world conflicts, even if its motives for doing so were different. Whether to advance an ideological agenda (Reagan's motivation) or to engage in 'international social work' (Clinton's agenda), the realist critique was the same: US foreign policy had lost sight of core national interests in favour of embarking upon moral crusades which have little relevance to the survival and influence of the United States. As Condoleezza Rice, the key national security adviser to incoming President George W. Bush argued during the 2000 presidential campaign, US foreign policy 'must proceed from the firm ground of national interest, not from the interests of an illusionary international community'.[8]

Liberals retorted that narrow, interest-oriented realist postulates could not by themselves possibly inspire the American people to sustain security commitments abroad in an increasingly complex global environment where threats had become more diffuse. They further argued that ideals could be pursued by Washington's policy makers in a systematic fashion without indulging in the messianism which realists feared would cause the United States to lose its way in a self-interested world.[9]

In the Asia-Pacific, American idealism translated itself into an increasing interest in institution-building and regional diplomacy as the means to achieve both a stable regional security order and sustainable economic growth. Yet the Clinton Administration was indecisive and ambiguous in pursuing institutionalism as its preferred approach to Asia-Pacific security. It instead 'equivocated between recommending that US bilateral alliances be strengthened "as the heart" of US strategy for the region, and tacitly acknowledging the need for the United States to develop "layers of multilateral ties" in Asia that would not erode the credibility of the existing US alliance system'.[10]

The United States adopted an engagement strategy to realise Clinton's vision of a 'Pacific Community'.[11] This posture clearly embraced the liberal approach to regional security. As defined by the President's national security strategy report released in early 1996, engagement was designed to prevent major threats to regional stability and to build stronger partnerships with Asia-Pacific states. It was further defined as the selective application of 'preventive diplomacy' – a combination of military power and non-military initiatives to ease regional tensions and avoid conflict. Economic assistance, support for democracy, a low-key but still credible US military presence, interaction between US and foreign militaries and involvement in multilateral dialogues and negotiations were all important ingredients of the engagement posture. If applied correctly, the report argued, engagement should work to further American security interests while promoting democracy and prosperity in the region.[12]

Engagement, however, failed to reconcile US goals and interests in the Asia-Pacific with the means to achieve them. While the region is clearly a vital component of US global strategy, the Clinton Administration failed to structure and convey a clear explanation of why this is the case and how American global and regional interests might be reconciled in the region.[13] This chapter argues that US interests would be better served if key aspects of both the realist and liberal outlooks were effectively integrated thus reflecting a key component of the 'convergent security' strategy that is the subject of this book. Specifically, the success of US strategy in Asia will be determined by how well key American strategic policy interests are justified and pursued on the basis of values that the American people can support. It is a truly daunting task to identify and establish rationales and strategies which generate widespread support among the American populace for helping Asian liberals to build a twenty-first century equivalent of the postwar European integration movement in their own region. To do so will require a concerted effort aimed at overcoming Americans' historical preference for isolationist policies. Yet Washington has little choice other than to meet this challenge by incorporating a judicious mix of realist and liberal strategies or face the prospect of confronting formidable threats and even fighting future wars in Asia.

This chapter will initially evaluate key US interests as they apply to the Asia-Pacific region. It will then discuss the George Bush Snr (1989–93) and Clinton Administrations' (1993–2001) approaches to pursuing these policy objectives and the difficulties that they faced in trying to achieve them. A third section will evaluate prospects for the United States to shape a more viable strategic policy agenda for Asia-Pacific. In particular, it will address those aspects of realism and liberalism that could be adopted by US policy planners to implement such a policy agenda and to enhance overall regional stability.

**US Policy Interests in the Asia-Pacific**

American grand strategy has had an Asia-Pacific component for at least a century. The annexation of the Philippines by the United States and its intensified penetration of Asian trading lanes during the 1890s was a logical extension of its westward continental expansion and a visible manifestation of American determination to create a sphere of influence in the Asia-Pacific region. It also marked the beginning of a lengthy period of strategic competition with Japan. This reached a climax with Japan's total defeat in the Pacific War of 1941–45. Following that conflict, the United States sought to impose its version of an international order throughout

Eurasia through both power balancing and the creation of international organisations. This system was designed primarily to restrain the Soviet Union, although it was later brought to bear against the PRC.

James Kurth has recently argued that the United States' major geopolitical challenge in Asia during the Cold War was learning how to co-exist with a powerful and unified China – a China opposed to US interests and values, but which did not threaten Asia-Pacific sea lanes and American regional markets as overtly as did wartime Japan. China neutralised US grand strategy by declining to posit an explicit strategic challenge to the United States, except in extraordinary circumstances. The Chinese response to the US deployment of troops in North Korea during 1950 and American attempts to undermine the survival of North Vietnam in the early 1960s need to be seen in this light. They were *responses* to incursions by US military forces into areas that China saw as vital strategic buffer zones rather than manifestations of an expansionist Chinese agenda. Accordingly, little real policy consensus was generated within the American electorate about the nature of the 'China threat'.[14] Furthermore, many Americans found it problematic that the United States was seeking to contain Asian political movements (even those of a Marxist nature) that were based on ideals of national self-determination and anti-colonialism when those very themes and values were so much a part of their own political heritage.

George Kennan's 'Long Telegram' (later appearing in the widely respected journal *Foreign Affairs*) spelled out the geopolitical premises which justified Washington's adoption of a global containment posture.[15] No equivalent treatise was offered, however, to explain in concise and convincing terms why the United States needed to sustain and protect an Asia-Pacific regional sphere of influence and how the United States needed to relate to other indigenous and external powers in the region to achieve this objective. Successive American postwar administrations lurched from crisis to crisis in Asia, only responding to what they perceived as incessant communist expansionism (what came to be known as the 'domino theory') with deployments of massive land and offshore forces to intervene against or to deter the threat.[16] When events forced policy adjustments to be made from the 1970s onward, the 'Nixon' (1969–73), 'Pacific' (1975), and 'Weinberger' (1983) doctrines all assumed America's strategic role in Asia to be self-evident. They therefore focused exclusively on the problem of how a more qualified level of strategic commitments would not compromise the role of the United States, even though that role was poorly defined.

The end of the Cold War has intensified concerns among US policy makers and independent analysts as to just what American interests in the Asia-Pacific justify a continuation of their strategic commitment to the region. A general consensus has developed among US policy planners on this point and several key interests that need to be protected have been identified. This is in stark contrast to the confusion and dissent that underscored US policy formulation during the Korean and Vietnam conflicts. The key US interest is to prevent major Asia-Pacific wars from erupting as these could lead to strikes against US territory or forces. Corollaries of this interest are the need to avert limited Asia-Pacific conflicts that could escalate into large-scale regional wars and to prevent the proliferation of WMD in the hands of those who would contemplate such an option. A second critical American interest is to prevent China, or a Chinese-led coalition of hostile powers, achieving regional hegemony at the United States' expense. China cannot and should not be contested in developing a regional sphere of influence. But Washington cannot allow Beijing *carte blanche* to subjugate the region. Nor is it in the interest of the United States for counter-coalitions to emerge that would oppose the Chinese and possibly lead to a major regional confrontation. A third US interest is to facilitate Asia-Pacific regional prosperity by encouraging open markets and free trade. A fourth, less strategic and more controversial, political interest is to project successfully democratic values into the region.[17]

Other US interests certainly exist, such as accessing and, where necessary, controlling critical sea lanes of communication in the region; stemming nuclear proliferation and regional arms races; and protecting human rights and cultivating regional confidence-building. These, however, are less central to the United States' physical survival or its ability to preclude a hostile hegemon from dominating the region.[18]

The nature and ramifications of the core American interests are interrelated in increasingly complex ways. War avoidance in the Asia-Pacific – and, more directly, the introduction of US military forces in what contingencies may erupt – will become more difficult as strategic threats will apply to longer distances, involve more advanced and lethal stand-off weapons technologies and introduce elements of strategic coercion into the region that previously could be dominated by American offshore military power operating in forward deployed positions. Certainly, greater free trade throughout Asia could reinforce the United States' legitimacy as a key politico-economic actor in the region. Yet it could also heighten the risk that a more 'globalised' marketplace, shaped by American technology and exports, will precipitate the spread of advanced strategic capabilities to potential US adversaries in the region. Intensified long-range strategic threats originating from more diversified locales than the traditional Northeast Asian area of Cold War focus could even draw the US into conflicts where vital interests might not be at stake. While the adoption of democratic values and institutions by Asian states could reduce this prospect, it is improbable that many Asian cultures will adopt or develop distinctly American or 'Western' forms of governance or civil society over the short-term. If not carefully managed, economic integration and information transparency could thus generate asymmetric regional threats and tensions and magnify previously local conflicts just as easily as fostering a more benign 'Pacific Community'.[19]

### The Asia-Pacific and War Avoidance

US global power has been largely predicated on its ability to influence from great distances the ways other states relate to each other – what Kurth has characterised as being an 'order-giver'.[20] Its status as a large and powerful geopolitical entity separated by two oceans has made the United States relatively invulnerable to a land invasion but its concentration of military and industrial power on its east and west coasts makes it a target for potentially devastating missile strikes.[21] As a maritime power, its ability to deploy forces rapidly and with great concentration of firepower to distant points is perhaps its most distinctive strategic asset. In the postwar Asia-Pacific, it has applied this capability to orchestrate an effective balance of power as a war avoidance strategy. It has usually been successful in preventing great-power confrontation and it has been highly successful in deterring nuclear conflicts.

It has been much less adept in avoiding the outbreak of limited conflicts. These have, at times, impeded regional economic development and have involved US forces in disputes not directly related to American national security interests. The United States has also tended to assume too many strategic commitments relative to the actual resource levels it deploys.[22] The 'two-and-a-half war' doctrine adopted by the Kennedy Administration was designed to allow the United States to fight and win a European, an Asian and a smaller war all at the same time. It was undermined by the Vietnam conflict which greatly strained American financial and military resources. The subsequent 'one-and-a-half war' posture adopted by the Nixon Administration was made possible by *detente* with China. It was undermined, however, by the Carter Administration's nearly disastrous miscalculation in contemplating a withdrawal of all US land forces from South Korea and by Washington's subsequent acknowledgment that an 'arc of crisis' had emerged with the 'loss' of Iran and the Soviet invasion of Afghanistan. A fundamental lesson of geopolitics was rediscovered in the 1970s: the strategic wellbeing of the United States is directly inter-related to its defence of Eurasia's rimlands and littorals. All else can fail, but if hostile powers launch successful air and sea offensives against US forces deployed in Western Europe or Northeast Asia, the

American homeland would become vulnerable to blockades, interdiction campaigns or offshore tactical missile strikes with WMD.[23]

The stakes for the United States in Asia-Pacific conflict prevention are high. The technological prowess of several Asia-Pacific states is sufficiently advanced for them to develop and deploy over the next decade or two nuclear, chemical or biological warheads and delivery systems which could be targeted against either the United States proper or its forward deployed forces.[24] This latent threat means that Washington must seek long-term alternatives to its traditional postwar deterrence strategy. These would be aimed at ensuring that negotiation will prevail over confrontation if local tensions escalate into conflicts with the potential to threaten the North American continent. Global arms control and disarmament initiatives offer substantial promise of achieving this over the long term; TMD and other defensive technologies consistent with the terms of the 1972 Anti-Ballistic Missile Treaty provide one (but not necessarily the best) short to mid-term option for reducing vulnerability to nuclear intimidation by potential Asia-Pacific adversaries.

US deterrence and war-fighting capabilities are complicated by an increasing difficulty to distinguish between tactical and strategic weapons systems. The current US nuclear posture, for example, has reduced the American tactical nuclear force to Air Force dual-capable aircraft and Navy Tomahawk missiles (the Bush Administration removed tactical nuclear weapons from South Korea and other sites during 1991–92). Yet, by themselves these systems could still render immense damage to an adversary's ability to deliver nuclear bombs against US or allied targets. Such systems would be considered 'tactical' in the strategic calculations of states such as Russia and China which deploy extensive and diversified nuclear capabilities, but could be 'strategic' with respect to North Korea or Pakistan which have more limited nuclear weapons inventories and delivery systems. Recent breakthroughs in missile defence technology, however, may well blur the past distinctions between strategic and tactical nuclear weapons. For example, the US deployment of either an effective national missile defence system on the American homeland or of theatre missile defences in Japan or Taiwan would be viewed by China as a major compromise of its own strategic capabilities. China's official no-first-use commitment, extended after its first nuclear test in 1964, could then become tenuous.[25]

The demise of the Soviet Union left American strategic planners without an immediately obvious rationale for sustaining high levels of force projection capabilities in the Asia-Pacific theatre of operations. The loss of US bases in the Philippines and the subsequent emphasis on the ability of the US Pacific Fleet to retain access to 'places, not bases' initially appeared to vindicate those in the United States who were arguing for a reduced American military presence in the region.[26] They posited that the one distinct threat to the physical security of the United States (Soviet naval power) had been removed and that the US navy was simply a service in search of a new Pacific mission. A self-declared 'minimalist' faction of the realist camp (yet one most likely to be labelled 'neo-isolationist' by most realists) disdained the need for the United States to maintain extended deterrence commitments against imaginary regional hegemons or on behalf of allied interests for which the United States should not risk war. It argued instead that the United States should adhere to an 'offshore balancing' strategy, taking advantage of its insularity and allowing Asian rivalries to counter-balance each other. It also insisted that Asian economic growth – most graphically represented by Japan's economic wealth – was not a strategic advantage for the United States but a direct attack on American prosperity and survival, employing the weapons of trade rather than those of war.[27]

The majority of realists, however, joined the liberal camp in rejecting these arguments. So too did those invested in formulating US strategic policy. Perhaps the most authoritative rebuttal was an article appearing in *Foreign Affairs*, written by US Assistant Secretary of Defense Joseph Nye. Long known as a scion of the liberal cause, Nye embraced an expedient combination of realist and liberal postulates to counter the minimalists' arguments. He observed that few people take the minimalist or neo-isolationist strategy seriously because: (1) history, geography, demographics, and economics unavoidably make the United States a Pacific power; (2) the Asia-Pacific region is not capable of orchestrating a 'normal' or stable balance of power without full American participation, and would move toward arms racing and the creation of regional security dilemmas if the United States detached itself from Asian security politics; and (3) Japan's defence burden-sharing role allows the United States to more readily project global power. Nye concluded that US security interests were met more effectively by continuing to pursue a strategy of regional engagement from a position of leadership and strength while simultaneously seeking greater economic and politico-strategic interdependence with other Asia-Pacific states. This entails developing and sustaining a policy consensus in the United States on Asia-Pacific security policy, maintaining and strengthening existing bilateral security alliances in the region and cultivating multilateral security dialogues as an active participant in regional security politics.[28]

Ultimately, US vital interests are served best by incorporating selected aspects of both arguments. The strength of the minimalist argument is its encouragement of policy discrimination between 'vital' and 'less vital' interests. Nye is correct in arguing that geography is a critical part of the Asia-Pacific policy calculus for any US administration. Yet America's great distance from Eurasian shores could conceivably eliminate or minimise the otherwise high cost of maintaining forward deployed US forces in the Asia-Pacific if no immediate threat exists in Europe or Asia which can directly threaten the United States. Moreover, strategic officials in the United States and in allied countries have tended to place too broad an interpretation on defence guarantees in the bilateral security agreements between the United States and its various Asia-Pacific friends and allies. These alliances, as they currently operate, are predominantly realist policy instruments with provisions for consultation but not necessarily automatic strategic commitment under all circumstances. They require constant re-evaluation 'in terms of the most probable threats to regional stability'.[29]

### China as a Hostile Hegemon?

Since becoming a Pacific power in the mid-nineteenth century, the United States has sought to prevent a hostile power or hostile group of powers from achieving regional dominance. By doing so it seeks, as a global maritime power, to maintain its access to the Asia-Pacific to safeguard its trans-Pacific trading lanes and the oil routes from the Persian Gulf to its key industrial allies in the region, Japan and South Korea, and to secure the western flanks of the Western Hemisphere. While this book's concluding chapter will evaluate strategic primacy or hegemony as a general problem for Asia-Pacific regional security, this subsection will address the more specific issue of how the United States has perceived and responded to a stronger and wealthier China – the most likely contender for supplanting or neutralising US power and influence in the Asia-Pacific.

Hardline realists assert that US strategic power must balance growing Chinese tendencies to be more assertive on irredentist issues (Taiwan and the South China Sea) and to acquire more sophisticated military capabilities. They conclude that if the United States accepts this challenge, a relatively stable bipolar regional power balance will emerge which is preferable to either a hegemonic or anarchical Asia-Pacific security environment.[30] Liberals counter that this reasoning reflects an unfortunate tendency by both the Americans and the Chinese to translate 'worst case planning' into strategic policy. They further assert that American policy makers would better serve their nation's interests by relating to their Chinese counterparts more positively and by affording the Chinese leadership the opportunity to win domestic support by interacting positively with the United States. This would be preferable to promoting an endless series of confrontations over weapons proliferation, human rights, trade and irredentism.[31] They believe Chinese interests are best served by engagement with the United States and by pursuing national security and economic interests in multilateral settings, preferably via international organisations or possibly by adopting concert politics – informal agreements among Chinese, American, Japanese and Russian leaders to meet regularly to coordinate their interests and policies on regional security issues. Moving towards agreements with rival claimants on the Spratly Islands dispute through institutional venues, such as ASEAN, is illustrative of the former approach; working with the United States and constantly consulting with Japan and Russia regarding a permanent peace settlement for the Korean Peninsula exemplifies a concert approach.

Once more, both the realist and liberal arguments have strengths that are applied most effectively by US policy makers in an integrated fashion. A necessary precondition for any approach to be successful, however, is that there be effective communication between China and the United States. These two countries must be able to enunciate their interests and intentions directly to each other without distortion. Neither the deterrence/containment approach supported by most realists nor the engagement postures backed by the liberal camp will work if this basic framework is lacking. Such a framework was mostly absent in Sino–American ties between the 1989 Tiananmen Square incident and the last year of President Clinton's first term of office (1996).[32] More recently, both sides have reconstituted channels of diplomatic, economic and even military dialogue. The summits between President Clinton and Chinese leader Jiang Zemin, during 1997 and 1998, are indicative of progress. However, with the notable exception of preventing conflict escalation on the Korean Peninsula, these consultations have often appeared to be short on efforts to identify and act on mutual *interests* and long on discussions over mutual *grievances*. This creates an atmosphere which makes it difficult for Chinese officials to break the cycle of politely disagreeing with their American counterparts on the international stage before turning to attack American policies on the domestic stage in order to engender nationalist sentiment at home.[33] The challenge Washington faces is to break this pattern of incessantly competitive or 'zero-sum' interaction with the PRC. In a wide-ranging interview on the incoming George W. Bush Administration reported in early January 2001, China's top foreign policy official, Deputy Prime Minister Qian Qichan, demonstrated sensitivity toward this problem. Calling on the new American President not to view 'China as a strategic competitor', Qian argued that China and the United States 'have no need to begin a war against each other' over Taiwan and insisted that 'anything could be discussed'.[34]

By their very nature, multilateral institutions may offer a basis for Beijing and Washington to identify more positive bilateral agendas. Neither China nor the United States will allow third parties to dictate their own policy agendas, but a broader forum presents opportunities for more diverse and more frequent lines of communication to be developed. Both China and the United States have recently demonstrated a greater level of interest in pursuing their relations with Asia-Pacific states within the ASEAN, ARF and APEC frameworks. China is also exploring the policy benefits of collaborating with Asian states in more exclusive regional bodies (see chapter 2). Both Washington and Beijing are determined to avoid being isolated by the rise of 'middle-power diplomacy' in the region. The major alternative to regional power management – concert diplomacy – appears less viable, as China has intensely criticised what it views as an American acquiescence to a greater and more independent Japanese security role in the region while the United States is watching with concern the evolution of Russian–Chinese strategic ties.[35] Some liberals would take comfort in the evolution of such 'concerted bilateralism' or regular summit diplomacy between major powers. Unless carefully managed and constrained, however, these bilateral relationships could precipitate security dilemmas where none previously existed.

Realist concerns about regional power vacuums thus cannot be discounted in the absence of a Sino–American reconciliation. Moreover, despite Qian's entreaty cited above, there is evidence that the Chinese are not willing to comply with such regional and international security norms as negotiating territorial disputes (regarding the Spratly Islands), honouring other polities' processes of political self-determination (in Taiwan and Burma) and complying with restraints on the transfer of materials applicable to nuclear weapons production (Pakistan). Nor have the Chinese exhibited a genuine readiness to enter into the Strategic Arms Reduction Talks (START) with the United States, Russia and other declared nuclear powers. This posture has serious long-term implications for US nuclear deterrence strategy. If China's nuclear arsenal and commensurate delivery systems (which are increasing and diversifying) are not addressed effectively, the United States will have little choice but to continue its extended deterrence strategy in the Asia-Pacific on behalf of its regional allies. Otherwise, if the United States were to disengage, China's nuclear force could become the catalyst for a highly destabilising nuclear arms race, involving possibly Japan, one or both Koreas, Taiwan, India, Pakistan and other regional actors.

*Economics and Security*

Economic relations are viewed by US policy planners as a crucial aspect of national security policy.[36] They are particularly relevant in the Asia-Pacific region that generates approximately one-quarter of the world's gross national product (GNP), a substantial part of which can be applied to military-related spending. However, American analysts are often less concerned than are their Asian and Australian counterparts about exploring precisely how the economics-security inter-relationship works in the context of reinforcing or undermining Asia-Pacific regional stability.[37] With few exceptions their attention has been directed towards specific microanalytical problems relating to trade flows. They have been particularly obsessed with the need to minimise or remove structural impediments to US exports to the region.[38]

A minority of American policy analysts, particularly those of the isolationist or 'minimalist' faction mentioned previously, have argued that trade relations cannot be separated from security considerations. They have damaged the credibility of their position by tending to accuse Japan (most frequently) or other Asian states (increasingly) of consciously conspiring to seek relative gains and long-term dominance over the United States by waging economic warfare. Such arguments only serve to precipitate a siege mentality among Japanese and Asian policy makers, serve forces in Asia which favour greater protectionism against US products and greater resistance to 'Western' democratic values, and abet the interests of Chinese strategists who favour undermining the US–Japan security alliance. Linkages between the economic and security ties binding the United States are always present. They are best approached in terms of how they can positively reinforce each other (absolute gains) rather than how one sector can be applied to extract leverage in the other (relative gains).[39]

There is little evidence that American policy planners view China's spectacular economic growth or the continued prosperity of other Asia-Pacific states, assuming they fully recover from the Asian financial crisis over the next few years, as a prelude to heightened tensions in the region. Instead, as noted previously, American policy tends to 'compartmentalise' security and economic issues in the Asia-Pacific. US security interests are pursued mostly through its bilateral alliance network while the American economic agenda is approached through APEC and the WTO.[40] US security alliances are decidedly realist in their orientation, based on strategies of deterrence and, more recently, power balancing. The United States' economic strategy is clearly advertised as liberal but it is perceived by many Asian observers as obsessed with extracting leverage and cultivating relative gains. American rhetoric calling for the transformation of intra-regional trading competition into a process of 'open regionalism' through tariff reductions and by encouraging greater high technology and information flows is viewed with scepticism. They have obvious difficulty in reconciling open regionalism with the comparative advantage dimensions of American trading strategies and behaviour.

The Asian financial crisis has likewise sobered ASEAN policy planners to the realities of economic growth and to the limitations of regional interdependence as a catalyst for international prestige. Their lingering doubts about US strategic involvement in Southeast Asia have nevertheless 'spilled over' to shape their security perceptions: increasingly, China, Japan, and their relationship with each other are viewed as the keys to future regional economic stability, with the United States needed only to counter-balance Beijing's and Tokyo's prospective ambitions and strategic rivalry.[41]

Such pessimism has been challenged by those liberals who argue that the United States retains sufficient regional influence to bargain effectively within APEC and the WTO for the adoption of rules and norms that facilitate its own interests while simultaneously promoting greater regional cooperation on both economic and security matters. But for US bargaining to be effective it will need firstly to be based on a more sensitive understanding of the needs of other regional states. In particular it will need to accommodate the conceptual inter-relationship between economic and non-economic interests so widely supported within the region.[42] Congressional pressure on future administrations to project hard-line trading postures against Japan and South Korea will have to be balanced against the prospect of those states adopting more nationalistic postures. Acceptance of this essential balancing principle, even if of limited dimension, was in evidence when the Clinton Administration modified its human rights stance against China – a China, it should be noted, that was prepared to confront Washington and risk losing its Most Favoured Nation (MFN) trading status in order to preserve what it saw as its sovereign prerogatives.

### Reconciling 'American' and 'Asian' Values

Recent efforts by various Asian elites to define and project a distinctly regional identity have illuminated a fundamental tension in US postwar foreign policy. Liberal American political ideology draws sharp normative lines between what is 'good' and 'bad' and what is 'democratic' and 'authoritarian'. By contrast, 'interest-driven' American geopolitics tends to subordinate concerns about the types of governments Washington is dealing with where such states are positioned strategically.[43] The former approach often is labelled 'neo-Wilsonianism', after the American President Woodrow Wilson whose normative vision of democratic ideals justified the United States entering World War I 'to end all wars'. It is predicated on the assumption that modern democracies are peaceful trading states that do not fight wars against each other. If this premise is valid, US foreign policy should work towards encouraging other states to strengthen their democratic practices and institutions. Multilateralism and liberalism are supported by this policy approach because the UN and other international organisations encourage negotiation, bargaining and other non-authoritarian forms of political participation and decision making.

The Clinton Administration wrestled with merging neo-Wilsonianism with its international free trade objectives by promoting the concept of 'good governance', that is the efficient management of free market reform evolving simultaneously with 'the creation of transparent mechanisms for the accountability of the state and its officials and a political system able to guarantee individual rights and freedoms'.[44] In November 1996 President Clinton argued in an address to Chulalongkorn University in Bangkok that the citizens of Thailand, Japan, South Korea, Hong Kong and the Philippines have recently demonstrated that 'accountability and rule of law can thrive in an Asian climate'.[45] However, in the Asia-Pacific, as in other 'non-Western' regions, the United States has continued to advance the pre-eminence of the individual over collective society – the 'enlargement' theory – and has stressed that no conflict exists between individual liberty and advancing economic prosperity.[46]

In an Asia-Pacific context, the application of this agenda has been impeded by the 'Asian Values' movement. The extent to which this movement is driven by either some Asian leaders actually believing their values are superior to Western principles or by their resentment to having external values imposed upon them is a question which may never be resolved. At least two specific aspects of the 'Asian Values' posture, however, have undermined efforts by Washington and other Western governments to combine idealism with policy pragmatism in fashioning their policies towards the Asia-Pacific region. These factors will be surveyed briefly here in the context of American policy.

First, Malaysian, Singaporean, Chinese and other regional elites have strongly resisted what they view as an American effort to undermine their own policies for economic competitiveness. These policies allegedly embody values of: (1) family loyalty and thrift; (2) the primacy of community interests over those of the individual; (3) the need to act through carefully derived consensus among legitimate state authorities rather than through flawed compromises emanating from confrontations among unwieldy representative political bodies; and (4) the imperative for strong governments acting to safeguard economic growth and social cohesion on behalf of its citizens.[47] Taken together, it is argued by the proponents of 'Asian Values' that these characteristics, which comprise a distinctively 'East Asian' economic culture, are superior to those ideals or values which prevail in Western societies and cultures.

As Malaysian Prime Minister Mohamad Mahathir has argued, 'enlargement' is an American campaign which threatens Asian core values because it fails to take into account that 'too much freedom is dangerous'.[48] In other words, if allowed to penetrate Asian societies unchecked, American-style democracy could threaten the social cohesion and international competitiveness of an 'Asian' bloc united in its determination not to be culturally swayed or politically dominated by the United States.

Such rhetoric is often targeted as much towards a domestic audience as it is toward the US government. As two Western analysts have correctly noted in their recent assessment of the US–ASEAN discourse on human rights, 'increasingly sharp rebuttals to Western criticism … suggest that the calculation seems to be that the minimal economic costs of standing up to the West, and especially to the United States, on human rights issues are more than offset by domestic political benefits'.[49]

Second, by connecting human rights to economic and strategic issues, the Clinton Administration complicated US relations with Asian governments by linking compliance with American values to American national interests.[50] This is particularly true with respect to Washington's posture toward China. However, it also extends to American resistance to Burma's participation in ASEAN and, intermittently, to US sanctions on various arms deals with Indonesia over the latter's administration of East Timor and behaviour leading to that province's independence referendum.[51] However, this linkage is not consistent since America has a tendency to express concern about human rights practices in various ASEAN settings while still conducting 'business as usual' in strategic relations. For example, Singapore has assumed the largely self-appointed role of being a major Southeast Asian critic of the human rights rhetoric emanating from Washington. Yet American investment levels in Singapore remain largely unaffected while the US navy and air force continue to deploy and train with their Singaporean counterparts on a rotating basis.[52]

Washington's strategic policy makers are concerned that the human rights debate does not spill over to affect American access to Asia-Pacific bases and markets. They worry that influential liberals within future administrations or within Congress will press for the United States to consistently promote human rights as a fundamental component of US foreign policy. Those realists who concede that American ideals cannot be totally absent in such policy nevertheless advocate that human rights should be promoted through quiet diplomacy. In addition, they also conclude that it should be focused more at the universalist level, that is, the UN, so that it does not appear to be directed towards Asia as a specific region.[53] Such an approach, they argue, would send a more positive message of engagement and reconciliation to Asian governments and elites that are resentful of any current US campaign to impose Western ideals on their own polities.

### The Pursuit of US Interests: The Bush and Clinton Administrations[54]

The Administration of George Bush, Snr (1989–93) largely disregarded or resisted arguments that the experience of building multilateral security institutions in Europe could be replicated in the Asia-Pacific. The Clinton Administration offered qualified and largely rhetorical support for such Asia-Pacific institutions. The important point is that the United States has been consistent in assigning much greater importance to preserving its regional bilateral security treaties than to building a new multilateral security framework.

### *The Bush (Snr) Administration (1989–93)*

In late 1991 President Bush's Secretary of State, James A. Baker, identified three 'pillars' for maintaining a stable and prosperous Pacific Community. These were: (1) a free trading system supported by regional economic integration; (2) greater regional democratisation; and (3) a revised defence structure designed to mitigate or minimise regional conflict. The United States would maintain a forward military presence in the region 'to provide geopolitical balance, to be an honest broker, to reassure against uncertainty' while cultivating intensified and liberalised trade relations with Asian states and encouraging political pluralism throughout the region.[55] Whatever defence network was to be pursued, however, would still be within the framework of America's postwar bilateral alliances. The Bush Administration regarded this as constituting 'a balancing wheel of an informal, yet highly effective, security structure' with the United States as the 'hub', the US–Japan alliance as 'the key connection' and US bilateral security ties with South Korea, the Philippines, Thailand and Australia as other important 'spokes' in the network.[56] This doctrinal approach, with its emphasis on an America-centric bilateral alliance system, confirmed that realism still prevailed in Washington's strategic thinking.

This perspective was immediately challenged in US domestic political circles by increasing calls to cut defence spending in response to the relative decline in Soviet power. Effectively, the US Congress and the American electorate were looking for a 'peace dividend' in the form of lower defence spending. It became clear that if the interests cited by Baker and other US officials were to be supported, something more in the way of justification was required than a mere reaffirmation of the existing, status quo-oriented policies. The response came in April 1990 when the US Defense Department released a report which, along with an update released in July 1992, became known as the East Asia Strategy Initiative (EASI).[57] 'EASI I' and 'EASI II' offered rationales for US forces to remain deployed in the Asia-Pacific (although at reduced strength) and advanced a number of arguments as to why increased allied defence burden-sharing would need to accompany the modest US force reductions which were planned over a ten-year, three-phase period.[58]

EASI was designed to complement the Bush Administration's 'Base Force' strategy for downsizing and reconfiguring the global US military presence. The downsizing part of the strategy was to be achieved by reducing total personnel strength from 3.2 to 2.6 million. The reconfiguration revolved around a shift from the emphasis on the forward deployment of forces in distant theatres of potential combat to a focus on maintaining forces that were both more mobile and flexible. It was anticipated that these forces would increasingly be deployed directly from the United States to points of conflict. If fully implemented, the Base Force concept would have reduced US defence spending by 25 per cent in real terms before the end of the twentieth century.[59] The US Defense Department endeavoured to reassure America's allies and domestic realists that forward deployed forces would be maintained to 'strengthen alliances [and] show [US] resolve'. However, the Bush Administration's so-called 'Regional Defense Strategy' appeared to reflect the strategic probability that the Persian Gulf War would be the last major American overseas operation of the post-World War II era.[60] The costs of that conflict alone, largely defrayed by allied financial contributions, reinforced the arguments of those who were asking when the long-promised peace dividend would emerge.[61] By the end of the Bush Administration's term of office (January 1993), US annual defence outlays had declined in real terms by over 15 per cent ($60 billion) and troop levels permanently stationed overseas had been reduced by over 225 000 personnel (44 per cent).[62]

Neither EASI I nor EASI II provided uniquely different rationales from those in effect during the Cold War as to why the United States should project military power into the Asia-Pacific. The US force presence was characterised as an instrument of power balancing to prevent regional hegemonism and as insurance for American economic involvement in the region. By 1990 US trade to the region exceeded $300 billion annually, 50 per cent more than the volume of US–European trade.[63] Even at reduced levels, American air and naval assets were expected to facilitate US control over regional sea lanes of communication and strategic chokepoints in order to guarantee continued American access to regional markets. Base Force/EASI projections called for US force levels in the

Asia-Pacific to decline from 135 000 in 1990 to approximately 100 000 personnel by 1995. This assumed that the region's security environment would continue to reflect continued progress and improvement.[64]

These force reductions were largely achieved. A notable exception was in South Korea where a proposed withdrawal of 6000 troops was frozen in November 1991 in response to growing tensions on the Peninsula. At this point, North Korean efforts to develop nuclear weapons led Washington to conclude that the United States would have to re-invest in ground forces if it wanted to seriously deter Pyongyang.[65]

The Bush Administration's doctrinal espousal of an 'honest broker' or regional power-balancing strategy failed to establish a universally accepted raison d'être for preserving US security commitments and defence resources in the Asia-Pacific. At that time it was unclear precisely which power, apart from North Korea, needed to be balanced in the region in an immediate post-Cold War era of American strategic primacy. Moreover, the American Congress and electorate were sceptical about increasingly wealthy Asia-Pacific friends and allies not being able to defend themselves. US policy critics argued that grand strategy and strategic doctrine had not taken into account the growing inter-relationship of military strategy and international political economics and that no specific US national security interest had been defined.[66]

The Bush team was further criticised for continuing to identify Japan as both a state that needed to be protected from itself (arguing that US security guarantees were required to prevent its remilitarisation) and one that posed an economic threat.[67] China was implicitly viewed by most in Washington as a potential threat to the American version of a new world order. The Bush Administration also advanced the dubious proposition that it could continue to exercise a strategic preponderance in the Asia-Pacific and prevent the emergence of power vacuums despite planned force reductions, particularly in Korea. US basing closures in the Philippines elicited questions about the United States' future role as an engaged power balancer in Southeast Asia. Vietnam's diplomatic and economic overtures to ASEAN called into question what an offshore US force presence would do in Southeast Asia apart from generating contracts for naval replenishment and re-supply.[68] Those arguing for wholesale US strategic disengagement from Asia were at least advocating a doctrinal approach that was clearly understood even if it lacked widespread policy support.

### The Clinton Administration

President Clinton entered office determined to formulate a clear and comprehensive doctrinal approach to Asia-Pacific security. Several key policy statements attempted to set the context. The most important of these included testimony before the Senate Foreign Relations Committee in March 1993 by Winston Lord (the Assistant Secretary of State for East Asian and Pacific Affairs) and speeches by President Clinton to Waseda University in Japan and to the South Korean National Assembly in July of the same year.[69] A focus on trade, security and human rights comprised the nucleus of the new administration's approach to the region. These policy sectors, administration officials argued, were closely inter-related and needed to be addressed jointly as part of a comprehensive policy approach. Manifestations of this new approach quickly became apparent. By mid-1995, for example, US trade tensions with Japan were being tacitly linked to America's propensity to sustain its security commitments under the US–Japan MST.

The Clinton Administration believed that Japan and other Asian states would need to improve on their previously poor record with respect to supporting the principles of free trade if the American public was going to continue to support US strategic involvement in the region. If they did not, the United States reserved the right to impose 'managed trade' initiatives, pressing Asian states to import selected American products or face retaliatory sanctions.[70] In the meantime, US human rights policy was embodied in a policy of democratic 'enlargement', wherein the promotion of human rights and political liberalisation throughout the Asia-Pacific was linked to continued US access to and influence within the region.

Most significantly, the idea of multilateral security dialogues was endorsed. This contrasted sharply with the Bush Administration's reluctance to involve the United States in such proceedings. Clinton believed that the United States shared common security interests with enough Asian states to merit Washington's visible, if qualified, participation in such processes. These shared interests included curbing regional arms races and nuclear proliferation, seeking conflict prevention, and strengthening regional peacekeeping.[71] The term 'engagement' was used to identify this common approach to regional security. It entailed preventing regional threats from overwhelming regional stability and working under US leadership toward regional peace and stability. US friends and allies, however, were expected to assume greater responsibility in achieving that common objective.[72] US security officials also employed the term 'cooperative engagement' to describe the application of US military power for reinforcing regional alliances and ensuring effective crisis response.[73] The Clinton Administration was less concerned about how multilateralism might erode US regional influence by undercutting its ability to deal with key allies in a bilateral context, and about regional power balancing, than was its predecessor. But it differed from the understanding many Asia-Pacific states had about the term 'engagement'. To the ASEAN states, in particular, cooperative engagement implied ensuring that parties deemed potentially destabilising to regional security, especially China, were included in any dialogue or consultative process for resolving regional differences and disputes.[74]

Initially, the Clinton Administration's policies reflected a highly liberal, values-oriented outlook towards international security. However, this approach was soon tested and found wanting by several developments in US–Asia-Pacific relations. Instead of relenting to American trade pressure and seeking greater interdependence with the United States, the Japanese Government hardened its resistance by petitioning the WTO for the lifting of US retaliatory sanctions on the import of Japanese luxury cars. In doing so, Japan signalled its insistence that trade issues were to be kept separate from US–Japan defence relations.[75] US policy credibility was actually enhanced by the Clinton Administration's decision not to link China's human rights behaviour to a continuation of that country's MFN trading status.[76] ASEAN states were critical of American efforts to attach human rights standards to their management of domestic labour problems and political dissent. Australia condemned the United States for undercutting traditional Australian agricultural markets with subsidies for American farming exports. Some Australian officials began to question if strategic affiliation with Australia's traditional 'great and powerful friend' was still relevant in a world where Canberra and Washington had increasingly become economic competitors.[77] Even the initial American success in negotiating an Agreed Framework with North Korea in 1994 to stop that country from developing an indigenous nuclear weapons production capability was subsequently questioned; bilateral US–North Korean relations intensified during 1998–99 with the North Koreans agreeing to constrain their ballistic missile production and exports in return for the US lifting many of its former trade sanctions against the North.

These developments generated increasing doubts about the viability of American support for multilateralism. How can American participation in a multilateral security dialogue be successful if Washington's relations are complicated by a policy agenda viewed sceptically by both its old allies and its potential adversaries? More fundamentally, what specific US policy objectives are being pursued by engaging in such a dialogue? If they are to provide American leadership in organising defence coalitions to supplement or replace the postwar bilateral alliance network, what type of specific security commitments are Americans prepared to extend towards the region?

The ambivalence of future US strategic involvement in the Asia-Pacific was accentuated in September 1993 when the US Defense Department announced its 'Bottom-Up Review' (BUR) of US defence strategy.[78] The

BUR argued that overall US force levels should be sufficient to fight two regional conflicts 'almost simultaneously'. However, it speculated that regional allies would have to contribute substantially to the 'holding' of an invading North Korean force until such time that US units deployed to defeat a Persian Gulf aggressor could be relocated to Northeast Asia.[79] This provided little reassurance to South Korea or Japan while doing nothing to satisfy American neo-isolationists who feared that any such strategy would be likely to embroil the United States in regional conflicts not directly related to its vital security interests. Moreover, neo-isolationists attacked the administration for overstating the nature of regional threats given their relative lack of technological sophistication and inability to threaten the American homeland.[80]

Pro-defence observers, meanwhile, attacked the BUR's strategic assumptions and its overall policy credibility. They questioned its neglect to address all but the most obvious major regional conflicts. Neither Southeastern Europe nor the Taiwan Strait, for example, appeared to be part of the scenario. Yet two of the most substantial deployments of US forces in the late 1990s took place in these locales. Nor did the BUR offer hard analysis on the state or utility of America's alliance systems. Both the neo-isolationist and power projectionist factions were arguing the same point from their respective ends of the philosophical spectrum: the Clinton Administration had failed to stipulate clearly what the United States' critical strategic interests were and how to implement them.[81]

In early 1995 the United States moved to reassure its Asia-Pacific allies of its intent to stay engaged in the region by releasing yet another version of EASI.[82] The thrust of the East Asia Strategy Review or EASR (also labelled the 'Nye Doctrine' after its primary author, Assistant Secretary of Defense for International Security Affairs, Joseph S. Nye, Jr), proved to be no more than an endorsement of the status quo. Additional US force reductions were rejected as a hedge against newly emerging regional threats (the force strength would be maintained at about 100 000 personnel). The centrality of US bilateral alliances in the region was also reaffirmed. This 'muddied' the Clinton Administration's earlier shift towards multilateralism because it failed to specify how the two concepts (bilateralism and multilateralism) would relate to each other. Nye's observation, that developing subregional or regional security dialogues 'is like an overlapping plate of armor … a way to surround the hard core of our security alliances with a softer exterior of dialogues and consultations', appeared to further obfuscate rather than to clarify the US approach.[83] Left unexplained was how a preference for maintaining power-balancing alliances could be reconciled with an inclination to seek instruments for threat reduction and region-wide security collaboration. Alliances may be insurance in the event a preferred policy course of regional cooperation fails but this is different from assigning US bilateral security treaties continued strategic priority, as the EASR clearly opted to do.

### Cross-comparisons

Both the Bush and Clinton Administrations defined the United States' bilateral alliances in the Asia-Pacific as the most important components of US security politics in that region. They nevertheless posited two distinct approaches to the realist-liberal debate. Officials responsible for Asian security policies under President Bush, such as Richard Solomon (Assistant Secretary of State for East Asian and Pacific Affairs) and Paul Wolfowitz (Under Secretary of Defense for Policy), adopted a cautiously realist posture. They minimised trade differences with Japan in favour of preserving the sanctity of US–Japanese security relations; emphasised the value of insulating regional defence and strategic cooperation from human rights issues; resisted regional confidence-building, arms control and other multilateral security initiatives in favour of reinforcing the United States' postwar bilateral treaty network; and sought to maintain substantial US military power to underwrite extended deterrence.[84]

The Clinton Administration's foreign policy, on the other hand, was initially shaped by Nye, Anthony Lake, and other well known advocates of the liberal paradigm. US security doctrine concerning the Asia-Pacific became increasingly entangled in value-driven rules and norms. During the first two years of Clinton's presidency this visionary path to conducting security relations was unsuccessful. It was perceived by Asian and American critics alike as leading to US policy mismanagement and to ineffective American diplomatic and strategic behaviour in the region. By May 1994 Winston Lord was warning Secretary of State Warren Christopher that US politico-security relations with Asia-Pacific states were eroding to the point where a regional 'malaise' had developed concerning US interests and policies.[85] While corrective measures were undertaken, including a strong performance by Clinton at the APEC summit in Bogor (Indonesia) during November 1994, strong concerns persisted during the remainder of his first term in office that US strategic doctrine had been subsumed by excessive expectations.

### Doctrinal Planning and the Forces of Change

Assumptions that key Asia-Pacific states would conform to American efforts to link its economic agenda in the region to security politics proved especially ill-founded. The Clinton Administration's campaign to impose 'managed trade' criteria on US–Japan relations was a graphic case-in-point. Soon after Clinton's inauguration, US Special Trade Representative Mickey Kantor and Japan's Minister for International Trade and Industry (MITI), Hashimoto Ryutaro, began exchanging insults on Japanese and American trade practices.[86] The atmosphere became sufficiently poisoned to cause a breakdown in economic and trade negotiations at the Clinton–Hosokawa summit meeting in February 1994. The United States was insistent that managed trade would be applied to relations with Japan: linking the opening of Japan's domestic markets to US products and services to the overall health of bilateral ties. The reasoning was stipulated clearly by Secretary of State Christopher in a subsequent speech to the US Business Council in May 1996, 'economic diplomacy is not only essential to advancing our economic ties for achieving other foreign policy goals ... it is essential to undergird peace, stability and progress toward democracy'.[87]

Initial US pressure against Japan was positive but short-lived. Between 1993 and 1996 US exports to Japan increased 34 per cent. By early 1999, however, the US–Japan bilateral trade deficit had returned to record high levels (nearly US$66 billion). In the aftermath of the Asian financial crisis, US officials were lamenting Japan's economic 'sluggishness' as well as their own Congress' refusal to pass 'fast-track' legislation giving the President greater discretionary power to negotiate trade agreements with Asian and other trading partners. They were also pleading with Japan to deregulate and open its domestic markets still further.[88] Emerging factors of globalisation including asymmetrical demand for energy sources, differing rates of technology flows and intensified links between nationalist agendas and communications modes (that is, the media) presented the Clinton Administration's policy planners with little or no warning for adjusting trade policy to core US policy interests.

Yet the flawed calculation that the Asia-Pacific security environment would remain largely unchanged (with the Korean Peninsula being posited as the one possible exception) was implicit within the Clinton Administration's EASR. It assumed that China would not seek regional hegemony, that ASEAN would initiate symbolic but mostly cosmetic security dialogues, and that the common motive of pursuing wealth would remain so predominant in the region that it would effectively preclude conflict escalation. It also failed to address how declining US defence budgets and projections for even deeper cuts in the future would impact on US strategy and force commitments in the region.

There was growing evidence throughout 1996 that a few of the realists who occupied positions in the Clinton Administration were beginning to assert their views on Asia-Pacific security affairs. In part, external developments strengthened their case. These included China's confrontation with Taiwan in the lead up to the March 1996 Taiwanese presidential election, North Korea's denunciation of the UN armistice and its violations of the DMZ in April 1996, and signs emerging throughout the year of a qualified but still tangible Sino–Russian push to form a strategic partnership aimed at countering American global power.

In May 1997 two definitive reports mandated by Congress set the context for US strategy during the Clinton Administration's second term of office: a presidential report on *A National Security Strategy for a New Century* and the US Defense Department's 'Quadrennial Defense Review' (QDR) reviewing US defence strategy for the years 1998–2005.[89] An updated version of the East Asian Strategy Report (EASR II) was released in November 1998.[90] All of these documents emphasised the Asia-Pacific region's continued importance to US global strategy. The QDR was the most significant of these documents because it attempted to address specific criticisms directed towards the BUR.[91] The EASR II attempted to apply the QDR's strategic reasoning specifically to the Asia-Pacific region.

The QDR retained the BUR's emphasis on US forces capable of fighting two major regional conflicts simultaneously and noted that no other power would be able to contest the United States as a 'global peer competitor' until at least 2015. However, the QDR emphasised that in the event the United States became involved in one theatre war, 'it would need to be extremely selective in making any additional commitments to either engagement activities or smaller-scale contingency operations'. If engaged in two simultaneous conflicts, 'US forces would be withdrawn from peacetime engagement activities and smaller-scale contingency operations as quickly as possible'. The Defense Department argued that the QDR thus differed from the BUR by placing greater reliance on emerging technologies, by updating operational concepts and by achieving more efficient resource management'.[92] The QDR hedged on the type and timing of military contingencies which would involve US forces and it was more resource-sensitive than its doctrinal predecessor.

The QDR's integrated concepts of 'Shape, Respond and Prepare' were applied to EASR II. The United States intended to shape and promote a 'secure, prosperous and peaceful' Asia-Pacific community 'in which the United States is an active player, partner and beneficiary'. It would be capable, however, of responding to a full spectrum of regional crises. It would also prepare for future strategic uncertainties.[93]

The QDR's key planning assumptions were that the region would remain one 'mostly at peace' and that US deterrence strategy would be primarily directed towards 'critical localized areas such as the Korean Peninsula'. Approximately 100 000 US forces would remain stationed in both the European and Asia-Pacific theatres of operation as a political symbol of US strategic interest. In a two-conflict scenario, selected rapid response forces (that is, bombers and amphibious assault forces) would swing between the two theatres. The most important force capabilities, however, would be new weapons technologies introduced to enhance the precision and lethality of US firepower that could be deployed and projected quickly in future crises. Existing US bilateral security alliances would remain key components of the US deterrence posture in the Asia-Pacific, with US bases in Japan and Korea central to implementation of the QDR's rapid response strategy. China would remain critical to regional peace and stability and it would continue to be engaged as a 'responsible' rather than threatening regional player. Chinese military modernisation would be closely monitored, however, for signs that the PRC was becoming a major military competitor to the United States. The QDR projected this would be of greater concern to US force planners after the year 2015. 'Security pluralism' would also be pursued as part of the United States' overall regional strategy – the development of cooperative and complementary frameworks in which nations seek to address their security concerns through bilateral and multilateral relationships and dialogue.[94]

The QDR incurred similar criticisms to those directed towards the BUR by those convinced that US mission requirements far exceeded projected US force capabilities. Force readiness was a major issue. The QDR projected the US navy decommissioning twelve to fifteen surface ships and at least two submarines. Active duty personnel would be reduced by an additional 4 per cent (active US army divisions had already been trimmed from eighteen divisions maintained at the time of the Persian Gulf War to a projected ten by the end of the century). Fighter and bomber wings would be consolidated and quantities of new weapons procurements would also be reduced sharply. Assumptions about the efficiency of the RMA high technology were also attacked as assuming that 'any adversary will cooperate by being exactly when and where the RMA dictates', ignoring fundamental Clausewitzian principles on the 'fog of war'. The QDR was wedded to traditional threat analysis and to maintaining the status quo when real threats facing the United States could emanate from 'rogue states' such as North Korea or from various nuclear proliferants intent on compromising US global power as a means to achieve their own limited strategic ends. By early 1999 the Clinton Administration had relented to Congressional Republicans, who had led the charge for a more broadly based threat assessment spectrum. It concurred with increasing the defence budget by an additional $12 billion for the fiscal year 2000 (US defence spending had declined 38 per cent in real terms between 1985 and 1997). It also agreed to explore various options for deploying both a nationwide anti-missile defence system and TMD systems in both Europe and Asia.[95]

The sceptics also linked their overall concerns about inadequate means underwriting ill-defined policy ends to a specific Asia-Pacific context. Of greatest concern was the prospect that ongoing Chinese military modernisation programs discredited the Clinton Administration's engagement strategy. North Korean missile tests similarly undermined US diplomacy. These critics also viewed an effective TMD as a panacea for inadequate forward-deployed US forces to protect increasingly vulnerable friends and allies such as Taiwan and Japan.[96] In almost every instance, critics targeted liberal assumptions about trust building, arms control and integration of regional markets as the basis of their arguments.

In its last year in office, the Clinton Administration appeared to be moving increasingly towards accepting at least some of these realist postulates but was far from ready to discard completely its liberal world views. Indeed, the realists have pressed their case forcefully that the history of Asian security relations has been characterised by great-power domination and an absence of shared interests or values.[97] In his landmark study, *Diplomacy*, Henry Kissinger has argued that it would be wrong to deny the continued relevance of power balancing to this region and premature to expect most Asian states to jump on the liberal bandwagon:

> Wilsonianism has few disciples in Asia. There is no pretence of collective security or that cooperation should be based on shared domestic values ... The emphasis is all on equilibrium and national interest ... other Asian nations are likely to seek counterweights to an increasingly powerful China as they already do to Japan ... And that ... is why ASEAN is asking the United States to remain engaged in their region.[98]

Realism's 'relevance', however, is not necessarily synonymous with complete dominance as Kissinger might lead us to believe. The Clinton Administration was understandably reluctant to acknowledge that liberal policy approaches are completely irrelevant, even in such a physically and culturally diverse region. It continued to demonstrate a genuine enthusiasm for developing multilateral economic and security cooperation in such established forums as APEC and the ARF. Stanley Roth, US Assistant Secretary of State for East Asian and Pacific Affairs, argued to Congress in early 1999 that 'one of the main accomplishments of the Clinton Administration in Asia has been vigorous support for the establishment and strengthening of regional institutions'. APEC continued to be represented as the best possible vehicle for trade and investment liberalisation. The ARF and ASEAN itself were experiencing 'temporary difficulties' but their overall record of diplomatic achievements in Indochina and elsewhere still merited US support.[99] The President conducted two summits with his Chinese counterpart in 1997 and 1998, expressing confidence on both occasions that the world views of China and the United States were not all that different.

The major danger confronting American interests by adhering to such a liberal perspective, realists insisted, is that intra-regional actors would respond by becoming increasingly dismissive of US interests in their determination to forge a new regional security order on their own terms. Little alternative existed for maintaining American regional influence to strengthening the US bilateral alliance network at a time when ASEAN was shifting towards closer relations with China via the 'ASEAN + 3' grouping, involving as well, a reluctant Japan and somewhat more enthusiastic South Korea. A key foreign policy adviser to then-Presidential candidate George W. Bush argued that Asia was becoming a more organic geoeconomic and geopolitical whole (as demonstrated by the 'ripple effects' of the Asian financial crisis). Given this condition, US alliances in the region needed to be strengthened to cope with 'fresh sources of potential conflict' and to update allied security coordination in accordance with post-Cold War structural changes occurring in Asia.[100]

### Reconciling Strategy Approaches: Securing US Interests in the Asia-Pacific

At present, there is no one issue in Asia-Pacific which is viewed as so challenging to the United States' vital interests that American public opinion has been galvanised into supporting a single vision or strategy. As one long-time observer of US policy in the region has noted, any such policy malaise cannot be attributed to any one particular administration nor to the US Congress. It instead relates to a collective failure within the American polity to fully recognise or understand the pace and depth of change in Asia and how this process can transform latent threats into immediate crises.[101]

In a strategic context, the Asia-Pacific region, rather than Europe or the Middle East, fields the world's largest armed forces and these are becoming among the most capable as increasing regional wealth is gradually translated into military strength. The US Secretary of Defense may still be able to tell his Chinese and other Asian counterparts that the United States is the world's greatest power and one to be reckoned with in any regional dispute, but how much longer this warning will remain uncontested is uncertain. Southeast Asia is less defensible now that American forces are no longer permanently based in the Philippines. Northeast Asia would be too if the Okinawan installations were to become inaccessible and a reunified Korea precluded the deployment of American forces on the Peninsula. As Paul Dibb has correctly observed, 'the US will remain the predominant global power in the next century, but it will have difficulty responding to the diverse strategic challenges of the post-Cold War era while also attending to its pressing domestic problems and the decline in its power'.[102] Under such conditions, it is critical for American policy makers to continue demarcating what its vital interests are in the region and to adopt a coherent regional strategy to secure them.

### Balancing China and Russia

The first essential component of a focused US regional strategy is to prevent a Sino–Russian coalition directed against the United States. Russia and China are the only great powers in a position to threaten the survival of the United States in the early part of the twenty-first century under any rational warfighting scenario.[103] Like the United States, Russian power is also declining (its industrial power declined by more than half between 1991 and 1996). In dealing with this reality, Russia is likely to seek a coalition with either China or perhaps with a unified Korea, in order to maintain its position as an influential Asia-Pacific power. Fortunately, at this point in time, US *vital* interests are still not in conflict with either Moscow or Beijing.

From a realist viewpoint, this could change if Sino–Russian strategic collaboration were to intensify. As noted in previous chapters, such cooperation might be designed to exclude American access and influence in Eurasia (including the reconstitution of Russian land power in Eastern Europe and an open-ended expansion of China's maritime capabilities). From an institutionalist perspective, Russian and Chinese inclusion in multilateral regional security arrangements and forums might dampen the incentive for Moscow and Beijing to coalesce with each other. China's participation in regional and international arms control may minimise the risk that its nuclear force could eventually be rendered obsolete by emerging US missile defence technology. Finally, a wealthy China could eventually become a more democratic nation less hostile to the West.

### Combining Deterrence with Power Balancing

A major source of confusion about US strategic intentions in Asia has evolved from Washington's inability to reconcile two apparently diverse policy approaches. One is that the United States' bilateral alliances in the region must be strengthened, despite what appears to be a less threatening regional security environment in the post-Cold War world. This policy approach, however, has been obfuscated by the Clinton Administration's apparent decision to eschew power balancing as a means of pursuing regional stability. The second policy track – engagement – implies that the United States will employ what Jonathan Pollack has termed an 'integration-based logic'. Potential adversaries will be encouraged by the United

States to pursue their interests within a framework of dialogues and rules. But Washington also insists that preserving and strengthening the old instruments of Cold War containment – America's bilateral alliances – is compatible with this logic. There has been, understandably, widespread confusion among regional allies and potential competitors, and within the American electorate, as to just what the engagement strategy actually means.[104]

It is essential that these two diverse policy approaches be clarified, if not reconciled. Future US administrations will be required to convey more precisely how the postwar US bilateral alliance network in the Asia-Pacific is relevant to contemporary regional security trends. The alliances could be represented as:

- Components of a potentially critical infrastructure from which counter-coalitions may be formed to contend with hostile hegemonic contenders which may arise in the region; or
- Short-term deterrence mechanisms to prevent states from committing aggression against their neighbours; or
- Long-term instruments of strategic reassurance designed to instil confidence in regional friends and allies that the United States will remain strategically involved in the Asia-Pacific.

### Alliances, Counter-Coalitions, Transparency

As discussed earlier in the chapter, China is the most obvious candidate for hegemonic status in the region. Particularly since 1994, the Clinton Administration intensified its efforts to prevent Beijing from assuming this mantle by identifying and pursuing areas of mutual strategic cooperation. In doing so, it adhered to the liberal assumption that the Chinese leadership is intent on making its country prosperous and powerful and that, with Western financial and technological assistance, China will derive absolute gains. This outcome is preferable to that of China seeking relative advantage over its regional neighbours and great power competitors.

Realists discount the assumption that China would be content to join any multilateral regional security system in which it must share equal status with the United States. They believe that the Asia-Pacific region cannot remain at peace without the Americans actively balancing Chinese power through the establishment of effective counter-coalitions.[105] The Clinton Administration's EASR policy reviews acknowledged the growth of China's nuclear weapons force and overall military power. They also appeared deliberately reticent, however, in discussing the implications of such capabilities for US national security, apart from, that is, stating that 'the United States and China's neighbours would welcome greater transparency in China's defence programs, strategy and doctrine'.[106] Realists insist that US strategic doctrine must be more precise in specifying the contingencies under which China's use of military force would encroach on US vital interests. Yet the Chinese must also be assured that the United States will not oppose China as long as its interests are respected and its allies are not threatened. Failure to specify unacceptable Chinese behaviour, realists argue, could help escalate tensions between China and the United States in any future regional crises, needlessly triggering policy miscalculations. Three typical contingencies currently need to be addressed in this context: (1) an outright Chinese invasion of Taiwan which would threaten its survival; (2) a highly improbable Chinese decision to back its North Korean treaty ally if Pyongyang were to decide to invade South Korea; and (3) Chinese efforts to block or interdict US or allied shipping in the South China Sea.

Discussing these contingencies extensively in US policy-making circles may reinforce already strong Chinese perceptions that the United States is orchestrating a post-Cold War containment strategy in the Asia-Pacific directed against itself. It could therefore be less inclined to participate in various regional multilateral frameworks where the United States is involved. However, this risk is not unacceptably high as Beijing's leadership has demonstrated sufficient diplomatic sophistication in using these forums to press its own position when it has perceived that multilateralism is working to its advantage in the region. The benefits of embracing strategic ambiguity as a posture in dealing with Beijing must be weighed against the benefits of reducing US policy uncertainty. The benefits of maximising policy transparency in the pursuit of critical national security interests are especially apparent in regard to such critical issues as Taiwan, TMD and the future of US alliance politics in the region. Early signs posited by the new George W. Bush Administration concurred with such thinking.[107]

Another rationale for the United States sustaining its Asia-Pacific alliance network in a 'threat-fluid' environment corresponds with 'alliance mutuality'. This concept is defined as 'those collective or shared interests that cut across different alliances, particularly bilateral ones, to reinforce cooperation throughout an entire network of alliances'.[108] The United States functions as a benevolent alliance leader or hegemon by maintaining loose security commitments and providing economic gains (markets, investments, etc) to its regional allies and by precluding the rise of a hostile regional hegemon through selective crisis intervention and through deployments of superior military power in the region. This approach to alliance relationships challenges a fundamental axiom of the realist school: that alliances inevitably dissolve when there is a significant decrease in the level of threat its members face. It is debatable, however, if such relationships are viable on their own terms. Liberals would argue that they are merely interim phases to increasingly more comprehensive multilateral frameworks that will eventually underwrite regional security. Realists would view them as interim arrangements to emerging, more comprehensive alliances or coalitions that will become more explicit in response to emerging threats or security dilemmas.

### *Deterrence versus Reassurance*[109]

Continued US strategic involvement in the Asia-Pacific through maintaining alliance commitments can lend specificity and form to its regional interests and commitments until such time as multilateral security arrangements based on a level of regional consensus emerge. The challenge confronting US defence planners and their allies is how to devise ways and means of achieving a stable and orderly transition from dependence on their old alliance relations to new and effective forms of regional security in which the United States will still play a vital role. The timing and context of this transitional task is critical, involving a carefully planned and appropriately timed shift of American politics in the region from a strategy of postwar deterrence to one of strategic reassurance.

This transitional process is complicated even more by increasing allied expectations that military cooperation with the United States be conducted on the basis of greater equality and consultation in return for shifting from a tight bilateral security association with the United States to a broadened, less explicit relationship. Achieving strategic reassurance relates to pursuing shared interests in maintaining regional stability and, as importantly, ensuring that residual US commitments are retained, are credible, and are consistent.[110] Identifying the means by which alliance coordination and burden-sharing can be enhanced is critical. The revision of the US–Japan Defense Guidelines was illustrative of how this transition could be realised. The Japanese will expand their security role by providing greater logistical support, fuel supplies and related military assistance to US forces deployed in Japan that are involved in future regional conflicts. The United States also needs to consider how to incorporate other bilateral allies, particularly South Korea and Australia, more systematically into a web of regional security consultations without advertising these as a NATO-style joint high command which could only antagonise the Chinese. An informal but reliable network of security consultations among all of the United States' allies in the Asia-Pacific could facilitate trust-building as a necessary pre-condition for the development of more extensive regional multilateral security cooperation. Some American policy planners have coined the term 'enriched bilateralism' to describe this development.[111]

America's bilateral security alliances in Asia can thus be adjusted most effectively by reassessing the commitment rationales underlying their continuation. An effective bilateral alliance should facilitate a US presence in the Asia-Pacific that serves regional and/or international security, but ideally at a manageable cost to Washington. It should not be justified on the grounds of inertia; nor should it be allowed to assume a political life of its own. Balancing and continually re-evaluating mutual security interests and committing appropriate military capabilities within an alliance context to meet those interests is the best process for alliance maintenance. By applying this principle, the United States will be more likely to retain the confidence of its allies and to encourage a viable interim power equilibrium in Asia.

### Moving Towards Multilateralism?

By pursuing the procedures described above, the United States could revise its security posture in the Asia-Pacific more successfully and preserve its strategic influence in the region. It could then work with its bilateral security allies to create new consultative architectures directed towards defusing specific crises points and accommodating varying great and middle power interests. The implementation of the Four Power Talks between the two Koreas, China and the United States to negotiate a new peace accord for the Korean Peninsula in lieu of the existing UN armistice illustrates how this process could work. The United States conducted extensive consultations with both South Korea and Japan prior to the talks being formally proposed in April 1996 by President Clinton and South Korean President Kim Young-Sam. By including China in the talks the United States properly acknowledged Beijing's great-power status while at the same time reaffirming its determination to ensure the security of South Korea and Japan in the event that North Korea ultimately rejected the proposal. The United States may be well served by exploring other opportunities for integrating deterrence and reassurance strategy. For example, regional nuclear arms control initiatives with Russia, China and possibly India, as well as crisis avoidance on the high seas, both present themselves as policy areas where such an approach may be constructive.

Future American strategy and doctrine will need to acknowledge more explicitly that Southeast Asia constitutes a separate subregion with a different array of security challenges than those confronting Northeast Asia. Accordingly, the United States will need to take gradual steps to transform its existing Southeast Asia bilateral security ties into a multilateral system if its interests are to accord with the future policy agendas of ASEAN and the ARF. Formal US defence relations with at least three of the seven ASEAN states (Thailand and the Philippines by treaty and Singapore by a comprehensive Memorandum of Understanding) provide Washington with a natural point of entry into local discussions about conflict prevention. Keeping the Strait of Malacca and other key maritime chokepoints accessible to US military and commercial traffic is the one unquestionably critical US strategic objective in the Southeast Asian and Southwest Pacific subregions that has global strategic ramifications.[112] Current bilateral arrangements between the United States and the three ASEAN states with which it entertains formal security ties provide an adequate infrastructure, but one that can be multilaterally strengthened to fulfil this objective.

Any multilateral strategy for Southeast Asia must confront persistent and well-known policy constraints. Opportunities for security collaboration will be limited to contingencies where American and local ASEAN interests coincide to a high degree. Washington's effectiveness will be restricted by the precondition that key neighbouring states will need to support any US strategic presence in, or involvement with, any given subregional security issue. For example, American efforts to establish new, permanent basing facilities adjacent to Indonesia or Malaysia for safeguarding the Strait of Malacca would be strongly opposed by these two states. This would be the case even though they currently sustain logistical cooperation with the United States Navy via informal Memorandums of Understanding. These governments, along with the other ASEAN states, would prefer an indirect American involvement which would 'focus on assisting regional armed services in developing their own capacities to monitor and defend their maritime spaces'.[113]

Finally, Washington will need to find a basis for dialogue with Asian governments on the issue of values. The growing sense of Asian self-identity will make it virtually impossible for the United States to establish itself as the undisputed leader of a 'Pacific Community' in the twenty-first century. Most Asian governments want a continued American military presence in the region and continued American interest (if not a direct involvement) in Asia's political and economic affairs. However, they are not about to trade their new-found independence to achieve these goals. Asian nationalism and 'Asian Values' mean that the United States must play a subtle role in the region. This is particularly true in regard to an increasingly fragmented and vulnerable Indonesia. The United States can only manage this role if it demonstrates a clear understanding of the cultural and social roots of key regional actors.

## Conclusion

The future success of US security policies in the Asia-Pacific will be determined primarily by two developments. The first is how clearly Washington correlates its most important interests with the emerging strategic priorities of key regional actors. The second is whether or not Washington can actually allocate sufficient resources to secure its objectives. An adjunct to these two points is that it will also be essential that present and future US Administrations clearly and effectively communicate their policies, objectives, interests and commitments both to their domestic audiences as well as to their allies in the Asia-Pacific.

The 'Reagan Doctrine' discussed at this chapter's outset underscored the continuing 'interest-ideals' dilemma confronting US policy makers. Another postwar president, however, provided a more relevant policy doctrine to define the American 'national interest' as it applies to the Asia-Pacific region. If they are contemplating success, contemporary US policy makers will be required to formulate a successor to the 'Nixon Doctrine'. Introduced in 1969, this policy statement laid down the basic premises that have shaped most subsequent American approaches to Asia-Pacific security policy. They are: deter potential regional threats with cost-effective force assets; encourage regional allies to assume ever greater responsibilities for their own defence; and manage regional security through systematic consultations with Russia, China and Japan as the region's other great powers.[114] US doctrinal credibility has been undermined by Asian doubts about both the intensity and the scope of American commitments to the region. It is now confronted even more directly by structural change in the region that challenges the future relevance of American bilateral alliances – the traditional mechanism for translating American commitments into policy action. Clearly a successor to the Nixon Doctrine is long overdue.

The United States faces the prospect of having to deal with an increasingly capable Asia that can test its historical dominance over the eastern Eurasia rimlands and littorals. Its economic interdependence with the region will continue to intensify. Any successor doctrine must therefore take these capabilities and that interdependence into account in ways not apparent nearly three decades ago when the Nixon Doctrine came into force. America will be compelled to become a regional power balancer during the first part of this new century while simultaneously cultivating a regional order which will ultimately render power balancing unnecessary. This policy challenge is at least as difficult as that which confronted the United States at the outset of the Cold War when Kennan's Long Telegram prescribed an American grand strategy for the postwar period. Rallying American domestic support for a new strategic blueprint while simultaneously winning the confidence and respect of both friends and competitors in the Asia-Pacific makes that challenge all the more formidable.

CHAPTER 7

# Conclusion:
# Shaping Convergent Security

The strategic configuration of the Asia-Pacific region is in a major state of flux. Its economic and security institutions are confronting an intensification of irredentist and territorial disputes, a possible fragmentation of several key polities and uncertainties regarding both the intentions and capabilities of the region's key strategic actors.[1] These factors have generated internal and external security problems, many of which are inter-related, and all of which constitute major policy challenges for regional decision makers. Their resolution would create major opportunities for advancing regional security.

While the realist and liberal approaches are both concerned with ensuring long-term Asia-Pacific stability, they suggest different strategies for attaining it. These two approaches have forged a consensus, however, on at least two key points. One is the recognition that a new regional security complex is now emerging in the post-Cold War Asia-Pacific security environment. The other is the imperative of re-examining how regional security can be better managed to ensure stability in the Asia-Pacific during the course of the new century.

Both realists and liberals acknowledge the emergence in the Asia-Pacific of what Barry Buzan has termed a 'regional security complex'. A security complex is a group of states whose security concerns are so closely linked that the security concerns of one individual state cannot be considered in isolation from that of others.[2] The Cold War instigated distinct changes in the Asia-Pacific regional security order: from bipolar superpower dominance to regionalisation and localisation of conflict management. As the 1990s unfolded, however, it became clear that Asia-Pacific states could not isolate themselves from broader international security trends and that a complex interplay of cooperative security models at the regional level and realist power balancing at the global level was actually occurring.

Realists are looking for new explanations of the contemporary dimensions of power and state-centric competition in the region. Liberals are focusing on the evolution of the Asia-Pacific states' interactions – their attitudes towards each other and the rules or norms governing such interactions. They insist that conflict management must evolve from the politics of confrontation, represented by alliances and power balancing, to that of collaboration in multilateral approaches that emphasise strategic cooperation.

It is argued here that convergent security is a viable means for integrating realist and liberal approaches. This approach focuses on aspects of bilateral security cooperation other than the traditional mechanisms of deterrence and power balancing that underwrote American and Soviet postwar bilateral regional security commitments in Asia. It embraces the principle of inclusion as a major determinant of future strategic behaviour. It particularly honours and accommodates the value of middle-power participation in the definition and introduction of regional security norms and regimes. Although it incorporates selective dimensions of power-balancing strategy, it contests the long-term effectiveness of both hegemonic stability and great power concerts in ensuring a benign regional security order. It acknowledges, however, that the competition may well exist with cooperation during the initial stages of implementation. The immediate objective of convergent security is to modify the most dangerous confrontation scenarios now threatening regional peace and stability.

In postulating this framework, it is assumed that those Asia-Pacific states that have the greatest stake in resolving the various crises to which convergent security may be applied must assume primary responsibility for its implementation. However, the question raised in chapter 1 as to whether the realist or liberal faction is *more* correct in addressing security politics in the Asia-Pacific need not be answered by such states as they implement convergent security. Instead, the optimum convergent security strategy is to utilise the strengths of both approaches to realise peace and stability in the region.

Convergent security requires a two-tiered approach. The first tier must involve the great powers – China, Japan and the United States – collaborating to underwrite initially a mutually acceptable security environment. The second tier must consist of aspiring, middle and smaller powers that would take the lead in developing mechanisms for trust-building and conflict avoidance. In temporal terms, such second-tier initiatives must involve a series of incremental 'transitional phases'. These phases would be endorsed by the larger powers, particularly China and the United States (in a politico-military context) and Japan (in an economic and diplomatic context).

This chapter will initially provide a brief review of those realist and liberal approaches which have recently been postulated for the Asia-Pacific. It then offers convergent security as a preferred strategy for underwriting regional stability. After initially defining the strategy and its components, its ability to integrate the realist and liberal arguments will be described in relation to: (1) cooperative bilateralism; and (2) pan-regional multilateralism. Convergent security's value as a solution to the region's most pressing security challenges will then be discussed and recommendations for its implementation will be offered.

## Asia-Pacific Security: Alternative Visions

Various realist and liberal explanations have been offered in anticipation of what will constitute the Asia-Pacific region's emerging security complex and how its key actors should respond to it. Most of these concepts have been previously defined in chapter 1. The most prominent realist policy contenders are: (1) strategic preponderance (also referred to as 'strategic primacy'); (2) neo-isolationism; and (3) various prescriptions for regional power balancing. Liberal predictions centre upon the development of regional security norms and institutions and an eventual shift to pro forma multilateralism. Each of these alternative visions will be addressed in the following subsections.

### Strategic Preponderance/Primacy (Realist)

Some American realists have promoted a vision of a new world order led by a United States which actively subjugates hegemonic competitors.[3] This strategy of 'preponderance' (also called 'primacy') embodies both realist and liberal elements because its anticipated outcome of greater international interdependence in the economic realm is similar to that espoused by most institutionalists. It is essentially realist, however, because the means it prescribes for achieving such a condition are largely confrontational and based on threat anticipation. Geopolitical rivals constitute the threat, and extended deterrence is the assumed strategy for neutralising their influence over key regional actors.

In an Asia-Pacific context, this school of thought deems China and possibly Japan as potential competitors to the United States for regional influence and predominance in the Asia-Pacific. It advocates maintaining or increasing US military power to balance or contain either 'rising hegemon'. Among the Asian proponents of American strategic preponderance in the Asia-Pacific are those who fear Chinese intentions relating to territorial and irredentist disputes (that is, the current governments of the Philippines and Taiwan). Others are traditional US allies and friends like Japan, South Korea and Singapore, who would prefer the United States to retain strategic superiority in the region but are increasingly uncertain about American intentions or capabilities to do so.

A regional preponderance strategy presents some serious problems. One is that it may be fiscally unsustainable in the absence of a clearly defined threat. A second difficulty with preponderance strategy is that any hegemon's geopolitical mandate is contingent upon those who are dominated not becoming alienated.

Perhaps the most telling indictment against the application of strategic preponderance or primacy strategy to the contemporary Asia-Pacific is that there is little evidence that China is planning to radically challenge that region's contemporary security system. Apart from resolving its territorial and irredentist claims on favourable terms, Beijing has declined to posture any doctrinal blueprint signalling that it wants to expand its boundaries beyond the territory it already contests. China's current opposition to the US alliance system in the Asia-Pacific appears to be defensive rather than predatory and risk-adverse rather than radical.

### Neo-Isolationism (Realist)

Neo-isolationists are a second major realist camp. They are increasingly active on both sides of the Pacific, interpreting the end of the Cold War as an opportune time to reassess and de-emphasise the military option as a means of projecting power and underwriting stability. Neo-isolationists active in the United States are descended from a long line of 'America-first' advocates, faithful to the policy maxim of 'no foreign entanglements' first enunciated by President George Washington two centuries ago.

The rise of Asian advocates of this strategy is a more recent phenomenon. It has some affinity with the postwar non-alignment movement and, more recently, with ASEAN's ZOPFAN framework. Its major catalyst, however, has been the anti-basing movement directed against US forces deployed in Asia-Pacific allied countries.

As 'minimal' or 'defensive' realists, neo-isolationists often view the continued deployment of American military power in the Asia-Pacific region as less than beneficial. If a power transition in the Asia-Pacific is inevitable, they assert, future Asian conflicts can best be avoided by the United States withdrawing its forward basing presence from Northeast Asia and downgrading (or even abrogating) its formal alliance commitments in the region. Moreover, they posit, the Asian financial crisis has not so undermined the economies of America's more prosperous Asian allies that they cannot assume a substantial share of their own region's defence burden.[4]

Another important component of the neo-isolationist argument is the shape of American military power as it now exists and operates in Asian locales. The RMA, it is argued, will eliminate the need for such bases because the United States will be able to strike targets anywhere in the world with high technology weaponry.

The most powerful element working for the neo-isolationist cause, however, is the 'no-casualty' philosophy. In the contemporary American political environment there is an unmistakable public aversion to incurring military casualties in conflicts where US national security interests are not clearly understood and communicated. Ongoing pressures for achieving ever greater financial accountability in military spending are also compelling US force planners to make harder choices regarding mission priorities and deployment patterns.

Finally, neo-isolationists argue that the current US extended deterrence posture is far too open-ended and that its credibility may be undermined in any number of post-Cold War Asia-Pacific flashpoints.[5] An example is Washington coming under pressure from the Philippines to include the Spratly Islands under its deterrence umbrella. Furthermore, the risks of the United States maintaining a deterrence commitment in such contingencies that may involve nuclear escalation and possibly incurring nuclear strikes against the US homeland are too high.[6]

In rebuttal, implementing a predominantly neo-isolationist posture in the Asia-Pacific is too risky because it is likely to produce an anarchical regional security environment, devoid of any *real* constraints to avert likely crisis and war. It is not in the interest of either the United States or any state in the Asia-Pacific to allow the United States to default as a key strategic player in the region. China would lose the one proven means of restraining Japanese rearmament. Japan would confront the terrible choice of strategic impotence or genuine rearmament that it has been able to avoid for half a century. American forward force deployments continue to make a critical difference to regional stability. There is no present alternative.

### Regional Power Balancing (Realist)

Among realists, various forms of power balancing have become the most widely discussed scenarios for organising Asia-Pacific security.[7] That Asia-Pacific policy elites should endorse power balancing may seem somewhat puzzling, given the traditional concern of Asian elites with their own governments' political survival and their preference for pursuing strategies of national self-reliance or 'self-help' to ensure it.[8] However, the very diversity of governmental and societal forms and economic systems that coexist in the Asia-Pacific has meant that these sovereignties have had to reconcile their self-help orientations with the multipolar strategic setting now emerging in the region. Power balancing is regarded by many Asian governments as the best way to do this.

Several variants of power balancing have been prominent in discussions on managing the changing distribution of military power in the contemporary Asia-Pacific region. Prospects for a Sino–American duopoly emerging in Asia during the early twenty-first century have led a number of analysts to advocate an 'engagement' strategy to cultivate mutual Chinese and American leadership in regional diplomacy and institutions. The objective is to prevent the 'China threat' from becoming a self-fulfilling prophecy, with Asia hardening into pro-China and pro-American blocs.[9]

A second bilateral approach to power balancing can be labelled as 'modified containment'. Realists have a general affinity for the 'China threat' thesis, but concede that what others view as threatening behaviour may simply be an instance of China pursuing its own legitimate interests as a great power. A future Sino–American strategic rivalry would entail both cooperative and competitive dimensions, with neither side inclined to challenge the other directly in a military context. The strategy is a balancing mechanism because it concedes China greater diplomatic and economic influence in the region but contests any Chinese effort to pursue regional hegemony through the application of offensive military power.

Power-balancing advocates have also advanced multilateral formulas. Paul Dibb's proposal for a quintipartite great-power arrangement (involving China, India, Japan, Russia and the United States), supported by middle-power diplomacy, has commanded much attention.[10] Although not identical, Dibb's model comes closest to the convergent security concept that will be presented as this study's approach to pursuing regional security in the Asia-Pacific. The differences are primarily in the timing and nuances of implementation more than in the substance of what is being implemented.

Two other multipolar patterns of power balancing might be cited. One is what Richard Betts has termed 'a bipolarity of blocs organising a multipolarity of states'.[11] Two alliances would dominate the region: one a continental arrangement with Russia and China, and the other a maritime or offshore coalition led by the United States and Japan.[12] An initial evaluation would yield the impression that this construct is already in place, given the recent Sino–Russian rapprochement and the strengthening of the US–Japan defence guidelines. It is too soon, however, to conclude that this pattern will endure.

The final pattern of multipolar balancing is the prospect that something resembling the nineteenth-century European great-power concert may materialise in the Asia-Pacific during the early twenty-first century. The advantages of concert are self-evident. A small group of great powers may engage in quick and clear decision making in episodes of crisis management. This arrangement must be predicated, however, on the ability of great powers to put aside their differences over values and ideologies and to derive consensus over what type of regional order they collectively prefer. Neither of these abilities is presently evident in the Asia-Pacific. Nor is it clear that the middle powers would accede very readily to a four- or five-power consortium determining how their future security environment will function and what role they would play in it.

### Multilateralism and Security Regimes (Liberal)

In contrast to the arguments presented by realists, liberals argue that the rationales for sustaining the alliances and coalitions that dominated Asian security politics for most of the postwar era are increasingly being undermined by evidence suggesting growing regional interdependence. They further assert that economic and security cooperation among states is a more likely outcome than realists would concede – especially in instances where state interests are not diametrically opposed.[13]

For many liberals, the answer to future Asia-Pacific stability lies in how successful states in the region will be in defining and implementing multilateralism and, more specifically, multilateral security. There is no consensus among those favouring multilateralism, however, on what form of multilateral cooperation is most appropriate.[14] Some advocate the development of existing regional institutions, like APEC or ARF, implementing a common set of rules which, if consistently observed, would lead to these entities becoming fully fledged 'security regimes'.[15] Others propose formal arms control arrangements as a first step for replacing strategic deterrence in the region with strategic reassurance.[16] Still others maintain that the United States should exercise leadership in constructing a new, complementary security framework in Asia and creating a climate in which Asian actors can find a workable balance through dialogue and trust-building.[17] The question of what factors will determine the viability of multilateral institutions merits fuller consideration.

An appropriate starting point is provided by Robert Jervis who has identified four critical conditions required for security regime formation: (1) that great powers must want to establish a regime; (2) that prospective regime affiliates must be convinced that others share their underlying values which support mutual security cooperation; (3) that regimes cannot form if a potential deviant or defector state is bent upon seeking relevant gains at others' expense; and (4) that conflict or the individualistic pursuit of security must be regarded by all potential regime participants as more costly than collaboration.[18]

As the Cold War drew to a close, the region's two foremost powers, the United States and China, were qualified in their support for establishing multilateral security structures in the region. The United States still emphasised the preservation and viability of its traditional bilateral alliances in the Asia-Pacific, complemented by a low-key American participation in multilateral regional security dialogues outside that alliance framework. Multilateral security was regarded as a supplementary process to sustaining these bilateral relationships.[19] Left unexplained is how US deterrence strategy, traditionally directed against external threats to itself or its allies, complemented rather than contradicted these 'no threat' security dialogues.

Although it has agreed to participate in the ARF and APEC, China's overriding security objective remains to avoid compromising its sovereign interests. Beijing prefers to conduct individual bilateral negotiations with other regional security actors because it believes that this reduces the amount of collective pressure that can be applied against it in pursuing these interests.[20] Nor is it currently interested in discussing Taiwan's future political status with any external party.

At the multilateral level China continues to engage in ARF security dialogues and co-sponsored (with the Philippines) a major confidence-building workshop that convened in Beijing in 1996. It also regularly participates in CSCAP sessions and in the NEACD. Multilateral interaction is still qualified, however, by two key Chinese conditions for continued engagement: (1) participation on an equal footing; and (2) seeking common ground while reserving differences.[21] China remains highly sensitive to its own sovereign prerogatives and continues to guard against any tacit regional coalition forming to isolate it on key national interests such as territorial claims or excessive transparency on defence strategy and capabilities.

### Regional Security Norms and Institutions (Liberal)

Liberals within Asia and beyond counter that there is a distinct set of priorities shared by enough Asia-Pacific states to constitute the basis for norm identification and adherence. This includes the fact that these states must provide for security in both military and non-military sectors and must reduce their vulnerability to both internal and external sources of threat and instability. Building strong economic and political ties with both allies and potential adversaries as a 'hedging strategy' against policy miscalculations or changing state interests is a regional approach now being utilised. Japan has labelled this approach 'comprehensive security' while Indonesia has adopted a similar approach which it calls 'national resilience' (*ketahanan nasional*).

However, clashing national security interests are still too evident in the Asia-Pacific for comprehensive security or its 'common security' variant (the achievement of 'genuine' security by all states recognising and accepting the legitimate security concerns of others) to be effective.

Liberals have identified at least two major conditions under which states are more willing to collaborate in security regimes: (1) when security dilemmas are moderate or absent because threat perceptions are low; and (2) when the gains yielded by such collaboration are able to be shared equally.[22] Accordingly, liberals have concluded, states will collaborate most readily in security regimes if they are sure of their ability to calculate the future intensity of security dilemmas and to gauge more precisely the costs and mutual benefits of collaboration.[23]

### Regional Interdependence (Liberal)

Several key conditions need to be met before multilateralism can be effectively applied to the Asia-Pacific security environment. First, bilateral security arrangements need to be perceived less as power-balancing exercises and more as steps designed to achieve at least a proximate form of regional interdependence between the bilateral participants as well as other regional actors. Visible steps have been initiated along these lines with the region's three great powers (China, Japan and the United States) institutionalising regular bilateral dialogues into a process of 'concerted bilateralism' to address regional tensions and security issues. However, at this stage there is little evidence that these bilateral initiatives are facilitating the development of an integrated and comprehensive regional security framework.

Second, Asia-Pacific multilateralism, if it is to ultimately succeed, needs a distinct pan-regional imprimatur. At present, ASEAN is orchestrating processes in the ARF that may coincide with its ASEAN founding states' traditional 'regional resilience' posture, but, as noted above, these states have failed to cope with the core strategic issues shaping Northeast Asia's security environment. Even Southeast Asian strategic analysts are now conceding that the 'ASEAN Way' – focusing on common interest rather than on controversy – is a product of their region's own unique historical experiences and political culture and that this approach may not be applicable to Northeast Asia's very different security conditions and priorities.[24] Nor may it relate very effectively to the United States' global strategic agenda. The Clinton Administration's effort to launch an Asia-Pacific Regional Initiative in September 2000, for example, hardly touched upon core US security interests, instead focusing on the areas of peacekeeping and humanitarian disaster relief.[25]

Third, multilateralism can only work in the Asia-Pacific if it is kept distinct from multipolarity. Realists argue that those who would subscribe to a single architectural approach to achieve lasting security in Asia have always understated the difficulties involved. But it is important not to assign greater weight to short-term power balancing strategies, however essential, than long-term multilateral objectives. America's insistence that its regional bilateral alliances take precedence over multilateral security approaches, China's employment of ARF to promote 'equal security' with respect to those alliances, and Russia's initial ambivalence towards the Four Power Talks on Korea all illustrate the propensity of great powers to assign more emphasis to the politics of power balancing than to the promotion of regionalism, interdependence and multilateralism. Until this tendency to reinforce existing polarities is confronted and modified, norm identification and adherence – the basis of multilateralism – will be extremely difficult to achieve.

### The Case for Convergent Security

Several trends reinforce the need to integrate the realist and the liberal approaches to regional security in the Asia-Pacific. First, the 'exclusive' bilateral alliance networks either underwritten or precipitated by US deterrence strategy are gradually transforming into a more complex 'inclusive' architecture. Second, some major power support for overcoming different national interests and identifying common security norms appears to be present, although differences remain on whether bilateralism, multilateralism or a combination of the two approaches is best. Third, it is increasingly apparent that regimes for security collaboration in the Asia-Pacific can only be implemented if any security community that does materialise commands greater loyalty by its adherents than past multilateral security initiatives. If these generalisations are valid, how can the best of what both realists and liberals have to offer be integrated and applied to develop an effective interim Asia-Pacific security architecture? The following discussion posits the requisite components of such an effective convergent security approach.

*Moving From 'Exclusive' Bilateralism to 'Inclusive'*
*Convergent Security Strategy*

Although the Bush (Snr) and Clinton Administrations emphasised the continued relevance of US bilateral alliances in the Asia-Pacific, both acknowledged that these arrangements are no longer as effective as when they contained Soviet and Chinese power during the Cold War. President Bush's vision of a New World Order and President Clinton's rhetoric about a 'Pacific Community' embraced the multilateralist ethos of fostering collaborative security alignments.[26] In both cases, however, these were qualified by the condition that the bilateral alliance framework be preserved as insurance against the multilateral processes and structures that were increasingly underwriting Asia-Pacific security politics deteriorating into a new round of strategic rivalries and unresolved regional security dilemmas.

Critics of this approach have argued that it is 'riddled with paradoxes', with Washington practising a 'humble' form of multilateralism at a time when most Asians would welcome more US strategic involvement and leadership in the region. Issue-specific approaches to Asian security problems are more effective than region-wide dialogues or institutions, they conclude, because the latter cannot supply the cohesion and credibility needed for conflict resolution in a region which has no real history of multilateral security collaboration. Moreover, this is a region populated by states that have an established tradition of *not* openly declaring what their values and interests may be in case they conflict with each other or need to be changed when challenged by more powerful forces.[27]

If these critics are right, prospects are dim that ARF and other multilateral institutions will become sufficiently inclusive to generate needed levels of strategic reassurance. The flaw in such arguments, however, is their underlying assumption that implementing bilateral and multilateral security structures must be an 'either/or' proposition. 'Exclusive' bilateral alliances can, it is posited here, work in conjunction with more inclusive multilateral arrangements.[28]

This concept can be termed 'convergent security'. Convergent security envisions giving regional great powers such as China and the United States a collective stake in an evolving multilateral regional security order while encouraging middle and small powers to assume responsibility in shaping and preserving any such framework.[29] Bilateral security alliances would be adjusted to allow greater equality in alliance relations and to broaden the network of security consultations and trust-building mechanisms. Sensitivity would be extended towards each state's strategic prerogatives and concerns by identifying and implementing confidence-building measures and by conducting wide-ranging regional security dialogues. Strategic reassurance would be retained by sufficient deterrence commitments and guarantees to ensure that regional aggression could be avoided or defeated. Initially, these commitments would operate outside inclusive frameworks such as the ARF, but could gradually become incorporated procedures within such frameworks, developing norms that can command regional consensus.

The US bilateral alliances in the region – collectively known as the 'San Francisco System' – constitute the most obvious test case for applying convergent security to the transformation of postwar bilateral security relations. Traditional threat assessments and power-balancing tactics, underwriting the need for instituting military cooperation and other aspects of alliance cooperation, can no longer by themselves sustain bilateral alliance rationales. 'Alliance mutuality' – shared interests which cut across different sets of bilateral alliances to reinforce cooperation throughout the entire alliance network – will increasingly predominate within contemporary Asia-Pacific security politics. More specifically, the United States and its allies share a liberal commitment to promote continued regional prosperity and to defuse regional security crises. Accordingly, alliance affiliates prefer that the United States engage China on most regional security issues instead of containing it, particularly on the Taiwan issue. They also want the United States to exercise leadership in defusing Korean hostilities through systematic dialogue with the principal actors (North and South Korea) and with other major regional powers (China and Japan) rather than merely confront the North through traditional deterrence strategy.

Yet realist postulates retain significance in this alliance network since regional confidence-building cannot be sustained or expanded without the United States supplying an active and relatively benevolent alliance leadership. Despite tensions intermittently generated by the stationing of US forces in Japan and South Korea among the host countries' populations, successive Japanese and South Korean governments (and more recently North Korea as well) acknowledge the utility of that force presence as a balancing mechanism until more indigenous multilateral security arrangements emerge and mature in Northeast Asia. The ASEAN states and Australia value US power as an insurance against the unexpected rise of an intra-regional hegemon that may entertain geopolitical or mercantilist instincts inimical to their own prior to ASEAN or the ARF developing into fully credible multilateral security forums.

The challenge for each bilateral alliance is to demarcate those interests and initiatives that are relevant and desirable for transforming bilateralism into pluralistic security from those that actually detract from this process. Here interpretations by the United States and its respective allies can differ, at times markedly so. The United States insists that ballistic missile defence will be more appropriate than extended deterrence for dealing with selected regional threats of nuclear proliferation. Japan and Australia are reluctant allies at best in this context; South Korea remains unconvinced and the Philippines and Thailand are members of ASEAN's nuclear-free zone arrangement that symbolises a very different approach from that of missile defence to curbing nuclear weapons in the region. The Philippines argues that alliance coverage of its territorial claims in the Spratly Islands is integral to the US alliance commitment to defend that country; Washington demurs, instead focusing on the need for both Thailand and the Philippines to train and coordinate multilateral operations such as peacekeeping and humanitarian intervention with its own forces and those of other regional powers, including PLA contingents, as a means of preparing for collective response to diverse regional crises that may not have an obvious adversary. But the United States still demands allied loyalty as a condition for continued American affiliation with and commitment to these allies' core concerns over their own national survival and welfare. This raises issues pertaining to basing access, force interoperability and military assistance that must initially be addressed in a specific bilateral alliance setting. They will also affect calculations related to regional confidence-building in a multilateral security context and thus must be weighed within both frameworks.

### Retaining Great-Power Support

Neither the United States nor China will endorse convergent security if they perceive that they can simply apply *ad hoc* security diplomacy to meet their security interests in the Asia-Pacific. There is growing evidence that the Chinese have recently adopted a strategic 'grand design' that aspires to remove a fundamental structural characteristic of the Asia-Pacific region's postwar security order: the US bilateral alliance network. They increasingly regard the US–Japan and US–Australian alliances as pincers to contain Chinese power.[30] Accordingly, the ARF and other multilateral security initiatives in Asia should be viewed as instruments that can be used to minimise Beijing's major security concern – American hostility towards China. If such thinking ('pincer' containment) truly reflects Chinese concerns, Washington will need to develop and implement a more sophisticated China strategy than it has proven capable of doing until now. An Australian analyst has aptly summarised the American policy challenge as requiring both engagement and containment regarding China:

> Everyone wants China to be fully absorbed into international institutions and international rules-based regimes. But savage [Chinese] policy reversals, internal or external, cannot be wished away or ruled out, or even ruled unlikely. In such cases, it will be necessary at times to contain China as well as engage it.[31]

Recognising that China is prone to frequent policy shifts is an integral precondition to cultivating habits of cooperation and, ultimately, greater cooperative security in the region. It is critical that other Asia-Pacific powers project clear and consistent policy postures when China experiences such shifts. Only a short time ago, one of America's most prominent China watchers concluded that China had become a status quo power, defending an international system that operated on the premise of unmitigated state sovereignty, and that this shift would allow it to undertake wide-reaching industrial and economic reform. This was contrasted with the United States evolution into a 'revolutionary state', determined to press for global democratic reform.[32] Although the policy excesses of the Clinton Administration, embodied in its 'enlargement' strategy for pursuing global democratisation, have since been checked by a more pragmatic Congress and by the counsel of restraint offered by its regional allies, Beijing has refused to acknowledge that Washington's recent efforts to reaffirm its bilateral alliances are anything more than a new and fervent American containment strategy.

If US efforts to reiterate the contemporary importance of its alliance network have intensified China's sense of insecurity, how can a convergent security approach be used as a means to cultivate China's endorsement for regional security regimes? At least three specific steps can be implemented over the short-term. They involve exercises in reconceptualisation, trust-building and discriminate engagement.

First, the United States, Japan, South Korea, Thailand, the Philippines and Australia could release a joint declaration downplaying the term 'alliance' and emphasising the concept of 'network' to describe their security ties. The emphasis of these relationships would be shifted from collective defence to implementing regional stability through 'alliance mutuality'. Such shared interests should be defined to include regional prosperity, conflict avoidance, and avoiding strategic preponderance by hostile hegemons.

This symbolic reconceptualisation of alliance politics would be an integral part of convergent security. It conforms with what Muthiah Alagappa has termed a 'generic' type of security policy – not defining the nature of threats to be contested or values to be defended but applying sufficient abstraction to the concept of 'security' that its concepts and mechanisms can accommodate and adjust to diversity and change.[33] Annual security consultations would still be held between US policy officials and their regional counterparts in this network, and deterrence strategies would still be implemented or refined as appropriate. However, these talks would increasingly be directed towards how the bilateral security relationships could be tailored to fit into multilateral regional security initiatives. A recent Japanese study advocating this type of policy approach described it as 'providing the Asia-Pacific region as a whole with the "public good" of security'.[34] There is, moreover, a clear need for the United States to change its alliance management style to one that is less paternalistic and demanding than is currently the case.

Second, the United States and its bilateral allies could propose upgrading and consolidating the ongoing regional defence exchanges that they conduct separately with China and other regional powers into a more structured format for military consultation and planning. A reconstituted

Forum for Defense Authorities, a group of defence officials from nineteen Asia-Pacific countries which convened in Tokyo during late October 1996, could serve as the basis for such an organisation.[35] However, the new body would have to move beyond dialogue to create a network for achieving high levels of regional transparency and trust-building, involving the combined intelligence and logistical assets of the region's militaries. Those undertaking such a policy initiative should be under no illusion that strategic prerogatives traditionally regarded as highly sovereign assets would not have to be compromised to ensure credibility. The dissemination of sensitive intelligence would inevitably occur throughout the region in ways that American, allied and Chinese national military commanders would initially find to be unsettling to their perceived national security missions. In implementing such measures on an incremental basis in response to Chinese commitments to participate fully in the process, regional actors could demonstrate a willingness to address and alleviate China's ongoing concerns about neo-containment or military blocs jeopardising its own security. It will, however, be essential to include in this process effective steps to balance China's propensity to seek closer engagement with its regional neighbours with the evident intent to strategically isolate the United States in the region.

Third, priority needs to be given to applying effective conflict avoidance strategy to the region's two most urgent security problems – the Korean Peninsula and Taiwan. In Korea, the United States needs to support Kim Dae-jung's 'Sunshine Policy' of separating military strategy from economic and cultural interaction when dealing with the North Korean regime. Initiatives to build more meaningful politico-economic interaction with the North need to be afforded every opportunity if they are to succeed in defusing that isolated state's remaining hostility towards the outside world. Close coordination between South Korea, the United States, Japan and particularly China must occur for this approach to continue to succeed. Chinese leaders need to be reminded on occasions when North Korea is particularly assertive that the risks of war and escalation on the Peninsula outweigh any perceived benefits of an unstable and bellicose North Korean regime serving as a 'buffer zone' between Chinese and American power.

At the same time, the United States, South Korea and Japan need to work closely to reach consensus over how to effect an alternative policy of strategic response if the 'Sunshine Policy' should, despite apparent preliminary successes, prove to be unsuccessful. This would entail investigating ways to defend against the North's conventional military threat (especially its artillery capabilities) against the ROK, measures to neutralise the North's missile capabilities and a strengthening of US forward projection of 'rapid reaction' forces. Such measures would be costly in political and material terms, however, and should be adopted only if inter-Korean diplomacy should deteriorate beyond repair.

Resolving the Taiwan crisis is even more challenging because China regards it as an integral part of its territory. Any US forces committed to the defence of Taiwan's political independence from Beijing will be increasingly subject to an intensified Chinese missile threat. If it became clear that China had developed a preponderance of power in the East China Sea, the US Congress might become uncertain as to the level of its obligations under the Taiwan Relations Act or the TSEA (if passed). While China is frustrated by Taiwan's de facto independence it is, as this is written, sufficiently mollified by its wealth and by Taipei's investments in the Chinese economy to preclude an invasion. This will remain the case so long as Beijing's sovereign claims to Taiwan are not directly challenged by Taiwan's leadership or openly supported by the United States or other Asia-Pacific states. The 'breathing space' afforded by this situation buys time for all concerned parties to reach a consensus on a 'norm' that may emerge after further social and economic liberalisation in China leads to greater political moderation. The best diplomatic outcome from a region-wide perspective may well be a modified Hong Kong-type settlement – one that provides Taiwan genuine prospects of continued political autonomy and economic prosperity. Under such circumstances, Taiwan could emerge as a willing partner in the convergent security process. Alternatively, China's gradual political liberalisation may be the most promising – and perhaps the only – long-term remedy for preserving Taiwanese democracy short of major war.

Realists question the above measures because they view the risks of seriously modifying the deterrence aspects of the US bilateral security network as clearly outweighing the benefits of a China temporarily assuaged from confronting Washington and its regional friends. There is, they feel, no guarantee that Chinese policy would not once more become antagonistic if a future US government were to contest Chinese interests on a specific issue.

The problem with this argument is that it offers nothing more than the prospect of permanent confrontation. It also posits the continuing prospect of Sino–Japanese hostility. If the US–Japan alliance endures in something akin to its present form, China will inevitably attempt to dismantle it by pressuring the Japanese to expel the US force presence from their country. If the Americans withdraw, China will fear Japanese remilitarisation. Only by substantially changing the exclusively bilateral focus of the US–Japan MST can Washington and Tokyo together induce the Chinese to view their alliance as something other than a threat to China. Such a change must be instituted, however, without unduly shaking the confidence of the Japanese electorate in the American security commitment if multilateralism goes awry. The same policy challenge confronts US and Australian policy leaders but the significance of that alliance is obviously much less salient to Chinese assessments than US–Japan defence relations.

Realism supplements institutionalism in terms of fostering great power support for security regimes with a power equilibrium that discourages strategic opportunism and reinforces great power satisfaction with the status quo. The key goal from a realist perspective is to prevent any one crisis or grievance from intensifying before mechanisms are put into effect which are capable of rectifying grievances through negotiation; to assure that a power balance exists which guarantees that conflict will always be viewed as more costly than regime maintenance.

### Creating Incentives for Security Regime Formation

The above strategies reflect a process of 'muddling through', of maintaining regional security through balance of power alliances (although not calling them that) while establishing nascent security regimes. This is the best alternative currently available for the maintenance of Asia-Pacific security. More palliative is the ultimate prospect that effective security regimes will afford to states the opportunity to 'learn' how their interests are perceived by others. Converging interests can be better achieved if they assume the mantle of legitimacy provided by an institutional context. Resistance to specific interests and behaviour reinforces the need to compromise to the extent that the divergent interests of others can be accommodated. Defecting from a regime must invite punitive counteraction, bringing to bear a preponderance of power that exacerbates the defector's losses.

How can these principles apply to the long-term Asia-Pacific security environment? Achieving regime compliance behaviour entails a two-step process: (1) deriving specific rules for managing sensitive regional security issues; and, over time, (2) transforming these rules into fundamental norms or 'behaviour-guides' that enable a regime to shape future security interests and policies.[36]

Both these principles exceed the ARF's current capacities, which, as Michael Leifer correctly noted, merely represent 'an embryonic, one-dimensional approach to regional security among states of considerable cultural and political diversity ... a modest contribution to a viable balance of distribution of power within the Asia-Pacific by other than traditional means'.[37] The ARF's emphasis has been to establish and sustain 'comfort zones' within which participating officials can discuss and exchange views, rather than negotiate differences. With this emphasis, no agreement can be reached on developing norms for a regime, no innovation in bargaining or brokering tactics is likely to occur and, most importantly, no force can be applied to supporting those regimes or institutions. In short, no intellectual, entrepreneurial or structural leadership can be exercised in such an environment of extreme caution.

There are at least some signs, however, that ARF members are becoming more attuned to the role of ARF loyalty. The ARF's *Guiding Principles* on the Criteria for Participation, released in July 1996 at the Jakarta ARF meeting, call for any new participant to subscribe to, and work cooperatively to help achieve, the ARF's goals of regional peace and prosperity.[38] Regional stability has thus evolved as an organisational norm, although interpretations within ARF as to how compliance with such a subjective condition is measured obviously vary. Consensus is still lacking over more specific and substantive norms.

The ARF is, additionally, still commanding diplomatic credibility (despite the problems stipulated in chapter 6). This is evidenced by the recent softening of American scepticism towards its credibility and by increased applications for membership. Because of this, the *Guiding Principles* have imposed a 'geographical footprint' – a restriction on where future ARF member-states will originate (Northeast Asia, Southeast Asia and Oceania) in the interest of consolidating the ARF process before expanding its overall purview. The perceived prestige of membership, however, still does not necessarily translate into ARF principles finding their way into norms or other tangible indicators of regime compliance.

A key question is to what extent the ARF's 'go slow' approach to regime implementation will buy time for the learning process to mature. Politico-strategic discourse, compliance and interdependence must all be nurtured patiently if they are to prevail over the realist principle of self-help that has underwritten and characterised Asia-Pacific relations. In particular, domestic politics in China and in other developing states affiliating with the ARF must be allowed time to change. Such domestic political change may facilitate a paradigmatical change in the Chinese view that bilateral security alliances and their relationships to multilateral security networks are inherently antagonistic.

There is, in the opinion of many observers of the Asia-Pacific security community, a reasonable doubt that the ARF may not be able to respond to the challenge posed by the region's need for an effective multilateral organisation. If, unfortunately, this proves to be the case it will be the responsibility of the United States and its allies to initiate the implementation of a supplemental or replacement institution and to assure its inclusiveness of all the states in the region. The stakes are too high to accept the ARF failure in this regard; convergent security is essential to regional peace and bilateral alliances must have an organisation within which they may transition and operate.

Asia-Pacific regional elites can benefit from a 'learning' process focusing on how bilateral and multilateral frameworks can be combined to balance deterrence and reassurance in ways that underwrite regional stability and make effective ARF or other security regimes. Test cases illustrate such a learning process; the revived US bilateral security treaties with Japan and Australia (in April and June 1996, respectively) and the April 1996 Sino–Russian declaration in Shanghai have both been advertised as instruments of strategic reassurance in the Asia-Pacific and thus as stepping stones for greater regional stability. The 'test' in both cases is the extent to which their initiators can overcome the perceptions of outsiders that they were policy initiatives directed towards containing Chinese expansionism and American hegemonism respectively. Specific mechanisms clearly directed towards strengthening reassurance in the region will need to flow from these revived bilateral security ties if they are to conform with the convergent security model. Japanese and Australian contributions to the modification of US ballistic missile postures, greater Russian inclusion into the negotiation of a 'Korean solution' and a Chinese arbitration role leading to a Russian–Japanese resolution of the Northern Territories dispute are all hypothetical examples of how these arrangements could work to underwrite strategic reassurance over time. The extent to which these bilateral relationships work to defuse economic or strategic tensions among their signatories, and the understanding of those neighbouring powers most concerned with the implementation of these arrangements, will be critical in demonstrating how effective bilateralism can be in serving as a building block to more comprehensive multilateral ties.[39]

### The Way Ahead

A dual process of alliance revitalisation and regime-building is emerging in Asia-Pacific security politics. To what extent this process will lead to security cooperation prevailing over strategic confrontation in the region is still unclear. What is evident is that regional stability will be dependent upon several factors: how willing the United States and China will be to assert structural power to underwrite compliance with regional norms; the degree to which alliances become less exclusive and more inclusive in their orientation (leading to their eventual dissolution in favour of multilateral security institutions in the region); and how successful regime adherents prove to be in cultivating and sustaining habits of substantive bargaining, compromise and collaboration.

Despite ongoing apprehensions about the deterioration of Sino–American relations, there is evidence that Washington and Beijing are prepared to engage in regime-oriented, multilateral security collaboration on some of the most critical regional security issues. China's continuing participation in the Four Power Talks on Korean peace and reunification is illustrative. Beijing has also acceded to various arms control initiatives, such as the comprehensive nuclear test ban treaty, which have direct, long-term implications for Asia-Pacific security. The Chinese leadership, of course, insists that it will retain its prerogative to apply exclusive control over Taiwan and other issues it considers as integral to preserving its own sovereign legitimacy against 'outside interference'. Moreover, Beijing has made clear that it will not be bullied by threats of punitive action levied against it by Washington and its allies for engaging in behaviour that they may find offensive. The Hainan spy plane incident was illustrative. The Bush Administration quickly moderated the tone and content of its rhetoric after China made it clear it would not respond substantively to the President's initial tough language about the policy consequences of China's decision to detain the plane and its crew.

China has nevertheless demonstrated increased sensitivity over the years to negative views and perceptions that could affect its self-appointed quest to achieve great-power status. Its acknowledgment that the principles embodied within the International Law of the Sea should govern future negotiations over the contested Spratly Islands reflects this sensitivity. For its part, Washington has gradually shifted its regional security posture on the ARF towards one of more open support. The US Defense Department, for example, is now on record as acknowledging that the 'ARF can play a useful role in conveying governments' intentions, constraining arms races and cultivating habits of consultation and cooperation on security issues ... [and] ... it will develop over time into an effective region-wide forum for enhancing preventive diplomacy and developing confidence-building measures'.[40]

Multilateral security collaboration in Asia is still in its embryonic stages but it appears that it is having an effect on alliance politics in the region. Traditionally, major regional powers such as the United States, Japan and China sought to avoid multilateral involvement, believing it gave middle or small regional powers leverage to constrain their options. Increasingly, this 'exclusive bilateralist' approach is giving way to what has been termed 'extended bilateralism' – although bilateral alliances 'remain the primary structuring device for security regions' they are increasingly becoming 'extended or supplemented through multilateral mechanisms'.[41] This is not a trend restricted to the American alliance network: mid-level discussions on regional security issues such as the ARF's Senior Officials Meetings, and the annual quintilateral military policy planning staff sessions involving representatives from Australia, Canada, Japan, South Korea and the United States, exemplify this trend. While participation in some multilateral channels is reserved for long-standing bilateral collaborators, the overall tendency is towards greater inclusiveness, even if consensus is lacking over common goals or agendas.[42]

Consensus, as it is understood in a Western sense, may, in any case, be less relevant than the Asia-Pacific 'learning style'. This involves habits of informal policy adjustment and emphasises process as much as substance or outcome.[43] If so, leadership in security regime-building for this region will need to accommodate this style in ways much different than regime implementation in post-Cold War Europe. Bargaining and accommodation may well be more time-consuming and more intent on achieving face-saving mechanisms than on reaching closure on specific items or rigidly conforming to every precedent of international law.[44]

Perhaps the most challenging aspects confronting those who aspire to create Asia-Pacific security regimes are, in the short term, preserving stability and conflict avoidance in the region and, over time, reconciling the sheer diversity of the cultures, interests and elites who intersect in an 'Asia-Pacific' context, a variegated concept of 'region', at best. Peace in the region – including the Korean and Taiwanese flashpoints – must be assured by the region's major powers: the United States, China and Japan. Ultimately, there is a sense of shared experience and destiny for the Asian, Australasian and North American states who share both a Asia-Pacific geographic contiguity and an historical framework involving the world's greatest body of water. Security regimes offer one promising long-term approach for achieving an enduring regional security order but that promise rests upon the readiness of Asia-Pacific powers to accommodate rather than to compete. Convergent security – the maintenance of essential bilateral relationships while creating effective multilateral security regimes – is the key to peace and stability in the region.

# Notes

## 1 Introduction

1 Aaron L. Friedberg, 'Will Europe's Past Be Asia's Future?', *Survival* 42:3 (Autumn 2000), p. 149.
2 The concept of 'Asia-Pacific' employed here encompasses Northeast Asia (China, Japan, and the Korean Peninsula); Southeast Asia (constituting the ten ASEAN member-states); and the Southwest Pacific (primarily Australia). The Pacific dimensions of US policy planning are also included. Where appropriate, the study incorporates references to Russian and Indian policies.
3 Perhaps the seminal contribution recently emerging in this 'agenda-building' discussion is Muthiah Alagappa (ed.), *Asian Security Practice: Material and Ideational Influences* (Stanford: Stanford University Press, 1998). Other key books and articles, however, could be cited as shaping the direction of the debate. Although far from constituting an inclusive list, these include: Mohammed Ayoob and Chai-Anan Samudaranija (eds.), *Leadership Perceptions and National Security: The Southeast Asian Experience* (Singapore: Institute of Southeast Asian Studies, 1989); Michael E. Brown, Sean M. Lynn Jones and Steven E. Miller (eds.), *East Asian Security* (Cambridge, MA: The MIT Press, 1996); Barry Buzan and Gerald Segal, 'Rethinking East Asian Security', *Survival* 36:2 (Summer 1994), 3–21; and Paul Dibb, *Towards a New Balance of Power in Asia*, Adelphi Paper 295 (London: Oxford University Press for The International Institute of Strategic Studies, 1995).
4 George W. Bush appears to have adopted this approach during the early days of his Administration. A blueprint foreshadowing this trend was Robert D. Blackwill's 'An Action Agenda to Strengthen America's Alliances in the Asia-Pacific Region', in Robert D. Blackwill and Paul Dibb (eds.), *America's Asian Alliances* (Cambridge, MA: The MIT Press, 2000), pp. 121–2, 130.
5 For analysis, see Rosemary Foot, 'China's Role and Attitude', in Khoo How San (ed.), *The Future of the ARF* (Singapore: Institute of Defence and Strategic Studies, 1999), pp. 128–32; and Robyn Lim, 'The ASEAN Regional Forum: Building on Sand', *Contemporary Southeast Asia* 20:2 (August 1998), 130–3.
6 See 'The Chairman's Statement, The Seventh Meeting of the ASEAN Regional Forum, Bangkok, 27 July 2000' which notes that 'the Ministers …

agreed that with the 23 current participants, the focus should now be on consolidating the process of dialogue and participation ...' The statement can be
found at the official ASEAN website: [http://www.aseansec.org/].

7  The definitive treatises of the classical realist school of thought are E. H.
Carr's *The Twenty Years' Crisis 1919–1939*, 2nd edn (London: Macmillan,
1946); and Hans Morgenthau's *Politics Among Nations: The Struggle for Power
and Peace*, 5th edn (New York: Knopf, 1973).

8  These realist characteristics are summarised by John J. Mearsheimer, 'The
False Promise of International Institutions', *International Security* 19:3 (Winter
1994/95), 10. Mearsheimer cites five characteristics but the fourth and fifth
have been consolidated here. Other well known works on realism and its
more recent 'neorealist' derivative include Inis L. Claude, Jr., *Power and International Relations* (New York: Random House, 1962); Joseph M. Grieco, *Cooperation Among Nations* (Ithaca: Cornell University Press, 1990); John Herz,
*Political Realism and Political Idealism* (Chicago: University of Chicago Press,
1951); Arnold Wolfers, *Discord and Collaboration* (Baltimore: The Johns Hopkins Press, 1962); and Kenneth Waltz, *Theory of International Politics* (Reading,
Mass.: Addison-Wesley, 1979).

9  Joseph Grieco, a critic of liberal thought, nevertheless advances a useful
demarcation of 'liberal/institutionalist' school into four successive chrono-
logical phases: (1) functionalist integration theory in the 1940s and early
1950s; (2) neo-functionalist integration theory in the 1950s and 1960s; (3)
interdependence theory in the 1970s; and (4) neo-liberal/institutionalism in
the 1980s. See 'Anarchy and the Limits of Cooperation: A Realist Critique of
the Newest Liberal Institutionalism', *International Organization* 42:3 (Summer
1988), 486–7. Major works of the liberal school of thought include Robert
Axelrod, *The Evolution of Cooperation* (New York: Basic Books, 1984); Karl W.
Deutsch et al., *Political Community and the North Atlantic Area* (New York:
Greenwood Press, 1957); Joseph S. Nye Jr (ed.), *International Regionalism*
(Boston: Little Brown, 1968); Robert O. Keohane and Joseph S. Nye Jr, *Power
and Interdependence: World Politics in Transition* (Boston: Little Brown, 1977);
Stephen D. Krasner (ed.), *International Regimes* (Ithaca: Cornell University
Press, 1983); and Kenneth Oye, *Cooperation Under Anarchy* (Princeton: Prince-
ton University Press, 1986).

10  Recent examples include Alagappa (ed.), *Asian Security Practice*; Steve Chan,
*East Asian Dynamism: Growth, Order and Security in the Pacific* (Boulder, CO:
Westview, 1990); and Graeme Cheeseman and Robert Bruce (eds), *Discourses
of Danger and Dread Frontiers: Australian Defence and Security Thinking After the
Cold War* (St Leonards: Allen & Unwin in association with the Department of
International Relations and the Peace Research Centre, Australian National
University, 1996).

11  Ascertained by the author in numerous conversations with Asian colleagues
over the past two decades.

12  Philip Zelikow, a former analyst on the US National Security Council,
acknowledges that this problem is typical even in Western circles. When academics and other outsiders, he observes, find it difficult to diagnose the
cause of a policy's success or failure, they often 'write off the problem as unin-
tellectual ... and raise the study of international politics to a level of abstraction where the vagaries of particular policy episodes are eclipsed by the
grander forces shaping the global "system"'. Lacking "any common vocabu-
lary", policy practitioners retreat into characterising and justifying policy with

vague platitudes or oversimplified anecdotes, assuming "outsiders" will not endeavor to understand the actual dynamics underlying their decision-making'. See his 'Foreign Policy Engineering', *International Security* 18:4 (Spring 1994), 143–4. Also see Alexander George, *Bridging the Gap: Theory and Politics in Foreign Policy* (Washington, DC: United States Institute for Peace, 1993).

13 Brian Job, 'Multilateralism in the Asia-Pacific Region', in William Tow, Russell Trood and Toshiya Hoshino (eds), *Bilateralism In A Multilateral Era* (Tokyo/Nathan: The Japan Institute of International Affairs/Centre for the Study of Australia–Asia Relations, Griffith University, 1997), p. 161.

14 See Christopher Layne, 'Less is More: Minimal Realism in East Asia', *The National Interest* 43 (Spring 1996), 66–77. Layne, although a realist, is a critic of this posture. Among the best known advocates of this approach are Robert Kagan, 'The Case for Global Activism', *Commentary* 98:3 (September 1994), 40–4; Zalmay Khalilzad, 'Losing the Unipolar Moment? The United States and the World After the Cold War', *The Washington Quarterly* 18:2 (Spring 1995), 87–107; and Joshua Muravchik, *The Imperative of American Leadership: A Challenge to Neo-Isolationism* (Washington, DC: American Enterprise Institute, 1996). Although better known for his clash of civilisations argument, Samuel P. Huntington has also supported preponderance in some of his recent work. See his 'Why International Primacy Matters', *International Security* 17:4 (Spring 1993), 68–83. Other thoughtful critiques of maximal realism or primacy include Robert Jervis, 'International Primacy: Is the Game Worth the Candle?', *International Security* 17:4 (Spring 1993), 52–67; Michael Mastanduno, 'Preserving the Unipolar Moment: Realist Theories and US Grand Strategies After the Cold War', *International Security* 21:4 (Spring 1997), 49–88; and Christopher Layne, 'From Preponderance to Offshore Balancing: America's Future Grand Strategy', *International Security* 22:1 (Summer 1997), 86–124.

15 For American arguments supporting this posture, see Eugene Gholz, Daryl G. Press and Harvey M. Sapolsky, 'Come Home America', *International Security* 21:4 (Spring 1997), 5–48; Pat Buchanan, *The Great Betrayal* (Boston: Little, Brown and Company, 1998); and more generally, Ted Galen Carpenter, *America's Search for Enemies: America's Alliances After the Cold War* (Washington, DC: CATO Institute, 1992).

16 See for example, Richard Betts, 'Wealth, Power and Instability: East Asia and the United States After the Cold War', *International Security* 18:3 (Winter 1993/94), 34–77; Dibb, *Towards a New Balance of Power in Asia*; Michael Leifer (ed.), *The Balance of Power in East Asia* (Basingstoke and London: Macmillan, 1986); and Douglas T. Stuart and William T. Tow, *A US Strategy for East Asia*, Adelphi Paper 299 (London: Oxford University Press for The International Institute for Strategic Studies, 1995).

17 This definition is extracted from Robert O. Keohane, 'Multilateralism: An Agenda for Research', *International Journal* 45: 4 (Autumn 1990), 732.

18 John Gerard Ruggie (ed.), *Multilateralism Matters: the Theory and Praxis of an Institutional Form* (New York: Columbia University Press, 1993), p. 32.

19 Definitive sources include Charles Kegley (ed.), *Controversies in International Relations Theory: Realism and the Neo-Liberal Challenge* (New York: St Martin's, 1995); and Robert Keohane (ed.), *International Institutions and State Power* (Boulder: Westview, 1989).

20 John Baylis and Steve Smith (eds), *The Globalization of World Politics: An Introduction to International Relations* (Oxford: Oxford University Press, 1997), p. 161.

21  See Bjit Bora and Christopher Findlay (eds), *Regional Integration and the Asia-Pacific* (Melbourne: Oxford University Press, 1996); Kiichiro Fukasaku (ed.), *Regional Cooperation and Integration in Asia* (Paris: Organisation for Economic Co-operation and Development, 1995); and various selections in Michio Kimura (ed.), *Multi-layered Regional Cooperation in Southeast Asia after the Cold War* (Tokyo: Institute of Developing Economies, 1995).
22  See Richard N. Haas, 'Foreign Policy by Posse', *The National Interest* 41 (Fall 1995), 58–77.
23  See Condoleezza Rice, 'Promoting the National Interest', *Foreign Affairs* 79:1 (January/February 2000), 45–62. In January 2001 Dr Rice was sworn in as National Security Adviser for the George W. Bush Administration.

### 2 Great-Power Strategy I: China

*Note:* Foreign Broadcast Information Material (FBIS) material is not available in paperback after 31 July 1996. Page numbers after that date are not cited.

1  Lowell Dittmer and Samuel S. Kim, 'Whither China's Quest for National Identity?', in Dittmer and Kim (eds), *China's Quest for National Identity* (Ithaca and London: Cornell University Press, 1993), p. 283.
2  Examples include Denny Roy, 'Hegemon on the Horizon? China's Threat to East Asian Security', *International Security* 19:1 (Summer 1994), 149–68; Larry Wortzel, 'China Pursues Traditional Great Power Status', *ORBIS* 38:2 (Spring 1994), 157–75; Gerald Segal, 'East Asia and the "Constrainment" of China', *International Security* 20:4 (Spring 1996), 107–35; David Shambaugh, 'Containment or Engagement of China? Calculating Beijing's Responses', *International Security* 21:2 (Fall 1996), 180–209; and Aaron L. Friedberg, 'The Struggle for Mastery in Asia', *Commentary* (November 2000), 12–26.
3  Thomas J. Christensen, 'Chinese Realpolitik', *Foreign Affairs* 75:5 (September–October 1996), 37–9.
4  Examples of the institutionalist argument as it has been applied to China include various selections within Stuart Harris and Gary Klintworth (eds), *China As a Great Power: Myths, Realities and Challenges in the Asia-Pacific Region* (Melbourne/New York: Longman/St. Martins, 1995); Michel Oksenberg and Elizabeth Economy, 'Introduction: China Joins the World', in Oksenberg and Economy (eds), *China Joins the World: Progress and Prospects* (New York: Council on Foreign Relations, 1999), esp. pp. 29–35; and Alastair Iain Johnston and Paul Evans, 'China's Engagement With Multilateral Security Institutions', in Alastair Iain Johnston and Robert S. Ross (eds), *Engaging China: The Management of An Emerging China* (London: Routledge, 1999), pp. 235–72.
5  As cited by Yao Yunzhu, 'The Evolution of Military Doctrine of the Chinese PLA from 1985–1995', *The Korean Journal of Defense Analysis* 6:2 (Winter 1995), 62. Yao, a colonel in the PLA and an associate professor at Beijing's Academy of Military Science, is one of a rising number of Chinese military analysts whose writings concerning China's military policy are receiving widespread attention in the West.
6  On the importance of 'image' considerations as a determinant of China's security behaviour see Johnston and Evans, 'China's Engagement With Multilateral Security Institutions', pp. 251–4.

7  Alastair Iain Johnston, 'Prospects for Chinese Nuclear Force Modernization: Limited Deterrence Versus Multilateral Arms Control', *The China Quarterly* 146 (June 1996), 576. This 'special issue' of *The China Quarterly* addresses various aspects of Chinese strategy perhaps more comprehensively than any other compendium in recent times.

8  An early but still definitive article is by Xu Guangyu, 'Pursuit of Equitable Three Dimensional Strategic Boundaries', *Jiefangjunbiao* (3 April 1987), translation in Joint Publications Research Service, JPRS-CHI-88-016, (29 March 1988). Also see Yu Guang Ming, 'A Comparison of Chinese and Western Geostrategic Thinking', *Zhongguo Junshi Kexue* 4 (20 November 1995), 22–9, translation in Foreign Broadcast Information Service, FBIS-CHI-96-076 (18 April 1996), 44–50; and Yu Bin, 'East Asia: Geopolitique into the Twenty-First Century – A Chinese View', written for a research project on 'America's Alliances with Japan and Korea in a Changing Northeast Asia', Asia/Pacific Research Center, Stanford University, June 1997. The concept is assessed from a Western perspective by David Shambaugh, 'The Insecurity of Security: The PLA's Evolving Doctrine and Threat Perceptions Towards 2000', *Journal of Northeast Asian Studies* 13:1 (Spring 1994), esp. 14–16.

9  Hwang Byong-Moo, 'Changing Military Doctrines of the PRC: The Interaction Between the People's War and Technology', *The Journal of East Asian Affairs* 11:1 (Winter/Spring 1997), 221–3.

10  Assessments of a high-level symposium convened in November/December 1993 by the General Office of the Chinese Communist Party Central Committee and the Central Military Commission are offered by Shambaugh, 'The Insecurity of Security', esp. pp. 7–10.

11  Halford J. Mackinder, 'The Geographic Pivot of History', *Geographical Journal* 4:4 (April 1904), 435–7. For a recent assessment of Mackinder's contemporary relevance, consult Christopher J. Fettweis, 'Sir Halford Mackinder, Geopolitics and Policymaking in the 21st century', *Parameters* (Summer 2000), 58–71; and Geoffrey Sloan, 'Sir Halford J. Mackinder: The Heartland Theory Then and Now', *Journal of Strategic Studies* 22:2/3, Special Issue (June–September 1999), 31–2, see esp. map on p. 33. Analysis of geopolitics in a Chinese context is offered by Michael H. Hunt, *The Genesis of Communist Chinese Foreign Policy* (New York: Columbia University Press, 1996) esp. pp. 10–17; and by Zalmay Khalilzad, Abram Shulsky, Daniel Byman, Roger Cliff, David Orletsby, David Shlapak, and Ashley Tellis, *The United States and a Rising China: Strategy and Military Implications* (Santa Monica: RAND, 1999), pp. 21–4.

12  Nicholas J. Spykman, *The Geography of Peace* (New York: Harcourt Brace, 1944), pp. 40–1; and David Wilkinson, 'Spykman and Geopolitics', in Ciro E. Zoppo and Charles Zorgbibe (eds), *On Geopolitics: Classical and Nuclear* (Dordrecht: Martinus Nijhoff, 1985), p. 107.

13  William V. Kennedy, 'China's Role in a New US Deterrence Strategy', in Douglas T. Stuart and William T. Tow (eds), *China, the Soviet Union and the West* (Boulder: Westview, 1982), p. 252. See also John Erickson, '"Russia Will Not be Trifled With": Geopolitical Facts and Fantasies', *Journal of Strategic Studies* 22:2/3, Special Issue (June–September 1999), 263–5.

14  Sun Shuli, 'US–Mongolian Relations Are Developing Rapidly', *Xiandai Guoji Guanxi* (20 January 1996): 32–4, translation in FBIS-CHI-96-085 (1 May 1996), 6–9.

15  By way of illustration, see Chen Zhou, 'The Differences Between the Chinese Theory of "Modern Local War" and the US Concept of "Limited War"', *Zhongguo Junshi Kexue* 4 (20 November 1995), 43–7, translation in FBIS-CHI-

96-063 (1 April 1996), 49–54. Chen notes that 'US geopolitician [Nicholas] Spykman's "border zone" theory – "to control the fate of the world, it is necessary to control Eurasia, the control of which in turn necessitates control of the border zone" – is also a key ideological ground for the [American] containment policy and limited war theory'.

16  Yao Yunzhu, 'The Evolution of Military Doctrine', p. 66. Also see John Wilson Lewis and Xue Litai, *China's Strategic Seapower: The Politics of Force Modernization in the Nuclear Age* (Stanford: Stanford University Press, 1994), esp. pp. 209–30.

17  While not directly assessing China's nuclear policies in a 'geopolitical' context, Alastair Iain Johnston has written about the PRC's determination to apply greater control of nuclear weapons technology as a problem of international political status and image. See his 'China's New "Old Thinking": The Concept of Limited Deterrence', *International Security* 20:3 (Winter 1995–1996), 5–47; and 'Prospects for Chinese Nuclear Force Modernization'.

18  Michael D. Swaine, 'The PLA and Chinese National Security Policy: Leaderships, Structures, Processes', *The China Quarterly* 146 (June 1996), 360–93.

19  'Confident nationalism' is assessed by Michel Oksenberg, 'China's Confident Nationalism', *Foreign Affairs* 65:3 (Winter 1986/1987), 501–23. Also see David Shambaugh, 'Growing Strong: China's Challenge to Asian Security', *Survival* 36:2 (Summer 1994), 43–59; Allen S. Whiting, 'Chinese Nationalism and Foreign Policy After Deng', *The China Quarterly* 142 (1995), 295–316; and Christensen, 'Chinese Realpolitik', *passim.*

20  David M. Lampton, 'China and the Strategic Quadrangle', in Michael Mandelbaum (ed.), *The Strategic Quadrangle: Russia, China, Japan, and the United States in East Asia* (New York: Council on Foreign Relations Press, 1995), pp. 63–106; Michael D. Swaine, *China: Domestic Change and Foreign Policy* (Santa Monica: RAND, 1995), esp. pp. 81–98; and Stuart Harris and Gary Klintworth, 'Conclusion', in Harris and Klintworth (eds), *China As a Great Power: Myths, Realities and Challenges in the Asia-Pacific Region* (Melbourne/New York: Longman/St. Martin's, 1995), pp. 357–66.

21  Margaret M. Pearson, 'The Major Multilateral Economic Institutions Engage China', in Johnston and Ross (eds), *Engaging China*, p. 229.

22  Dittmer and Kim, 'Whither China's Quest for National Identity?', pp. 281–2.

23  Khalilzad et al., *The United States and a Rising China*, pp. 4, 59–60.

24  Xu Xiaojun, 'China's Grand Strategy for the 21st Century', in Michael D. Bellows (ed.), *Asia in the 21st Century: Evolving Strategic Priorities* (Washington, DC: National Defense University Press, Fort Lesley J. McNair, 1994), p. 41.

25  Excerpts from a speech by Tao Siju, reprinted in *Chiushih Nientai* (Hong Kong) (1 January 1992), 26–8, as cited by William Heaton, 'The People's Republic of China', in Douglas J. Murray and Paul R. Viotti (eds), *The Defense Policies of Nations* 3rd edn, (Baltimore: The Johns Hopkins University Press, 1994), p. 379. On China's response to the New World Order concept, see Richard Yang, 'The PLA and the New World Order: A ROC View', in Richard Yang (ed.), *China's Military: The PLA in 1992/1993* (Taipei: Chinese Council of Advanced Policy Studies, 1993), pp. 30–1.

26  'Special article' by Zhou Qi, 'Sino–US Relations After George W. Bush Assumes Office', *Wei Wei Po* (Hong Kong) (18 December 2000), translated and reprinted in FBIS-CHI-2000-1218 (18 December 2000).

27  See Tang Tianri, 'Sino–US–Japanese Triangle Must Be in Equilibrium', *Liaowang* 23 (3 June 1996), p. 44, translation in FBIS-CHI-96-127 (1 July

1996), 1–2; Shambaugh, 'Containment or Engagement', p. 206; Wang Wei-xing, 'Perfidy, Great Calamity – Commentary on the US Arms Sale to Taiwan', *Jiefangjun Bao*, 27 April 2001, reprinted in FBIS-CHI-2001-0426, 26 April 2001; and 'Foreign Ministry Spokesman Comments on US President's Speech Regarding US Development of Missile Defense', *Xinhua*, 3 May 2001, translated and reprinted in FBIS-CHI-2001-0503, 3 May 2001.

28  See Harry Harding, 'A Chinese Colossus?', *Journal of Strategic Studies* 18:3 (1995), 111–12; and Paul Godwin, 'From Continent to Periphery: PLA Doctrine, Strategy and Capabilities Towards 2000', *The China Quarterly* 146 (June 1996), 484–5.

29  Much of this discussion is adopted from Michael D. Swaine, 'China', in Zalmay Khalilzad (ed.), *Strategic Appraisal 1996* (Santa Monica: RAND, 1996), pp. 197–8; Swaine, *China: Domestic Change and Foreign Policy*, pp. 81–4; and Bi Jianxiang, 'The PRC's Active Defense Strategy: New Wars, Old Concepts', *Issues & Studies* 31:11 (November 1995), 77–87. The definitive Chinese statement on the concept was an address delivered by Admiral Liu Huaqing, 'Unswervingly Advance Along the Road of Building a Modern Army With Chinese Characteristics', *Jiefangjun Bao* (6 August 1993), pp. 1–2, translation in FBIS-CHI-93-158 (18 August 1993), 15–22.

30  Swaine, 'China', in Khalilzad (ed.), *Strategic Appraisal 1996*, p. 198.

31  See, for example, an article by Sino–Russian Association Vice President He Fang, 'With a Multi-Polar Order Now Evolving, the Super-Powers Are Going To Become History', *Jiefang Ribao* (22 April 1996), p. 4, translation in FBIS-CHI-96-131 (8 July 1996), 5–6.

32  See a Japanese press report in the *Mainichi Shimbun* (18 July 1996), p. 7, translation in FBIS-CHI-96-139 (18 July 1996), 5.

33  Background is provided by Greg Austin and Stuart Harris (eds), *Japan and Greater China: Political Economy and Military Power in the Asian Century* (London: C. Hurst, 1999). For a typical Chinese perspective, see Xu Zhixian and Yang Bojiang, 'New Acts: A Historical Retrogression', *Beijing Review* (14 June 1999), 12–14.

34  Chen Lineng, 'The Japanese Self-Defense Forces Are Marching Toward the 21st Century', *Guoji Zhanwang* 2 (8 February 1996), 18–20, translation in FBIS-CHI-96-085 (1 May 1996), 11; and Zuo Feng, 'Who Is Threatening Asia?', *Renmin Ribao* (3 July 1996), 6, translation in FBIS-CHI-96-145 (26 July 1996), 7.

35  Excellent background is provided by Tai Ming Cheung, 'Ties of Convenience: Sino–Soviet/Russian Military Relations in the 1990s', in Yang (ed.), *China's Military*, pp. 61–76.

36  In January 1992 Chinese President Yang Shangkun visited Malaysia and expressed China's 'full support' for the then proposed East Asian Economic Caucus (EAEC), linking such a forum's establishment with the importance of promoting 'Asianisation'. See Lam Lai Sing, 'A Short Note on ASEAN–Great Power Interaction', *Contemporary Southeast Asia* 15:4 (March 1994), 458. A Chinese assessment of the 'ASEAN plus three' grouping is offered in 'ASEAN Plus Three Agree on Some Economic Issues', *Xinhua* (2 May 2000), reprinted in FBIS-CHI-2000-0502 (2 May 2000). In late November 2000, Chinese Premier Zhu Rongji used this forum to push for an Asian monetary fund. See an Agence France Presse report (22 November 2000), available on the Taiwan Security Research website, [http://www.taiwansecurity.org].

37  The definitive article on China's South China Sea policy remains John Garver's 'China's Push Through the South China Sea: The Interaction of

Bureaucratic and National Interests', *The China Quarterly* 132 (December 1992), 999–1028. Also see Mark J. Valencia, *China and the South China Sea Disputes*, Adelphi Paper 298 (London: Oxford University Press for the International Institute for Strategic Studies, 1995).

38 Michael Leifer, *The ASEAN Regional Forum*, Adelphi Paper 302 (London: Oxford University Press for the International Institute for Strategic Studies, 1996), p. 36.

39 Jusuf Wanandi lists Chinese efforts to accommodate the ASEAN states on the South China Sea issue in 'ASEAN's China Strategy: Towards Deeper Engagement', *Survival* 38:3 (Autumn 1996), 122–3. For a generally negative assessment on Sino–Vietnamese relations see Luo Chin-i, 'Undercurrent of Improvement in Sino–Vietnamese Relations', *Hsin Pao* (Hong Kong Economic Journal) (29 March 1996), p. 19, translation in FBIS-CHI-96-070 (10 April 1996), 5–7.

40 Sangwon Suh and David Hsieh, 'From Suspicion to Trust', *Asiaweek* (26 July 1996), p. 22.

41 State Council of the People's Republic of China, *China's National Defense 2000* (Beijing: State Council Information Office, October 2000). An English language version of this document is posted at [http://www.chinaguide.org/e-white/2000] (accessed 2 January 2001).

42 Allen S. Whiting, 'The PLA and China's Threat Perceptions', *The China Quarterly* 146 (June 1996), 598.

43 See Weixing Hu, 'Beijing's New Thinking On Security Strategy', *The Journal of Contemporary China* 3 (Summer 1993), 51–5; Wortzel, 'China Pursues Traditional Great Power Status', pp. 160–2; and Shulong Chu, 'The PRC Girds for Limited, High Tech War', *ORBIS* 38: 2 (Spring 1994), 180–3.

44 As Whiting notes, 'in terms of rhetoric, quantitative and qualitative, the United States clearly ranks as the number one threat to the security of the People's Republic'. See 'The PLA and China's Threat Perceptions', p. 607. Also see Rex Li, 'Unipolar Aspirations in a Multipolar Reality: China's Perceptions of US Ambitions and Capabilities in the Post-Cold War World', *Pacifica Review* 11:2 (June 1999), 115–49.

45 Shambaugh, 'The Insecurity of Security', pp. 6–7. Also see Yu Bin, *East Asia: Geopolitique into the Twenty-First Century – A Chinese View*, Asia/Pacific Research Center Discussion Paper (Institute for International Studies, Stanford University, 1997), p. 9. Yu notes that 'the United States is the most important factor for China's future. Not only does it hold the trump card for China's modernization, it is the only country with the capability to jeopardize China's fundamental interests ... [and] is seen as a power with enormous sway to persuade other countries in the region, particularly Japan, to embark upon a path to contain China's rise in the next [twenty-first] century'.

46 Li Dan, 'Zhang Wannian on Sino–US Differences', *Cheng Min* (Hong Kong) (1 April 1999), translated and reprinted in FBIS-CHI-1999-0414 (1 April 1999).

47 In an interview with the Japan Broadcasting Corporation (NHK), Li Ruihuan, Chairman of the Chinese People's Political Consultative Conference, argued that critics of China link the 'China threat theory' with the pace and scope of its national development. China would be more of a 'threat', he contended, if it failed to develop steadily, in accordance with its abundant population and resources because domestic instability would intensify within the country. He concluded that the China threat theory should be relabelled as the 'China being threatened theory' by those with a vested interest in retarding Chinese

growth. See a *Xinhua* report of the interview, (13 December 1999), reprinted in FBIS-CHI-1999-1212 (13 December 1999).

48 Chinese TMD response options have been comprehensively outlined by Shannon Kile and Eric Arnett, 'Nuclear Arms Control', *SIPRI Yearbook 1996: Armaments, Disarmament and International Security* (Oxford: Oxford University Press, 1996), p. 621. Ambassador Sha Zukang, Director-General for Arms Control and Disarmament at China's Ministry of Foreign Affairs, recently warned that if one country deploys TMD, 'other countries will be forced to develop more advanced offensive missiles'. See his speech to the Carnegie International Non-Proliferation Conference in Washington DC, January 1999 and reprinted as 'China's Missile Warning', *Proliferation Brief* 2:2 (11 February 1999) at [http://www.taiwansecurity.org] (accessed 1 January 2001). Additional background is provided by Kori J. Urayama, 'Chinese Perspectives on Theater Missile Defense', *Asian Survey* 40:4 (July–August 2000), 599–621.

49 'Tang Jiaxuan's News Conference', Beijing Central Television One Network in Mandarin, (7 March 1999), translation in FBIS-CHI-1999-0308 (7 March 1999).

50 He Chong, 'The [words missing] of Taiwan's Patriot US TMD System', *Zhongguo Tongxun She* (Hong Kong) (3 February 1999), translation in FBIS-CHI-[document number unavailable] (3 February 1999). See also, Erik Eckholm, 'China Argues Against Planned US Missile Defense', *New York Times* (24 November 1999), accessed at [http://www.taiwansecurity.org/].

51 As confirmed in author discussions with various Chinese analysts at Stanford University, Stanford, California, April 1999.

52 A point appropriately reinforced by Whiting, 'The PLA and China's Threat Perceptions', p. 608.

53 Whiting, 'The PLA and China's Threat Perceptions', p. 607; and Friedberg, 'The Struggle for Mastery in Asia', p. 21.

54 Khalilzad et al., *The United States and a Rising China*, pp. 45–6; Anthony Cordesman, *China and the Asian Military Balance* (Washington, DC: Center for Strategic and International Studies, March 1999), pp. ii–iii; Godwin, 'From Continent to Periphery', pp. 478–80; and Michael G. Gallagher, 'China's Illusory Threat to the South China Sea', *International Security* 19:1 (Summer 1994), 169–94. China's production of a modern F-10 fighter has been delayed to 2003 and beyond due to technical problems, despite Russian and Israeli assistance. Estimates vary on the effects of Russia's jet aircraft sales to China. Cordesman concludes that the 'vast majority of China's combat aircraft … ranges from obsolete to mediocre at best'.

55 In late December 1999 the *Washington Times* reported that China took delivery of two Russian-built *Sovremenny*-class guided missile destroyers that could be applied to this purpose. The report was also carried by the Taiwan Security Research Centre on the Internet at [http://www.taiwansecurity.org/] (27 December 1999).

56 Chinese experts have admitted that most of their statements of concern about Japanese remilitarisation have a 'very high rhetorical component' but that the history of animosity between the two countries compelled China to remain vigilant over any Japanese gesture or action that may seem threatening. See Ian Wilson, 'Sino–Japanese Relations in the Post-Cold War World', in Harris and Klintworth (eds), *China As A Great Power*, p. 100.

57 An assessment typifying the Chinese perspective is offered by Chen Lineng, 'The Japanese Self-Defense Forces Are Marching Toward the 21st Century',

*Guoji Zhanwang* (8 February 1996), translated in FBIS-CHI-96-085 (1 May 1996), 9–12.

58 Office of Technology Assessment, US Congress, *Approaches to Civil–Military Integration: The Chinese and Japanese Arms Industries* (Washington, DC: USGPO, 1994), pp. 37–8.

59 Zuo Feng, 'Who Is Threatening Asia?', *Renmin Ribao* (3 July 1996), 6, translation in FBIS-CHI-96-145 (26 July 1996), 7.

60 See Greg Austin, 'Russian Influences and Mutual Insecurity', in Harris and Klintworth (eds), *China As A Great Power*, p. 123. Various strategic observers have recently intensified speculation about a Sino–Russian–Indian axis emerging to contest US 'unipolarity' at the beginning of this century. Indian press reports attribute Russian Premier Yevgeny Primakov's late-1998 visit to New Delhi as a preliminary effort to forge an Indian–Russian–Chinese axis. See B. K. Karka, 'The Eastern Axis', *The Pioneer* (in English) (18 February 1999), 5, reprinted in FBIS-NES-1999-0218 (18 February 1999). India's Ambassador to Moscow subsequently denied that India was attempting to fashion any such axis but did indicate that India supported the Sino–Russian push for a truly 'multipolar world'. See the Moscow Interfax report in English as reprinted in FBIS-CHI-1999-0813 (13 August 1999).

61 J. Mohan Malik, 'India's Relations with China Post-Soviet Union: Less Co-operation, More Competition', in Harris and Klintworth (eds), *China as A Great Power*, p. 147.

62 In early 1997 reports surfaced that Beijing saw NATO expansion as another US plan to 'contain' China's rise as a global power. See Michael Richardson, 'Beijing Fears US Plot in NATO Expansion', *The Australian* (21 January 1997), p. 9. For in-depth analysis typifying China's scepticism that Russia will acquiesce to NATO's eastward expansion, see Yan Zheng, 'Loud Thunder But Small Raindrops – NATO's Eastward Expansion Still Faces Numerous Difficulties', *Renmin Ribao* (28 May 1996), 6, translation in FBIS-CHI-96-124 (26 June 1996), 1–3.

63 On the constraints for a more enduring Sino–Soviet alliance, consult Alexei K. Pushkov, 'A Russian–Chinese Alliance Doesn't Look Likely', *International Herald Tribune* (24 April 1996), p. 8; Steven Mufson, 'Russia–China Ties Warm, In a Cool Kind of Way', *International Herald Tribune* (12 February 1996), p. 4; Rajan Menon, 'The Strategic Convergence Between Russia and China', *Survival* 39:2 (Summer 1997), 101–25; and Jennifer Anderson, *The Limits of Sino–Russian Strategic Partnership*, Adelphi Paper 315 (London: Oxford University Press for the International Institute for Strategic Studies, 1997).

64 Tsuneo Akaha, 'Russia and Asia in 1995: Bold Objectives and Limited Meetings', *Asian Survey* 36:1 (January 1996), 106; Greg Austin, 'Russian Influences and Mutual Insecurity', in Harris and Klintworth (eds), *China as a Great Power*, pp. 113–14; and Sherman Garnett, 'The Russian Far East as a Factor in Russian–Chinese Relations', *SAIS Review* 16:2 (Fall/Summer 1996), 1–20.

65 The International Institute for Strategic Studies (IISS), *The Military Balance 1996/97* (London: Oxford University Press for the International Institute for Strategic Studies, 1996), pp. 104–5.

66 China analysts argue that Russia severed its relationship of 'strategic dependency' on the West around 1994 and began to pursue a more independent foreign policy 'aimed at regaining its lost status as a global power'. See Chen Yurong, 'Russia Distances Itself From the West', *Beijing Review* 38:14/15 (3–16 April 1995), 22–4.

67 The Foreign Ministry policy paper is covered by Jen Hui-wen, 'Sino–Russian Relations as Viewed From Internal Report', *Hsin Pao* (Hong Kong Economic Journal) (28 June 1996), 18, translation in FBIS-CHI-96-129 (3 July 1996), 9–11. The Five Nation Agreement is explored in 'Five Nation Agreement Provides Model in Peace Conflict Resolution', *Jiefang Ribao* (27 April 1996), 4, translation in FBIS-CHI-96-145 (26 July 1996), 2. See also Erickson, 'Russia Will Not be Trifled With', pp. 263–5.

68 The Beijing Declaration is assessed in 'Jiang, Putin sign "Beijing Declaration" on Deepening Sino–Russian Relations', *Xinhua* (18 July 2000), reprinted in FBIS-CHI-2000-0718 (18 July 2000). See also Lynne O'Donnell 'Masked Game on Islam's Borders', *The Weekend Australian*, 16–17 June, 2001, p. 12. On recent Russian naval moves, see 'Russian Fleet Sails', *The Australian* (17 January 2001), p. 7.

69 See Amitabh Mattoo, 'India's Nuclear Status Quo', *Survival* 38:3 (Autumn 1996), 50.

70 As argued by Shambaugh, 'The Insecurity of Security', p. 13.

71 The most comprehensive assessment recently appearing in Western literature on the Sino–Indian rivalry is by J. Mohan Malik, 'China–India Relations in the Post-Soviet Era: The Continuing Rivalry', *The China Quarterly* 142 (June 1995), 317–55. For a Chinese interpretation, see Wang Hongyu, 'Sino–Indian Relations', *Asian Survey* 35:6 (June 1995), 546–54.

72 This point is analysed in depth by Malik, 'China–India Relations in the Post-Soviet Era', pp. 331–2.

73 See Devin T. Hagerty, *The Consequences of Nuclear Proliferation: Lessons from South Asia* (Cambridge, MA: The MIT Press, 1998), pp. 175–6. It has been observed that the *Agni* has to be tested and developed further because without a full-fledged intercontinental ballistic missile (ICBM) India cannot deploy a credible minimum deterrent against China. T. T. Poulouse, 'India's Deterrence Doctrine: A Nehruvian Critique', *The Non-Proliferation Review* 6:1 (Fall 1998), 80.

74 See Johnston, 'China's New "Old Thinking"', especially p. 34; and Colonel John Caldwell and Alexander T. Lennon, 'China's Nuclear Modernization Program', *Strategic Review* 23:4 (Fall 1995), 29.

75 John W. Garver, 'Sino–Indian Rapprochement and the Sino–Pakistan Entente', *Political Science Quarterly* 111:2 (Summer 1996), 335; and Pervaiz Iqbal Cheema, 'Arms Procurement in Pakistan: Balancing the Needs for Quality, Self-Reliance and Diversity of Supply', in Eric Arnett (ed.), *Military Capacity and the Risk of War: China, India, Pakistan and Iran* (Oxford: Oxford University Press for the Stockholm International Peace Research Institute, 1997), pp. 155–6, 158.

76 Ross Masood Husain, 'Threat Perception and Military Planning in Pakistan: The Impact of Technology, Doctrine and Arms Control', in Arnett (ed.), *Military Capacity and the Risk of War*, pp. 130–47.

77 Garver, 'Sino–Indian Rapprochement', pp. 344–5.

78 John Wilson Lewis and Xue Litai assert that Chinese thinking about India has generally coincided with its planning for small or medium-sized regional conventional conflicts. See Lewis and Xue, *China's Strategic Seapower*, p. 216.

79 Malik, 'China–India Relations in the Post-Soviet Era', p. 348; and Gary Klintworth, 'Chinese Perspectives on India as a Great Power', in Ross Babbage and Sandy Gordon (eds), *India's Strategic Future: Regional State or Global Power?* (Basingstoke: Macmillan, 1992), p. 101.

80  See 'Chinese Arms Bolster Burmese Forces', *Jane's Defence Weekly* 20:22 (27 November 1993), 11. In May 1998 Indian Defense Minister George Fernandes accused China of pursuing a 'virtual land and water encirclement of India' by helping the Burmese install surveillance and communications equipment on islands in the Bay of Bengal. Manoj Joshi, 'George in the China Shop', *India Today* 38:20 (12–18 May 1998), 10–12; and Far Eastern Economic Review, *Asia 1999 Yearbook*, p. 87. The *Yearbook* noted 'substantial evidence existed that China helped Burma install advanced radar equipment on naval bases stretching from the Arakan State adjacent to Bangladesh down to the Zadetkyi Island at the entrance of the Strait of Malacca'.

81  For recent Chinese refutations of the 'China threat' thesis in addition to those cited in notes 2 and 47, see Xu Xin, a former PLA Chief of Staff, on 'China Threat Theory', *Liaowang* 8/9 (19 February 1996), 48–9, translation in FBIS-CHI-96-056 (21 March 1996), 34–7; and Yan Xuetong, 'China's Security Goals Do Not Pose a Threat To World, Analyst Says', *China Daily* (4 March 1996), 4.

82  A translated English language text of the 1998 version is Information Office of the State Council, PRC, *China: 'Text' of Defense White Paper [China's National Defense]*, translation in FBIS-CHI-98-208 (27 July 1998). The 2000 version is cited in note 41.

83  China's National Defense in 2000 at [http://www.chinaguide.org/e-white/2000].

84  Representative sources of this nature include a comprehensive five part article on 'The Changing Military Pattern From Old to New – Development Trends in the World Military Situation', *Jiefangjun Bao* (24 April 1992), translation in FBIS-CHI-92-095 (15 May 1992), 20–2; (15 May 1992), translation in FBIS-CHI-92-103 (28 May 1992), 30–2; (29 May 1992), translation in FBIS-CHI-92-118 (18 June 1992), 26–7; (26 June 1992), translation in FBIS-CHI-92-142 (23 July 1992), 32–4; and (17 July 1992), translation in FBIS-CHI-92-153 (7 August 1992), 20–2; and Jiang Yanghong, 'Special Articles marking the 65th Anniversary of the Army's Founding – Commentaries on Implementing Deng Xiaoping's Thinking on Army Building in the New Period: Epoch-Making Strategic Change [and] Considering Overall Situation Advised', *Jiefangjun Bao* (17 July 1992), 1, translation in FBIS-CHI-92-153 (7 August 1992), 22–4.

85  For a lucid explanation of this problem see, Chong-Pin Lin, 'Chinese Military Modernization: Perceptions, Progress and Prospects', *Security Studies* 3:4 (Summer 1994), 740.

86  Shambaugh, 'Growing Strong', pp. 44–6.

87  Weixing Hu, 'China's Security Agenda After the Cold War', *The Pacific Review* 8:1 (1995), esp. 118–19; and Robert A. Scalapino, 'China's Multiple Identities in East Asia: China as a Regional Force', in Dittmer and Kim (eds), *China's Quest for National Identity*, pp. 215–36.

88  Khalilzad et al., *The United States and a Rising China*, pp. 17–20.

89  For one such interpretation see Liu Ming, 'Future International Conflicts Mostly Economic, Not Cultural', *Shehui Kexue [Social Sciences]* 170 (15 October 1994), 26–9, translated in FBIS-CHI-95-007 (11 January 1995), 2–5. The Clinton Administration's shift towards supporting regional, multilateral security dialogues and towards building a 'Pacific Community' was characterised by Chinese writers as an effort 'to control the world by using the power of other countries' and to restrict the power of other Asia-Pacific states. See Chang Xin, 'Inherent Contradictions and Future Trends of America's

Asia-Pacific Strategy', *Shijie Jingji* 10 (1 October 1994), 1–7, translated in FBIS-CHI-95-037 (24 February 1995), 6–12.

90 Yao Yunzhu, 'The Evolution of Military Doctrine', p. 60.

91 In 1996 Jiang Zemin convened a discussion group of distinguished Chinese historians to contemplate major issues in Chinese and world history. These sessions were later published by the Chinese Communist Party's central secretarial bureau. Among other arguments, it postulated the thesis developed by Zhang Hongyi that the US was attempting to control the world market by impeding Chinese development and undermining its socialist system. For a discussion of this work, see Xinhua Shen, 'Jiang Zemin's "Brave New World": The Formation of a Vision for the Next Century', *China Strategic Review* 2:6 (November/December, 1997), 85–96.

92 Zheng Yin has offered a comprehensive assessment of China's role in such a great power concert. See his 'One-Power Domination of Asian Pacific Region Unlikely', *Xiandi Guoji Guanxi* 10 (20 October 1994), 2–9, translated in FBIS-CHI-95-021 (1 February 1995), 1–7.

93 China's scepticism regarding institutionalist proscriptions is discussed in-depth by Swaine, 'China', in Khalilzad (ed.), *Strategic Appraisal 1996*, pp. 199–201.

94 Li Qinggong and Wei Wei, 'Chinese Army Paper on "New Security Concept"', *Jiefangjun Bao* (24 December 1997), translated and reprinted in FBIS-CHI-98-015 (15 January 1998).

95 'China: "Text" of Defense White Paper', *Xinhua* (22 July 1998), reprinted in FBIS-CHI-98-28 (28 July 1998); 'Text of Tang Jiaxuan Address to UNGA', (22 September 1999), translated and reprinted in FBIS-CHI-1999-0924 (22 September 1999); and 'Statement by President Jiang Zemin of the People's Republic of China at the Millennium Summit of the United Nations, 6 September 2000', translated and reprinted at the Chinese Foreign Ministry's official website, [http://www.fmpre.gov.cn/eng/].

96 For further information on Chinese perceptions see the dispatch, 'China Details Foreign Security Policy', *Beijing Review* 43:8 (21 February 2000), 5.

97 The paragraphs here have been adapted from a more detailed study of China's 'New Security Concept' by William Tow and Leisa Hay, 'Australia, The United States and China Going Strong', *Australian Journal of International Affairs* 55:1 (April 2001) 37–54; See also Kenneth Allen and Eric McVadon, 'China's Foreign Military Relations', report no. 32 (a project by the Henry L. Stimson Center, October 1999); Carlyle A. Thayer, 'China's "New Security Concept" and ASEAN', *Comparative Connections* (3rd quarter 2000) at [http://www.csis.org/pacfor/cc/], (accessed 11 October 2000); David Finkelstein and Michael McDevitt, 'Competition and Consensus: China's "New Security Concept" and the United States' Security Strategy for the East Asia Security Region', *Pacnet* 1 (8 January 1999), on the Internet at [http://www.nyu.edu/ globalbeat/asia/], (accessed 10 August, 2000).

98 David Shambaugh, 'China's Military View of the World', *International Security* 24:3 (Winter 1999), 52–79.

99 US intelligence analysis has anticipated China adopting this type of 'calculated multilateralism'. See Greg Sheridan, 'Caught in the Middle', *The Weekend Australian* (16–17 March 1996), p. 25. Also see Michael D. Swaine and Ashley J. Tellis, *Interpreting China's Grand Strategy: Past, Present and Future* (Santa Monica: RAND, 2000), esp. pp. 133–40.

100 Alastair Iain Johnston argues this point in 'Prospects for Chinese Nuclear Force Modernization', pp. 575–6.

101 Mao Tse-Tung [Zedong], 'On Protracted War [May 1938]', in *Selected Military Writings of Mao Tse-tung* (Beijing: Foreign Languages Press, 1967), pp. 226–7; Alice Langley Hsieh, *Communist China's Strategy in the Nuclear Era* (Englewood Cliffs, NJ: Prentice-Hall, 1962); Harlan Jencks, *From Muskets to Missiles: Politics and Professionalism in the Chinese Army 1945–1981* (Boulder: Westview Press, 1982); and Ellis Joffe, *The Chinese Army After Mao* (Cambridge, MA: Harvard, 1987), pp. 71–7.

102 Background on People's War Under Modern Conditions is provided by Ellis Joffe, 'People's War Under Modern Conditions: A Doctrine of Modern War', *The China Quarterly* 112 (December 1987), 555–71; and Paul H.B. Godwin, 'People's War Revised: Military Doctrine, Strategy and Operations', in Charles D. Lovejoy, Jr, and Bruce W. Watson (eds), *China's Military Reforms* (Boulder: Westview Press, 1986), pp. 1–13.

103 One of the best accounts of this decision is offered by Paul H. B. Godwin, 'Chinese Military Strategy Revised: Local and Limited War', *The Annals of the American Academy of Political and Social Science* 519 (January 1992), 192–3. Also see Nan Li, 'The PLA's Evolving Warfighting Doctrine, Strategy and Tactics, 1985–95: A Chinese Perspective', *The China Quarterly* 146 (June 1996), 443–63; Hwang Byong-Moo, 'Changing Military Doctrines of the PRC', pp. 230–1; Bi Jianxiang, 'The PRC's Active Defense Strategy', pp. 59–97; You Ji, *In Quest of High Tech Power: The Modernisation of China's Military* (Canberra: Australia Defence Studies Centre, 1996). The definitive Chinese account is a report by Liu Huinan on the CMC meeting in FBIS-CHI (Daily Report), (12 June 1985).

104 Chong-Pin Lin, 'Chinese Military Modernization', pp. 732, 736.

105 Tai Ming Cheung and Nayan Chanda, 'Exercising Caution', *Far Eastern Economic Review* (2 September 1993), p. 20.

106 Two Hong Kong newspaper accounts are illustrative. See Yen Chun, 'Unmasking the Secrets of Communist China's "Nuclear Counterattack Force"', *Kuang Chiao Ching* (16 March 1996), pp. 32–7, translation in FBIS-CHI-96-070 (10 April 1996), 59–65; and Yin Yen, 'China Owns 300 Nuclear Warheads, Destruction of United States Is Not a Cock-and-Bull Story', *Sing Tao Jih Pao* (30 July 1996), A–2, translation in FBIS-CHI-96-147 (30 July 1996), 2–3. On China's development and deployment of the *Dong-feng 31* mobile-launch strategic missile, see '"New Type Dongfeng" Missile Viewed', *Ta Kung Pao* (2 October 1999), p. 11, translation in FBIS-CHI-1999-1114 (2 October 1999). Applying data from the unclassified version of the 'Cox Report', Duncan Lennox argues that China has consistently assigned priority to defending its own territory and surrounding seas, thus assigning priority to its theatre and tactical nuclear weapons arsenals. See his 'A Consistent Policy: Briefing [on] Chinese Nuclear Forces', *Jane's Defence Weekly* (11 August 1999), 20–3.

107 As Alastair Iain Johnston has observed, 'limited deterrence' requires sufficient counter-force ('hard' or military targeting capability) and counter-value ('soft' or city/industrial-targeting capability) tactical, theatre and strategic nuclear forces to deter the escalation of *conventional* or nuclear war or to control its escalation if deterrence fails. China does not presently have the operational capabilities to implement this type of strategy. See Johnston, 'China's New "Old Thinking"', pp. 5–6, 14, 31.

108  Chong-Pin Lin, 'The Military Balance in the Taiwan Straits', *The China Quarterly* 146 (June 1996), 577–95; and Richard Betts, 'What Will It Take to Deter the United States?', *Parameters* 25:4 (Winter 1995–96), 77.

109  As of 2000, China was reported to have 20 DF-5 land-based missiles capable of targeting the United States. This number will increase when the *Dongfeng-31* enters service over the next few years. An advanced DF-41 may be added to China's strategic inventory between 2002 and 2005 and a new generation of submarine-launched ballistic missiles is projected for deployment after 2002. Given US intelligence and surveillance capabilities, the extent to which these delivery systems, even if deployed in hardened sites, could constitute a legitimate deterrent against US pre-emption in a highly intense future Sino–American crisis would be a matter of some debate among US military planners. See International Institute for Strategic Studies, *The Military Balance 2000/2001* (London: Oxford University Press for the IISS, 2000), pp. 179, 194; Godwin, 'From Continent to Periphery', p. 482; and Holly Porteous, 'China's View of Strategic Weapons', *Jane's Intelligence Review* 8:3 (March 1996), 135. Also see National Intelligence Council (US), Federal Research Division, *China's Future: Implications for US Interests*, Conference Report, CR 99-02 (24 September 1999); and Abram N. Shulsky, *Deterrence Theory and Chinese Behavior* (Santa Monica: RAND, 2000). A comprehensive study can be found in Suisheng Zhao (ed.), *Across the Taiwan Strait: Mainland China, Taiwan and the 1995–1996 Crisis* (London: Routledge, 1999).

110  See, for example, Mi Zhenyu, 'China's Strategic Plan for Active Defense', in *Zhongguo Guoqing Guoli* 11 (28 November 1995), pp. 4–5, translation in FBIS-CHI-96-034 (20 February 1996), 24–7.

111  A trend anticipated by Michael D. Swaine, *The Role of the Chinese Military in National Security Policymaking* (Santa Monica: RAND, 1996), pp. 75–6.

112  The geographic scope of the new Chinese maritime doctrine reportedly reaches from Vladivostok in the north to the Strait of Malacca in the south and 'the first island chain' (encompassing Japan, the Philippines and the South China Sea) to the east. See John Downing, 'China's Evolving Maritime Strategy – Part I: Restructuring Begins', *Jane's Intelligence Review* 8:3 (March 1996), 130.

113  A dissenting view is offered by Bryce Harland, 'China Isn't a Militarist Power', *International Herald Tribune* (15 November 1996), p. 8, who argues that since the PLA remains under the control of the Chinese Communist Party, there is no tradition of Chinese militarism which can be easily transposed into aggression against other countries. Yet Harland concedes that the CCP is increasingly dependent upon the support of a politically assertive PLA for sustaining its own power base.

114  John Wilson Lewis and Hua Di have noted that China's ballistic missile programs 'are linked both to independence and defense and the ability to enter the international system as an equal'. John Wilson Lewis and Hua Di, 'China's Ballistic Missile Programs', *International Security* 17:2 (Fall 1992), 40.

115  For an excellent discussion of this Chinese approach, see Lewis and Xue, *China's Strategic Seapower*, pp. 231–7.

116  The findings of the Congressional investigation into Chinese espionage of US military and commercial technologies are set out in United States House of Representatives, *Report of the Select Committee on US National Security and Military/Commercial Concerns With the People's Republic of China*, 105 Congress, 2nd Session, Report 105-851 (Washington DC: USGPO, 1999). The major

findings of the investigation were that: (1) the PRC has stolen design information on the United States' most advanced thermonuclear weapons; the PRC's next generation of thermonuclear weapons will exploit elements of stolen US design information; the PRC's penetration of US national weapons laboratories spans at least the past several decades and almost certainly continues today; (2) the PRC has stolen or otherwise illegally obtained US missile and space technology that improves the PRC's military and intelligence capabilities; (3) US and international export control policies and practices have facilitated the PRC's efforts to obtain militarily useful technology; and (4) the PRC seeks advanced US military technology to achieve its long term goals. See Vol I, pp. ii–xxxvii. The major critique of the Cox Report was the so-called 'Panofsky critique' authored by Alastair Iain Johnston, W. K. H. Panofsky, Marco Di Capra and Lewis R. Franklin, *The Cox Committee Report: An Assessment* (Stanford: Center for International Security and Cooperation, December 1999). This report was in turn savaged by Nicholas Rostow, Staff Director, US Senate Select Committee on Intelligence, 'The "Panofsky" Critique and the Cox Committee Report: 50 Factual Errors in the Four Essays'. An electronic version is available on the Internet at [http://cox.house.gov/sc/coverage/senintell.htm].

117  A special and authoritative issue of *Zhengming* magazine was banned from publication during the latter half of 1994 because it contained sensitive interviews by top Chinese nuclear scientists confirming China's application of this finite deterrence strategy. It was declassified in November of that year. See the *Kyodo* news agency report (6 November 1994), reprinted in FBIS-CHI-94-215 (7 November 1994), 1.

118  Nigel Holloway, 'A Chill Wind', *Far Eastern Economic Review* (15 June 1995), 15–16; and David Wallen, 'PLA Plans To Modernize, Expand Force', *South China Morning Post* (21 April 1995), p. 19, reprinted in FBIS-CHI-95-077 (21 April 1995), 25–6.

119  Paul Dibb, *Towards a New Balance of Power in Asia*, Adelphi Paper 295 (London: Oxford University Press for the International Institute of Strategic Studies, 1995), p. 27.

120  The 'Europe dimension' of this Chinese policy orientation is covered by Dong-Ik Shin and Gerald Segal, 'Getting Serious About Asia–Europe Security Cooperation', *Survival* 39:1 (Spring 1997), 141. The development of China–Europe relations on a broader institutional context is discussed by Michael Yahuda and Zhang Yunling, 'European and Asian Policies', in Hans Maull, Gerald Segal and Jusuf Wanandi (eds), *Europe and the Asia-Pacific* (London: Routledge, 1997), pp. 183–97. The APEC dimension is reviewed by Peter Drysdale and Andrew Elek, *China and the International Trading System*, Pacific Economic Papers no. 214 (Canberra: Australia–Japan Research Centre, Australian National University, 1992); and by Christopher Findlay, 'China and the Regional Economy', in Harris and Klintworth (eds), *China as a Great Power*, pp. 297–8.

121  See an interview with Pan Junfeng, Director of the Foreign Military Affairs Department of the Chinese Academy of Military Science, 'Have a Clear Picture of General Trends of Relaxation, Be Prepared for New Challenges', *Jiefangjun Bao* (8 January 1995), translation in FBIS-CHI-96-060 (27 March 1996), 27–32. For a Western assessment of the Chinese fear about other states using multilateral institutions to collaborate against the PRC in the Asia-Pacific, see Banning N. Garrett and Bonnie S. Glaser, 'Multilateral

Security in the Asia-Pacific Region and its Impact on Chinese Interests: Views from Beijing', *Contemporary Southeast Asia* 16:1 (June 1994), 14–34.
122 Wanandi, 'ASEAN's China Strategy', pp. 121–4.

### 3 Great-Power Strategy II: Japan

1 Kenneth Waltz, 'The Emerging Structure of International Politics', *International Security* 18:2 (Fall 1993), 44–79; Samuel P. Huntington, 'America's Changing Strategic Interests', *Survival* 33:1 (January–February 1991), 3–17; Christopher Layne, 'The Unipolar Illusion: Why New Great Powers Will Rise', *International Security* 17:4 (Spring 1993), 5–51; and Michael Mastanduno, 'Do Relative Gains Matter? America's Response to Japanese Industrial Policy', in David Baldwin (ed.), *Neorealism and Neoliberalism: The Contemporary Debate* (New York: Columbia University Press, 1993), pp. 250–66.

2 See Robert O. Keohane, 'Institutional Theory and the Realist Challenge After the Cold War', in Baldwin (ed.), *Neorealism and Neoliberalism*, p. 288. Also see John Gerard Ruggie, *Winning the Peace: America and World Order in the New Era* (New York: Columbia University Press, 1996), pp. 170–2. Ruggie envisioned the US supporting 'cooperative balancing mechanisms' in an East Asian context.

3 As Stuart Harris and Richard N. Cooper have observed, Japan in particular 'sees its involvement in multilateral institutions as encouraging the United States to resist its own unilateral tendencies and to participate in the management of common security issues in multilateral settings'. See Stuart Harris and Richard N. Cooper, 'The US–Japan Alliance', in Robert D. Blackwill and Paul Dibb (eds), *America's Asian Alliances* (Cambridge, MA: The MIT Press, 2000), p. 55.

4 Howard W. French, 'Koizumi Vows to Give Japan a Real Army', *International Herald Tribune*, 28 April 2001.

5 John E. Endicott, 'Japan', in Douglas J. Murray and Paul R. Viotti (eds), *The Defense Policies of Nations* 3rd edn, (Baltimore: The Johns Hopkins University Press, 1994), pp. 355–9.

6 As late as 1994, a poll conducted by the Japanese government revealed that 73 per cent of the populace thought that the SDF's main function was disaster relief. Cited in Hartwig Hummel, 'Japan's Military Expenditures After the Cold War: The "Realism" of the Peace Dividend', *Australian Journal of International Affairs* 50:2 (July 1996), 151.

7 A theoretical explanation for this is suggested by Sun-Ki Chai, 'Entrenching the Yoshida Defense Doctrine: Three Techniques for Institutionalization', *International Organization* 51:3 (Summer 1997), 389–412.

8 Extensive and authoritative background on Japan's postwar defence posture is provided by the Japan Defense Agency, *Defense of Japan 1992* (Tokyo: The Japan Times, Ltd., 1992), esp. pp. 60–84; and Kenneth B. Pyle, *The Japanese Question: Power and Purpose in a New Era* (Washington, DC: AEI Press, 1992).

9 Norm Levin, 'Japan', in Zalmay Khalilzad (ed.), *Strategic Appraisal 1996* (Santa Monica: RAND, 1996), pp. 147–50.

10 Toshiya Hoshino has underscored the prospect of future Japanese governments coming under greater pressure to 'normalise' the country's defence posture. See his 'The Second Generation Japan–United States Security Alliance', in William Tow, Russell Trood and Toshiya Hoshino (eds), *Bilateralism in a Multilateral Era* (Tokyo/Nathan: Japan Institute of International

Affairs/Centre for the Study of Australia–Asia Relations, Griffith University, 1997), p. 80.

11  The Comprehensive National Security Study Group, *Report on Comprehensive National Security*, 2 July 1980 (English translation draft in author's hands). Also see J. W. M. Chapman, R. Drifte, and I. T. M. Gow, *Japan's Quest for Comprehensive Security* (London: Frances Pinter, 1983), pp. xvi–xvii. This Study Group was one of seven created by Prime Minister Ohira to investigate matters of national interest.

12  This is the conclusion drawn by I. T. M. Gow, 'Defense Planning in Post-War Japan', in Chapman, Drifte, and Gow, *Japan's Quest for Comprehensive Security*, pp. 75–6.

13  Hisahiko Okazaki, *A Grand Strategy for Japanese Defense* (Lanham MD: University Press of America, 1986). An excellent summary of the Japanese national security debate as it evolved throughout the 1980s is provided by Mike M. Mochizuki, 'Japan's Search for Strategy', *International Security* 8:3 (Winter 1983/1984), 152–79.

14  Barry Buzan, 'Japan's Defense Problematique', *The Pacific Review* 8:1 (1995), 30.

15  Kenichiro Sasae, *Rethinking Japan–US Relations*, Adelphi Paper 292 (London: International Institute for Strategic Studies, 1994), p. 4. Mike Mochizuki has referred to Japan's post-Cold War strategic policy identity crisis as a tension between 'globalism' and 'regionalism', with the need to reconcile vital interests in distant areas (i.e. continued access to oil fields in the Middle East) with those in the Asia-Pacific (that is, overcoming regional hostilities incurred from memories of its aggression during World War II). See Mochizuki's 'Japan and the Strategic Quadrangle', in Michael Mandelbaum (ed.), *The Strategic Quadrangle: Russia, China, Japan, and the United States in East Asia* (New York: Council on Foreign Relations Press, 1995), pp. 113–14.

16  Kenichiro Sasae has observed that 'there was strong criticism of the US-led war' in Japan 'on the grounds that the war itself was wrong'. See his *Rethinking Japan–US Relations*, p. 48. Yet influential conservative politicians such as Ozawa Ichiro and Hashimoto Ryutaro were both concerned that Japanese money did not necessarily buy it American respect. Also see Bilveer Singh, 'Redefining Japan's Defense Policy in the Post Cold War Era: Inner to Outer Perimeter Defense?' *Asia Defense Journal* (February 1992): 28–30.

17  Akio Washio, 'Blood, Sweat and Fears', *The Japan Times Weekly* (International Edition), 23–29 January 1995, pp. 10–11.

18  Washio, 'Blood, Sweat and Fears', p. 10. Additional background on the debate as it evolved during the Persian Gulf conflict is provided by S. Javed Maswood, 'Japan and the Gulf Crisis: Still Searching for a Role', *The Pacific Review* 5:2 (1992), 149–55.

19  Advisory Group on Defense Issues, 'The Modality of the Security and Defense Capability of Japan: The Outlook for the 21st Century', 12 August 1994 and reprinted as *Recommendations for Japan's Security and Defense Capabilities*, translation in FBIS-EAS-94-209-5 (28 October 1994). For a succinct assessment of the report, see Peter Polomka, 'Out of the Shadows Towards Greater Self-Reliance', *Asia-Pacific Defense Reporter* 21:6/7 (December 1994/January 1995), 35–7. An excellent Japanese discussion on the report is provided by Akio Watanabe and Takeshi Igawashi, 'Japan Experts Discuss Peace Constitution, Defense Guidelines', *Tokyo Ushio* (September 1997), 124–33, translation in FBIS-EAS (Daily Report) (23 September 1997).

20 Advisory Group on Defense Issues, 'The Modality of the Security and Defense Capability of Japan', pp. 2-3.
21 Haruo Fujii, 'The Goal Is To Make the Self-Defense Force the Military Force of a "Normal Nation"', *Ekonomisuto* (30 August 1994), 66-9, translation in FBIS-EAS-94-209-S (28 October 1994), pp. 19-22.
22 Morimoto Satoshi, 'What Japanese Interests Are Protected by its Defense Capabilities?', *Ekonomisuto* (13 September 1994), 56-9, translation in FBIS-EAS-94-209-S (28 October 1994), pp. 23-4.
23 The basic stipulations of both these measures are outlined concisely in Charles E. Morrison (ed.), *Asia-Pacific Security Outlook 1998* (Tokyo: Japan Center for International Exchange, 1998), pp. 68-9. Also see Japan Defense Agency, *Defense of Japan 1997* (Tokyo: The Japan Times Ltd, 1997), pp. 116-19, 290-306, for a Defense Agency assessment of these documents. As leading Japanese politics analyst J. A. A. Stockwin notes, the term 'parliament' is now preferred to the hitherto commonly used 'Diet' when discussing the Japanese Parliament and is thus adopted for this study. See his *Governing Japan* 3rd edn, (Oxford: Blackwell Publishers, 1999), p. 229 n. 6.
24 Nakashizuka Keiichiro, 'Reliability of Japan–US Alliance – If Japan Neglects To Make Efforts, Relations With the United States Would Die Out', *Sankei Shimbun* (18 December 1995), translation in FBIS-EAS-95-248 (27 December 1995), p. 4. Also see 'New Defense Outline Adopted by Cabinet', *The Japan Times* (29 November 1995), pp. 1, 3; and Reiji Yoshida, 'Agency Prevails in Defense Restructuring', *The Japan Times* (1 December 1995), p. 3.
25 As reported by a *Nihon Keizai Shimbun* poll, 17 October 1995 and cited in Hoshino, 'The Second-Generation Japan–United States Security Alliance', p. 70. Some critics of US policy in Japan claimed that the opposition was much greater during the height of the crisis, asserting that nearly all Okinawans and 90 per cent of all Japanese wanted a complete US force withdrawal from their country. Chalmers Johnson, 'Okinawan Rape Incident and the End of the Cold War in East Asia', *Quadrant* 40:3 (March 1996), 25. Most polling data reviewed for this study does not corroborate this assertion.
26 *Asahi Shimbun* (21 January 1996), p. 5, reprinted in FBIS-EAS-96-014 (22 January 1996), p. 8.
27 'Text: US–Japan Joint Declaration On Security', reprinted in USIS, *Wireless File*, EPF304 (17 April 1996).
28 'Japan: Chief Cabinet Secretary Kajiyama on ACSA Conclusion', Statement of the Japanese Ministry of Foreign Affairs (in English) (18 April 1996), reprinted in FBIS-EAS-96-076 (18 April 1996), pp. 16-17.
29 Hoshino argues that uncertainty still remained as to what Japan could actually do to assist US forces in a future regional security crisis due to constitutional constraints and psychological barriers among the Japanese populace. See his 'The Second Generation Japan–United States Security Alliance', pp. 73-5.
30 Asahi Shimbun defence analyst Taoka Shunji, for example, has noted the resurgence of Japanese militarism that is expected if the US withdraws its forces makes this 'sympathy budget' ($US 4 billion) akin to 'prison guards receiving allowances from their prisoners'. See Taoka, 'The Way to Save the US–Japan Alliance', *NIRA Review* (Summer 1997), as reprinted at [http://gate.nira.go.jp/publ/]. Additional background is provided by Miyoshi Etsujiro, 'Redressing the Okinawan Base Problem', *The Japan Quarterly* 43:1 (January/March 1996), 27-32. For a report on the further incidents

see Stephen Lunn, 'New Okinawa Anger at US Troops', *The Australian* (16 January 2001), p. 7.

31  A text of the new Guidelines is found in USIS, *Wireless File* (23 September 1997). It can also be referenced in East Asian Strategy Report (EASR II), pp. 21–2.

32  This point is discussed more fully in an editorial, 'The Japan–US Security Relationship Enters a New Phase', *Nihon Keizai Shimbun* (18 April 1996), p. 2, translation in FBIS-EAS-96-077 (19 April 1996), pp. 10–11. Sato reportedly committed Japanese logistical support to any future American defence of South Korea.

33  See Kurt M. Campbell, 'Energizing the US–Japan Security Partnership', *The Washington Quarterly* 23:4 (Autumn 2000), 125–34; and Harris and Cooper, 'The US–Japan Alliance', pp. 53–4, 58–9.

34  'SDF Can Rescue Citizens Abroad', *The Japan Times* (9 August 2000), p. 2.

35  Information on this search and rescue exercise is provided by Victor D. Cha, 'Seoul–Tokyo Cooperation on North Korea, Tried, Tested and True (thus far)', *Comparative Connections* (3rd Quarter 1999) at [http://www.csis.org/pacfor/cc/] (accessed on 12 January 2001).

36  The relevant clause is Part II, Article 4. See 'The Guidelines for US–Japan Defense Cooperation'.

37  As pointed out in 'Japan: Experts Discuss Collective Security: Okinawa – Dialogue Between Motoo Shiina, Upper House Member and Hisahiko Okazaki, Former Ambassador to Thailand', *Chuo Koron* (July 1996), 62–9, translation in FBIS-EAS-96-122 (24 July 1996).

38  Patrick M. Cronin, 'The US–Japan Alliance Redefined', *Strategic Forum* 75 (May 1996), *passim*, at the website [http://www.ndu/edu/inss/strforum/].

39  Harris and Cooper, 'The US–Japan Alliance', pp. 38–9, 45–53.

40  Ho Kwang-Chun, 'Are Japan's Self-Defense Forces Ready to Take Off?', *Sisa Journal* (9 October 1997), 90–1, translation in FBIS-EAS-97-293 (20 October 1997). See also Victor D. Cha, 'Hate, Power and Identity in Japan–Korea Security: Towards a Synthetic Material-Ideational Analytical Framework', *Australian Journal of International Affairs* 54:3 (November 2000), 311–12; and Taewoo Kim, 'Japan's New Security Roles and ROK–Japan Relations', *The Korean Journal of Defense Analysis* 11:1 (Summer 1999), 147–68.

41  *Kyodo* dispatch (in English) (17 August 1997), reprinted in FBIS-EAS-97-229 (17 August 1997); and *Kyodo* dispatch (in English) (22 August 1997), reprinted in FBIS-EAS-97-234 (22 August 1997).

42  Edward Neilan, 'Does Taiwan Have a "Japan Card"?', *Free China Review* 47:12 (December 1997), 46–7.

43  See for example, the remarks of Hitoshi Tanaka, the Japanese Foreign Ministry's American Bureau Counsellor who helped negotiate the Guidelines in 'Panelists Discuss New Defense Guidelines', *Gaiko Forum* (December 1997), 12–28, translation in FBIS-EAS-97-356 (22 December 1997).

44  Nicholas Kristof, 'Japan Acts to Widen Role with US Military', *International Herald Tribune* (28 April 1999), pp. 1, 4. On 30 April 1999, a delegation of Japanese parliamentarians and officials with expertise in the defence area addressed a seminar attended by this author at Stanford University's Asia/Pacific Research Center and endeavoured to address such questions. It revealed that while the Japanese Government would still be 'accountable' to the Parliament during times of military emergencies, it could initiate responses to such circumstances in advance of Parliament approval. Among the most significant changes in Japanese MSDF policy, vessels would now be

allowed to evacuate Japanese nationals (previously only Japanese aircraft could do this).

45 Sayuri Daimon and Yoko Hani, 'New Defense Changes Lack Public Debate', *The Japan Times* (27 April 1999), p. 3. A number of parliamentary opposition members and independent analysts argued that the Defense Guidelines lacked necessary 'geographic specificity' and rejected government arguments that the concept 'areas around Japan' should be 'situational' rather than geographic. See Qingxu Ken Wang, 'Japan's Balancing Act in the Taiwan Strait', *Security Dialogue* 33:3 (Autumn 2000), 339.

46 This stipulation was conveyed to the author by a visiting delegation of Japanese parliamentarians and defence experts at Stanford University, 30 April 1999 and cited in note 44.

47 Kent Calder, *Asia's Deadly Triangle: How Arms, Energy and Growth Threaten to Destabilise the Asia-Pacific* (London: Nicholas Brealey, 1996), esp. pp. 13–42; Also see Francis Fukuyama and Kondan Oh, *The US–Japan Security Relationship After the Cold War* (Santa Monica: RAND, 1993), pp. 9–21; and Eugene Brown, 'Japanese Security Policy in the Post-Cold War Era: Threat Perceptions and Strategic Options', *Asian Survey* 34:5 (May 1994), 430–46.

48 Japan Defense Agency, *The Defense of Japan 1996*, available through the Agency's website at [http://www.jda.go.jp/].

49 Christopher W. Hughes, 'The North Korean Nuclear Crisis and Japanese Security', *Survival* 38:2 (Summer 1996), 90.

50 David Wright and Timur Kadyshev, 'The North Korean Missile Program: How Advanced Is It?', *Arms Control Today* 24:3 (April 1994), 9–12; David P. Hamilton, 'North Korea Threatens War Against Japan', *Asian Wall Street Journal* (10 June 1994), p. A–7; and 'North Korea Threatens Japan and South Korea', *International Herald Tribune* (10 June 1994), pp. 1, 5. Various Japanese reports, however, doubt the readiness of the *Nodong-1*, due to a lack of testing. See Shunji Taoka, 'The Superiority of the South Korean Forces is Unshakeable', *AERA* (25 October 1996), 43–7, translation in FBIS-EAS-96-211 (25 October 1996). But more recent reports note that the *No-dong-1* has been successfully tested with a 1300 km range – far greater than the 1000 km previously estimated maximum range, see *Sankei Shimbun* report (13 May 1997), translation in FBIS-EAS-97-54 (13 May 1997). For Japanese reaction on the *Taepo-dong-1* test, see 'Tokyo "Anxious", "Deeply Worried" Over DPRK Missile Test', *Kyodo* dispatch (in English) (1 September 1998), reprinted in FBIS-EAS-98-244 (1 September 1998).

51 Writing in 1996, Christopher Hughes observed that whilst the Japanese are obviously concerned about the long-term implications of North Korea's nuclear program, 'the immediate military threat is from a chemically armed [North Korean] ballistic missile'; see Hughes, 'The North Korean Nuclear Crisis', p. 95.

52 For a highly authoritative assessment of North Korean weapons of mass destruction delivery capabilities against Japan, see Shinichi Ogawa, 'North Korean Missile Proliferation Threat on Northeast Asian Security', *KNDU Review* 4 (1999), esp. 29–34. An evaluation more sceptical of North Korean missile capabilities is offered by Selig S. Harrison, 'The Missiles of North Korea: How Real a Threat?', *World Policy Journal* 17:3 (Fall 2000), 13–24.

53 Yoshida Yasuhiko, 'Pyongyang's Airborne Threat to Improved Diplomatic Ties', *Japan Quarterly* 46:1 (January–March 1999), 10–16.

54 'More Food Could Go to Pyongyang', *The Japan Times* (28 July 2000), p. 1.

55 Background on the fishing dispute is provided by Michael J. Green, *Japan–ROK Security Relations: An American Perspective* (Stanford: Asia/Pacific Research Center, Institute for International Studies, Stanford University, 1999), pp. 10–11.

56 'Japan To Express Regret Over ROK Island's Plan', *Kyodo* dispatch (in English) (2 June 1997), reprinted in FBIS-EAS-97-103 (2 June 1997); and 'Japan Protests Against ROK's Building on Island', *Kyodo* dispatch (in English) (6 November 1997), reprinted in FBIS-EAS-97-310 (6 November 1997).

57 These lingering sources of tension are assessed in some depth by Victor D. Cha, *Alignment Despite Antagonism: The United States–Korea–Japan Security Triangle* (Stanford: Stanford University Press, 1999).

58 A liberal Japanese interpretation of the future of Japanese–North Korean relations is offered by Odagawa Ko, 'Japan–North Korea Reconciliation', *Japan Quarterly* 47:4 (October–December 2000), 9–15. A representative realist assessment is projected by Nakanishi Terumasa who warns that Japan must be careful not to embrace either the West or 'Asianism' too firmly. The emotional pull of the latter, he asserts, could cause Japan to stake its future in an illusionary multilateral system of regional security or to see an 'Asian community as its preferred choice of the future'. See Nakanishi, 'Goals for Japan in its "Second Postwar Period"', *Japan Echo* 27:2 (April 2000), 13.

59 Background is provided by Ogawa, 'North Korea Missile Proliferation Threat', pp. 44–5.

60 'Japan Postpones Decision on Joining US Missile Plan', (undated), *Kyodo* dispatch (in English), reprinted in FBIS-EAS-97-221 (9 August 1997). 'Defense Agency Wants 80 Million Yen for TMD Research', *Mainichi Shimbun* (23 August 1997), translation in FBIS-EAS-97-237 (25 August 1997).

61 Stephen A. Cambone, 'The United States and Theatre Missile Defense in Northeast Asia', *Survival* 39:3 (Autumn 1997), 68–70. During a January 1999 visit to Tokyo, US Defense Secretary William Cohen reiterated Washington's desire to help Japan develop a space satellite plan compatible with a US coordinated regional TMD system, arguing that an indigenous Japanese satellite program would be 'expensive and complicated'. 'Cohen, in Japan, Offers Help for Satellite Program, Seeks Cooperation on Missile Defense', *International Herald Tribune* (12 January 1999), at [http://www.iht.com/].

62 'TMD Plan: There Are Objections to Hasty Decisions', (Editorial) *Mainichi Shimbun* (23 September 1998), translation in FBIS-EAS-98-271 (28 September 1998). In mid-2000 the National Space Development Committee was reportedly debating the possibility of 'space development' being considered part of 'comprehensive security'. See report in the *Asahi Shimbun* at [http://iij.asahi.com] (27 July 2000).

63 Yoshiteru Oka, 'Can "Nodong" Be Intercepted and Destroyed? Brain Racking Problem of TMD Study', *Sankei Shimbun* (29 June 1997), translation in FBIS-EAS-97-85 (4 July 1997). Also see Shunji Taoka, 'Pitfalls of Participating in Theatre Missile Defense Initiative', *AERA* (10 August 1998), 58–9, translation in FBIS-EAS-98-277 (4 October 1998); and an ITAR/TASS News Agency Report, 'Russia Believes US–Japan TMD May Bring Confrontation in Asia', (18 October 2000) at [http://www.comtexnews.com] (accessed 9 January 2001).

64 Kohei Murayama, 'Japan, US Agree to Joint TMD Research', *Kyodo* dispatch (in English) (20 September 1998), reprinted in FBIS-EAS-98-263 (20 September 1998).

65  'Japan, US to Share Missile Research', *Associated Press* (16 August 1999), available at the website, [http://www.taiwansecurity.org/AP/].

66  The Chinese response was conveyed by editorialist Shih Chun-yu, 'Japan and the United States Take Advantage of Situation to Upgrade Military Cooperation', *Ta Kung Pao* (a PRC owned daily published in Hong Kong), (14 August 1999), translation in FBIS-CHI-1999-0815 (15 August 1999). The article accused Japan of attempting to 'create a new imbalance in military strength in East Asia'.

67  Typical assessments include Christopher B. Johnstone, 'Paradigms Lost! Japan's Asia Policy in a Time of Growing Chinese Power', *Contemporary Southeast Asia* 21:3 (December 1999), 365–85; Nicholas D. Kristof, 'The Problem of Memory (Lasting Tensions in Asia)', *Foreign Affairs* 77:6 (November 1998), 37–49; and Michael J. Green and Benjamin L. Self, 'Japan's Changing China Policy: From Commercial Liberalism to Reluctant Realism', *Survival* 38:2 (Summer 1996), 35–58.

68  As noted by Yoichi Funabashi, *Alliance Adrift* (New York: Council on Foreign Relations Press, 1999), p. 439; the 'worst-case scenario' in Japan's policy directed towards both China and the US is being forced to make an ultimate choice between these two powers in a future regional crisis or, of equal concern, China and the US cutting a deal on regional security to its own exclusion.

69  'Let's Put War Behind Us, Zhu Tells Japan', United Press International report provided by the Comtex website at [http://www.comtexnews.com] (accessed 10 January 2001).

70  A. Doak Barnett, *China and the Major Powers in East Asia* (Washington, DC: The Brookings Institution, 1977), pp. 110, 120, and 361, n. 69; and Jin-Hyun Park, 'Exclusive Maritime Zone and Boundary Delimitations in Northeast Asia', in Sam Bateman and Stephen Bates (eds), *The Seas Unite: Maritime Cooperation in the Asia-Pacific Region* Canberra Papers no. 118 (Canberra: Strategic and Defence Studies Centre, Australian National University, 1996), p. 206, n. 20.

71  Michael Richardson, 'Oil Lies at the Bottom of China–Japan Dispute Over Islands', *International Herald Tribune* (17 September 1996), p. 4.

72  Steven Mufson, 'Li Peng Warns Japan To Cool Isles Dispute', *International Herald Tribune* (1 October 1996), p. 4.

73  Cited in a *Kyodo* dispatch (in English) (24 September 1996), reprinted in FBIS-EAS-96-186 (24 September 1996).

74  'Text of Jiang Zemin speech at Waseda University', *Xinhua* (28 November 1998), translation in FBIS-CHI-98-333 (29 November 1998).

75  Michael Richardson, 'What China Doesn't Want With Japan Is War (Because It Might Lose)', *International Herald Tribune* (3 October 1996), p. 7. Japanese defence experts have acknowledged that China's navy is weaker than the Japanese MSDF but have still attempted to sustain the 'China threat' thesis by arguing that Chinese naval prowess could nevertheless intimidate other, smaller neighbours. See Hiramatsu Shigeo, 'The Objectives of Naval Strength Buildup', *Tokyo Ekonomisuto* (27 January 1997), 36–7, translation in FBIS-EAS-97-015 (27 January 1997).

76  Reportedly communicated to Chas Freeman, former US Assistant Secretary of Defense for Regional Security Affairs during his visit to China in February, 1996. See a *Kyodo* dispatch (in English) (16 February 1996), reprinted in FBIS-EAS-96-035 (21 February 1996). See also Banning N. Garrett and Bon-

nie S. Glaser, 'Chinese Apprehensions About Revitalization of the US–Japan Alliance', *Asian Survey* 37:4 (April 1997), 383–402.

77  Frank Ching, 'Hashimoto to Face Chinese Ire', *Far Eastern Economic Review* (4 September 1997), p. 32.

78  Akihiko Ota, 'The Ministry of Foreign Affairs Handling of the China–Taiwan Tension Is Questioned – A Wrong Signal to China?', *Sankei Shimbun* (8 March 1996), p. 2, translation in FBIS-EAS-96-056 (21 March 1996), pp. 8–9.

79  *Mainichi Shimbun* (17 May 1997), translation in FBIS-EAS-97-109 (18 May 1997). In a March 2000 poll 84 per cent of Americans surveyed said they supported the US–Japan Security Treaty. See report in *Asahi Shimbun* at [http://iij.asahi.com/], 5 June 2000.

80  Office of Technology Assessment, United States Congress, *Other Approaches To Civil–Military Integration: The Chinese and Japanese Arms Industries* (Washington, DC: USGPO, 1995), p. 12.

81  Green and Self cite a *Yomiuri Shimbun* report that early drafts of the 1995 NDPO made explicit reference to China's military modernisation, nuclear testing and expansionist territorial behaviour in the East and South China Seas but this language was deleted at the insistence of influential Social Democratic Party members. See Green and Self, 'Japan's Changing China Policy', p. 44.

82  On Japanese concerns over Chinese missile developments, see Neville de Silva, 'Japan Shows "Concern" Over Military Strength', *Hong Kong Standard* (3 June 1995), p. 8. On concerns over China's general military build-up, see 'Japan: Defense Agency Voices "Concern" Over PRC Military Buildup', *Kyodo* (in English) and reprinted in FBIS-EAS-96-140 (19 July 1996), 8.

83  See remarks of the US Deputy Assistant Secretary of Defense Kurt Campbell, as reported by Nigel Holloway and Peter Landers, 'Menage A Trois?', *Far Eastern Economic Review* (9 October 1997), pp. 24–8. Campbell did modify his NATO comparison by noting that the Clinton Administration believed it was important for the US and Japan 'to give a window into this alliance to China'. Also see Michel Oksenberg and Elizabeth Economy, 'Introduction: China Joins the World', in Oksenberg and Economy (eds), *China Joins the World: Progress and Prospects*, (New York: Council on Foreign Relations, 2000), p. 32, where the authors note that the process of NATO expansion needs to be better explained by US policy makers to their Chinese counterparts: 'the message should be that those changes are an important means of enhancing the stability of both regions by continuing to anchor Germany and Japan in an alliance system in Europe and Asia respectively' and 'prevent the reappearance of age-old regional rivalries rather than spearhead an American strategy of global hegemony directed at China'.

84  Rajan Menon, 'Japan–Russia Relations and Northeast Asian Security', *Survival* 38:2 (Summer 1996), 60.

85  Background to the dispute is provided by John J. Stephen, *The Kurile Islands* (Oxford: Clarendon Press, 1974); Fuji Kamiya, 'The Northern Territories: 130 Years of Japanese Talks with Czarist Russia and the Soviet Union', in Donald S. Zagoria (ed.), *Soviet Policy in East Asia* (New Haven, CT: Yale University Press, 1982); Kenichi Ito, 'Japan and the Soviet Union: Entangled in the Deadlock of the Northern Territories', *The Washington Quarterly* 11:1 (Winter 1988), 33–44; and especially Peter Berton, *The Japanese–Russian Territorial Dilemma: Historical Background, Disputes, Issues, Questions, Solutions, Scenarios or A Thousand Scenarios for the Thousand Islands Dispute* (unofficial title),

Strengthening Democratic Institutions Project, (Cambridge, MA: John F. Kennedy School of Government, Harvard University, December 1992).

86 The Ministry of Foreign Affairs, Japan, 'Foreign Policies' can be accessed on the MFA website at [http://www.mofa.go.jp] (accessed in January 2000).

87 'Proposal for Building New Japanese Russian Relations, "Text" of Outline of Hashimoto-Yeltsin Summit', *Kyodo* dispatch (in English) (2 November 1997), reprinted in FBIS-EAS-97-307 (3 November 1997); Keiko Tatsuta, 'Japan–Russia Relations Entering New Stage', *Kyodo* dispatch (in English) (24 October 1997), reprinted in FBIS-EAS-97-297 (24 October 1997); and 'Gist of Hashimoto–Yeltsin Discussions in Denver', *Kyodo* dispatch (in English) (20 June 1997), reprinted in FBIS-EAS-97-171 (20 June 1997).

88 Menon, 'Japan–Russia Relations', p. 70.

89 For technical analysis of this point, see Alexei V. Zagorsky, 'Russian Strategic Policy After the Collapse of the USSR (1992–1994)', in Takashi Inoguchi and Grant B. Stillman (eds), *Northeast Asian Regional Security: The Role of International Institutions* (Tokyo: United Nations University Press, 1997), pp. 171–6; and Menon, 'Japan–Russia Relations', pp. 72–3.

90 For graphic examples, consult Stephen Blank, 'Why Russian Policy Is Failing in Asia', *The Journal of East Asian Affairs* 11:1 (Winter/Spring 1997), 288–93.

91 'Russia: Lukin Says Putin's Visits to Japan Step Towards Building Confidence', Moscow Interfax Report, (4 September 2000), as reprinted in FBIS-SOV-2000-0904 (4 September 2000). Putin's backdown from the year 2000 negotiating commitment is reported by Moscow Interfax, (3 September 2000) and is reprinted in FBIS-EAS-2000-0903 (3 September 2000). Background on how the Summit dealt with the issue is provided by Joseph Ferguson's 'Back to the Drawing Board?', *Comparative Connections* (3rd quarter 2000), at [http://www.csis.org/pacfor/cc/]; and Ferguson, 'Spy Mania and Familiar Rhetoric', *Comparative Connections* (1st quarter 2001), at [http:www.csis.org/pacfor/cc/].

92 The term 'supplement' is used in the 1997 Japan Defense White Paper as reported by *Kyodo* (15 July 1997), translation in FBIS-EAS-97-195 (15 July 1997).

93 Nakanishi, 'Goals for Japan in its "Second Postwar Period"', pp. 12–13.

94 See Akiko Fukushima, *Japanese Foreign Policy: The Emerging Logic of Multilateralism* (Basingstoke: Macmillan, 1999).

95 Yoshihide Soeya notes Nakayama's 1991 proposal was slightly 'readjusted' to an initiative ASEAN could call its own and which formed the basis for creating the ARF. Soeya, 'Japan: Normative Constraints Versus Structural Imperatives', in Muthiah Alagappa (ed.), *Asian Security Practice: Material and Ideational Influences* (Stanford: Stanford University Press, 1998), p. 222. For a more sympathetic treatment of this episode, see Paul Midford, 'Japan's Leadership Role in East Asian Security Multilateralism: The Nakayama Proposal and the Logic of Reassurance', *The Pacific Review* 13:3 (2000), 367–97; see also Yukio Satoh, 'Emerging Trends in Asia-Pacific Security: The Role of Japan', *The Pacific Review* 8:2 (1995), 273; and Sasae, *Rethinking US–Japan Relations*, p. 27.

96 Brown, 'Japanese Security Policy in the Post-Cold War Era', pp. 442–3; and Hisane Masaki, 'Japan Adopts a New Asian Policy', *The Japan Times* Weekly International Edition (11–17 January 1993), pp. 1, 6.

97 This view is epitomised in an essay by Kosaka Masataka, 'Diplomacy and Security in the Twenty-First Century', *Japan Echo* 23:4 (Winter 1996), 69.

98  Hisane Masaki, 'A Mechanism for Security Is Caught Up in Rhetoric', *The Japan Times* Weekly International Edition (2–15 January 1995), p. 3; Nishihara Masashi, 'Aiming at New Order for Regional Security – Current State of the ARF', *Gaiko Forum* (November 1997), 35–40, translation in FBIS-EAS-97-321 (17 November 1997); and Heung-Soon Park, 'Korea, Alliances and Multilateralism: Policies for a Transitional Era', in Tow, Trood and Hoshino (eds.), *Bilateralism in a Multilateral Era*, pp. 101–2.

99  'Beijing Invited to US–Japan Security Talks', *South China Morning Post* Internet Edition (27 September 1997) at [http://www.scmp.com/].

100  Michael Vatikiotis et. al., 'Fears of Influence', *Far Eastern Economic Review* (30 January 1997), 14–15; Michael Richardson, 'Hashimoto Sparks Southeast Asia Dilemma', *The Australian* (9 January 1997), p. 9; and Richardson, 'Japan Cements S-E Asian Security', *The Australian* (15 January 1997), pp. 1, 7.

101  In December 1997, for example, the Hashimoto government cut ¥92 billion from the Japan Defense Agency's annual defence budget in response to a worsening national economic situation. See *The Japan Times* (20 December 1997), p. 1.

102  The centrality of the Yoshida Doctrine in Japanese realist thinking is explored in Yoshihiko Nakamoto, 'Japanese Realism and Its Contribution to International Relations Theory', *Issues and Studies* 33:2 (February 1997), 65–86.

103  As reiterated by Okazaki Hisahiko in *This Is Yomiuri* (December 1996): 202–11, translation in FBIS-EAS-96-245 (1 December 1996).

104  These steps are addressed more extensively by Harris and Cooper, 'The US–Japan Alliance', pp. 55–60.

105  In this regard, Hideo Sato proposes that the MST be directed towards the creation of a Pacific Rim security community via Washington's and Tokyo's support for emerging confidence building and cooperative security measures. See his *Japan's China Perceptions and its Policies in the Alliance with the United States*, Asia-Pacific Research Center Discussion Paper (Stanford, CA: Institute for International Studies, Stanford University, September 1998), p. 22.

106  This position is argued by Inoguchi Takashi, 'The New Security Setup and Japan's Options', *Japan Echo* 23:3 (Autumn 1996), 37. Also see Terashima Jitsuro, 'Seeking an Integrated Strategy for Being Both Pro-American and Part of Asia', *Chuo Koron* (March 1996), 20–36, translation in FBIS-EAS-96-048 (11 March 1996).

107  Soeya Yoshihide, 'The Structure of Japan–U.S.–China Relations and Japan's Diplomatic Strategy', *Gaiko Forum* (September 1997), 36–49, translation in FBIS-EAS-97-288 (15 October 1997); Soeya, 'Northeast Asia Policy of Japan in the 21st Century: Japan's Dual Identity Amid Asia's Dual Structure of Flux', paper prepared for conference on 'International Security Environment in Northeast Asia in the 21st Century and Korea's Security Strategy', for the Association of International Studies, 9–10 June 1997, Seoul, Republic of Korea; and Soeya, 'The Japan–U.S. Alliance in a Changing Asia', *Japan Review of International Affairs* 10:4 (Fall 1996), 255–75.

108  See Barry Buzan and Gerald Segal, 'Rethinking East Asian Security', *Survival* 36:2 (Summer 1994), pp. 9–10 for an argument along such lines.

109  This point is emphasised by William T. Tow and Richard Gray, 'Asia-Pacific Security Regimes: Conditions and Constraints', *Australian Journal of Political Science* 30:3 (November 1995), 439–40, 447–9.

110 On the problems generated by incrementalism and consensus building within the Japanese polity, see Mike M. Mochizuki, *Toward A True Alliance: Restructuring US–Japan Security Relations* (Washington DC: Brookings Institute Press, 1997), pp. 17–23.

111 Mochizuki, 'Japan and the Strategic Quadrangle', p. 149. For a concurring Japanese assessment, see Kondo Takeshi, 'US–Japan Economic and Security Relations', *Securitarian* (1 July 1994), translation in FBIS-EAS-94-199 (14 October 1994), 3.

112 INSS Special Report, 'The United States and Japan: Advancing Toward a Mature Partnership', Institute for National Strategic Studies, National Defense University, Washington, DC (11 October 2000); available at [http://www.ndu.edu./ndu/SR], accessed 11 May 2001.

113 See the report by Howard W. French, 'US Official Asks Japan for a Closer Relationship', *International Herald Tribune*, 7 May 2001, pp. 1, 6.

### 4 Other Key Players I: Korea and Taiwan

1 See H. V. Evatt, *Australia in World Affairs* (Sydney: Angus & Robertson, 1946), p. 27; and Martin Wight, 'Power Politics', in Carsten Holbrad and Hedley Bull (eds), *Power Politics* (London: Leicester University Press for the Royal Institute of International Affairs, 1978), pp. 65–6.

2 These characteristics, among others, have been regarded as 'niche diplomacy' and are addressed in Andrew F. Cooper (ed.), *Niche Diplomacy: Middle Powers After the Cold War* (New York: St Martin's Press, 1997).

3 This argument is advanced by Paul Dibb, *Towards a New Balance of Power in Asia*, Adelphi Paper 295 (London: Oxford University Press for the International Institute of Strategic Studies, 1995).

4 Especially representative of such a view is Paul Evans, 'The Prospects for Multilateral Security Co-operation', in Desmond Ball (ed.), 'The Transformation of Security in the Asia/Pacific Region', *The Journal of Strategic Studies* 18:3 Special Issue (September 1995), 201–17.

5 A point raised by Kay Möller, 'How Much Insecurity in East Asia?', *The Pacific Review* 9:1 (1996), 123.

6 As Denny Roy has noted, 'while the North Koreans have been thoroughly deterred from a large-scale conventional military attack since the Korean War, Pyongyang may yet lash out if it is convinced that its enemies are determined to destroy it'. See his 'North Korea as an Alienated State', *Survival* 38:4 (Winter 1996/1997), 32.

7 This problem is ably addressed by both Norman D. Levin, 'What If North Korea Survives?', *Survival* 39:4 (Winter 1997/98), 156–74; and Marcus Noland, 'Why North Korea Will Muddle Through', *Foreign Affairs* 76:4 (July/August 1997), 105–18.

8 For interpretation of Clause Two, see Jong-chul Park, 'Challenges and Opportunities for the Two Koreas after the Summit Meeting: Climate, Process and Tasks', *The Journal of East Asian Affairs* 14:2 (Fall/Winter 2000), 321–2. A text of the Declaration can be found in the journal *Korea and World Affairs* 24:2 (Summer 2000), 313–14. Also see Young-ho Park, 'The 2000 South–North Summit: A Historic Overture to Peaceful Coexistence', *Korea and World Affairs* 24:2 (Summer 2000), 193–206. For further assessment see Han Sung-Joo, 'The Koreas' New Century', *Survival* 42:4 (Winter 2000–01), 85–96.

9  Kim Dae-jung, 'North and South Korea Find Common Ground', *International Herald Tribune* (28 November 2000), p. 8; and Son Key-young, '2001 Sees Inter-Korean Community-Building Process', *The Korea Times* [New Year Special] (31 December 2000).

10  Good accounts of these realist apprehensions are offered by Kent E. Calder, 'The New Face of Northeast Asia', *Foreign Affairs* 80:1 (January–February 2001), 106–22; 'Asia's Shifting Balance', *The Economist* (2 September 2000), 16; and Howard W. French, 'As 2 Koreas Reconcile, Anxiety is Spreading in Asia', *International Herald Tribune* (16 October 2000), p. 1.

11  Stephen Noerper, 'Military Ties Remain Vital Despite North–South Thaw', *Comparative Connections* (3rd Quarter 2000), at [http://www.csis.org/pacfor/cc/], (accessed 8 January 2001). Also see David E. Sangor, 'Offering North Korea a Carrot, US Plans to Lift Many Sanctions', *International Herald Tribune* (16 June 2000), p. 5; and Kim Dal Choong and Scott Snyder, 'If Korea is Changing, US Policies Should Change', *International Herald Tribune* (5 October 2000), p. 8.

12  Excellent analysis of these factors is offered by Nicholas Eberstadt, 'Assessing "National Strategy" in North and South Korea', *The Korean Journal of Defense Analysis* 8:1 (Summer 1996), 55–76. See p. 59 for an explanation of the term *sadae*.

13  Don Oberdorfer, *The Two Koreas: A Contemporary History* (Reading, MA: Addison Wesley, 1997), p. 7.

14  William E. Berry, Jr, 'The Political and Military Roles of US Forces in Korea: Past, Present and Future', in Tae-Hwan Kwak and Thomas L. Wilborn (eds.), *The U.S.–ROK Alliance in Transition* (Seoul: Kyungnam University Press, 1996), p. 204.

15  President Carter's outlook is treated particularly well by Oberdorfer, *The Two Koreas*, pp. 84–108.

16  William E. Berry Jr, 'The Political and Military Roles of US Forces in Korea', pp. 211–12.

17  On the 1998 South Korean defence budget cuts, see 'Budget Razor Sends North Wrong Signal on Seoul's Defence, Cohen Warns', *The Australian* (23 January 1998), p. 6; Robert Karniol, 'South Korea Postpones Programmes Amid Crisis', *Jane's Defence Weekly* 29:3 (21 January 1998), 14; and 'South Korea Proposes 4% Cut', *Jane's Defence Weekly* 29:7 (18 February 1998), 15. The Korean perspective on the Japan question is covered by Young-Sun Song, 'Korean Concern on the New U.S.–Japan Security Arrangement', *Korea and World Affairs* 20:2 (Summer 1996), 197–218. US differences on defence technology transfer and the host nation support issues are surveyed by Peter Hayes and Stephen Noerper, 'The Future of the US–ROK Alliance', in Young Whan Khil and Peter Hayes (eds), *Peace and Security in Northeast Asia* (New York: M. E. Sharpe, 1997), pp. 253–5.

18  'Annual Report on the Military Situation on the Korean Peninsula' (Defense Secretary's Year 2000 Report to Congress), 12 September 2000 at [http://usinfo.state.gov/regional/ea/easec/]; also 'ROK Def Min Paper: DPRK Keeps Large-scale Forward Deployment', *The Korean Times*, Internet edn (4 December 2000) and reprinted in FBIS-EAS-2000-2104, (4 December 2000).

19  This variant of the soft landing theme is discussed in depth by Christopher W. Hughes, 'Japanese Policy and the North Korean "Soft Landing"', *The Pacific Review* 11:5 (1998), 389–415, esp. p. 392. Also see Selig S. Harrison,

'Promoting a Soft Landing in Korea', *Foreign Policy* 106 (Spring 1992), 57–75; and Victor D. Cha, 'Engaging North Korea Credibly', *Survival* 42:2 (Summer 2000), 146–7.

20 General John H. Tilelli, Jr cited in Amos A. Jordon and Jae Ku, 'Coping With North Korea', *The Washington Quarterly* 21:1 (Winter 1998), 40–1.

21 Just prior to the end of the Clinton Administration in January 2001 the US Defense Secretary William Cohen admitted that the Patriot failed to work in the Persian Gulf War. See 'Weekly News' from Defence Aerospace at [http://www.defence-aerospace.com] 12 January 2001 (accessed on 20 January 2001).

22 Charles Bickers, 'Pie in the Sky?', *Far Eastern Economic Review* (24 September 1998), 21–2.

23 Stephen Lunn, 'Seoul Aims Missile Program at North', *The Australian*, 18 January 2001, p. 7.

24 Perhaps the most comprehensive – and most controversial – of recent studies is by Michael O'Hanlon, 'Stopping a North Korean Invasion', *International Security* 22:4 (Spring 1998), 135–70. Using data on US weapons systems performance in the 1991 Persian Gulf War, O'Hanlon argues that any North Korean invasion (even one which incorporated chemical weapons systems) would be halted well short of Seoul. A similar conclusion is reached by Nick Beldecos and Eric Heginbotham, 'The Conventional Military Balance in Korea', *Breakthroughs* 4:1 (Spring 1995), 1–8. Other assessments include 'North Korea: The Final Act', and related articles in *Jane's Intelligence Review*, 6:4 [Special Report No. 2] (April 1994), 3–5; Paul Bracken, 'Nuclear Weapons and State Survival in North Korea', *Survival* 35:3 (Autumn 1993), 137–53; David C. Kang, 'Preventive War and North Korea', *Security Studies* 4:2 (Winter 1994/95), 330–64; Stuart K. Masaki, 'The Korean Question: Assessing the Military Balance', *Security Studies* 4:2 (Winter 1994), 365–425; Hayes and Noerper, 'The Future of the US–ROK Alliance', pp. 240–68; Robert A. Manning, 'The United States and the Endgame in Korea: Assessment, Scenarios and Implications', *Asian Survey* 37:7 (July 1997), 579–90; and Hideshi Takesada, 'The North Korean Military Threat Under Kim Jong Il', in Thomas H. Henriksen and Jongryn Mo (eds), *North Korea After Kim Il Sung: Continuity or Change?* (Stanford, CA: Hoover Institution Press, 1997).

25 See Manning, 'The United States and the Endgame in Korea: Assessment, Scenarios and Implications'; and Takesada, 'The North Korean Military Threat Under Kim Jong Il', pp. 69, 77.

26 As reported in Hayes and Noerper, 'The Future of the US–ROK Alliance', pp. 246–7.

27 For an excellent chronology of the process of Sino–ROK diplomatic normalisation see Chae-Jin Lee, *China and Korea: Dynamic Relations* (Stanford, CA: Stanford University Press, 1996), pp. 105–31.

28 These factors are cogently discussed by David I. Steinberg, 'The Dichotomy of Pride and Vulnerability: South Korean Tensions in the US Relationship', in Wonmo Dong (ed.), *The Two Koreas and the United States: Issues of Peace, Security and Cooperation* (New York: M. E. Sharpe, 1999), pp. 94–115.

29 Han, 'The Koreas' New Century', p. 91.

30 These developments are recounted by Samuel S. Kim, 'North Korea in 1999: Bringing the Grand Chollima March Back In', *Asian Survey* 40:1 (January 2000), 151–63.

31 See Jongryn Mo, 'Security and Economic Linkages in the Inter-Korean Relationship', in Henricksen and Mo, *North Korea After Kim Il Sung*, pp. 108–19.

32  Sung-Han Kim, 'The Future of Korea–US Alliance', *Korea and World Affairs* 20:2 (Summer 1996), 191.
33  This 'decoupling' process is examined by Scott Snyder, *Challenges of Building a Korean Peace Process: Political and Economic Transition on the Korean Peninsula*, US Institute for Peace Working Group on US Policy Toward the Korean Peninsula (Washington, DC: USIP, June 1998), pp. 5–6.
34  The most definitive study of North Korean–US relations during the nuclear crisis leading to the Agreed Framework is by Leon Sigal, *Disarming Strangers* (Princeton: Princeton University Press, 1998). Sigal argues that the United States was only able to reach agreement with Pyongyang when it abandoned tactics of coercion and applied a strategy of 'cooperative threat reduction' consistent with liberal theory by inducing the North Koreans to work with IAEA inspectors and by implementing 'Track Two' (informal) diplomacy through former President Jimmy Carter's trip to North Korea to negotiate face-saving solutions directly with Kim Il-sung to resolve North Korean–American differences. Also see Michael J. Mazaar, *North Korea and the Bomb* (New York: St Martin's Press, 1995) who presents a decidedly more realist perspective on the American negotiating posture. A seminal and realist-oriented study on North Korean negotiating and diplomatic style is Scott Snyder's *Negotiating on the Edge: North Korean Negotiating Behaviour* (Washington DC: United States Institute for Peace, 1999). A Korean perspective is offered by Lee Dong-bok, 'Dealing With North Korea: The Case of the Agreed Framework', *Journal of Northeast Asian Studies* 14:2 (Summer 1995), 90–101.
35  Snyder, *Challenges of Building a Korean Peace Process*, pp. 2, 15. Also see Hyung-Kook Kim, 'US Policy Toward North Korea: From Positive Engagement To Constructive Containment', *Journal of East Asian Affairs* 13:1 (Spring/Summer 1999), 122–6.
36  'Text: GAO Report on US–North Korea Agreement on Energy' at [http://www.usia.gov/regional]; and House International Relations Committee, 'North Korea Advisory Group: Report to the Speaker', November 1999, reprinted at [http://www.house.gov/internationalrelations/].
37  'Text: US–DPRK Joint Communique Oct. 12', International Information Programs, at [http://usinfo.state.gov/regional] (accessed on 20 January 2001).
38  See remarks of Ambassador Wendy R. Sherman, US North Korea Policy Coordinator, 'Transcript: Albright, Sherman Briefing Oct. 12', International Information Programs, at [http://usinfo.state.gov/regional/ea/easec/]; Sherman observed that while 'progress' had been made in discussions about diplomatic representation, the North Koreans had still not met all of the criteria listed in the October 1999 Perry Report that guided American policy on this issue. Also see 'North Korea Opens to the West', *IISS Strategic Comments* 6:9 (November 2000), 1–2.
39  Banning N. Garrett and Bonnie S. Glaser, 'Looking Across the Yalu: Chinese Assessments of North Korea', *Asian Survey* 35:6 (June 1995), 528–45; and Michael Green, 'North Korean Regime Crisis: US Perspectives and Responses', *The Korean Journal of Defense Analysis* 9:2 (Winter 1997), 22.
40  Background to the events and trends which led to Pyongyang opposing Mikhail Gorbachev's retention of power during the Soviet Union's declining years is provided by Seung-Ho Joo, 'Soviet Policy Toward The Two Koreas, 1985–1991: The New Political Thinking and Power', *Journal of Northeast Asian Studies* 14:2 (Summer 1995), 23–46.

41  See Alexander Zhebin, 'Russia and North Korea', *Asian Survey* 35:8 (August 1995), 738–9; and Valentin Moiseyev, 'Russia and the Korean Peninsula', *International Affairs* (Moscow) 42:1 (January/February, 1996), 106–14. Moiseyev has been often characterised as the most pro-North Korean diplomat in Russia's foreign policy establishment.

42  'Putin Steps up NMD Pressure', *Jane's Defence Weekly* 34:5 (2 August 2000), 18.

43  See 'Einhorn Statement November 3 on North Korea Missile Talks', International Information Programs, at [http://usinfo.state.gov/regional/ea/easec/] (accessed 21 January 2001).

44  'Russian Parliament Ratifies Friendship Treaty with DPRK', *Xinhua* (19 July 2000), as reprinted in FBIS-CHI-2000-0719, (19 July 2000).

45  For an assessment of KEDO see Joel Wit, 'Viewpoint: The Korean Peninsula Energy Development Organization: Achievements and Challenges', *Non-Proliferation Review* 6:2 (Winter 1999), 59–69.

46  A joint US–DPRK communique outlining the Berlin Agreement is found in USIS, *Washington File* EDF121, (13 September 1999). Also see 'US–North Korean Detente: A New Approach in Pyongyang?', IISS, *Strategic Comments* 5:8 (October 1999), 1–2; and Andrew Koch, 'North Korean Shift Eases Tensions', *Jane's Defence Weekly* 32:13 (29 September 1999), 21.

47  The NEACD was formed in October 1993 and was intended to involve China, Japan, Russia, the United States and the two Koreas. North Korea's participation has been sporadic, at best, although a major rationale for creating this group was to engage the North and China into systematic multilateral dialogue. See Ralph A. Cossa, *The Major Powers in Northeast Asian Security*, McNair Paper no. 51 (Washington, DC: Institute for National Strategic Studies, National Defense University, 1996), p. 65, n. 4.

48  Scott Snyder, 'A Framework for Achieving Reconciliation on the Korean Peninsula: Beyond the Geneva Agreement', *Asian Survey* 35:8 (August 1995), 704.

49  For a representative expression of this argument, see Doug Bandow, 'Leaving Korea', *Foreign Policy* 77 (Winter 1989/90), 77–93.

50  For an argument that this trend is very probable, see Aaron L. Friedberg, 'Ripe for Rivalry', *International Security* 18:3 (Winter 1993–1994), 5–33. A Korean perspective offering a similar logic is offered by Kyongsoo Lho, 'The U.S.–ROK Alliance: Meeting the Challenges of Transition', in Kwak and Wilborn (eds), *The U.S.–ROK Alliance in Transition*, esp. pp. 34–5.

51  See, for example, Kyung-Won Kim, 'Maintaining Asia's Current Peace', *Survival* 39:4 (Winter 1997/1998), 52–64; and Tae-Am Ohm, 'Toward a New Phase of Multilateral Security Cooperation in the Asia-Pacific Region: Limited Multilateralism or Issue-Based Regionalism', *The Korean Journal of Defense Analysis* 9:2 (Winter 1997), 157–61.

52  Brian L. Job, 'Multilateralism in the Asia-Pacific Region', in William T. Tow, Russell Trood, and Toshiya Hoshino (eds), *Bilateralism in a Multilateral Era* (Tokyo/Nathan: Japan Institute of International Affairs/Centre for the Study of Australia–Asia Relations, Griffith University, 1997), p. 166.

53  Chung-in Moon, *Arms Control on the Korean Peninsula* (Seoul: Yonsei University Press, 1996), pp. 103–4; Kang Choi, 'Inter-Korean Confidence Building', in Tae-Hwan Kwak (ed.), *The Four Powers and Korean Unification Strategy* (Seoul: Kyungnam University Press, 1997), pp. 189–219; Byung-Joo Ahn, 'Arms Control and Confidence Building on the Korean Peninsula: A South Korean Perspective', *The Korean Journal of Defense Analysis* 5:1 (Summer 1993), 131–4; and Thomas J. Hirschfeld, 'Building Confidence in Korea: The Arms

Control Dimension', *The Korean Journal of Defense Analysis* 4:1 (Summer 1992), 23–55. All these articles focus on the Basic Agreement as a key arms control instrument.

54  Choi, 'Inter-Korean Confidence Building', esp. p. 208.

55  Sigal, *Disarming Strangers*, pp. 250–1.

56  This point is emphasised by Cossa, *The Major Powers in Northeast Asian Security*, p. 62.

57  For a graphic example of the North Korean resistance to NEASD, see 'Commentary Decries "Northeast Asia" Forum', KCNA (in English) (14 December 1996). Reprinted in FBIS-EAS-96-242 (14 December 1996). Background on the NEACD is provided by Cossa, *The Major Powers in Northeast Asian Security*, pp. 51–2, 65.

58  Anthony Davis, 'North Korea Inducted into the ASEAN Forum', *Jane's Defence Weekly* 34:6 (9 August 2000), 15; and Ohm, 'Toward a New Phase of Multilateral Security Cooperation', p. 158. Also see an Agence France Press (Hong Kong) report on a North Korean letter sent to ASEAN officials in May 1998 soliciting ARF membership, reprinted in FBIS-EAS-98-141 (21 May 1998).

59  As Thomas J. Christensen has noted, China's mistrust of Japan compounds the two Koreas' mistrust of each other to thwart a truly liberal Chinese outlook towards multilateral security approaches in Northeast Asia. See 'China, the U.S.–Japan Alliance', p. 73.

60  For background on the Albright-Paek meeting, see 'Transcript: Albright July 28 Press Stakeout on US–DPRK Bilateral' International Information Programs, at [http://usinfo.state.gov/regional/ea/easec/]. 'Security pluralism' is discussed in US Department of Defense, *The United States Security Strategy for the East Asia-Pacific Region* (Washington D.C.: USGPO, 1998), pp. 42–4.

61  This argument is advanced convincingly by Dong-Ik Shin, 'Multilateral CBMs on the Korean Peninsula: Making a Virtue Out of Necessity', *The Pacific Review* 10:4 (1997), 504–22.

62  Taiwan's GNP grew 6.8 per cent during 1997; its unemployment rate was only 2.74 per cent and its inflation rate was only 0.9 per cent. The New Taiwan Dollar declined in value by about 7.2 per cent against the US dollar during that year. See commentary by Peng Shu-nam, *Ching-Chi Jih-Bao* (4 February 1998), 4, translation in FBIS-CHI-98-110 (20 April 1998). Also see a Taiwan Central News Agency report, 'Taipei Protected From Asia Crisis By a Healthy Economy', (in English) (18 May 1998), reprinted in FBIS-CHI-98-140 (20 May 1998).

63  For background on the overall trade/investment flows and the 1996 Taiwan Strait crisis effect on these trends, see Heather Smith and Stuart Harris, 'Economic Relations Across the Taiwan Strait: Interdependence or Dependence?', in Greg Austin (ed.), *Missile Diplomacy and Taiwan's Future: Innovations in Politics and Military Power*, Canberra Papers on Strategy and Defence no. 122 (Canberra: Strategic and Defence Studies Centre, Australian National University, 1997), 171–211.

64  Points emphasised by Gary Klintworth, 'Introduction', in Klintworth (ed.), *Taiwan in the Asia-Pacific in the 1990s* (St Leonards/Canberra: Allen & Unwin/Department of International Relations, Australian National University, 1994), p. xiii; and Ron Montaperto, 'Commentary' to Harlan W. Jencks, 'Taiwan in the International Arms Market', in Robert G. Sutter and William R. Johnson (eds), *Taiwan in World Affairs* (Boulder: Westview, 1994), pp. 105–6.

65　See a *Renmin Ribao* editorial on 'An Important Declaration for Achieving the Great Course of National Reunification', [undated], translation in FBIS-CHI-95-022 (2 February 1995); and 'Jiang Zemin Puts Forward Important Proposals Aimed at Promoting Cross-Strait Relations', *Wen Wei Po* (31 January 1995), 2, translation in FBIS-CHI-95-023 (3 February 1995). Also see Frank Ching, 'Jiang Zemin Goes Fishing', *Far Eastern Economic Review* (2 March 1995), 40.

66　For background, see Jean Pierre Cabastan, 'The Mainland China Factor in Taiwan's 1995 and 1996 Elections: A Secondary Role', in Austin (ed.), *Missile Diplomacy*, pp. 9–28; You Ji, 'Missile Diplomacy and PRC Domestic Politics', in Austin (ed.), *Missile Diplomacy*, pp. 29–53; Weixing Hu, 'China's Taiwan Policy and East Asian Security', *Journal of Contemporary Asia* 27:3 (1997), 374–8; Weixing Hu, 'The Taiwan Strait and Asian-Pacific Security', *The Journal of East Asian Affairs* 11:1 (Winter/Spring 1997), 150–6; and Todd Crowell, 'Target Taiwan', *Asiaweek* (22 March 1996), 24–7.

67　On PLA military contingency planning, see a report on China establishing the Central National Security Leading Group in late 2000 to coordinate national security crises, 'especially those involving cross-Strait clashes and Sino–US tension', *South China Morning Post* (12 December 2000), cited on the 'Taiwan Security Research' website at [http://taiwansecurity.org] (accessed 21 January 2001). The PLA's use of bellicose rhetoric relative to crises over Taiwan for enhancement of its own status with the Chinese leadership is covered by Alan P. L. Liu, 'A Convenient Crisis: Looking Behind Beijing's Threats Against Taiwan', *Issues and Studies* 36:5 (October 2000), 104–15. Also see Hih Kainen, 'Taiwan White Paper: China Likely to Attack Taiwan 2005–2010', *Lien-Ho Bao* (29 March 1998), 9, reprinted in FBIS-CHI-98-092 (2 April 1998) which reports on an 'unofficial study' drawn up by Tamkang University experts; and a background article by Willy Wo-Lap Lam for *The South China Morning Post* (30 November 1995), pp. 1, 9, reporting on the Chinese Military Commission's '3-step plan' for taking Taiwan by force.

68　The realist–liberal debate's applicability in the China–Taiwan dispute has received little attention among either Chinese or Taiwanese analysts. An exception, however, is the work of I Yuan of National Chengchi University. See his 'Cooperation under Anarchy? Paradoxes of the Intra-Chinese Rapprochement', *Issues & Studies* 31:2 (February 1995), 54–66; and 'Cooperation and Conflict: The Offense–Defense Balance in Cross-Strait Relations', *Issues & Studies* 33:2 (February 1997), 1–20.

69　US Assistant Secretary of Defense for International Security Affairs Joseph S. Nye Jr. was most closely associated with this policy during the Clinton Administration, while his predecessor, Chas Freeman, postulated the same approach during the Bush Sr. Administration. See Cheng-yi Lin, 'The US Factor in the 1958 and 1996 Taiwan Strait Crises', *Issues & Studies* 32:12 (December 1996), 20.

70　Charles Babington and Dana Milbank, 'Bush Advisers Try to Limit Damage: No Change in China Policy toward Taiwan', *The Washington Post*, 27 April 2001.

71　In a report submitted to Congress in February 1999, the US Defense Department noted that China's 2.5 million strong armed forces dwarf Taiwan's defence force of about 400 000. However, 'only a portion of [China's] overall strength ... could be brought to bear against Taiwan at one time' and that 'despite the modest qualitative improvement in the military forces of both

China and Taiwan, the dynamic equilibrium of those forces in the Taiwan Strait has not changed dramatically over the past two decades, except in a few niche areas like China's deployment of short-range ballistic missiles'. See Department of Defense, *Report to Congress Pursuant to the FY99 Appropriation Bill*, internet version at [http://www.usia.gov/regional/ea/uschina/twnstrt.htm].

72 As noted by Alastair Iain Johnston, 'China's Militarized Interstate Dispute Behaviour 1949–1992: A First Cut at the Data', *The China Quarterly* 153 (March 1998), 3.

73 This point is discussed by Denny Roy, 'Tensions in the Taiwan Strait', *Survival* 42:1 (Spring 2000), 81–2.

74 The TSEA was proposed by Senator Jesse Holmes, Chairman of the US Senate Foreign Relations Committee, and Senator Robert Torricelli in March 1999 to accelerate US arms sales to Taiwan (in apparent contradiction to the 1982 Sino–American 'Shanghai Communique' pledging the US to a gradual reduction of such sales) and to increase direct military-to-military relations between the US and Taiwanese governments; see 'Text: S.693 Taiwan Security Enhancement Act', International Information Program, at [http://usinfo.state.gov/ regional/ea/uschina].

75 For background see Robert Ross, 'The 1995 and 1996 Taiwan Strait Confrontation: Coercion, Credibility and the Use of Force', *International Security* 25:2 (Fall 2000), 87–125; and Bernice Lee, *The Security Implications of the New Taiwan* Adelphi Paper 331 (London: International Institute for Strategic Studies, 1999), pp. 60–2.

76 See the proposal by Joseph S. Nye Jr in 'Clear Up the Dangerous Ambiguity About Taiwan', *International Herald Tribune* (12 March 1998), p. 8.

77 The proposal has been explicated more fully by Robert A. Pastor, 'The Paradox of the Double Triangle: Preempting the Next Crisis in Taiwan and Cuba', *World Policy Journal* 17:1 (Spring 2000), 28–9. For an explanation of the Clinton Administration's position on this point see Testimony of Deputy Assistant Secretary of State Susan Shirk, 'On Taiwan Relations Act at 20', International Information Programs, at [http://usinfo.state.gov/regional/ea/uschina].

78 These factions are summarised by Tuan Y. Cheng, 'The ROC's Security Strategies After the 1996 Taiwan Straits Crisis', *Issues & Studies* 32:12 (December 1996), 34–5.

79 Two of the most comprehensive force balance assessments of a Taiwan Strait contingency in the open literature have recently been offered by Felix K. Chang, 'Conventional War Across the Taiwan Strait', *ORBIS* 40:4 (Fall 1996), 577–607; and Michael O'Hanlon, 'Why China Cannot Conquer Taiwan', *International Security* 25:2 (Fall 2000), 51–86. Also see Martin Lasater, *Changing of the Guard: President Clinton and the Security of Taiwan* (Boulder: Westview Press, 1995), pp. 200–12; Andrew Nien-Dzu Yang, *Crisis, What Crisis? Lessons of the 1996 Tension and the ROC View of Security in the Taiwan Strait*, CAPS Papers no. 20 (Taipei: Chinese Council of Advanced Policy Studies, December 1997); and Department of Defense, *The Security Situation in the Taiwan Strait*, *passim.*

80 See, in particular, O'Hanlon, 'Why China Cannot Conquer Taiwan', pp. 74–9.

81 These steps are discussed by Cheng, 'The ROC's Security Strategies', *passim*; Hickey, *Taiwan's Security*, pp. 37–55 and 77–91, and O'Hanlon, 'Why China Cannot Conquer Taiwan', pp. 84–6.

82 Yang, 'Taiwan's Defensive Capabilities', in Austin (ed.), *Missile Diplomacy*, p. 148.

83  Chang, 'Conventional War Across the Taiwan Strait', p. 605. Also see Chen Pi-chao, 'The Military Balance Across the Taiwan Strait', *Taipei Times* (10 January 2000), reprinted on the 'Taiwan Security Research' website at [http://taiwansecurity.org]. Chen Pi-chao, a counsellor at Taiwan's National Security Council, concludes that China may eventually overtake Taiwan's qualitative superiority in conventional arms by acquiring advanced Russian weapons system, including precision guided munitions. Dissenting views are presented by O'Hanlon, 'Why China Cannot Conquer Taiwan', *passim*; and John Pomfret, 'Chinese Threat Tests Taiwan's Preparedness', *The Washington Post* (27 July 1999) and reprinted on the Taiwan Security Research web site. Pomfret reports that Taiwan's military confronts a number of 'software issues', a requirement for greater professionalisation and a need to cultivate more genuine *esprit de corp* within the general population that is otherwise too susceptible to Chinese tactics of psychological warfare. Michael D. Swaine, moreover, has warned that Taiwan's defence doctrine has become excessively narrow and 'keyed primarily to the separate interests and outlooks of the three services and an assumption of US intervention in a future major military confrontation with the mainland'; See Michael D. Swaine, *Taiwan's National Security, Defense Policy, and Weapons Procurement Processes* (Santa Monica: RAND, 1999).
84  Bitzinger and Gill, *Gearing Up for High-Tech Warfare*, p. 49; and Yuan, 'Cooperation and Conflict', pp. 9, 11, 16–18.
85  On these issues and the limited utility of *Aegis*, see O'Hanlon, 'Why China Cannot Conquer Taiwan', pp. 50–1, 77–8, 82; and Michael O'Hanlon, 'US Missile Defense Programs', a paper presented at a TMD workshop convened by the Nautilus Institute and the United Nations University, Tokyo, in June 2000. The text is available at [http://www.nautilus.org/nukepolicy/TMD-Conference/] (accessed 28 January 2001).
86  Tom Woodrow, 'Nuclear Issues', in Hans Binnendijk and Ronald N. Montaperto (eds), *Strategic Trends in China* (Washington, DC: Institute for National Strategic Studies, National Defense University, 1998), p. 88.
87  Chas Freeman, 'An Interest-Based China Policy', in Binnendijk and Montaperto (eds), *Strategic Trends in China*, p. 125.
88  David S. Chou, 'Cross-Strait Relations and US Roles in the Taiwan Strait Crisis', *Issues & Studies* 32:10 (October 1996), 14–15; and Robert Sutter, 'The Taiwan Crisis of 1995–96 and US Domestic Politics', in Austin (ed.), *Missile Diplomacy*, esp. pp. 60–73.
89  Barton Gelman, 'US and China Nearly Came to Blows in 96', *The Washington Post* (21 June 1998), p. A–1. Robert Ross's account is less dramatic, insisting that the US never believed that China would really attack Taiwan, despite China's ongoing missile 'tests'. See Ross, 'The 1995–96 Taiwan Strait Confrontation', pp. 109–10, 112. Also see Perry's own account in Ashton B. Carter and William J. Perry, *Preventative Defense: A New Security Strategy for America* (Washington DC: Brookings, 1999), pp. 92–3.
90  Bruce W. Nelson, 'Will We Have to Go to War for Taiwan?' *Time* Internet edn (22 June 1998); and a Reuters report 'House Votes 411–0 for Resolution Urging PRC To Renounce Force Against Taiwan', Taiwan Research Institute, (9 June 1998) accessible at [http://www.taiwaninformation.org/policy/uscong].
91  Such tensions were amply demonstrated when an editorial in the *People's Daily* 'slammed' the TSEA bill to enhance US–Taiwan military ties being considered by the US Congress in February 2000 in the shadow of the unfolding

US Presidential campaign. See Lynne O'Donnell, 'Beijing Blasts US Bill on Taiwan', *The Australian* (4 February 2000), p. 7.

92  Wang Ming-yi, 'Xu Shiquan: TMD Should Be Part of Cross-Strait Talks on Ending Hostility', *Chung-Kuo Shih-Pao* (10 March 1999), p. 2, translation in FBIS-CHI-1999-0324 (10 March 1999).

93  US Department of Defense, *Report to Congress on Theater Missile Defense*.

94  'Defend Taiwan if China Violates One-China Policy', GOP debate in Los Angeles, 2 March 2000, available at 'Issues 2000' website, [http://www.issues2000.org/china.htm#George_W_Bush].

95  See coverage of Chen's inaugural speech in 'New Taiwan Leader seeks "Reconciliation" with China', *The Washington Post* (20 May 2000), at the 'Taiwan Security Research' website [http://www.taiwansecurity.org].

96  See 'Washington–Taipei Relations and the ROC's Pragmatic Diplomacy: Questions and Answers', at the 'Taiwan Security Research' website [http://www.taiwansecurity.org]. For additional background, see Bernard T. K. Joi, 'Pragmatic Diplomacy in the Republic of China: History and Prospects', in Jason C. Hu (ed.), *Quiet Revolutions on Taiwan, Republic of China* (Taipei: Kwang Hwa Publishing Company, 1994), pp. 297–330; and Hickey, *Taiwan's Security*, pp. 113–31. For a mainland Chinese view, see Chen Qimao, 'The Taiwan Strait Crisis', pp. 1058–9.

97  On this point, see Jean-Pierre Cabestan, 'The Cross-Strait Relationship in the Post-Cold War Era: Neither Reunification Nor "Win–win" Game', *Issues and Studies* 31:1 (January 1995), 32–3.

98  The interview is reprinted on the Taiwan Security Research website under the special section, 'Special State-to-State Position', see [http://www.taiwanheadlines.gov.tw/state/]. Lee reiterated his stance in *Foreign Affairs* during late 1999, see Lee Teng-hui, 'Understanding Taiwan: Bridging the Perception Gap', *Foreign Affairs* 78:6 (November–December 1999), 9–21.

99  Jim Mann and Norman Kempster, 'US Warns China Again on Taiwan', *Los Angeles Times* (14 August 1999), reprinted on the Taiwan Security Research website [http://www.taiwanheadlines.gov.tw/].

100  'Mainland's Olive Branch to "Right" Taiwan President', *South China Morning Post*, (5 January 2000). Reprinted on the Taiwan Security Research web site [http://www.taiwanheadlines.gov.tw/].

101  Peter Lewis Young, 'Will Taiwanese Independence Become an Asia-Pacific Security Issue?', *Asian Defense Journal* (January 1994), 26.

102  This approach was suggested in November 2000 by a prominent analyst of Southeast Asian security affairs, Carolina Hernandez, President of the Philippines Institute for Strategic and Development Studies. See 'International Seminar Stresses Taiwan, ASEAN Ties', accessed 5 May 2001 at [http://www. taiwanheadlines.gov.tw/].

103  'Taiwan Says it Favors an Asia-Pacific Security System to Settle Disputes', *The Sunday Times* (London) (11 July 1993), p. 8. For additional development of this viewpoint, see Gary Klintworth, 'Taiwan's Asia-Pacific Policy and Community', *The Pacific Review* 7:4 (1994), esp. p. 450; and Kay Möller, 'A New Role for the ROC in the Cold War Era', *Issues & Studies* 31:2 (February 1995), 82–3. On APEC, see Gordon C. K. Cheung, 'APEC as a Regime for Taiwan's Interdependence with the United States and Mainland China', *Issues & Studies* 33:2 (February 1997), 21–39.

104  See the arguments advanced in 'ESCAP', *IISS Newsletter* (Spring 1995), p. 6. Track Two diplomacy in an intra-Chinese context is discussed by Ralph

Clough, *Reaching Across the Taiwan Strait* (Boulder: Westview, 1994). A somewhat favourable review of Clough's arguments supporting the concept is offered by James W. Robinson, 'Loosening the Straitjacket', *Free China Review* 44:10 (October 1994), 48–52.

105 An extensive background of the entire 'Taiwan case' for UN re-entry is offered by Parris Chang and Kok-ui Lim, 'Taiwan's Case For United Nations Membership', *Journal of Law and International Affairs* (April 1997) posted on the Internet at [http://www.law.ucla.edu/student/Organizations/JILFA].

106 Dennis Van Vranken Hickey, 'US Policy and Taiwan's Bid to Rejoin the United Nations', *Asian Survey* 37:11 (November 1997), 1034.

107 'Americans Support Taiwan Membership in UN and WTO', Taiwan Research Institute (20 March 1997), internet version at [http://www.taiwaninformation.org/].

108 A comprehensive Chinese analysis is provided by Yuan Yang, 'Floating Historical Dregs – Refuting Taiwan Authorities, Fallacy of "Rejoining the United Nations"', *Liaowang* (12 September 1994), 16–17, translation in FBIS-CHI-94-185 (12 September 1994). Also see Ross Munro, 'Giving Taipei a Place at the Table', *Foreign Affairs* 73:6 (November/December 1994), 118.

109 President Clinton also reiterated US commitments to upholding the TRA but the impact of this paled in comparison to an American chief executive fundamentally supporting the Chinese line on the Taiwan UN membership question.

110 'Winston Lord Before US Senate Panel Hearing, "'Balance" Key To US Adjustments To Its Taipei Policy', *Wireless File*, EPF303 (28 September 1994).

111 Lee, *The Security Implications of the New Taiwan*, p. 70.

112 See, for example, report and commentary by Don Kirk, 'Seoul Demands Tokyo Rewrite History', *International Herald Tribune*, 9 May 2001, p. 4; and Kak Soo Shin, 'Japan's Skewed History Books are Straining Ties with Korea', *International Herald Tribune*, 9 May 2001, p. 8.

## 5 Other Key Players II: ASEAN and Australia

1 For example, Japan's Foreign Ministry adopted a clearly liberal strategy in working with ASEAN to establish the ASEAN Regional Forum, although differentiating its own approach from that of Australia's which it regarded as more 'idealistic' than 'liberal'. See Tsuyoshi Kawasaki, 'Between Realism and Idealism in Japanese Security Policy: The Case of the ASEAN Regional Forum', *The Pacific Review* 10:4 (1997), 480–503.

2 A pioneering blueprint for this approach was provided in December 1989 by then Australian Minister for Foreign Affairs and Trade, Gareth Evans. See *Australia's Regional Security* (Canberra: Department of Foreign Affairs and Trade, December 1989). Principles of trust building, preventive diplomacy and conflict resolution were later incorporated into the ASEAN Regional Forum's seminal 1995 Concept Paper. For assessments of ASEAN's reaction and implementation of this strategy, see Michael Antolik, 'The ASEAN Regional Forum: The Spirit of Constructive Engagement', *Contemporary Southeast Asia* 16:2 (1994), 117–36; and Michael Leifer, *The ASEAN Regional Forum*, Adelphi Paper 302 (London: Oxford University Press for the International Institute for Strategic Studies, 1996), esp. pp. 53–60.

3 This point is developed by Amitav Acharya, 'Ideas, Identity and Institution-Building: From the "ASEAN Way" to the "Asia-Pacific Way"?', *The Pacific Review* 10:3 (1997), 319–46.

4  As argued by Julian Schofield, 'War and Punishment: The Implications of Arms Purchases in Maritime Southeast Asia', *Journal of Strategic Studies* 21:2 (June 1998), 76–8.

5  These typologies were originally developed by Oran Young. 'Entrepreneurial leadership' refers to the use of negotiating skills to reach agreement on rules or norms governing an organisation or regime that would otherwise not be attained. 'Intellectual leadership' is the generation of ideas that eventually are accepted and form the ordering principles of such organisations or regimes. See his 'Political Leadership and Regime Formation: On the Development of Institutions in International Society', *International Organization* 45:3 (Summer 1991), 281–308. For their application in a specific Asia-Pacific context, see David Rapkin, 'Leadership and Cooperative Institutions in the Asia-Pacific', in Andrew Mack and John Ravenhill (eds), *Pacific Cooperation: Building Economic and Security Regimes in the Asia-Pacific Region* (St Leonards: Allen & Unwin, 1994), pp. 98–129; and William T. Tow and Richard A. Gray, 'Asia-Pacific Security Regimes: Conditions and Constraints', *Australian Journal of Political Science* 30:3 (November 1995), 436–51.

6  What actually constitutes 'mainland' or continental Southeast Asia as opposed to 'peninsula' or maritime Southeast Asia is contentious. This study applies Lim Joo-Jock's concept which entails 'the large stretch of mountainous territory between northeastern India and the Tonkin highlands on the one hand and the area between China and its southern neighbours (the "southern lowland states") on the other'. Six states are placed within this geographic entity – India, Burma, Thailand, Laos, Cambodia, Vietnam and China. See Lim Joo-Jock, *Territorial Power Domains, Southeast Asia and China: The Geo-Strategy of an Overarching Massif* (Singapore/Canberra: Institute of Southeast Asian Studies/Strategic and Defence Studies Centre, Australian National University, 1984), pp. xi–xii.

7  Saul B. Cohen, 'Geopolitics in the New World Era: A New Perspective on an Old Discipline', in George J. Demko and William B. Wood (eds), *Reordering the World: Geopolitical Perspectives on the 21st Century* (Boulder: Westview Press, 1994), pp. 15–48.

8  Donald E. Weatherbee, 'Mainland Southeast Asia: Thailand, Malaysia, Singapore and Myanmar', in Mohan Malik (ed.), *Asian Defence Policies: Regional Conflicts and Security Issues* (Book Two) (Geelong: Deakin University, 1994), pp. 94–5.

9  For in-depth analysis on this trend and how it affected Southeast Asia's strategic balance, see Michael C. Gallagher, 'China's Illusory Threat to the South China Sea', *International Security* 19:1 (Summer 1994), 169–94.

10  International Institute for Strategic Studies, *The Military Balance 2000/2001* (London: Oxford University Press for the IISS, 2000), p. 182.

11  See Panitan Wattanayagorn, 'Thailand: The Elite's Shifting Conceptions of Security', in Muthiah Alagappa (ed.), *Asian Security Practice: Material and Ideational Influences*, (Stanford: Stanford University Press, 1998), pp. 429–32; and Noel M. Morada and Christopher Collier, 'The Philippines: States Versus Society?', in Alagappa (ed.), *Asian Security Practice*, pp. 559–66. Also see David Lamb, 'Military Retreats From Politics in Most of Southeast Asia', *Los Angeles Times* (12 December 1998), p. 4.

12  The Vietnamese white paper is covered by Micool Brooke, 'Vietnam's White Paper Aims to Win the "Hearts and Minds" of ASEAN Neighbors', *Asian Defence Journal* (October 1998), 24–6. Also see Richard Betts, 'Vietnam's Strategic Predicament', *Survival* 37:3 (Autumn 1995), 61–81. Kim Ninh has

observed that Vietnam continues to pursue national security within the framework of a 'cooperation-struggle' strategy which emphasises regional diplomacy and military professionalisation but not at the expense of Vietnamese ideology. See Kim Ninh, 'Vietnam: Struggle and Cooperation', in Alagappa (ed.), *Asian Security Practice*, pp. 455–60.

13  On the China–Burma military relationship, see IISS, *The Military Balance 2000/2001*, p. 180. Signs emerged in late 2000 and early 2001 that the military was beginning to loosen its grip but only slightly on the country's political dissidents. Opposition leader Aung San Suu Kyi was released from house arrest to meet with both a European Union delegation and some of the country's military leaders in January 2001 and the second ranking opposition leader in the country was released later the same month after being held in detention for four months. See the BBC News reports, at [http://news.bbc.co.uk/hi/english/world/asia-pacific/] entitled 'Suu Kyi Meets Military', (9 January 2001); and 'Burma Releases Key Opposition Figure', (25 January 2001) (accessed 26 January 2001). Increased international pressure and the threat of economic sanctions reportedly persuaded the Burmese generals to meet with Aung San Suu Kyi, their long-time political nemesis. For a more pessimistic assessment, see Bertil Litner, 'Tightening the Noose', *Far Eastern Economic Review* (16 November 2000), 30–3.

14  The ASEAN option for Vietnam is weighed by William S. Turley, 'Vietnamese Security in Domestic and Regional Focus: The Political Economic Nexus', in Richard J. Ellings and Sheldon Simon (eds), *Southeast Asian Security in the New Millennium* (New York: M. E. Sharpe, 1996), pp. 206–7.

15  Betts, 'Vietnam's Strategic Predicament', pp. 66–70.

16  See, for example, the BBC News report, 'China and Vietnam Hail Border Treaty' at [http://news.bbc.co.uk/hi/english/world/asia-pacific/] (accessed 26 January 2001). Background on negotiations leading to this agreement is provided by Charles E. Morrison (ed.), *Asia-Pacific Security Outlook 1998* (Tokyo: Japan Center for International Exchange, 1998), p. 159.

17  Robert Karniol, 'Vietnam Buys Submarines from North Korea', *Jane's Defence Weekly* 30:23 (9 December 1998), 14; and Karniol, 'Vietnam Seeks to Bolster Air Force with More Su-27s', *Jane's Defence Weekly* 31:6 (6 January 1999), 12.

18  Lim Joo-Jock, *Territorial Power Domains, Southeast Asia, and China*, p. 180.

19  Carlyle A. Thayer, *Beyond Indochina*, Adelphi Paper 297 (London: Oxford University Press for the IISS, 1995), pp. 46–7.

20  J. N. Mak, *ASEAN Defence Reorientation 1975–1992: The Dynamics of Modernisation and Structural Change*, Canberra Papers on Strategy and Defence no. 103, (Canberra: Strategic and Defence Studies Centre, Australian National University, 1993), p. 80. Mak cites the estimates of the Permanent Subcommittee for Economic and Security Coordination which was established in 1980.

21  See commentary on Thailand's 'geostrategic position' in Ministry of Defense, *The Defense of Thailand 1994* (Defense White Paper) (Bangkok: December 1993), pp. 35–7 of the English language edn; Weatherbee, 'Mainland Southeast Asia', in Malik (ed.), *Asian Defence Policies*, pp. 94–5; and Panitan Wattanayagorn, 'Thailand: The Elite's Shifting Conceptions of Security', in Alagappa (ed.), *Asian Security Practice*, pp. 436–7.

22  For background consult 'Thais Beef Up Security Along Burmese Border', *Bangkok Post* Internet edn (9 January 1999), reprinted in FBIS-EAS-99-0110 (10 January 1999). Thai military commanders are increasingly worried that frequent skirmishes between Burmese army elements and ethnic minorities

living in Thai villages along the 846 kilometre Thai–Burmese border could escalate, precipitating massive refugee flows.

23   Malaysia's construction of a wall in 1996 to partition the Thai–Malay border opposite Thailand's Satun province was a source of considerable tension between the two countries. In January 2001 the Thai–Malaysia Joint Boundary Coordination Office agreed to replace separate fences set up by the two countries with a single fence, to settle the 'no man's land' problem in the Sadao district. See *Bangkok Post* Internet edn (12 January 2001), reprinted in FBIS-EAS-2001-0112 (12 January 2001).

24   Mark Rolls, 'Thailand's Post-Cold War Security Policy and Defense Programme', *Contemporary Security Policy* 15:2 (August 1994), 97.

25   Kusuma Snitwongse, 'The Thai Attitude Toward Naval CSBMs', in Andrew Mack (ed.), *A Peaceful Ocean? Maritime Security in the Pacific in the Post-Cold War Era* (St Leonards: Allen & Unwin, 1993), pp. 140–1. Also see Thayer, *Beyond Indochina*, pp. 36–7.

26   The reality of the Thai military's limited 'staying power' is discussed by Amitav Acharya, *A New Regional Order in Southeast Asia: ASEAN in the Post-Cold War Era* Adelphi Paper 279 (Oxford: Brassey's for the IISS, 1993), p. 23. Background on organisational reform of Thai defence decision making is provided in Charles E. Morrison (ed.), *Asia Pacific Security Outlook 1997* (Honolulu: East-West Center, 1997), pp. 130–2. A Thai account of the bureaucratic impediments confronting Defense Ministry restructuring is in *The Nation* Internet edn (27 July 1998), reprinted in FBIS-EAS-98-208 (27 July 1998).

27   IISS, *The Military Balance 1998/99*, pp. 170, 172–3.

28   In December 1997 the Malaysian government cut the defence budget by 10 per cent and warned that another 8 per cent cut was likely in 1998. See Sheldon Simon, 'The Economic Crisis and Southeast Asian Security: Changing Priorities', *NBR Analysis* 9:5 (December 1998), 18–19.

29   Michael Richardson, 'Asian Military Spending: A Casualty of Bad Times', *International Herald Tribune* (23 October 1998), p. 6; and Simon, *The Economic Crisis and ASEAN States' Security*, p. 19. Malaysia's Fleet Operations Command Headquarters is at Lumut. Other bases are divided into 'naval areas' or 'naval patrol areas' and include Kuantan, Labuan, Sandakan (Sabah) and Sungei Antu (in Sarawak). A training base operates at Penerang. See IISS, *Military Balance 1998/99*, p. 190.

30   K. S. Nathan cites eight specific criteria of comprehensive security as that concept is interpreted and operationalised by Malay policy planners: (1) domestic social cohesion and a stable regional environment; (2) diplomacy as the first line of defence; (3) commitment to the UN; (4) facilitating regional security dialogues; (5) promotion of confidence-building as a part of crisis management; (6) emphasis on military diplomacy through contacts, exchanges, training and joint exercises; (7) promotion of bilateral and multilateral strategic cooperation such as the Five Power Defence Arrangements; and (8) modernisation of the Malaysian armed forces to defend Malay national sovereignty. Nathan, 'Malaysia: Reinventing the Nation', in Alagappa (ed.), *Asian Security Practice*, p. 535.

31   Abdul Razak Abdullah Baginda, 'Malaysia', in William M. Carpenter and David G. Wiencek (eds), *Asian Security Handbook* (New York: M. E. Sharpe, 1996), pp. 182–3; and David Boey, 'Singapore and Malaysia: Defense Modernisation and Cooperation?', paper prepared for a workshop on 'Arms and Defense Planning in Southeast Asia', June 1993, p. 23.

32 Paul Dibb has noted that, with the exception of Singapore, ASEAN's military forces 'have little capacity to respond effectively to a sudden incident and the serviceability of combat platforms beyond 2–3 days of real operations is doubtful ... quality-control procedures are poor and most ASEAN armed forces are hampered by the low level of technological expertise available'. Paul Dibb, 'The Revolution in Military Affairs and Asian Security', *Survival* 39:4 (Winter 1997–1998), 101–2; see also Boey, 'Singapore and Malaysia', pp. 25–6; and J. N. Mak, 'The Modernization of Malaysia's Armed Forces', *Contemporary Southeast Asia* 19:1 (June 1997) 33.

33 Author discussions with regional defence analysts, September 1999 (in Tokyo) and November 1999 (in Singapore). For a discussion of this and other recent disputes between the two countries see Dzirhan Mahadzir, 'Malaysia At Odds With Her Neighbours', *Asia-Pacific Defence Reporter* 25:1 (Annual Reference Edn 1999), 25–6.

34 Ian Stewart, 'Missile Deal Adds to Strain', *The South China Morning Post* (20 July 1999).

35 Andrew Tan, 'Singapore's Defence: Capabilities, Trends and Implications', *Contemporary Southeast Asia* 21:3 (December 1999), 451–74.

36 Tan, 'Singapore's Defence', p. 471, n. 2; and Tim Huxley, *Defending the Lion City: The Armed Forces of Singapore* (Crows Nest, NSW: Allen and Unwin, 2000), pp. 24–72.

37 Narayanan Ganesan, 'Singapore: Realist cum Trading State', in Alagappa (ed.), *Asian Security Practice*, p. 591. Singapore's trade-related activities generate three times the revenue of domestically generated goods and services.

38 Indonesia is especially regarded as having assumed an aggressive posture on this issue. See Stanley B. Weeks, 'Sea Lanes of Communication Security and Access', in Sam Bateman and Steven Bates (eds), *Shipping and Regional Security*, Canberra Papers on Strategy and Defence no. 129 (Canberra: Strategic and Defence Studies Centre, Australian National University, 1998), 50.

39 See BBC News Reports, 'Singapore to Raise Funds for Malaysia' (23 November 1998) and 'Malaysia Rejects Singapore Water Offer' (17 December 1998) at [http://news.bbc.co.uk/hi/english/world/asiapacific/].

40 This argument is developed by Ganesan, 'Singapore', in Alagappa (ed.), *Asian Security Practice*, pp. 579–607. Also see Ministry of Defence, Singapore, *Defending Singapore in the 21st Century* (Singapore Defence White Paper), pp. 12–13; Tim Huxley, 'The ASEAN States' Defense Policies', in Morrison (ed.), *Asia-Pacific Security Outlook 1998*, pp. 143–5 which outlines Singapore's 'total defence' strategy in detail; Huxley, 'Singapore and Malaysia: A Precarious Balance?', *The Pacific Review* 4:3 (1991), 201–13; and Tan, 'Singapore's Defence', pp. 455–6 and 464–5.

41 Robert Karniol, 'Diplomacy Teams Up with Deterrence', *Jane's Defence Weekly* 27:17 (30 April 1997), 23; and author interviews with US officials in Singapore, November 1999.

42 Background on Singapore's approval for US access to its Changi naval facility which can accommodate American aircraft carriers, for example, is provided by Michael Richardson, 'In Asia, A New Mutual Defense', *International Herald Tribune* (3 December 1998).

43 Defence Intelligence Organisation, Australia, *Defence Economic Trends in the Asia-Pacific 2000* (Canberra: Commonwealth of Australia, 2001) p. 9.

44 Tim Huxley and David Boey, 'Singapore's Army – Boosting Capabilities', *Jane's Intelligence Review* 8:4 (April 1996), 174–80.

45 Simon, *The Economic Crisis and ASEAN States' Security*, p. 20; Tan, 'Singapore's Defence', pp. 460–1; and IISS, *The Military Balance 1998/99*, p. 174.

46 An assessment posited collectively by Mak, *ASEAN Defence Reorientation*, pp. 98, 103–4; Huxley, 'The ASEAN States' Defence Policies', pp. 143–5; Tan, 'Singapore's Defence', p. 459; and Willett, 'East Asia's Changing Defense Industry', pp. 116, 128–9.

47 The FPDA facilitates Singaporean and Malaysian interaction along just such lines. See Panitan Wattanayagorn and Desmond Ball, 'A Regional Arms Race?', *Journal of Strategic Studies* 18:3 (September 1995), 168. Malaysian military commanders are on record as endorsing joint exercises with Singapore as a means of developing 'mutual understanding' and transparency between the two countries. See 'S'pore–KL Military Exercises "Should Be Held Every Year"', *The Straits Times* (25 April 1992), p. 11. Malaysia announced in early 1999 that it would resume FPDA participation in May of that year. For comprehensive background and analysis of the FPDA, see Philip Methven, *The Five Power Defence Arrangements and Military Cooperation Among the ASEAN States: Incompatible Models for Security in Southeast Asia?*, Canberra Papers on Strategy and Defence no. 92 (Canberra: Strategic and Defence Studies Centre, Australian National University, 1992).

48 Indonesia was particularly concerned about Singapore's original 1990 Memorandum of Understanding to grant US naval ships access to its military bases after the closure of US bases in the Philippines in 1992. See John B. Haseman, 'Indonesia', in Carpenter and Wiencek (eds), *Asian Security Handbook*, pp. 160–1. In November 1998 US Secretary of Defense William Cohen and Singapore Deputy Prime Minister Tony Tan signed an agreement allowing American naval ships to berth at the Changi Naval base, including US aircraft carriers. See 'Singapore, United States Formalize Berthing Pact', *The Straits Times* Weekly edn (14 November 1998), p. 3.

49 This point is well covered by Donald K. Emmerson, 'Indonesia, Malaysia, Singapore', in Ellings and Simon (eds), *Southeast Asian Security*, pp. 67–8.

50 Dewi Fortuna Anwar, *Indonesia's Strategic Culture: Katahanan Nasional, Wawasan Nusantara and Hankamrata*, CSAAR Australia-Asia Papers no. 75 (Nathan: Centre for the Study of Australia–Asia Relations, Griffith University, 1996), pp. 20–5.

51 In November 1998, for example, General Wiranto, TNI's (ABRI's) supreme commander, announced that military personnel occupying political positions outside TNI's formal infrastructure had to relinquish their active military status. TNI's role as a 'sociopolitical initiator' was also modified and directed to undertake political reforms. See 'ABRI's Dual Functions and the Abolishment of the Title of Chief of Sociopolitical Section', *Jakarta Suara Pewmbaruan* Internet Edition (12 November 1998), translation in FBIS-EAS-98-316 (12 November 1998).

52 Lesley McCulloch, 'Business as Usual', *Inside Indonesia* 63 (July–September 2000), 13–14; Michael Vatikiotis and John McBeth, 'March Back', *Far Eastern Economic Review* (12 October 2000), 14–16; and John McBeth, 'Military Manoeuvres', *Far Eastern Economic Review* (9 November 2000), 32–4.

53 Sylvia Tiwon, 'From Heroes to Rebels', *Inside Indonesia* 62 (April–June 2000), 4–5; Ed Aspinall 'Whither Aceh?', *Inside Indonesia* 62 (April–June 2000), 6–7; and Smith Alhadar, 'The Forgotten War in North Maluku', *Inside Indonesia* 63 (July–September 2000), 15–16.

54 John McBeth and Michael Vatikiotis, 'Jakarta's Shame', *Far Eastern Economic Review* (21 September 2000), 16–21.

55 Anwar, *Indonesia's Strategic Culture*, p. 6. Bob Lowry has noted that fear of sovereign vulnerability is defined in Indonesian strategic doctrine at different levels of intensity: outright threat, annoyances, obstacles and challenges. Outright 'threat' is external aggression directly challenging Indonesia as a state; 'annoyances' are efforts to obstruct the implementation of national policy in all fields; 'obstacles' impede the national development effort; and 'challenges' arouse the capabilities of the nation in terms of alien ideas, the penetration of foreign cultural values or the effects of unbridled social change. Bob Lowry, *Indonesian Defence Policy and the Indonesian Armed Forces*, Canberra Papers on Strategy and Defence no. 99 (Canberra: Strategic and Defence Studies Centre, Australian National University, 1993), p. 10.

56 Anwar, *Indonesia's Strategic Culture*, pp. 33–4.

57 The term 'spider web' was initially used by Indonesian Vice President Try Sutrisno in describing Indonesian security ties during the mid-1990s. See Haseman, 'Indonesia', in Carpenter and Wiencek (eds), *Asian Security Handbook*, p. 161.

58 Lowry, *Indonesian Defence Policy*, p. 45; and Mak, *ASEAN Defence Reorientation*, p. 65.

59 Professor Mochtar Kusuma-Atmadja, 'A View from Asia', in Sam Bateman and Dick Sherwood (eds), *Australia's Maritime Bridge into Asia* (St Leonard's: Allen & Unwin, 1995), p. 216.

60 IISS, *The Military Balance 2000/2001*, pp. 180–1, notes that the Indonesian navy became the most important defence priority, with a cabinet post created to oversee maritime affairs and with a naval officer appointed commander of the Indonesian Armed Forces for the first time in history.

61 Minister of Defense and Security, Republic of Indonesia, *The Policy of the State Defense and Security of the Republic of Indonesia* (Jakarta: Departermen Pertahanan Keamanan, August 1995); and Minister of Defense and Security, Republic of Indonesia, *The Policy of the State Defense and Security of the Republic of Indonesia* (Jakarta: Departermen Pertahanan Keamanan, 1997).

62 Anwar, 'Indonesia' in Alagappa (ed.), *Asian Security Practice*, p. 496.

63 For background, see J. Soedjhati Djiwandono, 'Jingoism Rises to the Fore Over East Timor', *The Jakarta Post* (15 September 1999), p. 1. One of Indonesia's most respected analysts of international affairs, Djiwandono, criticises those Indonesian 'political and military elite' who opposed Australian participation in the East Timor peacekeeping force (INTERFET) on the basis of preserving the 'self-respect of the Indonesian nation'.

64 *Jakarta Media* Internet edn (15 July 1998), translation in FBIS-EAS-98-196 (15 July 1998); also, 'Cohen's Mission and US Interests', *Suara Pembaruan* (3 August 1998), translation in FBIS-EAS-98-218 (6 August 1998). A critical analysis of US policy motives regarding possible Indonesian basing is offered by Sudiono Kartohadiprodjo, former commander of the I/ITB Battalion, Mahawaran Regiment, 'Commentary: IMF Military Base Connection', *Jakarta Gatra* (18 March 1998), translation in FBIS-EAS-98-077 (18 March 1998). The latter analysis argues that the US loss of basing access in the Philippines and a pending, similar loss of basing access in Okinawa could prompt the Americans to pressure Indonesia for such access to the Natuna islands.

65 For background on the Indonesian response to Singapore's 1989 offer see Methven, *The Five Power Defence Arrangements*, pp. 78–81.

66 See an interview with Admiral Joseph Prueher, commander-in-chief of US Pacific Forces (CINCPAC) by Greg Sheridan, 'Admiral Warns US Wake Up to Jakarta', *The Australian* (8 December 1998), p. 9.

67  A text of the Security Agreement is found in Gary Brown, Frank Frost and Stephen Sherlock, *The Australian–Indonesian Security Agreement*, Research Paper no. 25 (Canberra: Department of Parliamentary Library, 1996), Appendix A.

68  For additional assessments see Brown, Frost and Sherlock, *The Australian–Indonesian Security Agreement*, pp. 9–10; and Bob Lowry, 'What the Jakarta Pact Means', *The Australian Financial Review* (20 December 1995), p. 15.

69  See a Hong Kong Agence France Presse report reprinted in FBIS-EAS-1999-0916 (16 September 1999).

70  Defence Intelligence Organisation, Australia, *Defence Economic Trends*, p. 3; and Thalif Deen, 'Indonesia Postpones Planned Arms Purchases', *Jane's Defence Weekly* 30:21 (21 October 1998), 21.

71  Stanley B. Weeks, *Sea Lines of Communication (SLOC) Security and Access* CAPS Papers no. 22 (Taipei: Chinese Council of Advanced Policy Studies, 1998), pp. 2, 12.

72  On the possibility of an unstable and weak Indonesia resulting in a leadership vacuum within ASEAN see Obaid Ul Haq, 'ASEAN: The Search For Regional Security in Southeast Asia', *World Affairs* 3:3 (July–September 1999), 37–9; and Anthony Smith, 'Indonesia's Role in ASEAN: The End of Leadership?', *Contemporary Southeast Asia* 21:2 (August 1999), 257–8.

73  Noel M. Morada and Christopher Collier, 'The Philippines: State Versus Society?', in Alagappa (ed.), *Asian Security Practice*, p. 550.

74  The AFP Modernization Program is outlined in Department of National Defense, *In Defense of the Philippines: 1998 Defense Policy Paper* (Manila, 1998), pp. 83–4. The *Policy Paper* strongly suggests that the allocation of 50 billion pesos for the first five-year phase of the program will be conditional relative to the country's overall economic performance and standing.

75  Rigoberto Tiglao, Andrew Sherry, Nate Thayer and Michael Vatikiotis, 'Tis the Season', *Far Eastern Economic Review* (24 December 1998), 18–20.

76  Powell's testimony is reprinted as 'US Looks to its Allies for Stability in Asia and the Pacific', *International Herald Tribune* Internet edn (27 January 2001) at [http://www.iht.com/articles/].

77  The SRDP is outlined by Commodore Francis T. Mallillin, the AFP's Deputy Chief of Staff for Material Development in First Philippine–Australia Defence and Security Conference, *Perspectives on National Security Policy Making*, Australian Defence Studies Centre Special Report (Canberra: Commonwealth of Australia, 1996), p. 11. At present, the Philippines has no credible defence production industrial base with only small guns and ammunition having reached international standards.

78  Diego C. Cagahastian, 'Estrada Unveils "New" 6-Point Defense, Security Program', *Bulletin* Internet Edition (27 November 1998), reprinted in FBIS-EAS-98-331 (27 November 1998). On the dour prospects for short-term force improvements, see Christina V. Deocadiz, 'Manila Defense Capability Called Pathetic', *Manila Business World* Internet edn (16 June 1998), reprinted in FBIS-EAS-98-167 (16 June 1998).

79  Jeannie Henderson, *Reassessing ASEAN*, Adephi Paper 328 (London: Oxford University Press for the International Institute for Strategic Studies, 1999), p. 34.

80  Various aspects of these challenges are discussed by Jorn Dosch and Manfred Mols, 'Thirty Years of ASEAN: Achievements and Challenges', *The Pacific Review* 11:2 (1998), 167–82.

81  An excellent account of Thailand's diplomatic efforts to support the flexible engagement concept leading to ASEAN's Hanoi Summit in December 1998 is provided by Jurgen Haacke, 'The Concept of Flexible Engagement and the Practice of Enhanced Interaction: Intramural Challenges to the "ASEAN Way"', *The Pacific Review* 12:4 (1999), 581–611.

82  See William T. Tow, 'Alternative Security Models: Implications for ASEAN' in Andrew T. W. Tan and J. D. Kenneth Boutin (eds) *Non-Traditional Security Issues in Southeast Asia* (Singapore: Select Publishing for the Institute of Defence and Strategic Studies, 2001) 257–85.

83  For realists, 'ASEAN's success in preventing latent tensions from escalating into open war is less due to a special ASEAN culture than to a combination of outside pressures (the Communist threat), and outside incentives (access to American markets and Japanese investments)'. See Robin Ramcharan, 'ASEAN Regional Forum: A Pitfall in Pacific Asia's Security?', *World Affairs* 3:3 (July–September 1999), 75.

84  On the problems generated by the recent inclusion of Burma and Cambodia, whose membership to ASEAN was postponed in 1997 after domestic political upheaval, see Carlyle A. Thayer, 'ASEAN Disunity Affects Regional Security', *Asia-Pacific Defence Reporter* 25:1 (Annual Reference Edn 1999), 11–12.

85  This is confirmed by the analysis of Obaid Ul Haq who contends that the central flaw of ASEAN is that, as of yet, 'the group has no surveillance mechanism to monitor trends and alert members to potential dangers', in 'ASEAN: The Search for Regional Security', p. 38.

86  Leifer, *The ASEAN Regional Forum, passim.*

87  Ramcharan, 'The ASEAN Regional Forum', p. 76; and Daljit Singh, 'ASEAN and the Security of Southeast Asia', in Chia Diow Yue and Marcello Pacini (eds), *ASEAN in the New Asia* (Singapore: Institute of Southeast Asian Studies, 1997), esp. pp. 138–42.

88  The 'middle power' concept has often been applied to describe various aspects of Australian foreign policy behaviour. There is little consensus on how to resolve the definitional problem inherent to the term 'middle power' but one respected study has argued convincingly that it is best regarded from a *behavioural* perspective rather from those dominated by positional, geographic, or normative considerations. See Andrew F. Cooper, Richard A. Higgott and Kim Richard Nossal, *Relocating Middle Powers: Australia and Canada in a Changing World Order* (Carlton: Melbourne University Press, 1993), pp. 16–27.

89  On the liberal agenda of the Hawke and Keating governments in particular see Pauline Kerr, Labor's Security Policy, 1983–1996: Towards A Liberal–Realist Explanation?, PhD dissertation, Australian National University, 1999, pp. 63–160.

90  These approaches and their underlying rationales are summarised by Simon Dalby, 'Continent Adrift? Dissident Security Discourse and the Australian Geopolitical Imagination', *Australian Journal of International Affairs* 50:1 (April 1996), 59–75. See also Graham Cheeseman and St John Kettle (eds), *The New Australian Militarism: Undermining Our Future Security* (Sydney: Pluto, 1990); and Gary Smith and St John Kettle (eds), *Threats Without Enemies: Rethinking Australia's Security* (Sydney: Pluto, 1992).

91  Peter Jennings, *Searching for Insecurity: Why the 'Secure Australia Project' is Wrong about Defence* (West Perth: Institute of Public Affairs, 1994). A rejoinder to Jenning's critique is by David Sullivan, 'The Poverty of Australian Defence and Security Studies: The "Secure Australia Project" and its Critics', *Australian*

*Journal of Political Science* 30:1 (March 1995), 146–57. This article focuses on enlarging the Australian public debate over defence issues in both conceptual and sectoral terms; it declines to address Jenning's arguments about Australia's defence force structure.

92  Department of Defence, Australia, *Defence 2000: Our Future Defence Force* (Canberra: Commonwealth of Australia, December 2000), pp. 29–32; and Robert Garran, 'A 3-zone Defence Strategy', *The Weekend Australian* (2–3 December 2000), p. 7.

93  Eric Jones, 'The People Next Door: Australia and the Asian Crisis', *The National Interest* 52 (Summer 1998), 80.

94  Cohen, 'Geopolitics in a New World Era', in Demko and Wood (eds), *Reordering the World*, p. 31. In a definitive strategic assessment released for public review in 1997, the Australian Defence Department concluded that the likelihood of a direct attack on Australia remains very low and the Department's force planning is therefore not based on any specific source of threat. See Department of Defence, *Australia's Strategic Policy 1997* (Canberra: Commonwealth of Australia, 1997), p. 30. Since the document's release, Department of Defence analysts have become less sanguine in their regional threat assessments.

95  In a wide-ranging interview with Australia's major weekly magazine, the Prime Minister put this view into context following the dispatch of Australian peacekeeping troops to East Timor: 'Gee, we were ourselves in Asia over the last few weeks ... we were defending the values we hold as Australians. We were willing to be in dispute with our nearest neighbour to defend those values'. Interview with Fred Brenchley, 'The Howard Defence Doctrine', *The Bulletin with Newsweek* (28 September 1999), 22.

96  'Australasia' can be described as 'bounded to the north by Southeast Asia and to the West by the Indian Ocean'. It encompasses the two relatively developed states of Australia and New Zealand, Papua New Guinea, which borders Indonesia, and a number of small island micro-states located throughout Oceania, west of the international dateline and inhabited by both Melanesian and Polynesian ethnic groups. See Jim Rolfe, 'The Prospects for Military and Economic Security in Australasia', in James Sperling, Yogendra Malik and David Louscher (eds), *Zones of Amity, Zones of Enmity: The Prospects for Military Security in Asia* (Leiden: Brill, 1998), pp. 20–2.

97  The landmark justification for this posture was Ross Garnaut, *Australia and the Northeast Asian Ascendancy* (Canberra: Australian Government Publishing Service, 1989), more popularly known as the 'Garnaut Report'.

98  Minister for Foreign Affairs and Trade, Australia, *Australia's Regional Security*, pp. 173–6.

99  Department of Foreign Affairs and Trade, Australia, *In the National Interest* (Canberra: Commonwealth of Australia, 1997), pp. 1, 27–8. A dissenting perspective is offered by Andrew Mack, 'Strategic Security Issues', in Bateman and Sherwood (eds), *Australia's Maritime Bridge*, pp. 81–94. Mack argues that strategic reassurance measures would largely neutralise any power disparities that Australia might confront.

100  Department of Defence, Australia, *Defence 2000*, pp. 29–32; and IISS, *The Military Balance 1998–1999*, pp. 175, 195.

101  For a detailed comparative assessment, see Derek Woolner, 'Back to Asia: Developments That Shape the Future Australian Defence Force', in McLachlan et. al., *Australia's Strategic Dilemmas*, pp. 128–38.

102  Commander James Goldrick, 'Developments in Regional Maritime Forces: Force Structure', in Bateman and Sherwood (eds), *Australia's Maritime Bridge*, pp. 103–4.

103  Department of Defence, Australia, *Australia's Strategic Policy*, p. 44.

104  Jennings, *Searching for Insecurity*, p. 21; and Ross Babbage, *A Coast Too Long: Defending Australia Beyond the 1990s* (Sydney: Allen & Unwin, 1990), p. 64.

105  Department of Defence, Australia, *Defence 2000*, pp. 29–32.

106  Stewart Woodman, 'Unravelling Australia's Strategic Dilemma', in McLachlan et. al., *Australia's Strategic Dilemmas*, p. 16.

107  Department of Defence, Australia, *Defence 2000*, pp. 23–4; and Garran, 'A 3-zone Defence Strategy'.

108  Woodman, 'Unravelling Australia's Strategic Dilemma', in McLachlan et. al., *Australia's Strategic Dilemmas*, p. 26.

109  John Short, 'Howard Bolsters US Links', *The Australian* (26 July 1996), pp. 1, 4.

110  Department of Defence, Australia, *Australia's Strategic Policy*, pp. 9, 14. Also see Woolner, 'Back to Asia', p. 116.

111  Paul Kelly, 'The Real Howard Doctrine', *The Australian* (7 December 2000), p. 4.

112  Department of Defence, Australia, *Defence 2000*, p. 31.

113  Powell, 'US Looks to Its Allies', see n. 76 above.

114  Cameron Stewart, 'Top US Spy Unit Sent to Pine Gap', *The Weekend Australian* (27–28 January 2001), pp. 1–2.

115  See an interview with Laurie Brereton, Opposition Foreign Affairs spokesman, by Paul Kelly, 'A Man of the World', *The Weekend Australian*, 5–6 May 2001, p. 24.

116  'The Howard Defence Doctrine', *The Bulletin with Newsweek* interview, pp. 22–4.

117  As noted by Cavan Hogue, 'Perspectives on Australian Foreign Policy 1999', *Australian Journal of International Affairs* 54:2 (July 2000), 146.

118  See Robert Garran, 'Howard's Doctrine Backflip', *The Australian* (28 September 1999), p. 1; and Paul Kelly, 'Jingoism Is a Luxury We Cannot Afford', *The Australian* (29 September 1999), p. 17.

119  See, for example, Tang Guanghui, 'Behind the Warming of Australia–US Relations', *Shijie Zhishi* (16 October 1996), translation in FBIS-CHI-97-021 (31 January 1997). For expanded analysis on this point, see Colin Mackerras, 'Australia and China', in F. A. Mediansky (ed.), *Australian Foreign Policy: Into the New Millennium* (Melbourne: Macmillan, 1997), pp. 212–28; and William T. Tow, 'Introduction', in Tow (ed.), *Australian–American Relations: Looking Toward the Next Century* (Melbourne: Macmillan, 1998), p. 7.

120  Indeed, an article in one of Australia's most respected newspapers has drawn attention to the danger of Australia being drawn into renewed Sino–US tensions over Taiwan. See Robert Garran, 'Sabre Rattling', *The Weekend Australian* (8–9 January 1999), p. 26.

121  *Defence 2000* stipulates that Defence Department policy makers 'do not envision that Australia would commit forces to operations beyond our immediate neighbourhood except to be part of a multilateral coalition', see p. 51. For analysis of the NMD factor compromising this posture statement, see Michael Richardson, 'Missile Shield Stirs Up Dissent in Australia', *International Herald Tribune* (19 July 2000), electronic version available at [http://www.iht.com/] (accessed on 10 January 2001).

122  Henry Albinski, 'Issues in Australian Foreign Policy: July to December 1999', *Australian Journal of Politics and History* 46:2 (June 2000), 194–5.

123 During INTERFET's creation, Prime Minister Howard estimated that the cost of sending 2000 troops to East Timor for six months would amount to $A500 million. But Australia committed up to 4500 troops and the government foreshadowed the sell-off of properties owned by the Defence Department to meet an annual financial commitment of $A2 billion. Access Economics, a respected private think-tank based in Canberra, has estimated that spending in the defence portfolio could reach $A3–4 billion annually for the duration of Australia's peacekeeping commitment in East Timor. See Tony Wright, 'Sell-Off To Pay for Timor', *The Age* (Melbourne) (30 September 1999), p. 1; and Sean Aylmer and Simon Evans, 'Treasurer Admits Funding Gap', *The Australian Financial Review* (23 September 1999), pp. 1, 4.

124 See, for example, the assessment of *Kompas*, Indonesia's largest daily newspaper the day after Indonesian President Habibie announced his government's approval of an international peacekeeping force deploying in East Timor, '[W]hat about Australia? The Prime Minister, Minister for Foreign Affairs Alexander Downer, Minister for Defence John Moore, the customs service and trade unions all of a sudden threaten Indonesia without a by your leave. They have not only stopped aid but Garuda has been boycotted as has the handling of Indonesian imports ... Australia, time and time again, has sent intelligence agents in UNAMET uniforms, encroached upon Indonesian territory, and mobilised troops on a large scale in Darwin', *Kompas* (13 December 1999), translation in FBIS-EAS-1999-0914, (14 September 1999).

125 For Australian reaction to Indonesia's cancellation of the AMS, see Greg Sheridan, 'It's a Blow to Lose the Pact We Had to Have', *The Australian* (17 September 1999), p. 6; Don Greenlees and Robert Garran, 'Jakarta Severs Ties with Canberra', *The Australian* (17 September 1999), p. 1; and Richard MacGregor, 'A Deal Struck by Yesterday's Men', *The Australian* (17 September 1999), p. 6.

126 A text of this document is available at the Australian Department of Foreign Affairs and Trade website, at [http://www.dfat.gov.au/neab/ai_partnership_agenda].

127 Department of Foreign Affairs and Trade, Australia, 'The Korean Peninsula Energy Development Organisation (KEDO)', (22 November 2000) at [http://www.dfat.gov.au/geo/dprk/kedo] (accessed on 29 January 2001).

128 See Rosemary Greaves, 'Australia's Bilateral Regional Security Dialogues', in *AUS–CSCAP Newsletter* 6 (April 1998), 8–9.

129 An account of these proceedings has been prepared by the Japan Institute of International Affairs and Hiroshima Peace Institute, 'Facing Nuclear Dangers: An Action Plan for the 21st Century', Tokyo, 25 July 1999.

130 Canberra Commission on the Elimination of Nuclear Weapons, *Report of the Canberra Commission on the Elimination of Nuclear Weapons* (Canberra: Commonwealth of Australia, 1996).

131 This section is partly extracted from the author's chapter on 'The Future of Alliances', in Desmond Ball (ed.), *Maintaining the Strategic Edge: The Defence of Australia in 2015*, Canberra Papers on Strategy and Defence no. 133 (Canberra: Strategic and Defence Studies Centre, Australian National University, 1999), pp. 259–305.

132 Dibb, 'The Revolution in Military Affairs and Asian Security', p. 96. A public version of a definitive Australian Government study of RMA was released by the Australian Defence Department's Office of the Revolution of Military Affairs, in January 2000, 'The Revolution In Military Affairs and the Australian Defence Force: A Public Discussion Paper'. See Robert Garran, 'War

Too Costly to Wage', *The Australian* (4 January 2000), p. 1 and Garran, 'High-Tech Hoopla Only One Part of the Military Equation', *The Australian* (4 January 2000), p. 2.

133 Department of Defence, Australia, *Australia's Strategic Policy 1997*, esp. pp. 43–57.

134 See Department of Defence, Australia, *Defence Review 2000 – Our Future Defence Force*, a public discussion paper, (Canberra: AGPS, June 2000), esp. pp. 28–47. It is sometimes referred to as 'The Green Paper'.

135 The case is made that the Australian–American alliance provides Australia with the needed access to RMA-related intelligence and technology by John Baker and Douglas H. Paul, 'The US–Australian Alliance', in Blackwill and Dibb (eds), *America's Asian Alliances*, pp. 95–6, 105–6.

136 'The Revolution In Military Affairs and the Australian Defence Force', sections 4–5, 4–6; and Tim Huxley and Susan Willett, *Arming East Asia*, Adelphi Paper 329 (London: International Institute for Strategic Studies, 1999): 65–6.

137 On the Northeast Asia dimension of this problem, see Cambone, 'The United States and Theater Missile Defense in Northeast Asia', pp. 66–84. On the South Asian aspect, consult Gregory Koblentz, 'Theater Missile Defense and South Asia: A Volatile Mix', *The Nonproliferation Review* 4:3 (Spring–Summer 1997), 54–62.

138 See Gary Brown and Gary Klintworth, *The US National Missile Defense Program: Vital Shield on Modern Day Maginot Line?* Research Paper 16 (Canberra: Parliament of Australia, Parliamentary Library, 5 December 2000), at [http://www.aph.gov.au/library/pubs/rp].

139 Department of Defence, Australia, *Australia's Strategic Policy 1997*, pp. 59–60.

140 These are assessed in depth by Desmond Ball and Pauline Kerr, *Presumptive Engagement: Australia's Asia-Pacific Security Policy in the 1990s* (St Leonards/Canberra: Allen & Unwin/Department of International Relations, Australian National University, 1996).

141 Department of Defence, Australia, *Australia's Strategic Policy 1997*, p. 18.

142 Examples include Roger C. Molander, Andrew S. Riddle and Peter A. Wilson, *Strategic Information Warfare: A New Force of War* (Santa Monica: RAND, 1996); and Martin C. Libicki, *What Is Information Warfare?* (Washington, DC: Center for Advanced Concepts and Technology, National Defense University, 1995).

143 See Adam Cobb, *Thinking About the Unthinkable: Australian Vulnerabilities to High Tech Risks*, Research Paper no. 18 (Canberra: Department of the Parliamentary Library, June 1998), esp. pp. 26–9.

144 See especially Points 23–4 of the 'Joint Communique of 1998 Australia–US Ministerial Talks', at [http://www.usis.australia.gov/ausmin/]; and Greg Sheridan, 'Friendship and the New Security', *The Australian* (31 July 1998), p. 13.

145 Australian Department of Defence, *Australia's Strategic Review* (Canberra: Commonwealth of Australia, 1997), pp. 8, 37–8.

146 This is the argument advanced by William T. Tow, 'Introduction', in Tow (ed.), *Australian–American Relations*, pp. 1–20. For opposing arguments, see Stephen Fitzgerald, *Is Australia an Asian Country?* (Sydney: Allen & Unwin, 1997); and Fitzgerald and Michael Wesley, *Should Australia Have an East Asian Doctrine?* (Sydney: Allen & Unwin, 1997), *passim.*

147 The term was initially developed by Karl Deutsch in Deutsch et al., *Political Community in the North Atlantic Area: International Organization in the Light of*

*Historical Experience* (Princeton, NJ: Princeton University Press, 1957). Amitav Acharya has done important work in applying the concept to the evolution of ASEAN. See his 'The Association of Southeast Asian Nations: "Security Community" or "Defense Community"?' *Pacific Affairs* 64:2 (Summer 1991), 159–78; 'A Regional Security Community in Southeast Asia?' *Journal of Strategic Studies* 18:3 (September 1995), 175–200; and *Constructing a Security Community in Southeast Asia* (London: Routledge, 2001).

148 Sheldon W. Simon, 'Security Prospects in Southeast Asia: Collaborative Efforts and the ASEAN Regional Forum', *The Pacific Review* 11:2 (1998), 197.

149 Michael Vatikiotis, 'Divided They Fall', *Far Eastern Economic Review* (17 December 1998), 26–7; and Nayan Chanda and Shada Islam, 'In the Bunder', *Far Eastern Economic Review* (6 August 1998), 24–5, 28.

150 Leifer, *The ASEAN Regional Forum*, p. 50. American preferences for a less ASEAN-centric ARF and for more ARF institutionalisation were outlined by Assistant US Secretary of State for East Asian and Pacific Affairs Stanley Roth, 'Multilateral Approaches to Regional Security', presentation at the Henry L. Stimson Center, July 21, 1998, reprinted in USIA, *Washington File*, EPF403 (23 July 1998).

151 This section of the chapter is extracted, in part, from William T. Tow, 'The Future of Multilateralism in the Asia-Pacific: The Korean Peninsula as a "Test Case"', in Kim Il Baek (ed.), *Comprehensive Security and Multilateralism in Post-Cold War Asia* (Seoul: Korean Association of International Affairs, 1998), pp. 347–82.

152 For background, see Pang Eng Fong and Chin Kin Wah, 'Nesting the Alliances in the Emerging Context of the Asia Pacific Multilateral Processes: A Southeast Asian Perspective', paper prepared for a workshop on America's Northeast Asian Alliances, Stanford University, August, 1998.

153 Alan Dupont, 'The Future of the ARF: An Australian Perspective', in Khoo How San (ed.), *The Future of the ARF* (Singapore: Institute of Defence and Strategic Studies, 1999), pp. 36–7.

## 6 The Super-Power Respondent: The United States

1 Institute for National Strategic Studies, *Strategic Assessment 1999: Priorities for a Turbulent World* (Washington DC: National Defense University, 1999), p. 5; also at the website [http://www.ndu.edu/inss] (accessed 3 January 2001).

2 Thomas E. Ricks, 'Changing Winds of US Defense Strategy', *International Herald Tribune* (27 May 2000).

3 Michael Howard, *The Causes of War and Other Essays* (Cambridge, MA: Harvard University Press, 1983), p. 103. Howard's frame of reference is the social passions generated by the French Revolution but the paradigm is equally applicable to the American experience.

4 For commentary on, and proposed remedies to, this condition, consult Josef Joffe, '"Bismarck" or "Britain"? Toward an American Grand Strategy after Bipolarity', *International Security* 19:4 (Spring 1995), *passim*.

5 Unlike some of his predecessors, President Reagan never presented his worldview in a formal or official document but relied upon his political charisma and oratorical skills to convince American voters to adopt his policies. There is no analytical dearth, however, of his general approach. Among the more notable sources are Christopher DeMuth, Owen Harries, Irving Kristol, Joshua Muravchik, Stephen Rosenfield and Stephen Solarz, *The*

*Reagan Doctrine and Beyond* (Washington, DC: The American Enterprise Institute, 1987); Charles Krauthammer, 'The Reagan Doctrine', *Time* (1 April 1985), 54–5; and Robert H. Johnson, 'Misguided Morality: Ethics and the Reagan Doctrine', *Political Science Quarterly* 103:3 (Fall 1988), 509–29.

6 John Mearsheimer, 'The False Promise of International Institutions', *International Security* 19:3 (Winter 1994–95), p. 48. Indeed, one of the Reagan Doctrine's major proponents justified its implementation on explicitly anti-realist premises. See Charles Krauthammer, 'The Poverty of Realism', *The New Republic* 3709 (17 February 1986), 14–23.

7 The definitive statement was postulated by Anthony Lake, President Clinton's National Security Adviser, in September 1993. It is reprinted as 'From Containment to Enlargement: Current Foreign Policy Debates in Perspective', *Vital Speeches of the Day* 60:1 (15 October 1993), 13–19. Also see a seminal address by Nancy Soderberg, President Clinton's Deputy Assistant for National Security Affairs as reprinted in United States Information Service (USIS), *Wireless File* (1 November 1996).

8 Condoleezza Rice, 'Promoting the National Interest', *Foreign Affairs* 79:1 (January/February 2000), 62. Another major critique was Michael Mandelbaum's 'Foreign Policy as Social Work', *Foreign Affairs* 74:1 (January/February, 1996), 16–32. Also see Joffe, '"Bismarck" or "Britain?"', pp. 94–117.

9 Although hardly viewed as a classical liberal, Robert Kagan emerged as a powerful exponent of this argument. See his 'American Power – A Guide for the Perplexed', *Commentary* 101:4 (April 1996), 21–31.

10 Douglas T. Stuart and William T. Tow, *A US Strategy for the Asia-Pacific*, Adelphi Paper 299 (London: Oxford University Press for The International Institute of Strategic Studies, 1995), p. 16.

11 Clinton's vision of a 'Pacific Community' was outlined in an address to the students and faculty of Waseda University, Tokyo on 7 July 1993. The speech is reprinted in *Vital Speeches of the Day* 59:21 (15 August, 1993), 642–5.

12 President William J. Clinton, *A National Security Strategy of Engagement and Enlargement* (Washington, DC: The White House, February 1996), pp. 11–12. For the concept's application to an Asia-Pacific context, see an address by US Secretary of Defense William J. Perry to the Japan Society, New York City, 12 September 1995. Reprinted in USIS, *Wireless File*, (14 September 1995).

13 See Jonathan Pollack, *Designing a New Security Strategy for Asia* Asia Project Working Paper, (New York: Council on Foreign Relations, March 1995), pp. 2–3.

14 James Kurth, 'America's Grand Strategy', *The National Interest* 43 (Spring 1996), 3–19.

15 X, 'The Sources of Soviet Conduct', *Foreign Affairs* 25:4 (July 1947), 566–82.

16 This process is traced extensively by William T. Tow, *Encountering the Dominant Player: U.S. Extended Deterrence Strategy in the Asia-Pacific*, (New York: Columbia University Press, 1991). Also see Marc S. Gallicchio, 'The Best Defense Is A Good Offense: Evolution of American Strategy in East Asia', in Warren I. Cohen and Akira Iriye (eds), *The Great Powers in East Asia: 1953–1960* (New York: Columbia University Press, 1990), pp. 63–85.

17 These stated interests are similar to US postwar power-balancing and extended deterrence strategies applied to Europe and the Middle East. An official statement of US interests recently disseminated is Office of International Security Affairs, Department of Defense, United States, *The United States Security Strategy for the East Asia-Pacific Region*, EASR 1998 (Washington, DC: USGPO, February 1998), pp. 9–10. For historical background of US strategic

and geopolitical interests in Eurasia, consult Robert J. Art, 'Defense Policy', in Robert J. Art and Seyom Brown (eds), *US Foreign Policy: A Search for a New Role* (New York: Macmillan Publishing Company, 1993), esp. pp. 102–22.

18  The classic in-depth treatment of this problem remains Nicholas Spykman's *America's Strategy in World Politics* (New York: Harcourt Bryce and Company, 1942).

19  These prospects are weighed in a series of scenarios on Asian security presented in Under Secretary of Defense (Policy), 1999 Summer Study Final Report, *Asia 2025*, organised by the Adviser to the Secretary of Defense for Net Assessment, (Newport, Rhode Island: US Naval War College, August 1999).

20  Kurth, 'America's Grand Strategy', p. 23.

21  Hugh Faringdon, *Strategic Geography* (London: Routledge, 1989), p. 142.

22  A tendency that the eminent historian Paul Kennedy has labelled 'imperial overstretch' and is part of his overall 'declinist' doctrinal thesis. See his *Rise and Fall of the Great Powers* (New York: Random House, 1987).

23  This, of course, conforms to the postulates of postwar US containment strategy. For an updated application directly related to the Asia-Pacific, see Robert H. Scales and Larry M. Wortzel, *The Future US Military Presence in Asia: Landpower and the Geostrategy of American Commitment* (Carlisle, PA: Strategic Studies Institute, US Army War College, 1999).

24  Institute for National Strategic Studies, National Defense University, *1996 Strategic Assessment* (Washington, DC: National Defense University, 1996), ch. 16 'Countering Weapons of Mass Destruction'. This document is on the Internet at [http://www.ndu.edu/inss/].

25  For in-depth analysis of this problem, see Alastair Iain Johnston, 'China's New "Old Thinking", The Concept of Limited Deterrence', *International Security* 20:3 (Winter 1995–96), 5–42. This line of Chinese thinking was confirmed in interviews with Chinese analysts undertaken for this study at Stanford University's Asia/Pacific Research Center, April 1999.

26  The emphasis shifted from all US offshore forces in the region being assigned priority missions within the Asia-Pacific theatre to their greater participation in a worldwide role and from permanently deployed US forward forces in the region to ready access for those forces to key regional bases in times of crisis. See US Department of Defense, Office of International Security Affairs, 'United States Security Strategy for the East Asia-Pacific Region', (Washington, DC: USGPO, February 1995), pp. 30–2; Stanley B. Weeks and Charles Meconis, *The Armed Forces of the USA in the Asia Pacific Region* (St Leonards, NSW: Allen & Unwin, 1999), pp. 52–60; and an interview with Admiral Charles R. Larson, Commander-in-Chief, US Forces in the Pacific by Michael Vatikiotis, 'Places, Not Bases', *Far Eastern Economic Review* (22 April 1993), 22.

27  Members of the 'minimalist' camp include Richard J. Ellings and Edward A. Olsen, 'A New Pacific Profile', *Foreign Policy* 89 (Winter 1992/93), 116–31; Chalmers Johnson and E. B. Keehn, 'The Pentagon's Ossified Strategy', *Foreign Affairs* 74:4 (July/August 1995), 103–14; and Christopher Layne, 'Less is More: Minimal Realism in East Asia', *The National Interest* 43 (Spring 1996), 64–77.

28  Joseph S. Nye, Jr, 'The Case for Deep Engagement', *Foreign Affairs* 74:4 (July/August 1995), 90–102.

29  Sheldon W. Simon, 'East Asian Security: The Playing Field Has Changed', *Asian Survey* 34:12 (December 1994), 1048. Also see William T. Tow,

'Contending Approaches in the Asia-Pacific Region', *Security Studies* 3:1 (Autumn 1993), 75–7.

30  Among the most discussed exponents of this position are Nicholas D. Kristof, 'The Rise of China', *Foreign Affairs* 72:5 (November/December 1993), 59–74; Denny Roy, 'Hegemon on the Horizon? China's Threat to East Asian Security', *International Security* 19:1 (Summer 1994), 149–68; and Gerald Segal, 'China's Changing Shape', *Foreign Affairs* 73:3 (May/June 1994), 149–68. Roy has explicitly linked the concept of 'power vacuum' to that of hegemony: that is, 'a power vacuum means that natural forces draw in a new hegemon to the old one' and concludes that 'on balance, the [Asia-Pacific] region appears susceptible to the vacuum scenario, with China the most likely new challenger'. See Denny Roy, 'Assessing the Asia-Pacific Power Vacuum', *Survival* 37:3 (Autumn 1995), 46–54.

31  See the prepared statements of Michel Oksenberg and Susan L. Shirk in a Hearing before the Subcommittee on Asia and the Pacific of the Committee on International Relations, House of Representatives, *The Future of the People's Republic of China: Perspectives on the Post-Deng Xiaoping Era*, 104th Cong., 1st Sess., 20 July 1995, pp. 39–54; and Gary Klintworth and Murray McLean, 'China and the United States: Neither Friends nor Enemies', in Stuart Harris and Gary Klintworth (eds), *China As a Great Power: Myths, Realities and Challenges in the Asia-Pacific Region* (Melbourne/New York: Longman/St. Martin's, 1995), pp. 65–90.

32  The ramifications of this are ably discussed by Chas W. Freeman, Jr., 'Sino–American Relations: Back to Basics', *Foreign Policy* 104 (Fall 1996), 3–17.

33  Freeman, 'Sino–American Relations', p. 6.

34  John Pomfret, 'Beijing Signals a New Flexibility Toward Taiwan', *International Herald Tribune* (5 January 2001).

35  For an account of the negative Chinese response to the US–Japan Defense Guidelines agreement, see Michael Richardson, 'China Criticizes Washington's Asian Allies as Tensions Rise', *International Herald Tribune* (8 July 1999), p. 1. In December 1999, Boris Yeltsin journeyed to Beijing and issued a joint declaration with his Chinese counterpart, Jiang Zemin, condemning 'unilateralism' and American efforts to 'break strategic stability'. See an ITAR-TASS report reprinted in FBIS-SOV-1999-1210 (10 December 1999). For a report on earlier American thinking regarding closer Russian–Chinese relations, see Todd Crowell, 'Two Giants Make Up', *Asiaweek* (19 April 1996), p. 28.

36  See President Clinton, *A National Security Strategy of Engagement and Enlargement* (Washington DC: USGPO, 1996), pp. 26–32.

37  Australian analysts appear to have taken the lead in this area of analysis. For example, see Stuart Harris, 'The Economic Aspects of Security in the Asia/Pacific Region', in Ball (ed.), 'The Transformation in the Asia/Pacific Region', pp. 32–51; Harris, 'The Impact of Economics in the New Asia-Pacific Region', in Denny Roy (ed.), *The New Security Agenda in the Asian-Pacific*, pp. 51–63; and Harris and Andrew Mack (eds), *Asia-Pacific Security: The Economics-Politics Nexus* (St Leonards, NSW/Canberra: Allen & Unwin/Australian National University, 1997). For other regional interpretations see Javed Maswood, 'The Rise of the Asia-Pacific' in Anthony McGrew and Christopher Brook (eds), *Asia-Pacific in the New World Order* (London and New York: Routledge, 1998), pp. 57–66; Lee Poh Ping, 'The Security and Economic Structure in the Post-Cold War Asia-Pacific Region: A Southeast Asian Perspective', in Michio Kimura (ed.), *Multilayered Regional Cooperation in Southeast Asia after*

*the Cold War* (Tokyo: Institute of Developing Economies, 1995), pp. 25–37; and Sueo Sudo, 'Development of Multilayered Regional Cooperation in Southeast Asia and Its Implications', in Kimura (ed.), *Multilayered Regional Cooperation in Southeast Asia after the Cold War*, pp. 43–59. Two exceptions to the general dearth of American analysis directly addressing the economics-security linkage are Henry S. Rowen, 'Catch-Up: Why Poor Countries Are Becoming Richer, Democratic, Increasingly Peaceable, and Sometimes More Dangerous', Asia/Pacific Research Center Discussion Paper, (Institute for International Studies, Stanford University, August 1999); and Sheldon Simon, 'The Economic Crisis and Southeast Asian Security', *NBR Analysis* 9:5 (December 1998).

38  See, for example, Council on Foreign Relations, Asia Project Panel, *Redressing the Balance: American Engagement with Asia* (New York: Council on Foreign Relations, 1996), p. 3.

39  Kent Calder, *Asia's Deadly Triangle: How Arms, Energy and Growth Threaten to Destabilise the Asia-Pacific*, (London: Nicholas Brealey, 1996), p. 202.

40  This point is discussed extensively by Jonathan Clarke, 'APEC as a Semi-Solution', *ORBIS* 39:1 (Winter 1995), 81–95. It was also emphasised by the then ASEAN Secretary-General William Bodde in a July 1993 interview with the author at APEC headquarters in Singapore.

41  Yoichi Funabashi, 'Bridging Asia's Economics-Security Gap', *Survival* 38:4 (Winter 1996/97), 105–11.

42  Helen E. S. Nesadurai, 'APEC: A Tool for US Regional Domination?', *The Pacific Review* 9:1 (1996), 37.

43  Mearsheimer, 'The False Promise of International Institutions', pp. 48–9; Keith L. Shimko, 'Realism, Neoliberalism and American Liberalism', *Review of Politics* 54:2 (Spring 1992), 281–301; and J. Bryan Hehir, 'The United States and Human Rights: Policy for the 1990s in Light of the Past', in Kenneth Oye, Robert Lieber and Donald Rothchild (eds), *Eagle in a New World: American Grand Strategy in the Post-Cold War Era* (New York: Harper Collins, 1992), esp. pp. 247–9.

44  Richard Robison, 'The Politics of "Asian Values"', *The Pacific Review* 9:3 (1996), 319–20, paraphrasing a report issued by the World Bank, *Managing Development: The Governance Dimension* (Washington, DC: 1991), p. 62.

45  Michael Richardson, 'Clinton's Stance on Rights Seen as Bad for Asian Ties', *International Herald Tribune* (2 January 1997), pp. 1, 4.

46  President Clinton, *A National Security Strategy of Engagement and Enlargement*, p. 33. Also see Stuart and Tow, *A US Strategy for the Asia-Pacific*, pp. 26–7.

47  Robison, 'The Politics of Asian Values', pp. 310–11.

48  Quoted by the *New Straits Times* (20 May 1995) and cited in Robison, 'The Politics of Asian Values', p. 313; and Alan Dupont, 'Is There An "Asian Way"?', *Survival* 38:2 (Summer 1996), 14–16.

49  Stephen A. Douglas and Sara U. Douglas, 'Economic Implications of the US–ASEAN Discourse on Human Rights', *Pacific Affairs* 69:1 (Spring 1996), 86.

50  Richardson, 'Clinton's Stance on Rights'.

51  On US–Burmese relations, see Hearing before the Subcommittee on Asia and the Pacific, Committee on Foreign Affairs, US House of Representatives, *US Policy Towards Burma*, 103rd Cong. 1st Sess., 25 March 1993; and Hearing before the Subcommittee on Asia and the Pacific, Committee on International Relations, US House of Representatives, *Recent Developments in Burma*,

104th Cong., 1st Sess., 7 September 1995. On how the human rights issue affected prospective US sales of jet aircraft to the Indonesians, see John McBeth, 'Plane Dealing', *Far Eastern Economic Review* (21 March 1996), 24–6.

52 Douglas and Douglas, 'Economic Implications', pp. 76–7. Also see a wide-ranging interview conducted by Fareed Zakaria, 'A Conversation with Lee Kuan Yew', *Foreign Affairs* 73:2 (March/April 1994), 109–26.

53 Council on Foreign Relations, *Redressing the Balance*, p. 28.

54 Parts of this subsection have been adapted from Douglas T. Stuart and William T. Tow, *Security Policy in the Asia-Pacific: A US Strategy for a New Century?*, Australia-Asia Papers no. 76 (Brisbane: Centre for the Study of Australia–Asia Relations, Griffith University, 1996), pp. 1–6.

55 James A. Baker, III, 'America in Asia: Emerging Architecture for a Pacific Community', *Foreign Affairs* 70:5 (Winter 1991/92), 3, 5.

56 Baker, 'America in Asia', 4–5.

57 Office of the Assistant Secretary of Defense for International Security Affairs, *A Strategic Framework for the Asian Pacific Rim* (Washington, DC: USGPO, April 1990) (hereafter cited as EASI I) and Office of the Assistant Secretary of Defense for International Security Affairs, *A Strategic Framework for the Asian Pacific Rim* (Washington, DC: USGPO, 1992) (hereafter cited as EASI II).

58 A concise assessment of EASI I and EASI II is offered by Richard D. Fisher, 'The Clinton Administration's Early Defense Policy Toward Asia', *The Korean Journal of Defense Analysis* 6:1 (Summer 1994), 104–6.

59 Lawrence J. Korb, 'The United States', in Murray and Viotti (eds), *The Defense Policies of Nations*, pp. 49–50; and Dov Zackheim and Jeffrey Ranney, 'Matching Defense Strategies to Resources: Challenges for the Clinton Administration', *International Security* 18:1 (Summer 1993), 51–78.

60 The Regional Defense Strategy was described in depth by US Secretary of Defense Dick Cheney in a Hearing before the Budget Committee, United States Senate, *The FY 1993 Budget for The Department of Defense*, 102nd Cong., 2nd Sess., 3 February 1992, pp. 18–27.

61 Weeks and Meconis, *The Armed Forces of the USA in the Asia-Pacific Region*, p. 34.

62 Institute for National Strategic Studies, *Strategic Assessment 1995: US Security Challenges in Transition* (Washington DC: National Defense University, 1995). Data retrieved from the Internet version of the document at [http://www.ndu.inss/Sa95/].

63 EASI I, p. 8.

64 Secretary of Defense, *Report of the Secretary of Defense to the President and the Congress* (Washington DC: USGPO, January 1993), p. 12.

65 The decision to delay the second phase of US troop reduction in Korea was taken at the twenty-fifth US–ROK Security Consultative Meeting convened in Washington during 7–8 October 1992. See Tae-Hwan Kwak, 'Basic Issues in the Peace Process on the Korea Peninsula', in Kwak and Olsen (eds), *The Major Powers of Northeast Asia*, p. 232.

66 See Anthony McGrew, 'Restructuring Foreign and Defense Policy: the USA', in McGrew and Brook (eds), *Asia-Pacific in the New World Order*, pp. 176–7; Jonathan Pollack, 'The United States in East Asia: Holding the Ring', in *Asia's International Role in the Post-Cold War Era* Part I, Adelphi Paper 275 (London: Brassey's for The International Institute for Strategic Studies, 1993), pp. 74–5; and Edward A. Olsen, 'A New American Strategy in Asia?', *Asian Survey* 31:12 (December 1991), esp. pp. 1140–1.

67 The seminal article calling for the US to view Japan as an economic threat and as a potential strategic challenger was by Samuel P. Huntington, 'Amer-

ica's Changing Strategic Interests', *Survival* 33:1 (January/February 1991), 3–17.

68  Comprehensive critiques of the Bush Administration's security policies in Japan and throughout Northeast Asia include Ellings and Olsen, 'A New Pacific Profile', *passim*; and Ted Galen Carpenter, 'Ending South Korea's Unhealthy Security Dependence', *The Korean Journal of Defense Analysis* 6:1 (Summer 1994), 175–94.

69  'Lord Lays Out 10 Goals for US Policy in East Asia', reprinted in USIA, *Official Text*, (5 April 1993); and 'Clinton Says Spread of Nuclear Weapons Must Not Replace Cold War', reprinted in USIA, *Wireless File*, (12 July 1993). The latter is a reprint of the President's address to the Korean National Assembly on 10 July. Also see Jonathan Friedland et al., 'Clinton's Clarion Call', *Far Eastern Economic Review* (22 July 1993), 10–11. An excellent overview of the Clinton Administration's policy approaches to the region is provided by Harry Harding, 'Asia Policy to the Brink', *Foreign Policy* 96 (Fall 1994), 57–74.

70  The general approach was outlined in testimony by various witnesses before the Subcommittee on Trade of the Committee on Ways and Means, US House of Representatives, *United States–Japan Trade Relations*, 104th Cong., 2nd Sess., 28 March 1996. In 1995 Japan was the second largest importer of US goods and services, assimilating $US64.3 billion.

71  *A National Security Strategy: Enlargement and Engagement*, pp. 28–9; and Pollack, *Designing a New American Security Strategy for Asia*, p. 12.

72  President William J. Clinton, *A National Security Strategy of Engagement and Enlargement* (Washington, DC: USGPO, July 1994), pp. 6–7.

73  See the testimony of Admiral Charles Larson, Commander-in-Chief of the US Pacific Command (CINCPAC) before the Senate Armed Services Committee, 21 April 1993. Reprinted in USIA, *Wireless File*, (21 April 1993) and 'Places, Not Bases: Pacific Commander Outlines New US Defense Role', *Far Eastern Economic Review* (22 April 1993), 22.

74  Michael Antolik, 'The ASEAN Regional Forum: The Spirit of Constructive Engagement', *Contemporary Southeast Asia* 16:2 (September 1994), 117–36.

75  See Yoshisuke Iinuma, 'Total Victory Means Seeking the Right Compromise', and Mitsuo Matsushita, 'Shore Up the WTO', *Tokyo Business Today* 63:8 (August 1995), 40–1. Japan had two objectives for taking this dispute to the WTO: (1) to end a trend of 'US-set quantitative targets' with the threat of sanctions if they were not met by Japan; and (2) to strengthen the WTO's credibility. The dispute was settled in late 1995.

76  In May 1993 President Clinton issued an Executive Order which approved renewal of China's MFN status but linked further extensions to 'certain realistic and obtainable human rights criteria'. By March 1994, however, Winston Lord testified that the Clinton Administration hoped that the 'annual [Congressional] debate [over renewing China's MFN] would be less central to our China policy. Our primary objective now must be to obtain progress that will enable us to renew China's MFN status and benefit both countries'. See Statement of Assistant Secretary of State for East Asian and Pacific Affairs Winston Lord before the House Subcommittee on Economic Policy, Trade and Environment; Subcommittee on International Security, International Organizations and Human Rights; and Subcommittee on Asia and Pacific of the Committee On Foreign Affairs, US House of Representatives, *China: Human Rights and MFN*, 103rd Cong., 2nd Sess., 24 March 1994, pp. 52–6 and esp. p. 55.

77 See, for example, Australian Department of Foreign Affairs and Trade (DFAT), *Australia–United States Trade and Investment Review* (Canberra: Commonwealth of Australia, August 1996), *passim.*

78 While the results of BUR were released in September, the comprehensive version of the study appeared the following month. See The Secretary of Defense, Les Aspin, *Report on the Bottom-Up Review* (Washington DC: USGPO, October 1993).

79 'Phase I' of US combat operations as envisioned by BUR is to 'halt the invasion'. During this phase, 'primary responsibility for the initial defence of their territory rests ... with our allies'. Secretary of Defense, US, *Report on the Bottom-Up Review*, p. 16.

80 'The Pentagon's Vision of the Post-Cold War World', in *In Search for Security*, Report by the National Priorities Project Inc., and ProPeace Action, 1994, pp. 4–7; and William W. Kaufmann, *Assessing the Base Force: How Much Is Too Much?* (Washington, DC: The Brookings Institution, 1992).

81 For critiques of BUR, see David Callahan, 'Saving Defense Dollars', *Foreign Policy* 96 (Fall 1994), esp. 102–10; Wyn Q. Bowen and David H. Dunn, *American Security in the 1990s: Beyond Containment* (Brookfield VA: Dartmouth, 1996), pp. 68–72; William Pendley, 'Mortgaging the Future to the Present in Defense Policy: A Commentary on the Bottom Up Review', *Strategic Review* 22:2 (Spring, 1994), 36–40; Eliot Cohen, 'Beyond "Bottom Up"', *National Review* (15 November 1993), pp. 40–3; and Dov Zackheim, 'Tough Choices: Toward a True Strategic Review', *The National Interest* 47 (Spring, 1997), 32–43.

82 Office of International Security Affairs, Department of Defense, United States, *United States Security Strategy for the East Asia-Pacific Region East Asian Strategy Report* (EASR) 1995 (Washington, DC: USGPO, February, 1995).

83 'Nye: Lingering Concerns Put US Troop Cuts in Asia On Hold', reprinted in USIA, *Wireless File* (7 March 1995).

84 Wolfowitz spelled out his thinking on these issues in an extensive press conference to journalists held at Kuala Lumpur in June 1992. See 'Wolfowitz Says US Performs Same Security Role With Smaller Force', reprinted in USIA, *Wireless File*, (23 June 1992). Also see Wolfowitz's assessments of East Asia in 'The New Defense Strategy', in Graham Allison and Gregory F. Treverton (eds), *Rethinking America's Security* (New York: W.W. Norton, 1992), pp. 187–8. Solomon's views are spelled out in Testimony before the Subcommittee on Asia and Pacific Affairs of the Committee on Foreign Affairs, US House of Representatives, *Overview of Recent Events In the East Asian and Pacific Region*, 101st Cong., 2nd Sess., 22 February 1990, pp. 25–52; and more recently, in Solomon, 'Who Will Shape the Emerging Structure in East Asia?', in Michael Mandelbaum, (ed.), *The Strategic Quadrangle: Russia, China, Japan and the United States in East Asia* (New York: Council on Foreign Relations, 1995), pp. 196–208.

85 Susumu Awanohara, 'About Face: US Asia Policy Architect Has a Change of Heart', *Far Eastern Economic Review* (19 May 1994), 22. Also see Harding, 'Asia Policy to the Brink', p. 71.

86 Yoichi Funabashi, *Alliance Adrift* (New York: Council on Foreign Relations Press, 1999), pp. 15–16.

87 Secretary of State Warren Christopher, 'Remarks before the Business Council', Williamsburg VA, (10 May 1996), as reprinted at International Information Programs, 'US Commitment to Security on the Asia-Pacific' at [http://usinfo.state.gov/regional/ea/easec] (accessed 6 January 2001).

88  Assistant Secretary of State for East Asia and Pacific Affairs, Stanley Roth, Testimony on the US–Asia Relations before the US House of Representatives, House International Relations sub-committee on Asia and Pacific, (10 February 1999) at [http://www.usinfo.state.gov/regional/ea/easec] (accessed on 6 January 2001).

89  President William Clinton, *A National Security Strategy for the New Century* (Washington, DC: USGPO, May 1997); and William S. Cohen, Secretary of Defense, *Report of the Quadrennial Defense Review* (Washington, DC: USGPO, May 1997).

90  Office of International Security Affairs, US Defense Department, *US Security Strategy for the East Asia-Pacific Region* (Washington, DC: USGPO, November 1998).

91  Weeks and Meconis, *The Armed Forces of the USA in the Asia-Pacific Region*, p. 60.

92  *The Quadrennial Defense Review*, p. 13. Also see testimony of members of the National Defense Panel which was largely responsible for QDR formulation in a Hearing held before the Committee on National Security, House of Representatives, *The Quadrennial Defense Review*, 105th Cong., 1st Sess., 16 April 1997, pp. 1–49; and data provided by the Research Institute For Peace And Security, Tokyo, *Asian Security 1997–98* (London: Brassey's, 1997), pp. 45–6.

93  Office of International Security Affairs, EASR 1998, p. 8.

94  Office of International Security Affairs, EASR 1998, p. 42.

95  Frederick H. Barnes, 'QDR and the Likely Impact on US Defenses', *Defense & Foreign Affairs Strategic Policy* 24: 11/12 (November/December 1997), 16–17; Pat Towell and Chuck McCutcheon, 'Right-Face on Defense Policy', *Congressional Quarterly Weekly Report* 87:4 (January 23, 1999), 181; Research Institute for Peace and Security, *Asian Security 1997–98*, p. 45; and Charles E. Morrison (ed.), *Asia-Pacific Security Outlook 1998* (Tokyo: Japan Center for International Exchange, 1998), pp. 152–4.

96  See the testimony of Edwin J. Feulner, President, The Heritage Foundation. 'Challenges In US–Asia Policy', summary of Statement before the Subcommittee on Asia and the Pacific Committee on International Relations, House of Representatives, (10 February 1999), for an example of such criticism.

97  See Paul Dibb, *Towards a New Balance of Power in Asia*, pp. 6–16; and William T. Tow, 'Reshaping Asia-Pacific Security', *The Journal of East Asian Affairs* 8:1 (Winter/Spring 1994), esp. 101–14 and 129–34.

98  Henry Kissinger, *Diplomacy* (New York: Simon & Schuster, 1994), pp. 826–7.

99  'Stanley Roth Testimony on US–Asia Relations: This Year Will Not Be a Repeat of Last Year', remarks to the International Relations Subcommittee, House of Representatives, (10 February 1999), reprinted in USIA, *Washington File*, EPF303 (10 February 1999).

100  Robert D. Blackwill, 'An Action Agenda to Strengthen America's Alliances in the Asia-Pacific Region', in Robert D. Blackwill and Paul Dibb (eds), *America's Asian Alliances* (Cambridge, MA: The MIT Press, 2000), pp. 115–16.

101  Richard Halloran, 'The Rising East', *Foreign Policy* 102 (Spring 1996), 5–6.

102  Dibb, *Towards a New Balance of Power in Asia*, p. 37.

103  Betts, 'Wealth, Power, and Instability', p. 48. Betts ranks Japan in this category as well. However, Japan's strategic vulnerability in modern nuclear

warfare is often underestimated. As Michael May has argued, Japan could develop and field survivable nuclear forces but could not survive a nuclear war, given its small land mass, its high population density and its inability to reconstitute itself alone. Michael May, 'Correspondence: Japan as a Super-power?', *International Security* 18:3 (Winter 1993/94), 185–6.

104 Pollack, *Designing a New American Security Strategy for Asia*, pp. 4–6. Also see Stuart and Tow, *A US Strategy for the Asia-Pacific*, pp. 12–13 and 16–17.

105 Blackwill, 'An Action Agenda', pp. 124–34; and Roy, 'Assessing the Asia-Pacific Power Vacuum', pp. 54–5.

106 Office of International Affairs, EASR 1998, p. 21.

107 Rice, 'Promoting the National Interest', *passim*.

108 William T. Tow, 'Alliances and Coalitions', in Marianne Hanson and William T. Tow (eds), *International Relations in the New Century: An Australian Perspective* (South Melbourne: Oxford University Press, 2001), pp. 21–2.

109 Much of this subsection and the next major subsection are derived from Stuart and Tow, *Security Policy in the Asia-Pacific*, pp. 36–41.

110 Paul Dibb, 'The Strategic Environment in the Asia-Pacific Region', in Black-will and Dibb (eds), *America's Asian Alliances*, p. 17; and Dibb, 'Comments', in Blackwill and Dibb (eds), *America's Asian Alliances*, p. 136.

111 This approach was postulated by the Commander-in-Chief of the US Pacific Command, Dennis C. Blair. See Dennis C. Blair and John T. Hanley, 'From Wheels to Webs: Reconstructing Asia-Pacific Security Arrangements', *The Washington Quarterly* 24:1 (Winter 2001), 7–18.

112 Australia, the US and other maritime countries have previously been con-cerned that Indonesia is attempting to apply overly restrictive interpreta-tions of the UNCLOS rules of passage concerning international shipping. See John McBeth, 'Water of Strife', *Far Eastern Economic Review* (29 February 1996), 30; and Patrick Walters, 'Sea Lane Talks Begin', *The Australian* (24 April 1996), p. 4.

113 Sheldon W. Simon, 'Regional Security Structures in Asia: The Question of Relevance', in Inis L. Claude et al. (eds), *Collective Security in Europe and Asia* (Carlisle, PA: Strategic Studies Institute, US Army War College, 1992), p. 48.

114 Robert S. Litwak, *Detente and the Nixon Doctrine: American Foreign Policy and the Pursuit of Stability, 1969–1976* (Cambridge: Cambridge University Press, 1984); Robert E. Osgood et al., *Retreat From Empire? The First Nixon Adminis-tration* (Baltimore: The Johns Hopkins University Press, 1973); Earl C. Rave-nal, *Large-Scale Foreign Policy Change: The Nixon Doctrine as History and Portent* (Berkeley: Institute of International Affairs, University of California, 1989); and Tow, *Encountering the Dominant Player*, pp. 48–50.

## Conclusion

1 Aaron L. Friedberg, 'Ripe for Rivalry', *International Security* 18:3 (Winter 1993–94), 17–19; and Susan L. Shirk, 'Asia-Pacific Regional Security: Balance of Power or Concert of Powers?', in David M. Lake and Patrick M. Morgan (eds), *Regional Orders: Building Security in a New World* (University Park: Penn-sylvania State University Press, 1997), pp. 245–70.

2 Barry Buzan, *People, States and Fear: The National Security Problem in International Relations* 2nd edn, (Boulder: Lynne Rienner, 1991), p. 190. Also consult Patrick Morgan, 'Regional Security Complexes and Regional Orders', in Lake and Morgan (eds), *Regional Orders: Building Security in a New World*, p. 25.

3  Among the best-known advocates of this approach are Robert Kagan, 'The
   Case for Global Activism', *Commentary* 98:3 (September 1994), 40–54; Zalmay
   Khalilzad, 'Losing the Moment? The United States and the World After the
   Cold War', *The Washington Quarterly* 18:2 (Spring 1995), 87–107; Joshua
   Muravchik, *The Imperative of American Leadership: A Challenge to Neo-Isolationism*
   (Washington, DC: American Enterprise Institute 1996). Samuel P. Hunting-
   ton has also supported preponderance in some of his recent work. See, for
   example, his 'Why International Primacy Matters', *International Security* 17:4
   (Spring 1993), 68–83. Thoughtful critiques of preponderance/primacy
   include Robert Jervis, 'International Primacy: Is the Game Worth the Can-
   dle?' *International Security* 17:4 (Spring 1993), 52–67; Michael Mastanduno,
   'Preserving the Unipolar Moment: Realist Theories and US Grand Strategies
   After the Cold War', *International Security* 21:4 (Spring 1997), 49–88; and
   Christopher Layne, 'From Preponderance to Offshore Balancing: America's
   Future Grand Strategy', *International Security* 22:1 (Summer 1997), 86–124.
4  The concepts of 'maximal' and 'minimal' realists are discussed by Christopher Layne, 'Less is More: Minimal Realism in East Asia', *The National Interest*
   43 (Spring 1996), 64–77. As a 'minimal realist', Layne is properly classified as
   belonging to the neo-isolationist faction. For other arguments supporting
   these assumptions, see Eugene Gholz, Daryl G. Press and Harvey M. Sapolsky,
   'Come Home America', *International Security* 21:4 (Spring 1997), 5–48; Pat
   Buchanan, *The Great Betrayal* (Boston: Little, Brown and Company, 1998), p.
   317; and, more generally, Ted Galen Carpenter, *America's Search for Enemies:
   America's Alliances After the Cold War* (Washington, DC: CATO Institute, 1992).
   The defence burden-sharing argument has been most forcefully projected by
   Chalmers Johnson and E. B. Keehn, 'The Pentagon's Ossified Strategy', *Foreign Affairs* 74:4 (July–August 1995), 103–14.
5  Layne, 'From Preponderance to Offshore Balancing', pp. 104–9.
6  Gholz, Press and Sapolsky, 'Come Home, America', p. 14.
7  See, for example, Richard K. Betts, 'Wealth, Power and Instability: East Asia
   and the United States after the Cold War', *International Security* 18:3 (Winter
   1993–94), pp. 73–7; Paul Dibb, *Towards a New Balance of Power in Asia*, Adelphi Paper 295 (London: Oxford University Press for the International Institute of Strategic Studies, 1995); Josef Joffe, '"Bismark" or "Britain"? Toward
   an American Grand Strategy After Bipolarity', *International Security* 19:4
   (Spring 1995), 94–117; James A. Kelly, 'US Security Policies in East Asia:
   Fighting Erosion and Finding a New Balance', *The Washington Quarterly* 18:3
   (Summer 1995), 21–35; Michael Leifer (ed.), *The Balance of Power in East Asia*
   (Basingstoke and London: Macmillan, 1986); Gerald Segal, 'East Asia and
   the "Constrainment" of China', *International Security* 20:4 (Spring 1996),
   159–87; and Douglas T. Stuart and William T. Tow, *A New US Strategy for East
   Asia*, Adelphi Paper 299 (London: Oxford University Press for the IISS, 1995).
8  As noted by Muthiah Alagappa in the conclusion to his book, Alagappa (ed.),
   *Asian Security Practice: Material and Ideational Influences*, (Stanford: Stanford
   University Press, 1998), pp. 625–6, 631–3.
9  Representative of this view is Robert Ross, 'Beijing as a Conservative Power',
   *Foreign Affairs* 76:2 (March/April 1997), 33–44.
10 Dibb, *Towards a New Balance of Power in Asia*. Also see a review of Dibb's proposals by Kay Möller, 'How Much Insecurity in East Asia?', *The Pacific Review*
   9:1 (1996), 114–24.
11 Betts, 'Wealth, Power and Instability', p. 70, n. 71.

12  This geopolitical framework, of course, parallels that which Robert Ross claims already exists in the region. See Robert S. Ross, 'The Geography of Peace: East Asia in the Twenty-First Century', *International Security* 23:4 (Spring 1999), *passim.*

13  Representative examples from the liberal camp making this case include Robert Axelrod and Robert O. Keohane, 'Achieving Cooperation Under Anarchy: Strategies and Institutions', *World Politics* 38:1 (October 1985), 226–54; Charles Lipson, 'International Cooperation in Economic and Security Affairs', *World Politics* 37:1 (October 1984), 1–23; Kenneth Oye, 'Explaining Cooperation Under Anarchy: Hypothesis and Strategies', *World Politics* 38:1 (October 1985), 1–24; and Arthur Stein, *Why Nations Cooperate: Circumstance and Choice in International Relations* (Ithaca: Cornell University Press, 1990).

14  Much of this paragraph is extracted from William Tow, 'Bilateral and Multilateral Security in the Asia-Pacific: Key Concepts', in Tow, Russell Trood and Toshiya Hoshino (eds), *Bilateralism in a Multilateral Era* (Tokyo: Nathan: The Japan Institute of International Affairs/Centre for the Study of Australia–Asia Relations, Griffith University, 1997), p. 46.

15  For an in-depth analysis of what constitutes 'security regimes', see Robert Jervis, 'Security Regimes', *International Organization* 36:2 (Spring 1982), 357–78. For an analysis in an Asia-Pacific context, consult David Rapkin, 'Leadership and Cooperative Institutions in the Asia-Pacific', in Andrew Mack and John Ravenhill (eds), *Pacific Cooperation: Building Economic and Security Regimes in the Asia-Pacific Region* (St Leonards, NSW: Allen & Unwin, 1994), pp. 98–129; William T. Tow and Richard Gray, 'Asia-Pacific Security Regimes: Conditions and Constraints', *Australian Journal of Political Science* 30:3 (November 1995), 436–51; and Suisheng Zhao, 'Soft versus Structured Regionalism: Organizational Forms of Cooperation in Asia-Pacific', *The Journal of East Asian Affairs* 12:1 (Winter/Spring 1998), 96–134.

16  Keith Krause, 'Constructing Regional Security Regimes and the Control of Arms Transfers', *International Journal* 45:2 (Spring 1996), 386–423.

17  Hee Kwon Park, 'Multilateral Security Cooperation', *The Pacific Review* 6:3 (1993), 251–66.

18  Jervis, 'Security Regimes', pp. 360–2.

19  See the Office of International Security Affairs, *EASR 1995*, pp. 7–8.

20  Banning N. Garrett, and Bonnie S. Glaser, 'Multilateral Security in the Asia-Pacific Region and its Impact on Chinese Interests: Views from Beijing', *Contemporary Southeast Asia* 16:1 (June 1994), 14–34. In a penetrating article on China's contemporary world view, Samuel S. Kim argues that 'the most basic characteristic of post-Tienanmen Chinese multilateral diplomacy is the supremacy of state sovereignty: *no state sovereignty, no world order*'. Kim, 'China in the Post-Cold War Order', in Stuart Harris and Gary Klintworth (eds), *China As a Great Power: Myths, Realities and Challenges in the Asia-Pacific Region* (Melbourne/New York: Longman/St. Martin's, 1995), p. 48. Emphasis is in the original text.

21  As stipulated in China's 1998 Defense White Paper, reprinted and translated in FBIS-CHI-98-209 (28 July 1998).

22  Robert Powell, 'Absolute and Relative Gains in International Relations Theory', *American Political Science Review* 85:4 (December 1991), 1311–14; and Duncan Snidal, 'Relative Gains and the Pattern of International Cooperation', *American Political Science Review* 85:3 (September 1991), 701–26.

23 Müller describes this form of regime collaboration as the 'neoliberal-utilitarian approach'. See 'The Internationalization of Principles, Norms and Rules', in Volker Rittberger (with the assistance of Peter Mayer) *Regime Theory and International Relations* (Oxford: Oxford University Press, 1993), p. 362.

24 See Jose T. Almonte, 'Ensuring Security the "ASEAN Way"', *Survival* 39:4 (Winter 1997–98), 80–92; and Narine Shaun, 'ASEAN and the ARF: The Limits of the ASEAN Way', *Asian Survey* 37:10 (October 1997), 961–78. As noted by David B. H. Denoon and Evelyn Colbert, the ARF provides additional opportunities for ASEAN to encourage the United States to remain in the region and for China to participate in 'the regional community'. Nevertheless, it 'seems unlikely' that ARF will become a vehicle for common action against the real regional threats to peace which currently originate in Northeast Asia and 'where the policies of the United States, Japan and China continue to play the dominating role'. See their 'Challenges for the Association of Southeast Asian Nations (ASEAN)', *Pacific Affairs* 71:4 (Winter 1998/1999), 515.

25 See 'Transcript: Secretary of Defense [William] Cohen, Sept 17 Singapore Briefing, (17 September 2000), International Information Program, at [http://usinfo.state.gov/regional/].

26 This point is well developed by Patrick M. Cronin, 'Pacific Rim Security: Beyond Bilateralism?', *The Pacific Review* 5:3 (1992), 209–11.

27 As asserted by Gerald Segal in 'What Is Asian About Asian Security?', in Jim Rolfe (ed.), *Unresolved Futures: Comprehensive Security in the Asia-Pacific* (Wellington: Centre for Strategic Studies, 1995) pp. 116–17.

28 Patrick Cronin refers to this approach as a 'system-reforming' model, focusing 'for the foreseeable future on an evolutionary, incremental, step-by-step, phased building-block approach', linking a number of existing organisations, alliances and frameworks together to form a foundation of a more comprehensive regional framework. Also see Paul Dibb and Gareth Evans, *Australian Paper on Practical Proposals for Security Cooperation in the Asia Pacific Region*, (Canberra: Department of Foreign Affairs and Trade/Strategic and Defence Studies Centre, 1994); and Lee Poh Ping, 'The Security and Economic Structure in the Post-Cold War Asia-Pacific Region: A Southeast Asian Perspective', in Michio Kimura (ed.), *Multilayered Regional Cooperation in Southeast Asia after the Cold War* (Tokyo: Institute of Developing Economies, 1995), esp. pp. 32–5.

29 The concept has been developed extensively by William T. Tow, 'Contending Security Approaches in the Asia-Pacific Region', *Security Studies* 3:1 (Autumn 1993), 104–7. It has been addressed further under the label 'moderate multipolar balancing' by Stuart and Tow, *A New US Strategy for East Asia*; and Stuart and Tow, *Security Policy In The Asia-Pacific*, Australia-Asia Papers no. 76 (Brisbane: Centre for the Study of Australia–Asia Relations, Griffith University, 1996).

30 A representative Chinese assessment is by Wang Jisi, 'US China Policy: Containment or Engagement?', *Beijing Review* 39:43 (21–27 October 1996), 6–9.

31 Greg Sheridan, 'Caught in the Middle', *The Weekend Australian* (16–17 November 1996), p. 25.

32 David M. Lampton, 'China and the Strategic Quadrangle', in Michael Mandelbaum (ed.), *The Strategic Quadrangle: Russia, China, Japan, and the United States in East Asia* (New York: Council on Foreign Relations Press, 1995), p. 101.

33 Alagappa, *Asian Security Practice*, p. 688.

34 Akio Watanabe et al., *The Perspective of Security Regimes in the Asia-Pacific Region* (Tokyo: The Japan Forum on International Relations, Inc., 1996), p. 15.
35 Robert Garran, 'Tokyo Forum Covers Security Hot Spots', *The Australian* (30 October 1996), p. 11.
36 Müller, 'Internationalization of Principles, Norms and Rules', p. 383.
37 Michael Leifer, *The ASEAN Regional Forum*, Adelphi Paper 302 (London: Oxford University Press for the International Institute for Strategic Studies, 1996), p. 59.
38 ASEAN, 'Chairman's Statement', p. 3.
39 The point is discussed cogently by Frank Ching, 'Sino–Russian Pact a Good Sign', *Far Eastern Economic Review* (23 May 1996), 40.
40 Office of International Security Affairs, *EASR 1995*, p. 19.
41 Brian Job, 'Bilateral and Multilateral Security Options', paper prepared for the fourth workshop on the 'Bilateral System of Alliances in the Changing Environment of the Asia-Pacific', Tokyo, 10–12 June 1996, p. 4 of draft manuscript.
42 Gareth Evans, 'The Prospects for Multilateral Security Co-operation', in Ball (ed.), 'The Transformation of Security in the Asia-Pacific Region', pp. 205–7; and Young Whan Kihl and Kongdan Oh, 'From Bilateralism to Multilateralism in Security Cooperation in the Asia-Pacific', *Korea Observer* 25:3 (Autumn 1994), p. 396.
43 Evans, 'The Prospects for Multilateral Security Co-operation', in Ball (ed.), 'The Transformation of Security in the Asia-Pacific Region', pp. 213–14; and Desmond Ball, 'Strategic Culture in the Asia-Pacific Region', *Security Studies* 3:1 (Autumn 1993), 44–74.
44 Müller argues that the norm *pacta sunt servanda* 'puts a heavy burden' on those who want to breach legally fixed regimes. He also notes that there is an inherent linkage between treaty obligations and their translation into domestic legislation. See 'Internationalization of Principles, Norms and Rules', p. 385. If those arguing that an Asia-Pacific 'strategic culture' is what is really driving that region's multilateral security dynamics are correct, these factors are less consequential.

# Selected Bibliography

Note: The books and articles listed below constitute only a representative citation of relevant works. More comprehensive citations can be found in the endnotes.

Accinelli, Robert, *Crisis and Commitment: United States Commitment Toward Taiwan, 1950–1955*, Chapel Hill and London: University of North Carolina Press, 1996.

Acharya, Amitav, *Constructing a Security Community in Southeast Asia*, London: Routledge, 2001.

Adler, Emanuel and Barnett, Michael (eds), *Security Communities*, Cambridge: Cambridge University Press, 1998.

Akaha, Tsuneo and Langdon, Frank (eds), *Japan in the Posthegemonic World*, Boulder: Lynne Rienner, 1993.

Alagappa, Muthiah (ed.), *Asian Security Practice: Material and Ideational Influences*, Stanford: Stanford University Press, 1998.

Anderson, Jennifer, *The Limits of Sino–Russian Strategic Partnership*, Adelphi Paper 315, London: Oxford University Press for the International Institute for Strategic Studies, 1997.

Anwar, Dewi Fortuna, *Indonesia's Strategic Culture: Katahanan Nasional, Wawasan Nusantara and Hankamrata*, CSAAR Australia-Asia Papers no. 75, Nathan: Centre for the Study of Australia–Asia Relations, 1996.

Austin, Greg (ed.), *Missile Diplomacy and Taiwan's Future: Innovations in Politics and Military Power*, Canberra Papers on Strategy and Defence no. 122, Canberra: Strategic and Defence Studies Centre, Australian National University, 1997.

Axelrod, Robert, *The Evolution of Cooperation*, New York: Basic Books, 1984.

Ayoob, Mohammed and Samudaranija, Chai-Anan (eds), *Leadership Perceptions and National Security: The Southeast Asian Experience*, Singapore: Institute of Southeast Asian Studies, 1989.

Baek, Kwang Il (ed.), *Comprehensive Security and Multilateralism in Post-Cold War East Asia*, KAIS International Conference Series no. 9, Seoul: Postcom, 1998.

287

Baker, James A. III, 'America in Asia: Emerging Architecture for a Pacific Community', *Foreign Affairs* 70:5 (Winter 1991–92), 1–17.

Baldwin, David (ed.), *Neorealism and Neoliberalism: The Contemporary Debate*, New York: Columbia University Press, 1993.

Ball, Desmond (ed.), 'The Transformation of Security in the Asia/Pacific Region', *The Journal of Strategic Studies* 18:3 (September 1995), Special Issue.

—— *Maintaining the Strategic Edge: The Defence of Australia in 2015*, Canberra Papers on Strategy and Defence, no. 133, Canberra: Strategic and Defence Studies Centre, Australian National University, 1999.

Ball, Desmond and Kerr, Pauline, *Presumptive Engagement: Australia's Asia-Pacific Security Policy in the 1990s*, St Leonards/Canberra: Allen & Unwin/Department of International Relations, Australian National University, 1996.

Bateman, Sam and Sherwood, Dick (eds), *Australia's Maritime Bridge Into Asia*, St Leonards: Allen & Unwin in Association with the Royal Australian Navy, 1995.

Bellows, Michael D. (ed.), *Asia in the 21st Century: Evolving Strategic Priorities*, Washington, DC: National Defense University Press, Fort Lesley, J. McNair, 1994.

Bergin, Anthony and Soesastro, Hadi (eds), *The Role of Security and Economic Cooperation Structures in the Asia Pacific Region*, Jakarta/Canberra: Centre for Strategic and International Studies/Australian Defence Studies Centre, 1996.

Bernstein, Richard and Munro, Ross H., *The Coming Conflict With China*, New York: Alfred A. Knopf, 1997.

Betts, Richard K, 'Wealth, Power and Instability: East Asia and the United States after the Cold War', *International Security* 18:3 (Winter 1993–94), 34–77.

Binnendijk, Hans and Montaperto, Ronald N. (eds), *Strategic Trends in China*, Washington, DC: Institute for National Strategic Studies, National Defense University, 1998.

Bitzinger, Richard A. and Bates, Gill, *Gearing Up For High Tech Warfare? Chinese and Taiwanese Defense Modernization and Implications for Military Confrontation Across the Taiwan Strait*, CAPS Papers no. 11, Taipei: Chinese Council of Advanced Policy Studies, 1996.

Blackwill, Robert D. and Dibb, Paul (eds), *America's Asian Alliances*, Cambridge, MA and London: The MIT Press, 2000.

Blair, Dennis C. and Hanley, John T., 'From Wheels to Webs: Reconstructing Asia-Pacific Security Arrangements', *The Washington Quarterly* 24:1 (Winter 2001), 7–18.

Booth, Ken and Trood, Russell (eds), *Strategic Cultures in the Asia-Pacific Region*, Basingstoke: Macmillan, 1999.

Bora, Bjit and Findlay, Christopher (eds), *Regional Integration and the Asia-Pacific*, Melbourne: Oxford University Press, 1996.

Brown, Gary, Frost, Frank and Sherlock, Stephen, *The Australian–Indonesian Security Agreement*, Research Paper no. 25, Canberra: Department of the Parliamentary Library, 1996.

Brown, Michael E., Lynn Jones, Sean M. and Miller, Steven E. (eds), *East Asian Security*, Cambridge, MA: The MIT Press, 1996.

Buszynski, Leszek, *SEATO: The Failure of an Alliance Strategy*, Singapore: Singapore University Press, 1983.

Buzan, Barry, *People, States and Fear: The National Security Problem in International Relations* (2nd edn), Boulder: Lynne Rienner, 1991.

Buzan, Barry and Segal, Gerald, 'Rethinking East Asian Security', *Survival* 36:2 (Summer 1994), 3–21.

Calder, Kent, *Asia's Deadly Triangle: How Arms, Energy and Growth Threaten to Destabilise the Asia-Pacific*, London: Nicholas Brealey, 1996.

Cambone, Stephen A., 'The United States and Theatre Missile Defence in Northeast Asia', *Survival* 39:3 (Autumn 1997), 66–84.

Carnegie Commission, *Designing a Pacific Community*, Washington, DC: Carnegie Commission 1994.

Carpenter, Ted Galen, *America's Search for Enemies: America's Alliances After the Cold War*, Washington, DC: CATO Institute, 1992.

Cha, Victor D., *Alignment Despite Antagonism: The United States–Korea–Japan Security Triangle*, Stanford: Stanford University Press, 1999.

—— 'Hate, Power and Identity in Japan–Korea Security', *Australian Journal of International Affairs* 54:3 (November 2000), 309–23.

Chai, Sun-Ki, 'Entrenching the Yoshida Defense Doctrine: Three Techniques for Institutionalization', *International Organization* 51:3 (Summer 1997), 389–412.

Chan, Steve, *East Asian Dynamism: Growth, Order and Security in the Pacific*, Boulder: Westview, 1990.

Chang, Felix K., 'Conventional War Across the Taiwan Strait', *ORBIS* 40:4 (Fall 1996), 577–607.

Chapman, J. W. M., Drifte, R. and Gow, I. T. M., *Japan's Quest For Comprehensive Security*, London: Frances Pinter, 1983.

Chinworth, Michael W., *Inside Japan's Defense*, Washington, DC, New York and London: Brassey's, 1992.

Christensen, Thomas J., 'Chinese Realpolitik', *Foreign Affairs*, 75:5 (September–October 1996), 37–52.

—— 'China, The US–Japan Alliance and the Security Dilemma in East Asia', *International Security* 23:4 (Spring 1999), 49–80.

Christensen, Thomas J. and Snyder, Jack, 'Chain Gangs and Passed Bucks: Predicting Alliance Patterns in Multipolarity', *International Organization* 44:2 (Spring 1990), 138–68.

Cohen, Saul B., 'Global Geopolitical Change in the Post-Cold War Era', *Annals of the Association of American Geographers* 81:4 (December 1991), 551–80.

Cohen, Warren I. and Iriye, Akira (eds), *The Great Powers in East Asia: 1953–1960*, New York: Columbia University Press, 1990.

Colbert, Evelyn, *Southeast Asia in International Politics 1941–1956*, Ithaca: Cornell University Press, 1977.

Comprehensive National Security Study Group, *Report on Comprehensive National Security*, Tokyo: Office of the Prime Minister, 1980.

Cooper, Andrew F. (ed.), *Niche Diplomacy: Middle Powers After the Cold War*, Basingstoke and London: Macmillan, 1996.

Cossa, Ralph A., *The Major Powers in Northeast Asian Security*, McNair Paper no. 51, Washington, DC: Institute for National Strategic Studies, National Defense University, 1996.

Cronin, Patrick M., 'Pacific Rim Security: Beyond Bilateralism?', *The Pacific Review* 5:3 (1992), 209–20.

Crowe, William J. Jr and Romberg, Alan D., 'Rethinking Security in the Pacific', *Foreign Affairs* 70:2 (Spring 1992), 123–40.

Deutsch, Karl W., Burrell, Sidney A., Kann, Robert A., Lee, Maurice Jr, Lichterman, Martin, Lindgren, Raymond E., Loewenheim, Francis L., Van Wagenen, Richard W., *Political Community and the North Atlantic Area: International Organization in the Light of Historical Experience*, New York: Greenwood Press, 1957 (1969).

290     SELECTED BIBLIOGRAPHY

Di, Hua and Lewis, John Wilson, 'China's Ballistic Missile Programs: Technologies, Strategies, Goals', *International Security* 17:2 (Fall 1992), 5–40.

Dibb, Paul, *Towards a New Balance of Power in Asia*, Adelphi Paper 295, London: Oxford University Press for the International Institute of Strategic Studies, 1995.

—— 'The Revolution in Military Affairs and Asian Security', *Survival* 39:4 (Winter 1997–98), 93–116.

Dibb, Paul and Evans, Gareth, *Australian Paper on Practical Proposals for Security Cooperation in the Asia Pacific Region*, Canberra: Department of Foreign Affairs and Trade/Strategic and Defence Studies Centre, 1994.

Dorsch, Jorn and Mols, Manfred, 'Thirty Years of ASEAN: Achievements and Challenges', *The Pacific Review* 11:2 (1998), 167–82.

Eberstadt, Nicholas, 'Assessing "National Strategy" in North and South Korea', *The Korean Journal of Defense Analysis* 8:1 (Summer 1996), 55–76.

Ellings, Richard J. and Simon, Sheldon (eds), *Southeast Asian Security in the New Millennium*, New York and London: M. E. Sharpe, 1996.

Fisher, Richard D., 'The Clinton Administration's Early Defense Policy Toward Asia', *The Korean Journal of Defense Analysis* 6:1 (Summer 1994), 103–22.

Frankel, Benjamin (ed.), *Roots of Realism*, Security Studies 5:2 (Winter 1995), Special Issue.

—— *Realism, Restatement and Renewal*, Security Studies 5:3 (Spring 1996), Special Issue.

Friedberg, Aaron L., 'Ripe for Rivalry', *International Security* 18:3 (Winter 1993–94), 5–33.

—— 'Will Europe's Past Be Asia's Future?', *Survival* 42:3 (Autumn 2000), 147–60.

Fry, Greg (ed.), *Australia's Regional Security*, Sydney: Allen & Unwin, 1991.

Fukushima, Akiko, *Japanese Foreign Policy: The Emerging Logic of Multilateralism*, Basingstoke: Macmillan, 1999.

Fukuyama, Francis and Oh, Kondan, *The U.S.–Japan Security Relationship After the Cold War*, Santa Monica: RAND, 1993.

Funabashi, Yoichi, *Alliance Adrift*, New York: Council on Foreign Relations, 1999.

Gaddis, John Lewis, 'International Relations Theory and the End of the Cold War', *International Security* 17:3 (Winter 1992), 5–58.

Gallagher, Michael G., 'China's Illusory Threat to the South China Sea', *International Security* 19:1 (Summer 1994), 169–94.

Garnaut, Ross, *Australia and the Northeast Asian Ascendancy*, Canberra: Australian Government Publishing Service, 1989.

Garrett, Banning N. and Glaser, Bonnie S., 'Multilateral Security in the Asia-Pacific Region and its Impact on Chinese Interests: Views from Beijing', *Contemporary Southeast Asia* 16:1 (June 1994), 14–34.

Garver, John W., *The Sino–Soviet Alliance: Nationalist China and American Cold War Strategy in Asia*, New York: M. E. Sharpe, 1997.

George, Alexander, *Bridging the Gap: Theory and Politics in Foreign Policy*, Washington DC: United States Institute for Peace, 1993.

Gholz, Eugene, Press, Daryl G. and Sapolsky, Harvey M., 'Come Home America', *International Security* 21:4 (Spring 1997), 5–48.

Godwin, Paul H. B., 'From Continent to Periphery: PLA Doctrine, Strategy and Capabilities Towards 2000', *The China Quarterly* 146 (June 1996), 464–88.

Green, Michael J., *Japan–ROK Security Relations: An American Perspective*, Stanford: Asia/Pacific Research Center, Institute for International Studies, Stanford University, 1999.

Green, Michael J. and Self, Benjamin L., 'Japan's Changing China Policy: From Commercial Liberalism to Reluctant Realism', *Survival* 38:2 (Summer 1996), 35–58.

Grieco, Joseph M., 'Anarchy and the Limits of Cooperation: A Realist Critique of the Newest Liberal Institutionalists', *International Organization* 42:3 (Summer 1988), 485–507.

Griffith, Samuel B., *Sun Tzu: The Art Of War*, London: Oxford University Press, 1963.

Gurtov, Mel and Hwang, Byong-Moo, *China's Security: The New Roles of the Military*, Boulder: Lynne Rienner, 1998.

Haacke, Jurgen, 'The Concept of Flexible Engagement and the Practice of Enhanced Interaction: Intra-Mural Challenges to the "ASEAN Way"', *The Pacific Review* 12:4 (1999), 581–611.

Haggard, Stephen and Simmons, Beth A., 'Theories of International Regimes', *International Organization* 43:3 (Summer 1987), 491–517.

Halloran, Richard, 'The Rising East', *Foreign Policy* 102 (Spring 1996), 3–21.

Harris, Stuart and Mack, Andrew (eds), *Asia-Pacific Security: The Economics–Politics Nexus*, St Leonards/Canberra: Allen & Unwin/Department of International Relations, RSAPS, Australian National University, 1997.

Hayes, Peter and Kihl, Young Whan (eds), *Peace and Security in North-east Asia*, New York and London: M. E. Sharpe, 1997.

Henderson, Jeannie, *Reassessing ASEAN*, Adephi Paper 328, London: Oxford University Press for the International Institute for Strategic Studies, 1999.

Henricksen, Thomas H. and Mo, Jongryn (eds), *North Korea After Kim Il Sung: Continuity or Change?*, Stanford: Hoover Institution Press, 1997.

Hewison, Kevin, Robison, Richard and Rodan, Garry (eds), *Southeast Asia in the 1990s*, Sydney: Allen & Unwin, 1993.

Hickey, Dennis Van Vranken, *Taiwan's Security in the Changing International System*, Boulder and London: Lynne Rienner, 1997.

Hosokawa, Morihiro, 'Are U.S. Troops in Japan Needed? Reforming the Alliance', *Foreign Affairs* 77:4 (July–August 1998), 2–5.

Hu, Weixing, 'China's Security Agenda After the Cold War', *The Pacific Review* 8:1 (1995), 117–36.

Hughes, Christopher W., 'The North Korean Nuclear Crisis and Japanese Security', *Survival* 38:2 (Summer 1996), 79–103.

Hummel, Hartwig, 'Japan's Military Expenditures After the Cold War: The "Realism" of the Peace Dividend', *Australian Journal of International Affairs* 50:2 (July 1996), 137–56.

Huntington, Samuel P., 'America's Changing Strategic Interests', *Survival* 33:1 (January/February 1991), 3–17.

—— 'Why International Primacy Matters', *International Security* 17:4 (Spring 1993), 68–83.

Huxley, Tim, *Defending the Lion City: The Armed Forces of Singapore*, Crows Nest, NSW: Allen & Unwin, 2000.

Huxley, Tim and Willett, Susan, *Arming East Asia* Adelphi Paper 329. Oxford: Oxford University Press for the International Institute for Strategic Studies, 1999.

Ina, Hisayoshi, *A New Multilateral Approach for the Pacific: Beyond the Bilateral Security Network*, Washington DC: The Johns Hopkins Foreign Policy Institute, 1993.

Inoguchi, Takashi and Stillman, Grant B. (eds), *North-East Asian Regional Security: The Role of International Institutions*, Tokyo, New York and Paris: United Nations University Press, 1996.

Ito, Kenichi, 'Japan and the Soviet Union: Entangled in the Deadlock of the Northern Territories', *The Washington Quarterly* 11:1 (Winter 1988), 34–44.

Jervis, Robert, 'Security Regimes', *International Organization* 36:2 (Spring 1982), 357–8.

—— 'Realism, Neoliberalism and Cooperation: Understanding the Debate', *International Security* 24:1 (Fall 1999), 42–63.

Joffe, Ellis, 'People's War Under Modern Conditions: A Doctrine of Modern War', *The China Quarterly* 112 (December 1987), 555–71.

Johnson, Chalmers and Keehn, E. B., 'The Pentagon's Ossified Strategy', *Foreign Affairs* 74:4 (July–August 1995), 103–14.

Johnson, William R. and Sutter, Robert G. (eds), *Taiwan in World Affairs*, Boulder: Westview Press, 1994.

Johnston, Alastair Iain, *Cultural Realism: Strategic Culture and Grand Strategy*, Princeton: Princeton University Press, 1995.

—— 'China's New "Old Thinking": The Concept of Limited Deterrence', *International Security* 20:3 (Winter 1995–96), 5–47.

—— 'Prospects for Chinese Nuclear Force Modernization: Limited Deterrence Versus Multilateral Arms Control', *The China Quarterly* 146 (June 1996), 548–76.

Johnston, Alastair Iain and Ross, Robert S. (eds), *Engaging China: The Management of An Emerging Power*, London and New York: Routledge, 1999.

Kagan, Robert, 'American Power: A Guide for the Perplexed', *Commentary* 101:4 (April 1996), 21–31.

Kang, David C., 'Preventive War and North Korea', *Security Studies* 4:2 (Winter 1994–1995), 330–64.

Katzenstein, Peter J. (ed.), *The Culture of National Security: Norms and Identity in World Politics*, New York: Columbia University Press, 1996.

Kaufmann, William W., *Assessing the Base Force: How Much Is Too Much?* Washington, DC: The Brookings Institution, 1992.

Kawasaki, Tsuyoshi, 'Between Realism and Idealism in Japanese Security Policy: The Case of the ASEAN Regional Forum', *The Pacific Review* 10:4 (1997), 480–503.

Keohane, Robert O., 'Multilateralism: An Agenda for Research', *International Journal* 45:4 (Autumn 1990), 731–64.

—— (ed.), *Neorealism And Its Critics*, New York: Columbia University Press, 1986.

Keohane, Robert O. and Nye, Joseph S. Jr, *Power and Interdependence: World Politics in Transition*, Boston: Little Brown, 1977.

Kerr, Pauline, Labor's Security Policy, 1983–1996: Towards A Liberal–Realist Explanation?, PhD dissertation, Australian National University, 1999.

Khalilzad, Zalmay, 'Losing the Moment? The United States and the World After the Cold War', *The Washington Quarterly* 18:2 (Spring 1995), 87–107.

Khoo, How San (ed.), *The Future of the ARF*, Singapore: Institute of Defence and Strategic Studies, 1999.

Kihl, Young Whan and Oh, Kongdan, 'From Bilateralism to Multilateralism in Security Cooperation in the Asia-Pacific', *Korea Observer* 25:3 (Autumn 1994), 395–419.

Kim, Dae Jung, 'Is Culture Destiny? The Myth of Asia's Anti-Democratic Values: A Response to Lee Kwan Yew', *Foreign Affairs* 73:6 (November–December 1994), 189–94.

Kimura, Michio (ed.), *Multi-layered Regional Cooperation in Southeast Asia after the Cold War*, Tokyo: Institute of Developing Economies, 1995.

Kissinger, Henry, *Diplomacy*, New York: Simon & Schuster, 1994.

Klintworth, Gary (ed.), *Taiwan in the Asia-Pacific in the 1990s*, St Leonards/Canberra: Allen & Unwin/Department of International Relations, Australian National University, 1994.

Krasner, Stephen D. (ed.), *International Regimes*, Ithaca: Cornell University Press, 1983.

Krugman, Paul, 'The Myth of Asia's Miracle', *Foreign Affairs* 73:6 (November–December 1994), 62–78.

Kugler, Richard L., *Changes Ahead: Future Directions for the U.S. Overseas Military Presence*, Santa Monica: RAND, 1998.

Kurth, James, 'America's Grand Strategy', *The National Interest* 43 (Spring 1996), 3–19.

Kwak, Tae-Hwan (ed.), *The Four Powers and Korean Unification Strategy*, Seoul: Kyungnam University Press, 1997.

Kwak, Tae-Hwan and Olsen, Edward (eds), *The Major Powers of Northeast Asia: Seeking Peace and Security*, Boulder: Lynne Rienner, 1996.

Lake, David M. and Morgan, Patrick M. (eds), *Regional Orders: Building Security in a New World*, University Park, PA: Pennsylvania State University Press, 1997.

Layne, Christopher, 'Less is More: Minimal Realism in East Asia', *The National Interest* 43 (Spring 1996), 64–77.

—— 'From Preponderance to Offshore Balancing: America's Future Grand Strategy', *International Security* 22:1 (Summer 1997), 86–124.

Leaver, Richard L. and Richardson, James L. (eds), *The Post-Cold War Order: Diagnoses and Prognoses*, St Leonards/Canberra: Allen & Unwin/Department of International Relations, Australian National University, 1993.

Lee, Bernice, *The Security Implications of the New Taiwan* Adelphi Paper 331, London: International Institute for Strategic Studies, 1999.

Lee, Chae-Jin, *China and Korea: Dynamic Relations*, Stanford: Hoover Press, 1996.

Lee, Suk Jung, *Ending the Last Cold War: Korean Arms Control and the Security of Northeast Asia*, Aldershot: Ashgate, 1997.

Leifer, Michael, *The ASEAN Regional Forum*, Adelphi Paper 302, London: Oxford University Press for the International Institute for Strategic Studies, 1996.

Leifer, Michael (ed.), *The Balance of Power in East Asia*, Basingstoke: Macmillan, 1986.

Levin, Norman D., 'What If North Korea Survives?', *Survival* 39:4 (Winter 1997–98), 156–74.

Lewis, John Wilson and Xue Litai, *China's Strategic Seapower: The Politics of Force Modernization in the Nuclear Age*, Stanford: Stanford University Press, 1994.

Li, Nan, 'The PLA's Evolving Warfighting Doctrine, Strategy and Tactics, 1985–95: A Chinese Perspective', *The China Quarterly* 146 (June 1996), 443–63.

Lim, Joo-Jock, *Territorial Power Domains, Southeast Asia and China: The Geo-Strategy of an Overarching Massif*, Singapore/Canberra: Institute of South-East Asian Studies/Strategic and Defence Studies Centre, Australian National University, 1984.

Lim, Robyn, 'The ASEAN Regional Forum: Building on Sand', *Contemporary Southeast Asia* 20:2 (August 1998), 115–36.

Lin, Cheng-yi, 'The U.S. Factor in the 1958 and 1996 Taiwan Strait Crises', *Issues & Studies* 32:12 (December 1996), 14–32.

Litwak, Robert S., *Detente and the Nixon Doctrine: American Foreign Policy and the Pursuit of Stability, 1969–1976*, Cambridge: Cambridge University Press, 1984.

Liu, Alan P. L., 'A Convenient Crisis: Looking Behind Beijing's Threats Against Taiwan', *Issues and Studies* 36:5 (October 2000), 83–121.

Lowry, Bob, *Indonesian Defence Policy and the Indonesian Armed Forces*, Canberra Papers on Strategy and Defence no. 99, Canberra: Strategic and Defence Studies Centre, RSAPS, Australian National University, 1993.

Mack, Andrew and Kerr, Pauline, 'The Evolving Discourse in the Asia-Pacific', *The Washington Quarterly* 18:1 (Winter 1995), 123–40.

Mack, Andrew and Ravenhill, John (eds), *Pacific Cooperation: Building Economic and Security Regimes in the Asia-Pacific Region*, St Leonards: Allen & Unwin, 1994.

Mackinder, Halford J., 'The Geographic Pivot of History', *Geographical Journal* 4 (April 1904), 435–7.

Mahan, Alfred T., *The Influence of Sea Power Upon History*, New York: Hill & Wang, [1890] 1960.

Mak, J. N., *ASEAN Defence Reorientation 1975–1992: The Dynamics of Modernisation and Structural Change*, Canberra Papers on Strategy and Defence no. 103, Canberra: Strategic and Defence Studies Centre, Australian National University, 1993.

Malik, J. Mohan (ed.), *Australia's Security in the 21st Century*, St. Leonards: Allen & Unwin, 1998.

Mandelbaum, Michael (ed.), *The Strategic Quadrangle: Russia, China, Japan, and the United States in East Asia*, New York: Council on Foreign Relations Press, 1995.

Manning, Robert A. and Stern, Paula, 'The Myth of a Pacific Community', *Foreign Affairs* 73:6 (November–December 1994), 79–93.

Mao Tse-tung [Zedong], 'On Protracted War [May 1938]', in *Selected Military Writings of Mao Tse-tung*, Beijing: Foreign Languages Press, 1967.

Mastanduno, Michael, 'Preserving the Unipolar Moment: Realist Theories and U.S. Grand Strategies After the Cold War', *International Security* 21:4 (Spring 1997), 49–88.

Mazaar, Michael J., *North Korea and the Bomb*, New York: St. Martin's, 1995.

McCafferie, Jack and Hinge, Alan (eds), *Seapower in the Next Century: Maritime Operations in the Asia-Pacific Beyond 2000*, Canberra: Australian Defence Force Academy, 1997.

McInnes, Colin and Rolls, Mark G. (eds), *Post-Cold War Security Issues in the Asia-Pacific Region*, Newbury Park: Frank Cass, 1994.

Mearsheimer, John, 'The False Promise of International Institutions', *International Security* 19:3 (Winter 1994–95), 5–49.

Menon, Rajan, 'The Strategic Convergence Between Russia and China', *Survival* 39:2 (Summer 1997), 101–25.

Methven, Philip, *The Five Power Defence Arrangements and Military Cooperation Among the ASEAN States: Incompatible Models for Security in Southeast Asia?*, Canberra Papers on Strategy and Defence no. 92, Canberra: Strategic and Defence Studies Centre, RSAPS, Australian National University, 1992.

Michisita, Narushige, 'Alliances After Peace in Korea', *Survival* 41:3 (Autumn 1999), 68–83.

Milner, Anthony, Cotton, James, Kerr, Pauline and Kikuchi, Tsutomu (eds), 'Perceiving National Security: A Report on East Asia and Australia', *Australian Journal of International Affairs* 47:2 (October 1993), 221–38.

Milner, Helen, 'International Theories of Cooperation Among Nations: Strengths and Weaknesses', *World Politics* 44:3 (April 1992), 466–96.

Mochizuki, Mike M., *Toward A True Alliance: Restructuring US–Japan Security Relations*, Washington DC: Brookings Institute Press, 1997.

Molander, Roger C., Riddle, Andrew S. and Wilson, Peter A., *Strategic Information Warfare: A New Force of War*, Santa Monica: RAND, 1996.

Moltz, James Clay, 'Missile Proliferation in East Asia: Arms Control vs. TMD Responses', *The Nonproliferation Review* 4:3 (Spring–Summer 1997), 63–71.

Moon, Chung-in, *Arms Control on the Korean Peninsula*, Seoul: Yonsei University Press, 1996.

Morgenthau, Hans, *Politics Among Nations: The Struggle for Power and Peace* (5th edn), New York: Alfred A. Knopf, 1973.

Morrison, Charles E., Kojima, Akira and Maull, Hanns, *Community–Building With Pacific Asia*, New York, Paris and Tokyo: Trilateral Commission, 1997.

Muravchik, Joshua, *The Imperative of American Leadership: A Challenge to Neo–Isolationism*, Washington, DC: American Enterprise Institute, 1996.

Nakamoto, Yoshihiko, 'Japanese Realism and Its Contribution to International Relations Theory', *Issues and Studies* 33:2 (February 1997), 65–96.

Niou, Emerson M. S. and Ordeshook, Peter C., 'Less Filling, Tastes Great: The Realist–Neoliberal Debate', *World Politics* 46:2 (January 1994), 209–34.

Nye, Joseph S. Jr, *Bound to Lead: The Changing Nature of American Power*, New York: Basic Books, 1990.

—— 'The Case for Deep Engagement', *Foreign Affairs* 74:4 (July–August 1995), 90–102.

Oberdorfer, Don, *The Two Koreas: A Contemporary History*, Reading, MA: Addison Wesley, 1997.

O'Hanlon, Michael, 'Stopping a North Korean Invasion', *International Security* 22:4 (Spring 1998), 135–70.

—— 'Why China Cannot Conquer Taiwan', *International Security* 25:2 (Fall 2000), 51–86.

Ohm, Tae-Am, 'Toward a New Phase of Multilateral Security Cooperation in the Asia-Pacific Region: Limited Multilateralism or Issue-Based Regionalism', *The Korean Journal of Defense Analysis* 9:2 (Winter 1997), 137–64.

Okazaki, Hisahiko, *A Grand Strategy For Japanese Defense*, Lanham, MD: University Press of America, 1986.

Oksenburg, Michel and Economy, Elizabeth (eds), *China Joins the World: Progress and Prospects*, New York: Council on Foreign Relations, 1999.

Oye, Kenneth, *Cooperation Under Anarchy*, Princeton: Princeton University Press, 1986.

Paik, Jin-Hyun, 'Multilateralism and the Korean Peninsula', *Korea and World Affairs* 21:1 (Spring 1997), 5–19.

Pollack, Jonathan, *Designing a New Security Strategy for Asia*, Asia Project Working Paper, New York: Council on Foreign Relations, March 1995.

Posen, Barry and Ross, Andrew L., 'Competing Visions for Grand Strategy', *International Security* 21:3 (Winter 1996/97), 5–53.

Powell, Robert, 'Absolute and Relative Gains in International Relations Theory', *American Political Science Review* 85:4 (December 1991), 1303–20.

Pye, Lucian W., *Asian Power and Politics: The Cultural Dimensions of Authority*, Cambridge, MA: The Belknap Press of Harvard University Press, 1985.

Rice, Condoleezza, 'Promoting the National Interest', *Foreign Affairs*, 79:1 (January/February 2000), 45–62.

Richardson, James L., 'Asia-Pacific: The Case for Geopolitical Optimism', *The National Interest* 38 (Winter 1994–95), 28–39.

Rittberger, Volker R. (with the assistance of Peter Mayer) (ed.), *Regime Theory and International Relations*, Oxford: Oxford University Press, 1993.

Robinson, Thomas W. and Shambaugh, David (eds), *Chinese Foreign Policy*, Oxford: Clarendon Press, 1994.

Robison, Richard, 'The Politics of "Asian Values"', *The Pacific Review* 9:3 (1996), 319–20.

Rolfe, Jim (ed.), *Unresolved Futures: Comprehensive Security in the Asia-Pacific*, Wellington: Centre for Strategic Studies, 1995.

Ross, Robert S., 'The Geography of Peace: East Asia in the Twenty-First Century', *International Security* 23:4 (Spring 1999), 81–118.

Roy, Denny, 'Assessing the Asia-Pacific Power Vacuum', *Survival* 37:3 (Autumn 1995), 46–54.

—— (ed.), *The New Security Agenda in the Asia-Pacific Region*, Basingstoke: Macmillan, 1997.

Rozman, Gilbert, 'Flawed Regionalism: Reconceptualizing Northeast Asia in the 1990s', *The Pacific Review* 11:1 (1998), 1–27.

Ruggie, John Gerard, *Winning the Peace: America and World Order in the New Era*, New York: Columbia University Press, 1996.

—— (ed.), *Multilateralism Matters: the Theory and Praxis of an Institutional Form*, New York: Columbia University Press, 1993.

Sasae, Kenichiro, *Rethinking Japan–U.S. Relations*, Adelphi Paper 292, London: Brassey's for the International Institute for Strategic Studies, 1994.

Satoh, Yukio, 'Emerging Trends in Asia-Pacific Security: The Role of Japan', *The Pacific Review* 8:2 (1995), 267–82.

Sawyer, Ralph D. (trans.), *The Seven Military Classics of Ancient China*, Boulder: Westview Press, 1993.

Scales, Robert H. and Wortzel, Larry M., *The Future U.S. Military Presence in Asia: Landpower and the Geostrategy of American Commitment*, Carlisle, PA: Strategic Studies Institute, US Army War College, 1999.

Segal, Gerald, 'East Asia and the "Constrainment" of China', *International Security* 20:4 (Spring 1996), 107–35.

Shambaugh, David, 'China's Military in Transition: Politics, Professionalism, Procurement and Power Projection', *The China Quarterly* 146 (June 1996), 265–98.

—— 'China's Military Views the World', *International Security*, 24:3 (Winter 1999), 52–79.

Shaun, Narine, 'ASEAN and the ARF: The Limits of the ASEAN Way', *Asian Survey* 37:10 (October 1997), 961–78.

Shimko, Keith L., 'Realism, Neoliberalism and American Liberalism', *Review of Politics* 54:2 (Spring 1992), 281–301.

Shirk, Susan and Twomey, Christopher P. (eds), *Power and Prosperity: Economics and Security Linkages in the Asia-Pacific*, New Brunswick and London: Transaction, 1996.

Shulsky, Abram N., *Deterrence Theory and Chinese Behavior*, Santa Monica: RAND, 2000.

Sigal, Leon, *Disarming Strangers*, Princeton: Princeton University Press, 1998.

Simon, Sheldon W., 'Realism and Neoliberalism: International Relations Theory and Southeast Asian Security', *The Pacific Review* 8:1 (1995), 5–24.

—— *The Economic Crisis and Southeast Asian Security: Changing Priorities*, NBR Analysis, 9:5, December 1998.

Snidal, Duncan, 'Relative Gains and the Pattern of International Cooperation', *American Political Science Review* 85:3 (September 1991), 701–26.

Snyder, Glenn H., *Alliance Politics*, Ithaca: Cornell University Press, 1997.

Snyder, Scott, *Negotiating on the Edge: North Korean Negotiating Behaviour*, Washington, DC: US Institute of Peace, 1999.

Soeya, Yoshihide, 'The Japan–U.S. Alliance in a Changing Asia', *Japan Review of International Affairs* 10:4 (Fall 1996), 255–75.

Spykman, Nicholas J., *The Geography of Peace*, New York: Harcourt Brace, 1944.

Stuart, Douglas T. and Tow, William T., *A U.S. Strategy for the Asia-Pacific*, Adelphi Paper 299, London: Oxford University Press for the International Institute of Strategic Studies, 1995.

Stubbs, Richard, 'Subregional Security Cooperation in ASEAN: Military and Economic Imperatives and Political Obstacles', *Asian Survey* 32:5 (May 1992), 397–410.

Swaine, Michael D., *Taiwan's National Security, Defence Policy and Weapons Procurement Processes*, Santa Monica: RAND, 1999.

Swaine, Michael D. and Tellis, Ashley J., *Interpreting China's Grand Strategy: Past, Present and Future*, MR1121-AF, Santa Monica: RAND, 2000.

Tang, James T. H., *Multilateralism in Northeast Asian International Security: An Illusion or a Realistic Hope?*, North Pacific Cooperative Security Dialogue, Working Paper no. 26, Ontario: York University, 1993.

Thakur, Ramesh and Thayer, Carlyle A. (eds), *Reshaping Regional Relations: Asia-Pacific and the Former Soviet Union*, Boulder: Westview Press, 1993.

Thayer, Carlyle A., *Beyond Indochina* Adelphi Paper 297, London: Oxford University Press for the International Institute for Strategic Studies, 1995.

Tow, William T., *Encountering the Dominant Player: U.S. Extended Deterrence Strategy in the Asia-Pacific*, New York: Columbia University Press, 1991.

—— 'Contending Security Approaches in the Asia-Pacific', *Security Studies* 3:1 (Autumn 1993), 75–116.

Tow, William T. and Gray, Richard, 'Asia-Pacific Security Regimes: Conditions and Constraints', *Australian Journal of Political Science* 30:3 (November 1995), 436–51.

Tow, William T., Trood, Russell and Hoshino, Toshiya (eds), *Bilateralism in a Multilateral Era*, Tokyo/Nathan: Japan Institute of International Affairs/Centre for the Study of Australia–Asia Relations, 1997.

Valencia, Mark, *China and the South China Sea Disputes*, Adelphi Paper 298, London: Oxford University Press for the International Institute for Strategic Studies, 1995.

Walt, Stephen M., 'Why Alliances Endure or Collapse', *Survival* 39:1 (Spring 1997), 156–79.

Waltz, Kenneth, 'The Emerging Structure of International Politics', *International Security* 18:2 (Fall 1993), 44–79.

Wanandi, Jusuf, 'ASEAN's China Strategy: Towards Deeper Engagement', *Survival* 38:3 (Autumn 1996), 117–28.

Wang, Jisi, 'U.S. China Policy: Containment or Engagement?', *Beijing Review* 39 (21–27 October 1996), 6–9.

Wang, Qingxu Ken, 'Japan's Balancing Act in the Taiwan Strait', *Security Dialogue* 33:3 (Autumn 2000), 337–42.

Watanabe, Akio, Tsutomu Kikuchi and Yasuhide Yamanouchi, *The Perspective of Security Regimes in the Asia-Pacific Region*, Tokyo: The Japan Forum on International Relations, Inc., 1996.

Weeks, Stanley B. and Meconis, Charles A., *The Armed Forces of the USA in the Asia–Pacific Region*, St Leonards: Allen & Unwin, 1999.

Whiting, Allen S., 'The PLA and China's Threat Perceptions', *The China Quarterly* 146 (June 1996), 596–615.

Wiseman, Geoffrey, 'Common Security in the Asia-Pacific Region', *The Pacific Review* 5:1 (1992), 42–59.

Wohlforth, William C., 'Realism and the End of the Cold War', *International Security* 19:3 (Winter 1994–95), 91–129.

Wurfel, David (ed.), *Southeast Asia in the New World Order*, Basingstoke: Macmillan, 1996.

Yahuda, Michael, *The International Politics of the Asia-Pacific, 1945–1995*, London: Routledge, 1996.

Yao, Yunzhu, 'The Evolution of Military Doctrine of the Chinese PLA from 1985–1995', *The Korean Journal of Defense Analysis* 7:2 (Winter 1995), 57–80.

You, Ji, *In Quest of High Tech Power: The Modernisation of China's Military*, Canberra: Australian Defence Studies Centre, 1996.

—— *The Armed Forces of China*, St Leonards: Allen & Unwin, 1999.

Young, Oran R., 'Political Leadership and Regime Formation: On the Development of Institutions in International Society', *International Organization* 45:3 (Summer 1991), 281–308.

Yuan, I, 'Cooperation and Conflict: The Offense–Defense Balance in Cross-Strait Relations', *Issues & Studies* 33:2 (February 1997), 1–20.

Zackheim, Dov and Ranney, Jeffrey, 'Matching Defense Strategies to Resources: Challenges for the Clinton Administration', *International Security* 18:1 (Summer 1993), 51–78.

Zakaria, Fareed, 'A Conversation with Lee Kuan Yew', *Foreign Affairs* 73:2 (March/April 1994), 109–26.

# Index

299